Achievement Motivation in Perspective

Achievement Motivation in Perspective

HEINZ HECKHAUSEN
Max-Planck-Institut für Psychologische Forschung
München, Federal Republic of Germany

HEINZ-DIETER SCHMALT
Bergische Universität
Gesamthochschule Wuppertal
Wuppertal, Federal Republic of Germany

KLAUS SCHNEIDER
Psychologisches Institut
Ruhr-Universität Bochum
Bochum, Federal Republic of Germany

Translated by
MARGARET WOODRUFF
ROBERT WICKLUND

1985

ACADEMIC PRESS, INC.
(Harcourt Brace Jovanovich, Publishers)
Orlando   San Diego   New York   London
Toronto   Montreal   Sydney   Tokyo

ARCHBISHOP ALEMANY LIBRARY
DOMINICAN COLLEGE
SAN RAFAEL, CALIFORNIA

ACADEMIC PRESS, INC.
Orlando, Florida 32887

United Kingdom Edition published by
ACADEMIC PRESS INC. (LONDON) LTD.
24–28 Oval Road, London NW1 7DX

LIBRARY OF CONGRESS CATALOGING-IN-PUBLICATION DATA

Heckhausen, Heinz.
    Achievement motivation in perspective.

    Translation of: Fortschritte der
Leistungsmotivationsforschung.
    Bibliography: p.
    Includes indexes.
    1. Achievement motivation.   I. Schmalt, Heinz-Dieter.
II. Schneider, Klaus, DATE   .   III. Title.
BF503.H3913   1985   153.8   84-12463
ISBN 0-12-336160-5 (alk. paper)

PRINTED IN THE UNITED STATES OF AMERICA

85 86 87 88   9 8 7 6 5 4 3 2 1

Contents

3

Interaction of Motive and Task Difficulty 58

4

Revisions and Extensions of the Risk-Taking Model 88

5

The Contribution of Attribution Theory 125

6

Self-Concepts and Reference Norms 192

Preface

Since the early 1950s, achievement motivation has been widely regarded as a prototypical human motive. Not only is it a standard topic in psychology textbooks, but also the term has become a part of everyday language. So much theoretical and empirical work has been included under the rubric of achievement motivation — appropriately or inappropriately — that there has been a tendency to assume premature closure on the topic. As a result, new developments and critical afterthoughts have tended to go unnoticed. Such an inclination was reinforced, paradoxically enough, by the sheer volume and increasing diversity of research efforts during the 1970s.

Achievement Motivation in Perspective first provides a general framework that organizes and integrates the diversity of perspectives. Then it summarizes the state of research up to the mid-1960s and organizes the history of the subsequent 20 years under primary research areas. Chapter 2, "Motive Arousal and Motive Differences," examines developments in the measurement of the achievement motive, as well as historical change and cross-cultural and gender differences in achievement motives. The third chapter focuses on the interaction of motives and task difficulty and examines the predictive power of Atkinson's risk-taking model for such diverse behaviors as choice, information seeking, persistence, and performance. The fourth chapter follows with a discussion of the risk-taking model and introduces new aspects such as overmotivation, personal standards, and future orientation. The impact of attribution theory on an understanding of achievement motivation, particularly with regard to self-evaluative reactions, is discussed in the fifth chapter, and the sixth chapter examines the role of self-concepts and reference norms. The last chapter, entitled "Broadened Perspectives," introduces new ideas, models, and experimental paradigms, some of them from adjacent fields, such as industrial psychology.

The book describes and critically appraises the conceptual progress made in the last 20 years. It sets in perspective successive attempts to reconsider old questions and add new ones. In addition, each chapter documents new practical applications, including new measurement devices.   The book also acquaints an English-speaking readership with the substantial influence of non-English work on the present state of the art in achievement motivation research.

The book will be valuable for all who are interested in human motivation — not only for psychologists, but also for social scientists and educators.   To address a wide audience, conceptual issues and research data are illustrated by concrete descriptions of specific studies, aided by 57 figures and 22 tables, in language that avoids technical jargon.

1

Introduction

The earliest overview of research on achievement motivation, *The Anatomy of Achievement Motivation* (Heckhausen, 1967a), was undertaken in the mid-1960s. In the best sense of the word, that overview has been superseded. This does not mean that the concepts and methods reported at that time have proven to be inadequate, nor the results incorrect. Nor does "superseded" imply merely that the amount of detailed knowledge has multiplied since the mid-1960s. Instead, a series of new theoretical and methodological approaches have been opening up new points of view — extending, refining, and enriching our understanding of achievement-related behavior and how it differs among individuals. Thus it is time to describe the rapid and continuing development of this research in the order in which each new impulse for change has arisen. Such an attempt serves to clarify the present complicated state of research, which even for experts is becoming increasingly difficult to grasp. Since the mid-1960s, the concepts and results of earlier research in achievement motivation have been established in the repertoire of textbooks and as material for courses in psychology and related disciplines. After pointing out the extent to which this material has become part of an established body of knowledge, we can attempt to replace some of it with more recent insights.

For the 1967 book it was possible to survey almost all the research that had been published up to that time. Today that would no longer be possible, nor would it be desirable. Now, in retrospect, the primary lines of development have become more apparent. In order to obtain a clear picture, therefore, we can and should indicate only the most prominent tendencies in research, illustrating them with typical findings. The closer this brings us to the current state of research, the less certain we become as to which approaches will turn out to be productive. At this point the authors attempt to outline as many approaches as possible, including some that have developed apart from achievement motivation research, such as instrumentality theory or studies of learned helplessness.

Expansion of Research

Since 1967, when *The Anatomy of Achievement Motivation* appeared, the number of publications per year has increased rapidly. This can be illustrated by examination of the index of *Psychological Abstracts,* simply counting the instances of the key terms "achievement need" and "achievement motivation" (since the 1960s, the first key term has gradually been replaced by the second). Figure 1.1 shows the increase in number of publications from 1954 to 1981, with frequencies averaged over 3-year periods. Achievement motivation research can be said to have begun in 1953 with the publication of *The Achievement Motive* by McClelland, Atkinson, Clark, and Lowell. Research activity in the new field increased only gradually in the following decade, but after that period of incubation, the figures shot up rapidly. Such a pattern is surely typical and can be encountered in other productive new fields of research. In this case, the sudden upswing after the mid-1960s seems to have been inspired primarily by Atkinson's formalization of the interaction of person (motive) and situation (task difficulty). This formalization was introduced in 1957 as the "risk-taking model," and by the mid-1960s had produced impressive results described in two books: Atkinson's textbook, *An Introduction to Motivation* (1964), and the collection of individual studies edited with Feather in *A Theory of Achievement Motivation* (1966).

By the mid-1970s the output of publications on achievement motivation showed signs of having reached an asymptote such as one expects from any process of development. To be sure, a subgroup under the key term "aca-

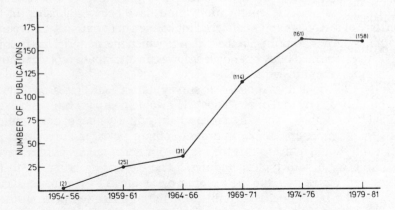

FIGURE 1.1 Annual number of publications on achievement motivation from 1954 to 1981, as listed in *Psychological Abstracts,* with frequencies averaged over 3-year periods.

demic achievement motivation" began to appear in 1974–1976, constituting 22% of achievement motivation research; in 1979–1981 it reached 30%. The quality of these studies is uneven, and in part questionable in nature, relative to the usual standards for achievement motivation research. Many of the studies indicate the popularity of the concept more than they contribute to motivational psychology. If we consider only the key term "achievement motivation," we could perhaps say that the culmination was reached in 1977 with 211 articles in that year, for after that, the figures drop sharply to 154 (1978) and as low as 134 (1979) and 100 (1981).

By the early 1970s, researchers outside the United States had come to play an increasingly important part in the study of achievement motivation. This was notable in Germany (especially at the University of Bochum), Norway, Holland, and Belgium, and outside Europe in Australia, India, and Japan. In German-speaking countries alone, the number of publications per year rose from 11 in 1971 to over 20 in the period from 1975 to 1979 and to 30 in 1980 (see Dambauer's annual bibliography).

In this book we intend to document the expansion of research since 1965, not with regard to its quantitative increase, but in terms of the conceptual progress made (see also Atkinson's foreword to the second edition, 1976, of the 1953 book by McClelland and his associates).

Directions in Research Development

In *The Anatomy of Achievement Motivation* the attempt was made to explore the entire field, systematically and with attention to particular phenomena, especially in regard to the individual phases of achievement-related behavior. Thus some of the phenomena mentioned there were only later conceptualized and explored: for example, future orientation, calculation of effort, reference norms, and self-evaluation, which have since become fields of research in their own right.

This book is not intended to be a mere updated version of its predecessor. Rather, a succession of the most significant tendencies in the development of achievement motivation research is described from the contemporary point of view in separate chapters. These approaches have served as an impetus to initiate new stages of research, without earlier impulses having thereby lost their momentum. Old and new tendencies take their courses simultaneously, they overlap, and they merge. Throughout all the developments in this field, the phenomena of risk taking, persistence, and performance have remained the central ones in achievement-related behavior. At every stage, researchers have attempted to clarify these matters anew, more fully, or in a more precise manner.[1] Whenever theoretical progress has been made, new problems of diagnostic measurement have arisen along with possibilities of practical application, some of which have been tested and used. Measurement problems, as well as practical applications, are mentioned in almost every chapter.

We start with the pioneering work of David McClelland and his colleagues at the beginning of the 1950s. The content analysis method developed by McClelland *et al.* (1953) for measuring the achievement motive focused on motive arousal and motive differences (Chapter 2, this volume). Soon after, in 1957, followed interaction of motive and task difficulty (Chapter 3, this volume) in John Atkinson's formalization of the risk-taking model. Along with the two motivational tendencies "hope of success" and "fear of failure" (Heckhausen, 1963a), these two approaches were described in detail in the earlier book, although no particular attempt was made to distinguish one approach from the other. Anyone seeking information about the extensive results of these pioneering efforts should consult *The Anatomy of Achievement Motivation.* In the present book we trace achievement motivation back as far as the beginnings and early stages — in a condensed version, to be sure — in order to outline the elements that served as a foundation for all later development.

The fourth chapter presents a number of revisions of the risk-taking model. Each revision has increased the requirements for mastery of methodological problems to such an extent that even today complete clarity has not been attained in regard to these revisions. More recently, Bernard Weiner and his associates (1971) introduced a new approach, applying causal attribution theory to achievement-related behavior. The explanation of one's own success and failure acquired the status of an indispensable intermediary cognitive process, influencing the alteration of expectancies and the occurrence of affective consequences. The elaboration of achievement motivation research through attribution theory is the theme of the fifth chapter. Such experimental paradigms as learned helplessness, which have been applied to areas other than achievement motivation research, can also be analyzed profitably from the perspective of attribution theory.

Self-concepts and self-evaluation can be treated as influencing actual motivation. For example, self-concepts of competence determine expectancies of success. Self-centered cognitions can impair task-processing efficiency; thus, apparently, the self is a focal point for achievement motivation. But what is the ultimate motivating factor in self-evaluation: affective satisfaction, or the information obtained about one's own competence? Questions

---

[1] Diagrams derived from a basic model of motivation (see Figure 1.2) illustrate the differentiation of the theoretical network in this book.

of this sort are treated in Chapter 6, "Self-Concepts and Reference Norms." Reference norms are the measure for any evaluation of achievement, whether self-evaluation or evaluation by others. The norms affect motivation and have proven to be leading factors in motive-modification programs.

The seventh chapter broadens our perspectives on methods and models. First, new methods for measuring motives and motivational states are introduced. Two opposing "metamotivational" directives or motivational states, action orientation versus state orientation, can promote or retard the conversion of intentions into action. As for the new explanatory models, they do not integrate merely the various stages of development in achievement motivation research. They also draw in aspects of theory from neighboring and previously separate areas of research. For example, instrumentality theory, taken from industrial psychology, inspired the formation of an extended motivation model. This model distinguishes among various kinds of expectancies and among consequences of the action outcome with their incentives.

The extended motivation model applies only to individual behavioral episodes and can thus be described as episodic. In contrast, the dynamic theory of action is designed to explain change in the stream of consecutive episodes. In order to determine both the initial strength of the various motivational tendencies and their subsequent waxing and waning, the dynamic model is combined with the episodic model.

Chapter 7 ends the book with the rediscovery of a problem that has been concealed for at least a half century by the simple but false assumption that the motivational tendency that is strongest at the moment determines behavior. Up to now psychologists have concentrated on explaining how motivational tendencies are aroused in a given situation and to what extent such tendencies influence subsequent behavior. Currently, however, we are seeking the missing links in the causal chain leading from motive arousal to action outcome. Once more we must investigate the way in which motivational tendencies become intentions and under what circumstances intentions are transformed into actions. Thus some of the current approaches to achievement motivation research involve such basic problems of general motivational psychology as the aspects of volitional processes that generate behavior and the motivational control of behavior.

On looking back, it appears that the compact nature of the earlier achievement motivation research has by now evolved into a number of separate areas. It is too early to tell whether the impulses from some of the approaches will give the original theoretical body new momentum. Thus the present situation is particularly stimulating.

On the whole, achievement motivation research has developed much as other research areas have. Trait concepts, such as the motive construct, have disappeared in favor of process constructs. The interactive connection of personality factors and situation factors has increased. There has been a widespread reversion to the use of intermediary cognitive processes, although there is still little agreement as to whether these are merely hypothetical or perhaps even real. The development of achievement motivation research also includes methodological limitations on the refinement of models and applications such as motive-modification programs, in which one of the important functions is to test the productivity of the development of theories.

A comparison with the state of research in other motive areas is also appropriate. While the investigation of social motives, such as helping behavior and aggression, has consisted almost exclusively of differentiating among situational factors and has neglected personality factors, achievement motivation research has taken the opposite course. A gradual convergence has become apparent. Those attempting to reconstruct social motivations have turned more toward individual differences in the form of motive constructs, and those attempting to reconstruct achievement motivations are searching increasingly for distinctions in the appraisal of situations. Thus a number of prospects can be outlined. Whether they will be pursued by researchers and made productive is yet to be seen.

An important part of achievement motivation research is not described in this book. That is the development of motivation — the general development of achievement-related behavior and its numerous cognitive roots, up until mid-adolescence. A survey of recent research in this area is available elsewhere (Heckhausen, 1982b; see also Ruble, 1980). The development of motives — that is, the formation of individual differences in achievement-related behavior — must be distinguished from the development of motivation. Until the 1970s, questions of the development of motives were very much in the foreground, although next to nothing was known about the general development of motivation. The results of this somewhat premature research are also summarized elsewhere (Heckhausen, 1972a, 1980b; Trudewind, 1982).

A Basic Model of Motivation

A basic model of motivation will serve as an illustrative summary of the theoretical progress that is described in the individual chapters. Since it is designed to assist the reader in orientation, the basic outline appears in this introductory chapter. Figure 1.2 shows a series of states or events that constitute stages of a goal-directed (i.e., motivated) course of action, from an initial situation to the attainment of a superordinate goal. Specifically: the demand characteristics of a situation activate a motivation that is also in-

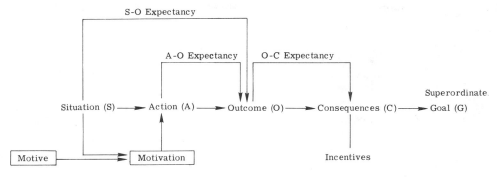

FIGURE 1.2 A basic model of motivation.

fluenced by a dispositional variable of the individual in question, called a motive. "Motivation" and "motive" are hypothetical constructs and thus appear in boxes. They are seen as mediators between situation and action. Motivation consists of the anticipation of possible actions expected to lead to an outcome that will have certain consequences, which will possibly bring the person closer to a superordinate goal.

Two kinds of variables are fundamental for the theoretical reconstruction of the motivation process: incentives and expectancies. We are motivated to act by the positive or negative incentive values of the expected consequences stemming from a possible outcome of our own action. In identifying goals that motivate action, we distinguish between the outcomes of an action and its consequences, for three reasons. First, as a rule, an action outcome has a number of consequences, each with its respective incentive value: There are consequences for self-evaluation, for evaluation by others, for costs and benefits, for the attainment of superordinate goals, and so on. Second, the consequences can vary considerably even though the outcome is the same, since they are subject for the most part to outside influences. Third, the same action outcome can lead to different consequences in self-evaluation for different people, depending on such factors as the strictness of their standards.

In regard to expectancies, we must distinguish among the following. Situation-outcome expectancies (S-O) have to do with the subjective probability that the existing situation (S) will lead to a particular outcome (O) on its own — that is, without the person involved taking any action. Of greater importance in achievement motivation research are action-outcome expectancies (A-O) — that is, the subjective probability of success: the probability that one's own action (A) will lead to the desired outcome (O). Finally, another kind of expectancy, which, though important, was overlooked for a long time, is the outcome-consequence expectancy (O-C). This is the subjective probability that the outcome (O), once attained, will actually have the particular consequences (C) that are desired or feared. The outcome-consequence expectancy and the situation-outcome expectancy are both distinguished from the action-outcome expectancy through one important peculiarity: The connection between outcome and consequences (or between situation and outcome) cannot be influenced by one's own actions, or at least not directly. With regard to these expectancies, then, we speak of perceived instrumentality instead of subjective probability of success. These few conceptual distinctions may suffice to introduce the basic system from which we can derive versions of a model of the motivational process at various levels of differentiation.

Some Frequent Abbreviations

To simplify communication, we use several abbreviations. Most of them describe variables basic to the achievement motive. In American research the following measures are generally used:

n Ach	*need* Achievement (from the TAT procedure developed by McClelland *et al.,* 1953)
TAQ	Test Anxiety Questionnaire (Mandler & Sarason, 1952)

Instead of *n* Ach a similar, equivalent measure is occasionally used:

FTI	French Test of Insight (French, 1955, 1958a)
MARPS	Mehrabian Achievement Risk Preference Scale (Mehrabian, 1968, 1969)

The following are occasionally used instead of the TAQ:

MAS	Manifest Anxiety Scale (Taylor, 1953)
AAT	Achievement Anxiety Test (Alpert & Haber, 1960)

In German-speaking countries, Heckhausen's TAT procedure (1963a) is generally used, with the following variables:

HS	hope of success
FF	fear of failure
NH	net hope ($HS - FF$)
Tm	total motivation ($HS + FF$)

A semiprojective measure of the same variables was devised by Schmalt (1976a, 1976b):

LMG	Achievement-Motive Grid *(Leistungsmotivgitter)*

To indicate that the LMG measure is being used rather than the TAT measure, the abbreviation LMG is appended to the four motive variables *HS*, *FF*, *NH*, and *Tm* (e.g., *HS*, LMG). When the achievement motive is measured by Schmalt's grid test, FF_1 means Self-Concept of Low Ability; NH_1, LMG is Net Hope when FF_1 is subtracted from HS_1 (Self-Concept of High Ability). FF_2 means Fear of Failure.

Motive differences between experimental groups are usually described as follows in the text: strongly motivated versus weakly motivated when the groups are divided merely on the basis of the values for *n* Ach or for *Tm*. Groups that differ with respect to their dominant motive tendencies are characterized as success motivated versus failure motivated. The precise measure used is indicated in parentheses whenever this is not already clear from context. Thus "success motivated (*n* Ach > TAQ)" means that *n* Ach values were determined to be relatively higher than TAQ values, usually on the basis of a median split or use of extreme groups. Likewise, "success motivated (*NH*)" means that $HS > FF$. On the other hand, "success motivated (*HS*)" is merely a division on the basis of the *HS* distribution. For failure-motivated groups as well—whether determined on the basis of *n* Ach < TAQ, or *NH*, or *FF*—the measure used is indicated. Finally, the following two abbreviations occur frequently throughout:

TAT   Thematic Apperception Test
Ps   subjective probability of success (varies between .00 and 1.00).

2

Motive Arousal and Motive Differences

At the end of the 1940s the group of researchers associated with D. C. McClelland began to analyze experimentally some questions associated with motivation in humans. As Atkinson (1964, pp. 222–223) emphasizes, there existed neither a general theoretical concept of the nature of a motive, nor a widely accepted view of how an instrument for measuring motives should be constructed and how the validity of such an instrument could be determined.

Experimental research in motivation was concerned almost exclusively with the analysis of primary needs (especially hunger) in animals. Researchers claimed universal applicability for the results, tracing back all motivational phenomena in the more highly organized beings to simple organismic factors such as hunger. According to this view, complex phenomena of human motivation are learned on the basis of their connection with primary needs.

However, the clinical and diagnostic psychologists influenced by Murray (1938) had unearthed extensive material concerning human motivational phenomena. This material caused McClelland and his associates to question the simple reductionism of traditional theories of motivation and to seek a new approach. The research was to be limited initially to exploration of the achievement motive. However, it was difficult to find a starting point, owing to the inadequate stock of theories and procedures for gathering data. McClelland (1958a, p. 8) decided to begin by developing a procedure that would not introduce any assumptions about the construct to be measured (the motive). To be sure, the general behavioral characteristics indicating the operation of motives were specified. According to this criterion, behavior is caused by or partially attributable to motives in the case of a coordinated, goal-directed "response sequence, which terminates when the organism arrives somewhere with respect to a source of affect" (McClelland *et al.,* 1953, p. 38).

But this criterion alone was still somewhat ambiguous, for such response sequences can also be influenced by two other behavioral determinants: the situation itself, and stable habits or traits (McClelland, 1951a; McClelland *et al.*, 1953, pp. 35–42). However, McClelland felt that in fantasies the influence of situation and habits would be random and minimal, especially with fantasies that are reactions to semistructured stimuli. In such a novel situation there are no learned habits to determine behavior, nor are the situational cues in themselves specific enough to determine a response sequence (McClelland, 1951a, p. 412). Thus the presence of motives was supposed to be indicated most clearly in fantasies by goal-directed response sequences and affect in connection with evaluation (McClelland *et al.*, 1953, p. 79).

Contents of Fantasies as Motivation Indexes: Preliminary Experimental Studies

A procedure for analyzing fantasies produced by semistructured stimuli and recorded in writing was provided by Murray in his Thematic Apperception Test (TAT)(1938). Before the onset of research on achievement motivation, the TAT had been used for some time in clinical psychology to analyze motivational phenomena. However, compelling evidence for the validity of this procedure was lacking, as was conclusive evidence for the appropriateness of the theoretical assumptions (Atkinson, 1964, p. 222).

McClelland and his associates decided first of all to demonstrate the validity of the TAT by means of a theme that had already been analyzed considerably: the hunger motive. It was sufficiently well known how to stimulate such a motive, to bring it to the point where it could affect behavior — that is, by means of withholding nourishment. It was clear which fantasy content would indicate the presence of hunger themes. It was also useful to assume that, given equally specific stimuli, real-life behavior would center on the same contents as the description of motivated acts in TAT stories, and that behavioral components would relate to the specific motives in a thematically unambiguous and direct manner. Thus these behavioral components and the TAT themes can be analyzed according to the same principles, using the same set of categories (McClelland, Clark, Roby & Atkinson, 1949, p. 245).

In an initial experimental exploration of their new medium for the analysis of motivational processes, Atkinson and McClelland (1948) used three groups of subjects. These were deprived of food for 1, 4, or 16 hours respectively. They were then shown a set of six pictures, each for twenty seconds, that had something to do with food and eating (projected slides designed on the basis of Murray's TAT and some magazine pictures).

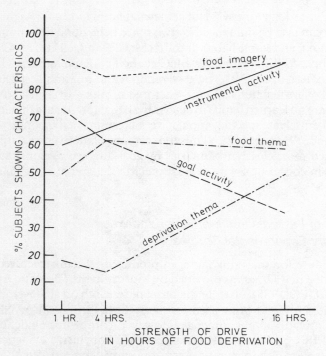

FIGURE 2.1 Percentage of subjects showing selected food-related content categories in their TAT stories as a function of increasing food deprivation. (From Atkinson & McClelland, 1948, p. 649.)

Subjects were led to think that this was a test of creative imagination. They were asked to tell the most interesting story possible and to include responses to the following questions:

1.   What is happening? Who are the persons?
2.   What has led up to this situation; that is, what has happened in the past?
3.   What is being thought? What is wanted; by whom?
4.   What will happen? What will be done?

(McClelland et al., 1953, p. 98)

The next task was to develop a scoring key with definitions of certain content categories that would reflect most clearly the distinctions between the stories of the hungry and nonhungry subjects. This was done on the basis of a general theory of basic needs, since it was assumed that the characteristics of real-life actions parallel those actions described in fantasies. The

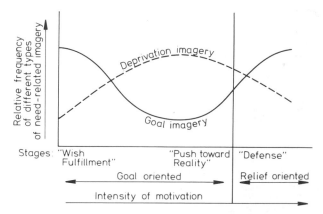

FIGURE 2.2 The hypothetical effect of increasing motive strength on thought processes. (Adapted from McClelland, 1951a, p. 495.)

scoring key contained categories such as description of needs, activities instrumental in the attainment of goals and overcoming of obstacles, goal anticipations, and positive and negative emotional states upon approaching the goal.

The categories varied with the length of deprivation of food; however, they did not increase in a monotonic manner along with deprivation, as was first assumed. Some categories, such as consummatory goal activity, actually occurred less frequently in a hunger-motivated condition than in a neutral condition (see Figure 2.1).

In light of the assumption of parallelism, this outcome is quite understandable, for as hunger motivation increases, it becomes more effective to concern oneself with one's deprivation state and with instrumental activity for overcoming it than with goal-related activity; that is, with food itself.

In his model, McClelland (1951a, pp. 494–497) has summarized the hypothetical effects of various motivation intensities on thought processes and fantasy processes. He suggests that when motivation intensities are low, goal-directed wish-fulfilling thoughts predominate. Increasing motivation strength initiates a "push toward reality" (p. 495): The need is seen clearly and thoughts are dominated by obstacles to the satisfaction of the need and activity that might be instrumental in overcoming them. Thoughts of deprivation replace wish-fulfilling thoughts, which quite clearly fulfill an adaptive function. If motivation increases still further, the hungry person is tormented by thoughts of deprivation. This leads to avoidance of such thoughts and to renewed preoccupation with goal-related activity, this time of a defensive nature (see Figure 2.2).

TABLE 2.1

Arousal Conditions for the Achievement Motive and Mean Motive Scores[a]

Arousal conditions	Motive scores[b]
Relaxed (The experimenter pretends to be trying out a new test)	1.95
Neutral (Standard situation)	7.33
Achievement-oriented (The experimenter pretends to be using a test of important intellectual capabilities)	8.77
Success (Like achievement, but followed by the induction of success)	7.92
Failure (Like achievement, but followed by the induction of failure)	10.10
Success–failure (A combination of success and failure)	10.36

[a] Adapted from McClelland, Atkinson, Clark, and Lowell, 1953, p. 184.
[b] Combined values for all content categories.

The actual goal of the investigation was, however, the analysis of the achievement motive. Now that research had justified the search for motivation products in fantasy productions, the researchers decided to conduct an analogous experiment to analyze the achievement motive.

First of all it was necessary to find situations that would activate the achievement motive. On the basis of the hunger study it was assumed that success, like satiation in the case of the hunger motive, was the goal of the achievement motive. Correspondingly, strength of arousal was assumed to be a direct function of deprivation — that is, failure — and an inverse function of satiation — that is, success. Thus McClelland et al. (1949) established six different arousal conditions ranging from a relaxed condition to a highly achievement-oriented condition (see Table 2.1). The subjects worked on an achievement test under various conditions. Afterward they were shown TAT pictures with achievement themes.

The original key for scoring achievement-related content categories resembled that of the hunger study in form, but it was adapted in such a way that it discriminated clearly between the relaxed and failure conditions (see Table 2.1). However, since it turned out that the difference between the relaxed and success conditions also produced a substantial difference on the TAT measure, the deprivation theory behind the original approach of setting up graded arousal conditions became questionable (McClelland et al., 1953, pp. 100–106). Instead of assuming that failure creates the strongest arousal,

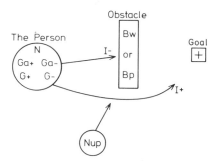

FIGURE 2.3 Position of the scoring categories in the adjustive behavioral sequence. (From McClelland, Atkinson, Clark, & Lowell, 1953, p. 109.)

it was now assumed that the achievement-oriented condition was maximally arousing, while success and failure were merely characteristic outcomes of an achievement motive that had already been aroused. The n Ach key was thus revised again in a replication study for the purpose of optimal differentiation between the relaxed and achievement-oriented conditions. In its final form it contains the following categories:

1. Stated need for achievement (N)
2. Instrumental activity with various outcomes (I+; I?; I−)
3. Anticipatory positive and negative goal states (Ga+; Ga−)
4. Obstacles or blocks (Bp; Bw)
5. Nurturant press (Nup)
6. Affective states (G+; G−)
7. Need achievement (n Ach Th)

In their general form these categories can also be used to describe components of spontaneous goal-directed response sequences, as is suggested by the assumed parallelism between certain structural characteristics of fantasy stories and spontaneous behavior. Thus an action can be said to begin with the arousal of a need (N) and the anticipation of positive or negative goal states (Ga+, Ga−). In the active phase, instrumental activity (I+, I?, I−) is undertaken for the pursuit or avoidance of the anticipated goal states, sometimes with assistance from other persons (Nup). Often personal blocks (Bp) or blocking of actions by the environment (Bw) must be overcome for this purpose. Finally, when a person attains or fails to attain a goal, positive or negative affective states (G+, G−) are experienced (see Figure 2.3).

However, points are assigned to these categories only when the entire action sequence during which they occur is achievement oriented. McClelland *et al.* (1949, p. 244) initially defined achievement orientation (still without detailed theoretical clarification) as preoccupation with the long-term problem of bringing oneself closer to ideal goals of personal development in academic or career areas, such as making outstanding discoveries.

Defining the Motive on the Basis of an Affect Model of Motivation

A few years after the early efforts of McClelland *et al.*, the state of knowledge had advanced far enough that an initial attempt at theoretical integration could be undertaken. In 1953, McClelland *et al.* defined the goal of the achievement motive as "success in the competition with a standard of excellence" (p. 110). A definite sign of the existence of such standards is that the outcomes of the action are evaluated. In order to ensure that the processes of evaluation are not only described objectively, but also actually serve to motivate, evaluation must be coupled with expressed affect. Thus the existence of affect in connection with evaluation is the most important indication of the existence of achievement themes (McClelland *et al.*, 1953, p. 79).

Primary affects such as pleasure and displeasure play a special role in McClelland's motivation theory. Psychogenic motives—for example, the achievement motive—are learned when particular affects or the expectancy of experiencing these affects come to be associated with particular situational cues.

Theoretically, these affects are aroused according to McClelland's discrepancy model (see Figure 2.4). Certain situational cues can deviate to a greater or lesser degree from that which is normally expected, causing the degree of discrepancy from the level of expectancy or adaptation to vary. The discrepancies determine the quality and intensity of the resulting affect. Low discrepancies lead to indifference and boredom, medium discrepancies to strong positive affect, and very high discrepancies to strong negative affect. If individuals who have learned these associations find themselves in situations resembling the original learning situation, the cues then redintegrate the original affect. The redintegrated affects, or anticipatory affects, such as hope and fear, have a motivating effect whenever the redintegrated affect represents a change from the affect that would normally have been aroused by the situation. These affects, in turn, determine approach or avoidance behavior in relation to goal states. Thus a motive is understood as the "redintegration by a cue of a change in an affective situation" (McClelland *et al.*, 1953, p. 28). That is, a motive is learned. For its arousal, two points on an affective continuum are needed. A momentary affect redintegrates a second affect on the basis of the person's learning history. This second affect

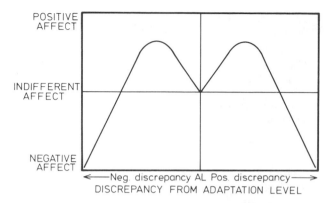

FIGURE 2.4 Affect as a function of positive and negative discrepancies from the adaptation level (hypothetical). (From Haber, 1958, p. 371.)

represents a change from the momentary affect in shadings of pleasure or pain (McClelland, 1951a, p. 467).

In later formulations (see Chapter 3) a sharper distinction is made between "motive"—a stable personality trait—and "motivation"—a tendency aroused by a specific situation. McClelland *et al.* (1953) had not yet distinguished so clearly between the two. Moreover, in McClelland's theory no specific affect is connected with any specific motive theme. Affects connected with achievement themes are those that occur in relation to performance judged against a standard of excellence. Thus—and here we come full circle—achievement motivation is indicated in the TAT by "affect in connection with evaluation" based on standards of excellence (McClelland *et al.,* 1953, p. 79).

Given that McClelland attaches motives exclusively to positive and negative affect, we can say that he shares the hedonistic view of "motive" that has been a part of motivation research since Aristippus of Cyrene and since Freud's formulation of the pleasure principle. This conception can basically be reduced to the idea that we seek that which is pleasant and avoid that which is unpleasant. Despite its plausibility, it has received considerable criticism, since its ultimate foundation is affect. To be sure, no one would deny that attaining or failing to attain a desired goal state has something to do with positive and negative affect. It is questioned, however, whether in the end, affect actually constitutes the motive goal toward which behavior is oriented. Thus affective theories of motivation can be contrasted— particularly in the area of achievement motivation—with so-called cognitive theories, which also deal with the cognitive determinants of the motivational process. In these latter theories, the significance of the process of evaluating the extent to which the desired goal was attained is emphasized more than the affective consequences of this evaluation in the motivational process (see Halisch, 1976; Heckhausen, 1980b).

Two Motives in Achievement Motivation

It became clear quite early that at least two distinct motives exist: a motive to approach success, and a motive to avoid failure. Yet, at first, the talk was always of *the* achievement motive (*n* Ach) in the sense of a monistic concept, and arousal studies paid no attention to the distinction between the two motives. Finally, the question of how to measure the two different motives became more urgent.

Although it might have seemed natural to score the various subcategories separately for positive and negative goal anticipations (hope and fear), the attempt at first was to assign the two motive tendencies to different sectors of the distribution of total *n* Ach scores. The first indication that the method of dividing the distribution into sectors was feasible came from an investigation by McClelland and Liberman (1949). These authors divided their subjects into three groups (low-, middle-, and high-motive groups) on the basis of *n* Ach scores and of scores on a behavioral measure. Then they attempted to relate this measure of motivation to the recognition of positive and negative achievement-related words that had been presented for a short time. While the group with the lowest scores showed no significant differences, the group with middle scores took a longer time to recognize negative achievement-related words, and the group with the highest scores took less time to recognize positive achievement-related words. The authors concluded that the motivation of the subjects with medium *n* Ach scores was directed primarily toward avoidance of failure, while the group with high scores focused more on the attainment of success.

Along the same lines, Atkinson (1950) reported that the number of completed tasks that were recalled increased across the following three conditions: relaxed, task oriented, and ego involved. However, with regard to the number of unfinished tasks that were remembered, there were some distinctions among the terciles of the *n* Ach distribution. As in the McClelland and Liberman study, the difference was between the upper and the middle thirds. While the upper third showed an increase in recall of unfinished tasks as conditions moved from relaxed to ego involved, the middle third recalled increasingly fewer unfinished tasks as ego involvement increased (see Figure 2.5). No systematic trends appeared for the lowest tercile.

The theoretical significance of these results is based on the assumption

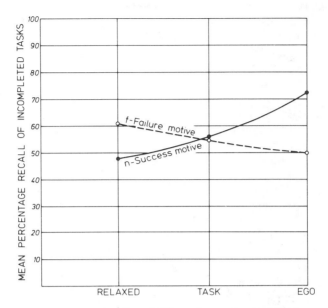

FIGURE 2.5 The effect of different instructional orientations on recall of interrupted tasks for two kinds of achievement motives. (From Atkinson, 1950; in McClelland, 1951a, p. 498.)

that the subjects in the upper third of the n Ach distribution were characterized by hope of success and those in the middle third by fear of failure (McClelland, 1951a, pp. 497–499). Elsewhere, however, McClelland (1951b, p. 99) continued to use a single achievement motive construct. He considered the success and failure motives to be mere subcomponents with a successively stronger effect on behavior as arousal of the achievement motive increased. According to this view, the achievement motive would initially be directed toward avoiding failure, while arousal was still relatively low. Only when arousal increased would the motive be directed toward attaining success.

Since 1950, researchers attempting to differentiate between the success and failure motives have tended not to use the tripartite division. Even as early as 1951, McClelland cited findings from studies with tripartite divisions only in respect to differences between subjects with high and low motivation. He already equated these differences with differences in orientation of the achievement motives, that is, hope of success and fear of failure (McClelland, 1951a, pp. 497–499; see Figure 2.5). Not until later do we read again of a division into three parts (McClelland *et al.,* 1953, p. 268 ff.).

McClelland also considered the possibility that the appearance of failure-oriented subjects in the middle or lower third of the distribution of scores might be a measurement artifact. However, differences in intensity of motivation led to the conclusion that the difference might be qualitative. This conclusion was based on the assumption that it should actually be possible to find subjects with high fear of failure, as well as subjects with high hope of success, in the upper range of the distribution. Fear of failure could be so intense, however, that its manifestation in fantasy and verbal behavior would be inhibited, and thus appear in only a few content categories.

Interest in the middle third has reawakened. Sorrentino and Short (1977) found, in a series of their own studies and in their reanalysis of studies by others, that a mere contrast of strongly and weakly motivated subjects, or success-motivated versus failure-motivated subjects (n Ach/TAQ), yielded results contradictory to the theory. Data from these studies tended more to support theory-based hypotheses, however, when the n Ach distribution was divided into three parts and only the upper and lower terciles compared with each other. Subjects from the middle tercile were discontinuous with the high- and low-motive groups on a number of behavioral dimensions. Those with scores in the middle range were neither strongly nor weakly motivated, and were neither confident of success nor fearful of failure. Thus their scores presumably showed particularly strong influences from other motives that were not measured in the study, or especially sensitive responses to situational cues (Sorrentino & Short, 1977, p. 483).

The difficulties that were identified in the TAT procedure led Moulton (1958) to attempt an independent measurement of the failure motive, again by means of content analysis. For this purpose he drew upon the TAT stories of subjects from Atkinson's study (1953, see above). Subjects in the achievement-oriented condition in this study showed relatively poor recall of interrupted tasks. This was interpreted as a behavioral manifestation of fear of failure. The key categories for the failure motive were adapted primarily from the negative categories in McClelland's key but were in part redefined and respecified. However, this approach, which the author himself saw as exploratory in nature, has not been pursued further or cross-validated; other researchers have chosen different methods of measurement for this purpose (see below).

Heckhausen (1963a) undertook a separate and independent measurement of the two motives "hope of success" and "fear of failure" by means of content analysis. Like Moulton (1958), Heckhausen determined his individual content categories on the basis of a behavioral criterion which, in this case, was goal setting in a level-of-aspiration experiment. The key was refined until it discriminated between story-telling groups having positive and negative goal discrepancies. After numerous revisions, the key finally consisted of the following behavioral categories (Heckhausen, 1963a, p. 67; pp. 287–302):

	HS		*FF*
N	Need for achievement and success	N_f	Need to avoid failure
I	Instrumental (goal-directed) activity	I_f	Instrumental activity directed toward avoiding failure
E	Expectancy of success	E_f	Expectancy of failure
P	Praise	C	Criticism
G+	Affective state: positive	G−	Affective state: negative
		F	Failure
Th	Success theme	Th_f	Failure theme

In the analysis of the stories, one point is scored for each of the content categories that appears, and the points for the entire set of six pictures are added together. The contents of each individual statement that receives a point must have an unmistakable achievement orientation. In contrast, McClelland's procedure first determines whether each separate story is achievement oriented at all; if so, an additional point is assigned for it. Compared with McClelland's procedure, Heckhausen's allows greater independence in the determination of the individual points and a closer approximation to a normal distribution of scores. With Heckhausen's procedure, besides the two scores for the hope of success *HS* and fear of failure *FF* motives, additional scores for compound measures can be determined: a measure of total motivation ($HS + FF = Tm$) and a measure of the dominant tendency in motivation, net hope ($HS - FF = NH$). Meyer, Heckhausen, and Kemmler (1965) have developed an equivalent procedure for measuring the achievement motive in children.

A projective procedure for measuring the failure motive alone was developed by Birney, Burdick, and Teevan (1969). These authors proceeded from the assumption that fear of failure is not openly admitted and thus cannot be measured by means of need-related contents. Accordingly, they developed a key based on specific forms of perception of one's environment as hostile and threatening, particularly with regard to the danger that one's self-esteem will be undermined publicly. This motive variable is called hostile press *HP*. As one would expect from the conceptual distinctions between the *HP* and *FF* measures, there appears to be little overlap in the areas of empirical validity of the two concepts (Birney *et al.*, 1969; Heckhausen, 1968a).

On the other hand, the *HS* and *Tm* scores in the procedure developed by Heckhausen (1963a) show a certain correspondence to the *n* Ach scores; the

TABLE 2.2
Correlations between n Ach (McClelland et al., 1976) and Heckhausen (1963a) TAT Variables[a]

	Hope of success (HS)	Fear of failure (FF)	Net hope (NH)	Total motivation (Tm)
Students at a teachers' college (N = 71)	+.73**	+.15	+.32*	+.63**
Students at a university (N = 77)	+.60**	+.21	+.27*	+.62**

[a] From Heckhausen, 1963a, p. 74.
$* p < .05; ** p < .01$.

FF scores, however, do not. With regard to the NH measure, there is a relatively low correlation (see Table 2.2). Thus we can assume that the n Ach measure developed by McClelland et al. (1953) primarily registers the success-oriented tendency of the achievement motive.

Psychometric Effectiveness of the Thematic Apperceptive Technique

Projective diagnostic techniques such as the TAT procedures described here are especially problematic when it comes to evaluating their quality as psychometric tests from the standpoint of classical test theory. Certain peculiarities of projective measures limit the usefulness of their evaluation according to criteria of classical test theory, even to the point where the development of new evaluative criteria (Kuhl, in press) is necessary.

Objectivity

As we have shown, the TAT is sensitive to a number of situational influences. This calls for particular care in the standardization of test conditions and procedures. It has become customary in TAT research to keep the arousal level of the pictures relatively strong and the arousal cues of the test situation relatively weak. We can create neutral experimental conditions in a natural and reliable fashion, without any achievement-related arousal from the situation or the instructions (Heckhausen, 1964, p. 245), so that the test procedure is sufficiently standardized.

The objectivity of the test scoring is another critical point. In the process of reducing story contents to the individual scoring categories, scorer bias could impair objectivity. Thus training programs have been developed in which the conventions of interpretation can be practiced (Heckhausen, 1963a; Smith & Feld, 1958). Trained scorers can attain interrater reliabilities of up to .95.

Reliability

The strongest criticism of the TAT procedure is directed at the fact that test – retest correlations tend to be disappointingly low. Entwisle (1972), and Winter and Stewart (1977) determined from published or otherwise accessible investigations an average test – retest coefficient of .30 (.28). Naturally, such low coefficients hardly encourage the use of this procedure. Thus authors such as Guilford (1964) and Entwisle (1972) have even recommended eliminating the TAT from the arsenal of measurement procedures useful in research.

However, we must question the appropriateness of the criteria used to evaluate the TAT, and also of the interpretation involved in evaluation. The test – retest method produces useful estimates of the reliability of a procedure when it is certain that the procedure can be used repeatedly under nearly identical internal and external experimental conditions. However, this prerequisite is not met in the case of the achievement motivation TAT. After all, the instructions call for the production of the most creative and imaginative story possible. When the procedure is repeated, the subject is uncertain whether to produce again the stories that have already been generated, which is by no means creative, or to invent a new story, which naturally involves considerable thematic variation (Tomkins, 1961, p. 279).

Winter and Stewart (1977) varied these subject attitudes experimentally. They found relatively high test – retest coefficients when they instructed their subjects to tell the same story (.61), and also when they instructed subjects not to concern themselves at all about whether they were inventing a new story or presenting the old story again (.58). However, when the subjects were encouraged to invent a new story, the test – retest coefficient dropped to the insignificant value of .27. In his instructions Heckhausen (1963a) also suggested the repetition of TAT stories that had already been told; he obtained a test – retest coefficient of .53. Moreover, both test and retest in these investigations employed identical TAT pictures, which had been carefully calibrated with respect to theme and cue content.

On the basis of these studies by Heckhausen and by Winter and Stewart, we can expect test – retest reliabilities to be close to .60 if arousal conditions are carefully controlled and an effort is made to create comparable conditions when giving the retest. This test – retest coefficient of approximately

.60, decidedly higher than the averages of .30 and .28 determined by Entwisle (1972) and by Winter and Stewart (1977), completely satisfies the standards for a research instrument. Taking into account the standard error, the procedure does make possible a reliable classification of subjects into three or four subgroups.

In addition, it is questionable whether classical test theory's assumption — that high test – retest reliability is a prerequisite for high validity — can be applied to the TAT. The statistically determined reliability of most questionnaire procedures is higher than that of the TAT, but this is often merely an apparent reliability. In addition to the well-known influence of memory factors and response sets (Rorer, 1965), another factor keeping these reliability statistics artificially high is the rather sweeping nature of the statements that subjects are willing to make about their past behavior. Here subjects rely on memory contents that are very stable over time but can in no way reflect recent changes in motive structures (McClelland, 1980). But precisely these changes are reflected in measures such as the TAT.

Homogeneity

Another frequent criticism of the TAT procedure is directed at its lack of homogeneity: that is, low inter-item consistency (Entwisle, 1972). This line of argument is directed primarily at the low correlations of the motive scores among the various TAT pictures. However, here too we must take into account a peculiarity of the achievement motivation TAT. The test provides information not only about the intensity of the achievement motive, but also about its extensity, that is, its potential for generalization to various situations. The TAT pictures are chosen specifically to represent the theme "achievement" in various areas of activity and to arouse success and failure themes in varying degrees. Obviously the motive indexes for such heterogeneous material can hardly be internally consistent (deCharms, 1968).

Moreover, the assumed need for consistency is based on principles that cannot be applied to motivation measurement with the TAT. We should not assume that motivation is comparable to certain mental skills and abilities available over a long period, which can be tapped under almost any circumstances in order to find expression in homogeneous test scores.[1] A motivational tendency, such as might be aroused by the confrontation with thematic picture material, does not remain constant. Instead, it is reduced by the amount that is satisfied by the production of stories. Thus, another important factor determining whether, and to what extent, fantasies containing achievement themes occur in response to a TAT picture is the nature

---

[1] This assumption has become questionable even for the measurement of skills (Atkinson, 1974b; Atkinson & Lens, 1980).

of the stories produced for the preceding pictures. Along these same lines, Reitman and Atkinson (1958) actually observed a sawtooth effect in the sequential analysis of fantasy productions on the basis of individual TAT pictures.

Thus, if we take advantage of the situational arousal of motives for diagnosis of motivation, we can hardly expect internal consistency in the testing procedure. In diagnosing motivation with operant procedures, we cannot assume that the reactions to various TAT pictures must be stochastically independent of each other.

The question is, then, whether despite inconsistent test behavior we may expect high validity from the TAT procedure. Atkinson, Bongort, and Price (1977) investigated this matter in a simulation study, assuming the motivational principles described above as the basis for the fantasy themes produced in response to individual TAT pictures. In the analysis of the thematic material produced for successive TAT cards, they found, on the whole, very low consistency values (Cronbach's α). Nevertheless, the test reflected the previously determined motive strength of the hypothetical subjects with great precision. Thus a completely inconsistent measurement instrument turned out to be a valid predictor.

The results of these rather technical analyses of procedure are implicit in McClelland's theoretical concept of motivation (1971). According to McClelland, the TAT assesses the frequency with which thoughts revolve around certain themes (here achievement). McClelland (1971, p. 13) orients his definition of the motive toward this fact: "The measure, in turn, helps define a motive as a recurrent concern for a goal state, normally detectable in fantasy, which drives, directs, and selects behavior."

It is a fallacy to conclude from classical test theory that a lack of consistency in test behavior necessarily indicates a lack of consistency in the latent dimension on which the behavior is based. This fallacy is typical of the trait-centered approach to model construction found in personality psychology and has led to a variety of difficulties. But in recent times, from an interactionist perspective, we have begun again to distinguish more sharply between mediating variables (intervening variables, hypothetical constructs) and behavioral variables, or between a behavioral phenomenon and its explanation (Bowers, 1977; Magnusson & Endler, 1977).

The conceptual distinction leads to the realization that inconsistency on the behavioral level is entirely compatible with the assumption of consistency on the level of mediating processes (Olweus, 1977). Thus, what we must require is not the demonstration of behavioral consistency, but rather of behavioral coherence: that is, "the lawful idiographic, cross-situational pattern of stable and changing behaviors that is characteristic for an individual" (Magnusson, 1976, p. 1).

From this point of view, the achievement motive as measured by the TAT is supposed to represent the fact that behavior can be oriented toward the same goal under changing situational conditions. Accordingly, the TAT provides information about situation-specific, achievement-related experiential contents that are standardized in content categories. Content categories may indeed correlate only insignificantly with each other over the various TAT pictures and thus be inconsistent. Yet at the same time, they can constitute actualizations of the achievement motive that are appropriate to the respective situations. Content categories need to be equivalent only in a conceptual sense. The functional equivalence of individual test contents, as indicated by high intercorrelations and correspondingly high degrees of consistency, need not be assumed by interactionist theories of personality (Alker, 1972, pp. 8–9).

Thus, the question as to the internal consistency of the TAT procedure refers, on one hand, to the question of the homogeneity of the picture set, but also, on the other hand, to the homogeneity of the content categories. This question involves aspects of measurement theory and of construct theory that are concerned with the dimensionality of the procedure and of the construct. From the standpoint of techniques of measurement, the question is, Which elements of a procedure can be combined and taken to be a measure of the same latent continuum (the trait being measured)? Posed in the sense of a theory of constructs, on the other hand, the question concerns the mutually independent dimensions that must be called upon to characterize a given construct area.

Sader and Keil (1968) were the first to devote themselves to this question. Through factor analysis of the content categories in Heckhausen's scoring key (1963a), they found an optimal three-factor solution in which, along with an HS component, two different FF components appear: "need to avoid failure," and "negative feeling state." Kuhl (1972) reports quite similar findings. Kuhl (1977, 1978b) also pursued the question of the dimensionality of the TAT (Heckhausen, 1963a), with the aid of an analysis by Rasch (1960). "Specific objectivity," examined by Kuhl, implies consistency in the latent determinants of response behavior (motives as personal determinants, and cue values as situational determinants). Kuhl attempted primarily to determine whether all content categories used to calculate HS or FF scores belong to an equivalent class—that is, whether they can be considered measures of the same construct. It turned out that the various HS categories are equivalent within a subject group and thus constitute consistent indexes for a latent personality dimension. However, this was not true of the FF categories, which did not prove to be unidimensional in the sense of the model.

It is important to distinguish between two groups of FF categories. One describes a tendency, in anticipations as well as actions, to focus on avoidance of failure; the other describes a tendency to concern oneself with failure that has already occurred, and with its affective consequences. These results correspond completely to those of investigations involving factor analysis. These investigations also showed that the failure-avoidance components of the achievement motive constitute a dimension lacking in consistency. Since these results are relevant not only from the standpoint of measurement techniques, but also for factorial validity from the standpoint of construct theory, it becomes necessary here to describe the two-component approach to fear of failure on a theoretical level as well (see Chapter 6).

Alternatives to the Indirect Measuring Device: Questionnaires

McClelland (1958a, 1971, 1972b) has tended to emphasize that the achievement motive could be measured only in an indirect, projective manner, with the aid of the TAT. Other procedures, he felt, could by no means measure the motives underlying behavior, but were at most capable of registering generally recognized value orientations and opinions about achievement. According to McClelland, this objection holds especially for questionnaires. In reality, however, only for the tendency to seek success has McClelland's assumption been generally accepted. Since the investigation by Atkinson and Litwin (1960), a questionnaire has been employed for the measurement of the failure motive.

This procedure, the Test Anxiety Questionnaire (TAQ), was developed by Mandler and Sarason (1952) on the assumption that two kinds of learned drives are aroused in test situations: a task drive and an anxiety drive. This anxiety drive, in turn, leads to two different classes of reactions. Reactions in the first class are oriented directly toward the task and contribute to task management; the other reaction class consists of feelings of inadequacy and helplessness in relation to task demands, as well as a number of psychophysiological symptoms of anxiety in connection with test situations (heart palpitations, perspiration, etc.). Reactions in the second class, which the questionnaire is supposed to measure, are characterized by Mandler and Sarason as anxiety symptoms that are irrelevant to the task and which thereby interfere with performance. The individual items of the questionnaire refer to general uneasiness, consciousness of an accelerated heartbeat, perspiration, feelings of emotional impairment of performance, and finally, worries about the quality of performance. Factor analyses have often revealed two kinds of factors: cognitive factors that can be characterized as worries and lack of confidence, and emotional factors as expressed in psychophysiological symptoms of agitation (Fisch & Schmalt, 1970; Liebert & Morris, 1967). We return to this topic in Chapter 6.

It is customary in research to measure the two motives separately—the success motive with the TAT, and the failure motive with the TAQ. Subsequently, the standardized TAQ score is subtracted from the standardized TAT score. In order to distinguish between success- and failure-motivated subjects, the resulting differential value is divided at the median. Another method is to divide each of the two distributions of scores at the median, in order to identify extreme groups. Subjects with the score combination high TAT – low TAQ are considered to be success motivated, while those with the opposite combination of scores are called failure motivated.

Although this latter procedure for measuring the failure motive is well established (primarily in the United States), a satisfactory theoretical foundation for the procedure has not yet been developed. Atkinson (1964, pp. 289 – 290) has suggested that the signs of anxiety measured by the TAQ are symptoms of the fear of failure as activated by work on achievement-related tasks. It is argued that the stronger the anxiety symptoms are, the more pronounced is the failure motive. However, the assumption of such a direct, linear relationship between the symptoms of psychophysiological arousal and the failure motive is problematic. We are justified in assuming that the symptoms of arousal expressed in a test situation also reflect other motives, perhaps even the success motive (Heckhausen, 1968a, p. 120). At the moment, there are apparently no reliable physiological indicators for the directional component of emotional processes connected with motivational processes (see Duffy, 1962; Grossmann, 1973).

McClelland (1971) tried once more to justify the use of the TAQ to measure the failure motive. His point of departure was Smith's (1969) discovery that mothers of highly anxious children (TAQ) consider their children less gifted and exert considerable pressure for achievement. McClelland (1971) suggests that failure-motivated persons are characterized primarily by a motive goal of winning approval from others. In that case, the anxiety reflected in the TAQ would correspond to the fear, aroused in achievement situations, of not being able to meet high external standards of achievement, and thereby losing maternal affection. However, the relevance of this explanation must be questioned, since it involves a motive definition that is nowhere included in the concept of the failure motive; the motive goal in McClelland's definition is different from the actual achievement goals. In summary, then, there is little theoretical justification for using the TAQ to measure the failure motive (see Winter, 1973, p. 78).

As we have seen, the origin and development of the theory of achievement motivation was closely connected with the development of a measuring device, the TAT. Nevertheless, from the beginning there have been many attempts to replace the TAT with a questionnaire and to measure the approach and avoidance components of the achievement motive directly (see Schmalt, 1976b, pp. 52 – 69). However, many of these questionnaires were constructed without explicit reference to the theory of achievement motivation. Instead, the formulation of item contents depended entirely on the intuitions of the author of the test. In no instance was the validity of the instruments, in conformity with theory, demonstrated in a replicable manner. At best, we can say that correlations with school grades and with external ratings of achievement motivation are reported frequently. To be sure, the construct "achievement motive" is not necessary for the explanation of such correlations. They can be explained more economically by a variable such as value achievement (see McClelland, 1958a, 1972b).

However, two procedures must be mentioned as exceptions, if only because the principles by which they were constructed distinguish them from all others. Items on these tests were derived theoretically. Individual items were designed to reflect various sorts of behaviors and experiences that correspond to theoretical formulations — behaviors and experiences that many investigations have shown to be typical of success-motivated and failure-motivated persons. The principal areas of behavior reflected in the item contents are goal setting, risk taking, self-reinforcement after success and failure, conformity, preference for achievement-related activities, persistence, differentiation among various time perspectives for achievement-related behavior, and finally, behavioral effects of finished and unfinished tasks.

The first procedure based on these principles was constructed by Mehrabian (1968, 1969). He described alternative actions and experiences characteristic of success- and failure-motivated persons for selected areas of behavior and recorded the degree of agreement or disagreement with the alternatives. This became a measure for the "resulting tendency" of achievement motivation. The following item is typical: "In my spare time I would rather learn a game to develop skill than for recreation."

The revised, shortened version of the questionnaire contains 26 items; these appear in slightly modified form in separate versions for male and female subjects. Since many different aspects of behavior are included, the heterogeneity of the procedure is relatively great. Indeed, factor analyses by its author have resulted in approximately 12 factors with eigenvalues of over 1.0.

Up to now an entire series of investigations has been carried out with Mehrabian's procedure, primarily by the group of researchers working with Weiner. The great majority of these studies have produced results consistent with theory and thus confirmed the construct validity of the procedure.

The usefulness of this questionnaire is apparently based on its relatively close dependence on theory and on the successful formulation of its items, which are not transparent and thus are hard to falsify.

Hermans (1970) has developed another procedure for measuring the resulting tendency, constructed on the same principles. The questionnaire

contains 29 items altogether, selected according to the size of the discrimina-
bility coefficients and their correlation (as low as possible) with an anxiety
measure. The validation studies reveal nothing more than some correla-
tions with achievement measures, and these correlations are difficult to
interpret because of methodological inadequacies of the investigation.
Thus the question as to whether this procedure actually measures the
achievement motive must be answered negatively at the moment.

Another procedure based on theory is that by Gjesme and Nygard (1970),
which has already been used successfully (Rand, 1978) in a number of
investigations designed to test theory (see Chapter 3, Chapter 4).

Construct Validity in Trait Psychology: Motive Differences and Their Nomological Network

McClelland began by demonstrating that the TAT reflects motivations
that are partly dependent on various situational arousal conditions. The
next step was to show that TAT scores also reflect stable differences in the
personality trait "achievement motive." The question here was whether the
scoring key, developed on the basis of goal-setting behavior, could be cross-
validated, and whether it would be valid for new areas of behavior.

The first step was to develop a nomological network for the concepts,
which were isolated on the operational level. Initially this involved investi-
gating connections between motive variables and achievement-related be-
havior, without taking into account any situational parameters. Behavioral
differences were attributed exclusively to differences in the strength of mo-
tive dispositions, generally disregarding the fact that motives as dispositions
do not influence achievement-related behavior directly. The extent to
which a motive can affect behavior depends on how strongly it is aroused in a
given situation. Thus predictions of behavior should be made not from
motive dispositions, but rather from aroused motives—that is, from actual
motivation.

Performance Outcome

Lowell (1952) was the first to investigate the intensity of efforts to
achieve. His subjects were given scrambled-word tasks in which progress in
learning was possible. At the beginning of the experiment there was no
difference between the performance of high- and low-motive groups. How-
ever, highly motivated subjects apparently used their opportunities for learn-
ing better, for they were able to improve their performance considerably (see
Figure 2.6). These results remained the same when the influence of intelli-
gence was factored out (McClelland *et al.*, 1953, p. 235).

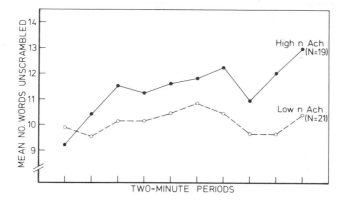

FIGURE 2.6 Performance of high and low need achievement groups on scrambled-word task. (From Lowell, 1952, "The effect of need for achievement on learning and speed performance," *Journal of Psychology, 33,* p. 36; a publication of the Helen Dwight Reid Educational Foundation.)

A second experiment (Lowell, 1952) involved simple overlearned addition tasks. This resulted in generally superior performance by highly motivated subjects (see Figure 2.7).

The question of the connection between the achievement motive and

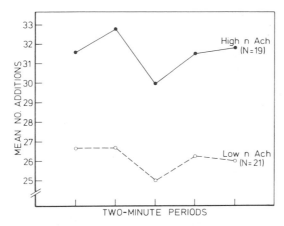

FIGURE 2.7 Performance of high and low need achievement groups on addition task. (From Lowell, 1952, "The effect of need for achievement on learning and speed performance," *Journal of Psychology, 33,* p. 38; a publication of the Helen Dwight Reid Educational Foundation.)

school or university performance has some practical significance; however, its theoretical significance is low. Such performance also depends on a whole series of other situational and motivational factors that are not taken into account and generally cannot be investigated with the monocausal experimental approach in question here (McClelland *et al.,* 1953, p. 237).

Early studies show that high, success-oriented achievement motivation is correlated with a higher level of performance in school or university (for example: Heckhausen, 1963a; McClelland *et al.,* 1953; Meyer *et al.,* 1965; Sader & Specht, 1967). Klinger (1966) reviewed studies of this sort in English-speaking countries and found that there are approximately as many studies showing the expected positive relationships as there are showing no relationship at all; however, results contrary to the expected positive relationship are rare (Wasna, 1972).

Such inconsistent results have been used inappropriately to cast doubts on the validity of the various measurement procedures and thus on the validity of the entire theory of achievement motivation—as if the experiments had been designed to test a theory. In fact, this body of literature consists primarily of correlational work, unrelated to theory (Entwisle, 1972; Wasna, 1972). To infer theoretical disconfirmation from such research is a crass violation of the principle that situational arousal of motives should be taken into account in predicting behavior. To be sure, we can generally assume —in predicting school performance, for example—that the achievement motive will be aroused by the teacher and by the topic being studied. Other things being equal, we can expect confirmatory, though low, positive correlations. However, the cases in which these correlations are absent do not falsify the theory. Rather, we must take care to examine and control the arousal conditions.

In general, these early studies soon made it clear that performance outcomes should not be attributed in a monocausal fashion to motives, but instead must be attributed to motivations. Yet for a long time no one asked in what fashion various motivational intensities can be translated into differences in performance. The suggested monotonic relationship between motivational strength and level of performance is not supported by many of the studies, especially when quality rather than quantity of performance of difficult tasks is examined. This question is discussed in the fourth chapter.

Goal Setting and Risk Taking

Setting the level of a goal that one hopes to attain in the course of an achievement-related activity is another important motive indicator. Goal setting has been used in research more frequently than any other criterion for individual differences in the achievement motive. Originally it seemed plausible to assume that a high, success-oriented achievement motive should be associated with a relatively high level of aspiration. The first study was by Atkinson (1950, cited by McClelland *et al.,* 1953). Students about to take their final exams were asked what grades they expected to receive. The correlation of expected grades with the achievement motive was .24 (n.s.). However, this value amounted to .45 (p < .05) for those subjects whose level of aspiration was unrealistic and who thus were apparently under motivational influence.

It soon became apparent that the level set for a goal does not increase monotonically with the level of approach motivation. McClelland (1958b) conjectured that achievement-motivated subjects tend to prefer moderate risks and thus would tend to set moderate goals. They should tend to avoid setting excessively high or low goals, because a very high level of aspiration would inevitably expose them to the likelihood of failure. If they succeeded, they would have to attribute their success to luck rather than to their own efforts. Likewise, if the goal is set very low, success would hardly provide them with any satisfaction about their own performance (McClelland, 1958b, p. 306). These conjectures about goal setting were confirmed in an experiment involving children playing a ringtoss game. Highly motivated children tossed their rings from a moderate distance more frequently than children with low motivation and also avoided extreme distances. This finding was soon confirmed by other experiments as well. There was also a new formalized approach to explaining these findings: Atkinson's risk-taking model (1957, 1964), which we discuss in the next chapter.

Persistence

French and Thomas (1958) investigated the behavioral parameter "persistence." Their subjects worked on complex tasks that they could abandon whenever they liked. Highly motivated subjects spent on the average twice as much time seeking a solution as did subjects with low motivation (27 vs. 14 minutes). Almost all the subjects who voluntarily worked until the end of the entire session were highly motivated (22 of 23), while most who discontinued participation had low motivation (44 of 69).

Other Behavioral Criteria

Only in this initial phase of achievement motivation research were motive scores correlated and connected with so many different variables. The goal was to delimit the meaning of the newly conceived motive construct in a network of nomological relationships. Thus the choice of behavioral criteria was frequently based on considerations of plausibility rather than derived from theory. The wealth of correlational studies is documented in *The Anatomy of Achievement Motivation* (Heckhausen, 1967a). Thus we mention only three kinds of behavioral criteria here, in order to indicate the variety available: perception thresholds, experience of time, and physiological activation.

McClelland and Liberman (1949) investigated recognition thresholds for words relevant to achievement concerns. As was mentioned, they found that subjects with high *n* Ach had a lower threshold for success-related words than did subjects with average or low *n* Ach. Criteria such as recognition threshold are among the variables that could cast light on an area that has been neglected in achievement motivation research up to the present: the extent to which motive-dependent differences exist in the perception and immediate appraisal of situations (see Ertel, 1964).

Differences in the achievement motive are expressed quite clearly in the structuring and experience of time. The length of future time perspective can be determined from the temporal frame of the sequence of events in TAT stories. Success-motivated subjects (*HS*) as well as highly motivated subjects (*Tm*) (see also Miessler, 1976) structure time spans further into the future (Heckhausen, 1963b). Success-motivated subjects also experience time in a more goal-directed and active fashion than do failure-motivated subjects. This was demonstrated with a method developed by Knapp and Garbutt (1958) involving the rating of the appropriateness of different sorts of time imagery. Factor analysis produced three groups of metaphors. The first type of metaphor involved high loadings on the factor "dynamic, fast-moving." This type can be divided into metaphors of "rapid goal-directed movement" (e.g., "Time is a galloping horseman") and metaphors of an "aimless, incessant stream of motion" (e.g., "Time is a rushing waterfall"). These categories reveal a clear difference in experience of time: goal-directed and rapid for success-motivated subjects (*HS*), but aimless and incessant for failure-motivated subjects. Not until later were motive differences in the experience of time taken into consideration again as a so-called future orientation (Raynor, 1969) and examined strictly according to theory for their effect (see Chapter 4).

Physiological variables were used more in the early phase of research as indicators of arousal within the central nervous system. Since the late 1960s their use (e.g., by Schönpflug & Heckhausen, 1976) has been rare. One example of early research in this area is a study by Mücher and Heckhausen (1962). Muscle tone in the thigh was measured during various sorts of mental activities and during rest breaks between activities. The rise and fall of muscle tone was not merely a function of alternation between activity and rest. In all phases of the experiment, highly motivated subjects (upper tercile of the *Tm* distribution) had higher activation scores than subjects with low motivation (lower tercile).

Incentive Studies: Motivation Effects as a Function of Motive and Situational Incentive

At first the principal aim of achievement motivation research was to uncover simple linear relationships between motive strength and behavioral criteria. Yet even in the initial phase there were already individual designs that were more challenging and productive because they varied situational cues as well as motive strength. Experimental designs involving analysis of variance replaced correlation and comparison of means, making it possible to measure interaction effects of person (motive strength) and situation (goal incentive).

A good example is an early incentive study by French (1958b). French varied two situational factors systematically in such a way that they corresponded to one or the other of the two motives whose relative strengths were being varied. In groups of four subjects, each subject received 5 sentences; the group was to compose a story with the 20 sentences. The performance of the group was the dependent variable. With regard to the strength of the two motives, each group was homogeneous. Either the achievement motive was high and the affiliation motive low (achievement motive group), or vice versa (affiliation motive group). The first situational factor was the instructions given for the task. Half of the groups were instructed to reach a consensus in the final solution; the other half were not required to do so (group orientation vs. individual orientation). The second situational factor was the incentive of the task outcome. The experimenter provided evaluative feedback during a pause in the experiment, praising the group either for competence or for cooperation (evaluative incentive for competence vs. cooperation).

As expected, in this $2 \times 2 \times 2$-factorial design, the achievement motive groups scored higher when the evaluative incentive was competence, while the affiliation motive groups scored higher when the incentive was cooperation (see Table 2.3). Group versus individual orientation had no effect at all

TABLE 2.3

Task-Score Means of Groups of Four for Eight Experimental Conditions[a]

| Feedback[b] | High achievement motive | | High affiliation motive | | |
	Group orientation	Individual orientation	Group orientation	Individual orientation	Mean
Competence	40.50	39.38	29.12	25.12	33.53
Cooperation	29.25	30.87	38.38	31.50	32.50
	34.88	35.12	33.75	28.31	

[a] Adapted from French, 1958b, p. 404.
[b] Positive feedback during the experiment from the experimenter.

on the achievement motive groups, whereas in the affiliation motive groups, group orientation was associated with somewhat better performance. The most favorable experimental constellation for subjects with a high affiliation motive consisted of group orientation and feedback during the experiment that emphasized good group work; the least favorable constellation was individual orientation with feedback about competence. None of the three main factors—neither motive pattern, nor task orientation (group vs. individual orientation), nor evaluative incentive in feedback—had a significant effect on performance when considered in isolation. In contrast, the interaction between motive pattern and kind of feedback was highly significant. The interaction of motive pattern and task orientation was also significant.

From French's study it was possible to draw two conclusions: (1) Motive differences affect behavior only when coupled with corresponding situational cues (i.e., as aroused motivation), and (2) Individual cue dimensions differ in their effects on individual motives. This study showed, therefore, that group versus individual task orientation is important only with affiliation-motivated subjects, but not with achievement-motivated subjects.

Sex Differences and Fear of Success

Female subjects have been exceptions to the rule since the beginning of achievement motivation research. The first arousal studies showed that n Ach scores for females did not increase along with the strength of the cue conditions, but were already quite high under neutral conditions (McClelland et al., 1949; Veroff, Wilcox, & Atkinson, 1953). It was suggested (McClelland et al., 1953, p. 178) that the cues referring to "intelligence and leadership qualities" that were given by the experimenter just before the TAT was administered were poorly suited for activating the achievement motive in women, in contrast with a cue such as "social acceptability." In other countries, such as Brazil (Angelini, 1959) or Japan (Hayashi & Habu, 1962), sex differences did not appear. Nor did sex differences appear in Germany with another motive scoring key (for HS and FF; Heckhausen, 1963a). These data in turn suggested that national differences in the proportion of women attending universities might be the determining factor. In Brazil, Japan, and Germany the participation of women in higher education was not as high as in the United States, so that a more selective portion of the age groups became students—presumably the portion with a more masculine role concept.

The unclear findings inspired a series of studies continuing until the middle of the 1960s. These studies examined various presumed factors for their effect: the degree of selectiveness in the female subject sample, their level of academic achievement, whether the institution of learning in question was coeducational and how competitive it was, value orientation (intellectual and career oriented vs. domestic and family oriented), the sex of the persons in the TAT pictures, the age and family status of the storyteller, and so forth. Alper (1974) and Horner (1974a, 1974b) gave overviews of various patterns of findings that left the field in some confusion. Characteristic is the title of Alper's review: "Achievement Motivation in College Women: A Now-You-See-It-Now-You-Don't Phenomenon."

The following results illustrate the lack of clarity in the findings. Subjects of both sexes had higher n Ach scores in TAT pictures involving males. This was attributed to the manner in which the educational institution in question selected students and to sociocultural sex stereotypes (Veroff *et al.,* 1953). As cues became stronger, female college students showed increasingly higher n Ach for male TAT pictures (Alper, 1957; Morrison, 1954); however, for female TAT pictures the scores increased only when a professional career was implied (Morrison, 1954).

In a highly selective high school for girls, students with similar IQs were divided into two groups: successful and unsuccessful students. When the effects of male and female TAT pictures and of neutral and achievement-oriented cue conditions were compared, the general cue effect was not significant (Lesser, Krawitz, & Packard, 1963). However, the effect was significant for successful students reacting to female pictures, though not when they reacted to male pictures. The reverse was true for unsuccessful students. The situational cue effect occurred only with male TAT pictures but was reversed with female pictures. The findings could not be clarified by taking into account individual differences in values (French & Lesser, 1964). N Ach was higher for all students when intellectual values were aroused for male TAT pictures and traditional feminine values were aroused for female TAT pictures, regardless of whether the students' own role concept was more intellectual or more traditionally feminine.

Had it not been for a dissertation by Horner (1968; see also 1969, 1970, 1974a), achievement motivation research in English-speaking countries might still be almost entirely restricted to male subjects. Horner's dissertation rapidly became widely known, literally caused a furor, and inspired a series of follow-up studies. Horner believed that she had cleared up the mystery behind the inconsistent findings by introducing an additional motive characteristic of women, "fear of success." Being a high achiever reduces the popularity of women, especially their popularity with men. Thus it is only seemingly paradoxical that women fear success.

Instead of TAT cards, Horner presented her male and female subjects with statements like those in the FTI (French, 1958a). The sixth and last was "At the end of the first-term final, Anne finds herself at the top of her medical school class." (For male subjects the name Anne was replaced by John.) Success-avoidance stories were told in response to this statement by 65% of Horner's female subjects, including an especially large number of successful students, but only 9% of her male subjects told such stories for the John version. The scoring key for fear of success is based on the presence of the following content categories in the story: negative consequences of success with respect to popularity and affiliation, expectation of negative consequences from success, negative affects associated with success, activities instrumental in moving away from present or future success (e.g., becoming a nurse instead of a doctor), directly expressed conflicts about success, reinterpretation of the situation (denial), or bizarre and unrealistic reactions. If one of these categories appeared, fear of success was attributed to the narrator (just as Scott, 1956, had done for fear of failure).

After the measurement of motives, subjects were assigned various tasks in a group experiment. In a second session subjects again performed various tasks, this time under one of three conditions: individual and noncompetitive, mixed sexes and competitive, or same sex and competitive. Some performance differences were found in the female subject groups. Subjects with fear of success performed better in the noncompetitive session than in the general group session, which Horner considered competitive. The reverse was true of subjects without fear of success.

The design of this experiment does not facilitate definitive conclusions, nor do the findings indicate that fear of success is an incentive effect based on competition with men that interferes with performance. It would be more fitting to see the noncompetitive condition (second session) as achievement oriented and the group condition (first session) as neutral. Then female subjects with fear of success would show a distinct cue effect. Along these same lines, Zuckerman and Wheeler (1975) also compared subject groups in the second session and found that female students with fear of success were generally superior in performance to other female students without fear of success. Only under the noncompetitive condition was the performance of subjects with high fear of success inferior. Nor did later studies generally find any difference in performance in Horner's sense (see Peplau, 1976).

Horner had gathered her first data in 1965. It seemed reasonable to see fear of success as a historical phenomenon in the sense of a generation effect or cohort effect. Accordingly, fear of success could have been expected to disappear with the awakening of the women's liberation movement at the end of the 1960s and the beginning of the 1970s. But Horner reported a sample of female students with 85% fear of success as late as 1972, and Alper (1974) reported 89% from the 1970–1971 school year. Soon it was discovered that male students produced only a little less or even more fear of success in response to the John version than female students did to the Anne version. In 9 of 16 samples taken between 1968 and 1974, female students showed more fear of success than male students; the opposite was true of the other 7 samples (Zuckerman & Wheeler, 1975, p. 936). A historical trend seemed to be manifesting itself in men rather than in women. Hoffman (1974) reported a percentage of 79 with fear of success in her sample of male students at the University of Michigan. Meanwhile, it was becoming increasingly clear that Horner's instrument might be measuring something different in men than in women; in any case, it did not measure fear of the extrinsic side effects of success.

It seemed reasonable to explain the fear of success results by means of cultural stereotypes rather than in terms of an epochal change in sex roles, especially since the medical profession continued to be dominated by men and the statement used by Horner referred to Anne's being in medical school. Such an explanation is partially supported by the fact that both men and women produced much more fear of success in response to the Anne version than to the John version (Alper, 1974; Monahan, Kuhn, & Shaver, 1974). But the contents of the fear of success stories show sex-related differences. Men (John version) question the value of achievement as such and reject the goals and life-style of a successful professional career. They do not fear success because of its unwanted extrinsic side effects. Instead, they have begun to question the intrinsic incentive value of academic and professional success. Women, on the other hand, are concerned about loss of their femininity and about social rejection (see Hoffman, 1974; 1977; Morgan & Mausner, 1973). Thus, they are not motivated by fear of success as such; rather, they fear extrinsic side effects of success, especially the thwarting of affiliation-motivated goals.

Even today the construct "fear of success" is "popular but unproven" (the title of an article by Tresemer, 1974). In a critical collective review, Zuckerman and Wheeler (1975) come to the following conclusions:

1. There are no reliable sex or age differences in the motive "fear of success."
2. Fear of success is apparently not related to sex-role orientation.
3. It is unclear whether a motive or cultural stereotypes are involved in the case of fear of success.
4. There are no consistent relationships between fear of success and achievement-related variables. The procedure for measuring fear of success is questionable and not especially reliable.

Hoffman (1977) has shed some light on this confusing state of affairs with the aid of a follow-up experiment involving Horner's original subjects. Nine years had passed between the 1965 experiment (Horner) and the 1974 experiment (Hoffman). A reevaluation of the original material revealed that a change had meanwhile taken place in the method of interpretation. The new method made it easier to register frequent occurrences of fear of success in men, so that a large part of the presumed epochal change in men seemed attributable to the method of analysis alone. After nine years the women in Horner's original sample showed on the average a decrease in fear of success, while the average for men had remained the same. Thus the average scores for men were somewhat higher than for women in the follow-up experiment. However, only for women were the scores consistent. Those who had no fear of success in 1965 had none in 1974; but nearly half of those who did fear it feared it no longer in 1974, being for the most part married and already mothers.

The fear of success measure turned out to be invalid for the men. Indeed, it had never been validated for them with behavioral criteria. It is here that most of the problems arose in evaluation. Again it turned out that men tended to find success intrinsically questionable rather than to fear extrinsic negative side effects as did the women. Such doubts about the incentive value of success tended both in 1964 and in 1975 to be associated with a low achievement motive in men.

On the other hand, Horner's instrument did indeed turn out to measure something like fear of extrinsic side effects of achievement in women. As Hoffman had expected, more than the statistically predictable number of women who had high fear of success scores in 1965 became pregnant in the next nine years, just at the point when they were faced not only with the decision of whether or not to have a child, but also with the prospect of an impending success that would change in their favor the established balance of achievement status between them and their male partners (husbands or life companions). What could be a better solution than a pregnancy when a woman fears that her own success will cause a strain in the relationship with her partner? A pregnancy, comments Hoffman (1977), "removes the wife from the achievement-career arena, confirms her femininity, and reestablishes affiliative ties" (p. 319).

The case of fear of success is typical for a phenomenon that is presumably enlightening but was prematurely conceptualized. From the perspective of our basic model of motivation (Figure 1.2), fear of success is apparently a complex motivation. An achievement outcome, whether expected or already attained, generates an extrinsic outcome-consequence expectancy (instrumentality). This expectancy is that a consequence with negative incentive will occur within a different motive area: for example, loss of social affiliation. Our motivation model brings out a number of points that were ignored in previous research and should be taken into account when determining the conditions under which this "now-you-see-it-now-you-don't" phenomenon (fear of success) appears. The first step is to measure the strength of those motives whose actualization can be threatened by achievement, such as the affiliation motive. The second step is to determine the strength of the outcome-consequence expectancy that a positive achievement outcome will automatically elicit a particular consequence with negative incentive. And last but not least, we need to bring into line with motivation theory the procedure for measuring fear of success, which needs improvement, as well as to define the situations in which fear of success behavior can be predicted and manifested.

Karabenick (1977) has begun these long-overdue projects. He took the first step mentioned above by measuring the strength of the affiliation motive. He then measured fear of success with a new procedure developed by Horner, which had been validated for achievement differences between competitive and noncompetitive conditions (Horner, Tresemer, Berens, & Watson, 1973). Karabenick's dependent variable was performance on an anagram test. After individual experiments, each female subject worked on anagrams again in competition with a male subject. Both the apparently masculine and the apparently feminine types of anagrams were assigned. In comparison with their performance when working alone, the more the women feared success, the greater was the drop in quality of performance during competition — but only with regard to masculine tasks. The results were the same with the negative version of the affiliation motive (fear of rejection), but here only for feminine tasks. For males the variance in performance is best explained by a combination of n Ach and TAQ.

Finally, the connections among the motive variables are also of interest. With women, fear of success showed a negative correlation with n Ach and a positive correlation with both tendencies in the affiliation motive (hope for affiliation and fear of rejection). In men, fear of success also correlated with both affiliation motives, but not with n Ach. From these studies conducted with students in the United States in the mid-1970s, we can conclude that when fear of success is high, the incentives for achievement and for affiliation interfere with each other, but only for women.

Although the explanatory construct "fear of success" did not turn out to be especially suitable for determining sex differences in achievement motivation, researchers' interest in this question has not lessened; if anything, it has increased. This interest is fostered by research in three different areas. The first stems from traditional studies in achievement motivation, in which sex differences on individual variables are regularly identified. For example, Crandall (1969) reported that among 7–12-year-old schoolchildren, girls had less expectation of success than did boys. She also found that their causal attributions frequently differed. In comparison with boys, girls tended less to attribute success to ability, and they tended less to attribute failure to bad luck or insufficient effort (Deaux & Farris, 1977; Dweck &

Repucci, 1973; Feather & Simon, 1975; Nicholls, 1975, 1978). Correspondingly, self-evaluation by girls was less favorable; their effort and persistence decreased and their performance dropped. Presumably, general prejudices about typical sex differences in competence are a factor in producing these differential patterns of attribution (Deaux & Emswiller, 1974).

The second and third sources of recent interest in researching sex differences in achievement motivation involve primarily those female researchers who have taken a closer look at the problem. Some of them have extended the concept "achievement" and the motivation model based on it, or even questioned it. Others have liberated achievement-related behavior from the narrowness of single episodes and, instead, have examined it as career motivation, with its complex opportunity structures.

As an example from the first of the three research areas—traditional achievement motivation research—Stein and Bailey (1973) have proposed that affiliative and nurturing values be included in the model of achievement motivation, thereby doing justice to women's achievement strivings. In this context, Bakans' (1966) "duality of human existence"—that is, agency versus communion—was especially influential. Bem's (1977) studies of androgyny (see also Spence & Helmreich, 1978) were also important. Parsons and Goff (1980) inserted two affiliation motives, conceived analogously to the two achievement motives, in the risk-taking model: a motive to gain affiliative success and another motive to avoid affiliative failure. To be sure, the attempt to consider both motives (or, as they can also be called, value dispositions) simultaneously could be more adequately formalized by using a model based on instrumentality theory, such as we outlined in the first chapter, instead of the risk-taking model. In our model, outcomes of achievement-related behavior are always accompanied by anticipated affiliation-related consequences for persons to whom affiliation means a great deal. Both the consequences and their instrumentalities determine a person's choice of achievement goals and the extent to which the goals are pursued.

The other approach to sex differences in achievement motivation (career motivation) involves developmental psychology. It is based on a psychology of individual differences in motives and early socialization of sex-role orientation, also taking into account the environmental forces that influence development in early and middle adulthood. This includes, above all, the expectations of significant others (parents, husbands, employers, etc.) and the socioeconomic structure (e.g., social support systems for working mothers, or laws to establish equal rights for both sexes).

Farmer and Fyans (1980) have drawn upon various psychological and environmental factors to explain the achievement motivation as well as the career motivation of women who return to college after raising a family. One of their findings for this group of subjects was that personality dispositions can be modified decisively through environmental factors. Thus, androgynous women who did not perceive their environment as supportive had no professional motivation, while women with a definitely feminine role orientation sought top-level careers if they felt themselves encouraged to do so by their social surroundings. Yet despite the importance of environment, since highly motivated women also face the greatest conflicts, they will still find themselves in complicated situations if they attempt to achieve professional success.

Historical Change and Sociocultural Differences

Early on it seemed reasonable to expect motive differences among various demographically defined population groups. This was suggested by Max Weber's thesis (1904 – 1905) of an inner connection between "the Protestant ethic and the spirit of capitalism." According to this thesis, the early Industrial Revolution had its religious roots in the activist, individualistic professional ethics of post-Reformation denominations, especially Calvinism with its theory of predestination. McClelland started his own line of research, the results of which he presented in 1961 in the book *The Achieving Society.* This book attracted considerable attention outside the field of psychology as well. McClelland proposed the following theory of psychological cause and effect: In the evaluative context of the Protestant ethic, childrearing emphasizes independence and responsibility for oneself. This encourages the development of a pronounced achievement motive. The achievement motive, in turn, leads to increased entrepreneurial activity, resulting in accelerated economic growth through continual reinvestment of profits and through the use of technological innovations (see Figure 7.3).

Accordingly, it should be possible to take advantage of economic categories for the analysis of motive differences among population groups. McClelland even ventured to suggest that the per capita consumption of electric energy was an indicator of the degree of economic expansion of a particular population as defined in historical, cultural, and spatial terms. For example, a comparison of the economic power of Protestant and Catholic countries around 1952 showed that Protestant countries were more powerful, even when national differences in natural resources were taken into account.

Historical Change

Such analyses call for a national motive index as well as an economic index. McClelland derived his motive index from the content analysis of stories from third-grade reading textbooks, using the *n* Ach scoring key. He assumed that in countries with universal compulsory education the national spirit is reflected more transparently in readers for young schoolchildren than in any other documents. In order to establish whether motive changes determine economic rise and fall as suggested by Weber, or whether the reverse is true, McClelland examined connections between earlier motive indexes and later economic indexes. In an initial comparison he correlated national n Ach indexes for 22 countries (European and non-European, capitalist and socialist) as of 1925, with the discrepancy between the expected and actual increase in per capita consumption of electricity that was observed in the individual countries in 1950, 25 years later. The expected degree of increase had been based on the extent of industrialization in 1925 and the amount of natural resources in the individual countries. The correlation was no less than $+.53$. Using the motive index from the same year (1950), the correlation disappears ($+.03$). It does indeed seem that a high national achievement motive leads to a disproportionally high growth rate, and low motive strength leads to a disproportionally low growth rate.

McClelland also found the same relationship over a shorter period, from 1950 to 1958, for 49 countries. Here the correlation between n Ach (1950) and the deviation from the expected growth rate (1952–1958) still amounted to $+.43$. Extending the period examined (1952–1976), on the other hand, did not result in a significant correlation ($+.11$) with the motive index of 1950 (Beit-Hallahmi, 1980).

Content analysis of linguistic documents makes it possible to determine motive indexes of much earlier times as well. Samples from literary texts that can be dated are assumed to reflect the achievement motive of the period in question. For ancient Greece from 900 to 100 B.C., for example, the texts were epigrams, lyric poems, martial orations, and funeral elegies; for Spain from 1200 to 1730 they were novels, poems, and legends; and for Tudor England from 1400 to 1830 they were dramas, reports of ocean voyages, and street ballads. The corresponding national economic indexes for ancient Greece were archaeological maps that show the increase in export of olive oil, as determined from excavated clay pitchers whose ornamentation makes it possible to establish their date of origin. In the case of medieval Spain, the indexes were documents from seaports concerning the tonnage of Spanish ships that sailed to the New World each year. Finally, the indexes for England were the annual coal import statistics for greater London. In all three cases, the increase and decrease in the n Ach index preceded the periods of economic growth.

deCharms and Moeller (1962) contributed an example from a less distant age — the United States between 1800 and 1950. They compared the n Ach index for the midpoint of 20-year periods (as determined from the average number of pages containing achievement imagery in schoolchildren's

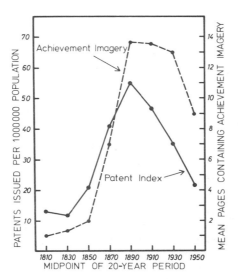

FIGURE 2.8 National index of the achieve-
ment motive (mean pages out of 25 containing
achievement imagery in school readers) and
number of patents issued per million popula-
tion in the United States between 1800 and
1950. (From deCharms & Moeller, 1962, p.
139.)

readers) with the number of registered patents per million inhabitants. Here
too, rise or fall in the national motive index was reflected in economic growth
or decline 20–40 years later, as measured by patents—that is, technological
innovation (see Figure 2.8).

Sociocultural Motive Differences

It also seemed reasonable to seek motive differences among sociologically
defined groups in the contemporary populations of industrialized nations
(see summary by Heckhausen, 1972a). Representative data were collected
for the United States (Veroff, Atkinson, Feld, & Gurin, 1960) and for Swit-
zerland (Vontobel, 1970). It was no longer possible to find differences
between Protestants and Catholics, but it was indeed possible to do so for
social classes. Table 2.4 contains the results of a sample of Swiss-German
army recruits. The TAT scores from the *HS* and *FF* scoring keys were
standardized (with 100 as the mean of the entire sample) to facilitate com-
parisons. The success motive, unlike the failure motive, diminishes as the

TABLE 2.4
Achievement Motive Patterns in Groups of Different
Social Origins[a]

Social origin[b]	HS	FF	NH	Tm
All regions				
Protestants	100	97	103	98
Catholics	101	107	94	104
upper class	114	107	108	111
middle class	108	102	106	105
lower class	84	108	76	96
Urban regions				
upper class	132	110	122	121
middle class	108	98	110	103
lower class	95	108	87	101

[a] Adapted from Vontobel, 1970, pp. 190–191.
[b] From a sample of 539 Swiss-German army recruits.

social class becomes lower; the correlation is highly significant. Corresponding differences were found for NH and Tm. Social class differences in the achievement motive are especially clear in the urban population. In contrast, no significant differences were found between the two religious denominations.

Vontobel (1970, pp. 66–146) worked out an ecological theory of optimal challenge in the sense of the historian A. Toynbee in order to explain the motive differences among sociocultural groups. In this connection, he differentiated among the following aspects: familial socialization and enculturation, family structure, religious denomination, social class, occupation, traditional versus modern orientation of the culture, type and ideology of the society, and tensions in the social structure.

Motive Constellations for Achievement, Power, and Affiliation

Motive influence on complex behavior as well as on the results of extended behavioral sequences can be described more precisely if not just one, but rather several motives are taken into account. This is especially true of complex situations in which various motives are activated. In a number of studies, individual constellations of two or three motives have been used to group subjects, or the constellations were determined subsequently. Motive constellations were controlled from the outset in some experimental bargaining games; such constellations were determined subsequently for some criterion groups such as prominent businessmen, political leaders, or radical students, and were in some cases used as national motive indexes for psychological shifts from one epoch to another.

Experimental Bargaining Games

Terhune (1970) arranged bargaining games of varying complexity, choosing subjects at the beginning by motive constellation. In his variant of the Prisoner's Dilemma game (1968a), used so frequently in conflict research, Terhune paired off the players in such a way that each was very high in one of the three motives — achievement, power, or affiliation — and very low in the other two. When the game matrix was not arranged in too threatening a fashion, definite motive differences appeared. Achievement-motivated subjects were the most cooperative; they also expected more cooperation from their partners. The affiliation-motivated subjects were the most defensive and most fearful of being deceived. The most competitive were the power-motivated subjects (as defined by Veroff, 1957). They attempted to deceive their partners, but at the same time they expected them to cooperate. The more threatening the game became — that is, the greater the temptation to deceive their partners and the greater the fear of being deceived — the more defensive the behavior of all subjects became. Motive differences disappeared.

Bludau (1976) found quite similar results by contrasting highly success-motivated subjects (*NH*) who had a weak power motive (as defined by Winter, 1973) with the opposite constellation. Success-motivated subjects preferred to cooperate and showed a preference for a game matrix that was neither too threatening nor too cooperation oriented. Power-motivated subjects showed ambivalent behavior, with a tendency to be competitive. They preferred conflict-oriented games (threatening matrix).

The game "International Connections" (Terhune, 1968b) is far more complex. The group consists of several subjects with similar motive constellations. Each "nation" can build up its armament level or develop its economy, declare war or make treaties, spread misleading propaganda or reveal its true intentions. The results are similar to those in the Prisoner's Dilemma game. Achievement-motivated subjects expended the most effort on cooperation and affiliation-motivated subjects expended the least effort, presumably because of their extreme withdrawal (in order not to become involved in any conflicts). For example, they sent the fewest messages. Power-motivated subjects (as defined by Veroff, 1957) were occupied more than the other two groups with an arms buildup, while achievement-motivated subjects spent the least money for arms. Power-motivated subjects also put the most effort into manipulating the others—that is, misleading them through public propaganda and confidential messages.

The image communicated by power-motivated subjects through bargaining games almost has the quality of manipulative exploitation. It is appropriate, however, to be skeptical of such a narrow, moralistic perspective. We must not forget that from the outset, bargaining games simultaneously define and call for such behavior. The situational dependency of behavior is emphasized by Terhune's discovery that all motive differences are blurred when the matrix for winning becomes too threatening. Moreover, Terhune found that motive differences became less relevant when 30 rounds were played in succession, particularly when the subjects were permitted oral communication. It is possible to see power-motivated subjects somewhat more clearly by examining these subjects as criterion groups in real-life contexts.

Criterion Groups

One example of a criterion group is a group of leading managers of commercial enterprises. McClelland (1961) had originally gathered proof that large numbers of highly achievement-motivated persons are to be found among successful business leaders. But it was necessary to correct, or at least to qualify this statement (see McClelland, 1975, pp. 252–253). Managers of large organizations need to delegate tasks, coordinate their execution, and motivate—if not inspire—their subordinates to work toward long-range goals: in short, to be leaders. Managers whose only qualification is high achievement motivation are apparently too individualistic to lead in this fashion; instead, they attempt to take full responsibility and do many things better on their own than they were done before. Lost in detail and unable to delegate, they are caught in an organizational maze. In order to function well, these leaders with high achievement motivation need that which only a manager can create for them: an atmosphere that facilitates their way of thinking and acting, and that creates a framework for it within the organizational structure (see Litwin & Stringer, 1968).

Andrews (1967) studied two large, comparable Mexican firms and discovered that the atmosphere in an organization is the major influence determining whether individual motives are expressed at all. Firm A, a branch of a U.S. company, was organized strictly according to the achievement principle. Those who were successful in terms of the firm's goals were promoted rapidly, even above the heads of former supervisors who had been with the firm for a long time. Firm B, a Mexican firm, had a strictly hierarchical organization and was managed in an almost patriarchal fashion. Years of service and loyalty to the firm were more important criteria for upward mobility than proof of accomplishment.   Distinctly different motives appeared in samples from the two firms, including subjects at various job levels.   Subjects with higher achievement motives held higher-ranked positions in Firm A; in Firm B, in contrast, subjects with higher power motives held higher-ranked positions.

Litwin and Stringer (1968) developed a procedure for measuring the atmosphere in an organization more precisely, on six dimensions:

1. conformity
2. responsibility
3. standards
4. rewards
5. clarity of organizational structure
6. team spirit

The co-workers of 49 top managers in large American firms described in detail how their area functioned with regard to these six points.   The indexes for clarity of organizational structure and team spirit were combined into an index of morale.   Of the 26 top managers whose co-workers showed above-average morale, 88% had higher TAT scores for the power motive than for the affiliation motive.   In contrast, higher power scores appeared for only 30% of the top managers whose co-workers had described an organizational atmosphere with lower morale.   When work morale was high, the power motive of managers was very strong in every respect and the affiliation motive weak; co-workers agreed that they were proud to belong to their manager's work group.

The findings of Litwin and Stringer suggest that the optimal organizational atmosphere for economic success would be produced by a combination of high power motive, high achievement motive, and low affiliation motive in leading managers.   Only part of this motive constellation appeared in an investigation by Wainer and Rubin (1971).   Wainer and Rubin measured power, achievement, and affiliation motives of 51 managers of small, recently established businesses in the technical sector.   The index of economic success was the growth rate of business turnover.   Figure 2.9 shows the results based on percentage of low, medium, and high scores for each motive in managers of firms with an above-average growth rate.   According to these results, which show each motive separately, a high achievement motive combined with a low affiliation motive encourages economic success, while the strength of the power motive is apparently irrelevant. However, two aspects of the experiment must be considered along with these findings.   In the first place, the study was restricted to small firms with simple organizational structures that did not require any especially demand-

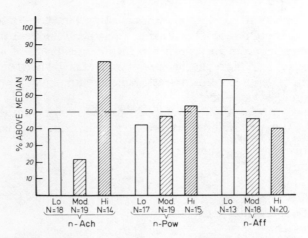

FIGURE 2.9 Percentage of companies with above-median growth rate whose managers exhibit low, moderate, or high achievement, power, or affiliation motive. $N = 51$ companies that were small or had been established for 3 years or less. (Adapted from Wainer & Rubin, 1971, p. 137.)

ing leadership or distribution of tasks. In the second place, an examination of motive constellations showed that the largest growth in turnover occurred in firms whose leaders had a high achievement motive and an average power motive.

On the basis of the constellation of high achievement and power motive combined with low affiliation motive, Kock (1965, 1974) predicted the destiny of some large businesses and checked 10 years later to see whether his prophecies had been fulfilled. Kock (1965) chose 15 similar firms from among 104 Finnish businesses in the knitted-goods industry. All of these firms had been founded at the same time, with the aid of state subsidies. Over a period of 10 years (1952–1961), data for various economic development factors were collected. At the end of this period, the achievement, power, and affiliation motives of the persons in charge of these firms were measured. Table 2.5 shows the correlations between the individual motives and the motive pattern "achievement plus power minus affiliation" ($Ach + Pow - Aff$) for company leaders, on the one hand, and five economic development criteria for the 10-year period, on the other hand. Over this period a noticeable change in direction had taken place in the industry: The production of fashion accessories had grown steadily. As we can see, the constellation $Ach + Pow - Aff$ correlated even more closely with the economic criteria than the achievement or power motive had ever done—or, in a negative sense, the affiliation motive.

TABLE 2.5

Relations between Managers' Motive Patterns and Economic Development[a]

	Motives of managers[b]			
	Ach	*Pow*	*Aff*	*Ach + Pow − Aff*
15 firms 1954–1961				
gross production value	.39	.49*	−.61**	.67**
number of employees	.41	.42	−.62**	.66**
turnover	.46*	.41	−.53*	.60*
gross investments	.63*	−.06	.20	.45*
profits	.27	.01	−.30	.34
10 firms 1962–1971				
gross production value	−.04	.44	−.42	.62
number of employees	.15	.55	−.26	.74
turnover	.04	.37	−.49	.60
gross investments	.05	.85	.20	.59
profits	.10	.56	−.13	.62

[a] Adapted from Kock, 1974, pp. 215–216.

[b] Correlations of five criteria of economic development for 15 knitted-goods companies in the period 1954–1961 with managers' achievement, power, and affiliation motives, as well as with the motive pattern "Achievement + Power − Affiliation," along with corresponding correlations for the 10 firms that survived the period 1962–1971.

* $p < .05$; ** $p < .01$

In an affiliation study, Kock (1974) predicted the economic development for the subsequent period, 1962–1971, on the basis of motive scores. Of the 7 firms with the lowest motive constellation scores, 5 failed during this period. One was combined with another firm, 1 became bankrupt, and the other 3 ceased to exist for other reasons. Table 2.5 contains the correlations for the remaining 10 firms. In contrast with a high power motive and a low affiliation motive, a high achievement motive alone no longer plays a decisive role. The overall motive pattern is important; again, it is a better predictor than any single motive.

Politicians holding government office constituted another criterion group in positions of power. Donley and Winter (1970) analyzed the inauguration speech of every president of the United States for power and achievement themes. Action-oriented presidents such as Franklin Roosevelt, John F. Kennedy, or Lyndon Johnson have much higher power motive and achievement motive scores than do relatively inactive presidents such as William Taft or Dwight Eisenhower. Motive differences are also reflected in the number of reorganizations of the Cabinet, in territorial extensions of the country, and in number of wars entered (Winter, 1973).

Activists in the student protest movement constituted another criterion group. Winter and Wiecking (1971) determined motive scores for male and female students at the end of the 1960s who worked full time in protest organizations instead of studying, and called themselves radicals. At first glance the results are surprising. The radicals were more motivated toward achievement and less toward power than a control group. These results were confirmed by nonreactive findings. In May 1969 students occupied the office of the president of Wesleyan University in order to protest campus reserve-officer recruiting for the Vietnam War. At the same time, other students passed a resolution against the occupation of the office. Both groups, the participants in the sit-in and the counterdemonstrators, signed resolutions. Among these names, Winter and Wiecking found approximately 55 students on both sides who had participated 3 – 15 months earlier in a TAT experiment measuring the power motive and the achievement motive. A comparison of the two groups showed that the protesters had a significantly lower power motive than the counterdemonstrators, who were concerned with law and order. The difference in achievement motive was in the expected direction, but not significant. The authors explain their findings thus: It is precisely the more highly achievement-motivated persons who attempt to change rigid and established conditions, while those who are highly power motivated attempt to use the existing state of affairs instrumentally.

Applications: Motive Training Courses

In 1961 McClelland began conducting training courses in developing countries in order to reinforce the achievement motive for owners of small- and medium-sized firms. Such training courses are still found, for example, in the intervention repertoire of the UNIDO (United Nations Industrial Development Organization). In a slightly altered form, similar training courses have also been set up as extracurricular training for schoolchildren. The theoretical bases and methodological procedures of these 10 – 14-day training courses were derived only loosely from contemporary achievement motivation theory and on the whole were quite eclectic. We will describe these motive training courses in this chapter and distinguish them from motive-modification programs, which are not described until Chapters 5 and 6. It is true that the motive-modification programs could hardly have been conceived without McClelland's motive training courses. Yet even though the two programs are very similar in some ways, there are two main differences. First of all, as a rule the motive-modification programs are not actually courses, but rather programs that are incorporated into everyday institutions such as school instruction. Second, and more important, motive-modification programs are much more closely derived from propositions of achievement motivation theory, especially such postulated cognitive intermediary processes as causal attribution of success and failure, self-reinforcement, and reference norms (developments that are described in Chapters 5 and 6).

McClelland began the first motive training courses in 1961, although the achievement motive was thought of at that time as a stable personality disposition. Even in early childhood, it was believed, firm connections are established between situational cues and expected affect with respect to success and failure, and these are redintegrated in all situations that promise such a change in affect. Indeed, the resistance of the established connections between situational cues and expectancy affects to any later relearning was precisely that which was believed to determine the dispositional nature of the motive. Fortunately, McClelland moved away from his earlier positions about the dispositional stability of the motive. Apparently the desire to do something and to give people that motivational basis on which economic prosperity was believed to depend was stronger in him than theoretical consistency.

McClelland did not offer any theoretical basis — or rather, justification — for his training courses (which were quite successful) until 1965. This justification was not based only on the optimism of missionaries, therapists, those who want to improve the world through ideology, and political leaders. McClelland also examined all areas of contemporary psychology that seemed to concern themselves with behavioral change in some form, especially learning theory, psychotherapy, and attitude change. The resulting theory was not only eclectic, but also so general that it was not very convincing. Motives were described as affectively toned "associative networks" related to each other by a hierarchy of dominance. Thus, in order to make a weak achievement motive dominant, the number of affective associations in its network was to be increased. But how? Simply causing concrete situations to be associated with expectancy affects as in early childhood would be far too time-consuming, to say nothing of problems of feasibility, given the limits to the ways in which it is permissible for psychologists to behave to other adults. Instead, it would seem that even imaginary couplings of situational cues with expectancy affects would weave the associative network more tightly and make it more dominant. McClelland was certain that this would work, since behavior and imagination are apparently mutually influential and may even constitute two sides of the same matter. Finally, it had been demonstrated that thought samples from the TAT can predict actual behavior.

In order for imagery and simulated behavior to trigger a process of motive change, participants in the training course needed to accomplish four goals: (1) to extend, strengthen, and improve the affective network, (2) to perceive more clearly and above all to name the various parts of this network, (3) to connect this network with the events of everyday life, and (4) to work out and harmonize the relationship of the new network with superordinate patterns of association such as the self, reality, and cultural values.

With these four goals in mind, McClelland chose a total of 12 inputs for the training course, organized into groups of three under the following categories: studying and practicing the achievement syndrome, self-study, goal setting, and social support. Examples of individual inputs include the following: content analysis of one's own TAT stories (using the n Ach key), finding examples of achievement-motivated behavior by entrepreneurs, practicing realistic goal setting in the context of self-experiencing games, and examining the desirability of achievement-motivated behavior for the conduct of one's own life in the context of one's personal life situation.

McClelland and Winter (1969) wrote a book documenting in detail several training courses conducted in the Indian state Andrah Pradesh. In contrast with control groups, the participants showed an increase in economic activity after the course, as well as higher capital investments, the creation of new jobs, and so on. In a follow-up experiment in 1971, the town Kakinada, in which the training courses had taken place in 1963, showed a far higher rate of employment than a comparable nearby town with a similar initial situation in 1963 (McClelland, 1978). The increased activity was particularly prominent for those participants who were generally in a position to make independent decisions in their work. In order for a motive change to have long-range effects on behavior, external conditions must also make it possible for the change to take place. Apparently, insufficient possibilities exist for those who do not work independently.

From a cost–benefit standpoint, the training courses were more helpful than many projects of aid to developing countries. For example, in Kakinada a 6-month course costing approximately $25,000 raised the standard of life for around 1000 families in the following years by increasing employment (McClelland, 1978). In the United States as well, the training courses turned out to be cost-effective for encouraging growth of small businesses and shops, as well as for increasing the rate of employment in minority groups.

In this sense the training courses were indeed successful. But did the motive actually change, as had been theoretically postulated? Immediately after the course the n Ach scores rose to a multiple of the precourse figure, and 2–3 years later they were still higher than the original figure, although they had dropped somewhat in the meantime. However, since the participants in the course had practiced writing TAT stories with n Ach content and had become familiar with the scoring key, the increase in scores is an effect of learning, memory, or social desirability more than an accurate reflection of motive change. The training course had made the TAT procedure a worthless instrument; the inflated TAT scores did not even allow differentiation between active and inactive participants after the course. Some years later, after training courses for schoolchildren (in contrast with those for managers) had been shown to be rather ineffective, McClelland came to the conclusion: "We think it is parsimonious and more theoretically sound to conclude that achievement motivation training courses improve school learning by improving classroom and life-management skills rather than by changing nAchievement levels directly" (McClelland, 1972a, p. 145).

However, McClelland's conclusion was apparently premature. Heckhausen (1971) reanalyzed the TAT stories from the Indian training course, using scoring keys for the success and failure motives (*HS* and *FF*). Since the participants in the course were not familiar with these keys, it would not have been possible for the keys to influence their stories. Above all, it was possible to determine the two opposite motive tendencies just as the course began and 2–3 years later (unfortunately, the TAT stories told immediately after the course had been lost). The reanalysis of the TAT material showed distinct motive differences between the participants who had become active after the course and those who had remained inactive. Those who had tended to be failure motivated before the course (*FF > HS*) offered the best proof of success, especially when they had a key position for business decisions in the firm. Two to three years later they showed a considerable motive change, to a dominant success motive (*HS > FF*). In contrast, those who had entered the course with a success-oriented achievement motive tended to leave the course as inactive, and — to the extent that they held a position in which they could make independent decisions — even with a dominant failure motive.

Figure 2.10a shows a motive change *NH* between the beginning of the course and 2–3 years later for active (successful) and inactive (unsuccessful) participants, without distinguishing participants in either group by the relative independence of the positions they occupied. Heckhausen (1971) interprets the results as follows:

> The motive change in the direction of a tendency to expect success that was attained after two to three years is based on an interaction between dominant failure motivation before the course and increased business activity after the course. Economic independence reinforces this interaction, which encourages motive change. Accordingly, the prerequisites for maximum motive change consist of two conditions, one of which precedes the other in time: (1) the greatest possible dissonance between initial motivation and the goals sought during the course, and (2) a long-term exploration of new behavioral possibilities such as

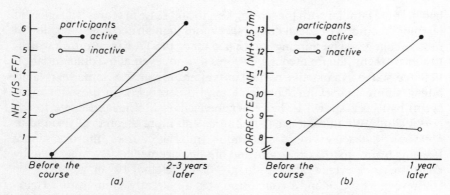

FIGURE 2.10   Change in motive score for net hope ($NH = HS - FF$) between the first measurement before the training course and a later measurement, for participants who turned out to be active or inactive after the course.   (a) Reanalysis of the Indian course conducted by McClelland and Winter (1969).   (Adapted from Heckhausen, 1971, p. 258.)   (b) Evaluation of UNIDO courses in Indonesia, Pakistan, Persia, and Poland.   (From Varga, 1977, p. 193.)

> were suggested in the completed course.   The first, short-term condition seems to have an initial accelerating effect on the motive change, but it will continue and persist only if it is coupled over a long period with a corresponding change in behavior.   (Heckhausen, 1971, p. 267)

Varga (1977) evaluated several training courses in Indonesia, Pakistan, Persia, and Poland for UNIDO, in order to determine whether the motive change observed by Heckhausen could be seen here too as an interaction between a dominant failure motive before the course and increased business activity after the course.   For this purpose Varga administered the TAT test (on the average 12 months after the course) and compared HS and FF scores with corresponding data from the TAT material obtained before the course. Varga used a corrected NH score ($NH + 0.5\ Tm$) to give HS scores more weight in comparison with FF scores when the total motivation Tm was high than when it was low.   The results (Figure 2.10b) corresponded to those of Heckhausen's reanalysis: The differences before and after the course and the increase for active participants were highly significant.   It is remarkable that the results were so clear after only one year.

Training Courses for Schoolchildren

Kolb (1965) was the first to adapt the structure and contents of the motive training course for businessmen for a group of schoolchildren with unexpectedly poor school performance and IQ over 120.   All children received tutoring during a 6-week vacation camp.   In addition, half of them participated in the motive training program (June 1961). Seven months later (January 1962) both groups performed better, but a year later (January 1963) performance sank again in the group that had not participated in motive training. In contrast, in the experimental group the performance of upper-class children had continued to increase sharply, while improvement had leveled off for lower-class children, as for children of both classes in the control group (i.e., without training).

In the following years a group of researchers working with McClelland at Harvard conducted a number of intensive extracurricular courses for schoolchildren, adapted to local needs and interests (see Alschuler, 1973; Alschuler, Tabor, & McIntire, 1970). None of these courses resulted in any significant improvements in school performance (McClelland, 1972a). Apparently the everyday school routine offered few possibilities for applying the new motivational tendencies, for on the one hand the courses took place outside of school, and on the other hand they were not connected with school subject matter or with tutoring. Nevertheless, the courses were not without effect. Achievement orientation increased in extracurricular activities, in career goals, and in precareer activities. This was observed, for example, in telephone interviews conducted a year after the end of the courses (see McClelland & Alschuler, 1971).

The nature of the effect of the Harvard training courses for businessmen and schoolchildren has not yet been determined, except for such general conclusions as the greater effectiveness of the more complete programs and those that extend over a longer period (Smith & Troth, 1975). Originally McClelland (1965a) wanted to reduce the 12 inputs one after the other, in order to find out by a subtractive method which individual inputs were essential and which were unnecessary. This was never carried out. Apparently the researchers (and perhaps also those who financed the programs) were more interested in practical effects than in clarifying theory. One particular difficulty was also that it was not possible to determine motive change by the TAT method because the n Ach scoring key was part of the content learned during the course. Motive change programs that were integrated directly into school instruction or derived from cognitive components of an external motivational theory (see Chapters 5 and 6) proved to be more conclusive.

3

Interaction of Motive and Task Difficulty

McClelland's achievement motivation research followed a general course toward the social and historical dimensions of human achievement-related behavior. At the same time, a second influential school of achievement motivation research, connected with the name Atkinson, directed its interest toward creating a formal model of achievement-related behavior and testing the model empirically. Although Atkinson's model dominated achievement motivation research in the 1960s, we shall restrict ourselves to a brief report of the findings gathered while testing this model. The model and the related findings have been incorporated into motivation research and have been summarized frequently (see Atkinson, 1957; Atkinson & Feather, 1966; Schneider, 1976).

The goal-setting research inspired by Lewin used concepts and models with a long history in the broader field of the social sciences to explain phenomena of achievement-oriented behavior. The setting of a goal or level of aspiration for an achievement-oriented task was explained by the combination of two factors in an individual's environment: (1) subjective evaluation, attractiveness, or valence of future success and failure; and (2) perceived probability of success and failure as outcomes of action.

As long as a task is neither too easy nor too hard, such that either success or failure is possible, anticipated success is said to be all the more valuable as the task becomes harder. Anticipated failure, on the other hand, is all the more aversive the easier the task appears (Escalona, 1940; Festinger, 1942; Lewin, Dembo, Festinger, & Sears, 1944).

Lewin and his colleagues developed a model of goal setting in achievement-oriented task situations, according to which the person weights the valences of success and failure with their estimated probabilities. As in classical models (see Stigler, 1950), this assumption is expressed in Lewin's model in the multiplicative association of the two factors, valence and subjective probability.

Like all factors in an individual's environment (see Lewin, 1938), valences are determined not only by objective characteristics of the environment—here, task difficulty—but also by personal factors: here, in particular, the motives "to seek success" and "to avoid failure" (Lewin *et al.,* 1944).

Atkinson (1957) adapted this model for the purposes of achievement motivation research by incorporating knowledge that had already been acquired on behavioral correlates and on ways of measuring the tendencies to seek success and to avoid failure. It was the independent measurement of personality factors that made it possible to predict those interindividual differences in goal-setting behavior that had also been observed by Lewin and his colleagues. At the same time, the introduction of Lewin's model made it possible to liberate achievement motivation research from its ties to McClelland's heuristically unproductive discrepancy model.

Atkinson's Risk-Taking Model

Following the example of Lewin and his colleagues, the evaluation of a future success—represented according to Atkinson (1957) by anticipated joy or pride about a possible success—is weighted by the strength of expectancy for success. The negative evaluation associated with a possible failure (anticipated irritation and embarrassment) is weighted by the extent of the expectancy that this feared event will occur.

Expectancy of Failure and Success

Atkinson borrowed from Tolman (1955) the idea that expectancies are factors of internal cognitive states. They are based on particular perceived situational characteristics and the evaluation of one's own ability (Atkinson, 1957; 1964, p. 254) and can be represented in subjective probabilities. The expectancy of the success of an action, represented by the subjective probability of success Ps, and that of failure, represented by the subjective probability of failure Pf, should add up to 1.0. Logically, the action outcomes success and failure are two mutually exclusive and exhaustive events. To be sure, Atkinson and his colleagues did not have great confidence in subjects' statements about subjective probability. Such statements are instrumental actions. Like other actions, they too must be understood as the expression of situationally aroused motivational tendencies (Atkinson & Feather, 1966). Thus greater value was placed on the control of objective task characteristics that were supposed to induce various expectancies of success. This will be described in more detail later.

Valence of Success and Failure

Lewin's valences are divided into an environmental part—the incentives of success and failure (Atkinson takes this concept too from Tolman)—and a hypothetical personality part—the more permanent motives to seek success and to avoid failure (Atkinson, 1957; 1964). Accordingly, the valence of a possible success Vs is defined as a multiplicative function of the motive to seek success Ms and the incentive of success Is; the valence of a possible failure Vf is a function of the motive to avoid failure Maf and the incentive of failure If:

$$Vs = Ms \times Is \qquad Vf = Maf \times If.$$

Instruments for measuring the motives already existed; Atkinson derived the incentive values of success and failure from subjectively perceived task difficulty, as Lewin and his colleagues had done. Escalona (1940) and Festinger (1942) had suggested that an S-shaped curve best expressed the relationship of the valences of success or failure to the subjective probability of success. Atkinson (1957), in contrast, made the simple assumption of an inverse linear connection between subjective probability and the incentives of success and failure: $Is = 1 - Ps$; $If = 1 - Pf$. The harder the task, the more attractive is a possible success and the more joy and pride are anticipated. The easier the task, the more irritation and embarrassment are feared from a possible failure.

Escalona and Festinger had made the psychologically plausible assumption that when human beings reach the limits of their ability—that is, when a task is either too difficult or too easy—they cannot discriminate as well between the valences of success and failure as they can in an intermediate range of difficulty. Atkinson, on the other hand, offers no justification for the assumption of a linear connection between the valences or incentives and the probabilities of success and failure. Certainly this is the simplest assumption; however, neither in psychology nor in biological disciplines can one find many examples of linear relationships between observable quantities.

Motivational Tendency

The motivational tendencies to seek success Ts and to avoid failure Tf are understood to be functions of the valences of success and failure as defined here, weighted with the subjective probabilities of these events.

$$Ts = (Ms \times Is) \times Ps, \qquad \text{and} \qquad Tf = (Maf \times If) \times Pf,$$

or, in more detail,

$$Ts = (Ms \times [1 - Ps]) \times Ps, \qquad \text{and} \qquad Tf = (Maf \times [1 - Pf]) \times Pf.$$

Both tendencies can be aroused in the same person in certain task situations, as long as the subjective probability of success is neither 0 nor 1 and neither of the two motives is 0. If approach and avoidance tendencies are aroused simultaneously, the avoidance tendency will inhibit achievement-oriented behavior in proportion to its strength. The model does not recognize any other forms of conflict solution between approach and avoidance.

In the model, this assumption is reflected by an additive connection of the tendencies to seek success and to avoid failure. The so-called resulting tendency Tr can be calculated:

$$Tr = Ts - Tf,$$

or, in more detail,

$$Tr = ([Ms \times (1 - Ps)] \times Ps) - ([Maf \times (1 - Pf)] \times Pf).$$

Since the subjective probabilities of success and failure, which are mutually exclusive and exhaustive events, must add up to 1.0, this formula can be simplified:

$$Tr = ([Ms \times (1 - Ps)] \times Ps) - ([Maf \times Ps] \times [1 - Ps]), \quad \text{and}$$

$$Tr = (Ms - Maf) \times Ps\,(1 - Ps).$$

Thus, subjective probability of success is the only variable besides the motives to seek success Ms and to avoid failure Maf that must be controlled when the model is tested.

The correlations between incentives for success and failure, on the one hand, and probabilities of success and failure on the other hand, can be determined empirically. The approach and the avoidance tendency show reverse U-shaped correlations with the subjective probability of success. Both tendencies reach their peak at moderate probability of success (.50) and fall evenly toward both ends of the continuum of difficulty. When probability of success is 0 or 1, these correlations have a value of 0. Subjects facing these extreme subjective difficulties are not expected to be motivated for approach or avoidance. Depending on whether the motive to seek success or the motive to avoid failure is dominant, the approach or avoidance tendency will dominate the entire area in which the probability of success is not 0 or 1. The extent of domination of a given tendency will depend on the extent to which one motive is dominant over the other.

Thus, Atkinson's model includes only one of the expectancies introduced in our basic model of motivation, presented in Chapter 1 (Figure 1.2): that is, action-outcome expectancies. Moreover, it includes only direct action outcomes — affective reactions to success and failure.

Measuring the Achievement Motive

Atkinson and his colleagues used the TAT procedure only for measuring the motive Hope of Success. Previously it had been assumed that fear of failure, as a form of the achievement motive, was manifested in low TAT

scores (Atkinson, 1953; McClelland, 1951a), and some experimental find-
ings supported this (McClelland *et al.,* 1953). However, Atkinson and
Litwin (1960) assumed that the avoidance of failure was a separate motive,
manifested in symptoms of excitement and anxious concern in test and
examination situations. Subjects were able to observe these symptoms in
themselves and communicate them to others through responses on a ques-
tionnaire, according to Atkinson and Litwin. As a rule, the Test Anxiety
Questionnaire (TAQ) by Mandler and Sarason (1952) was used to measure
these self-observed anxiety symptoms (see Chapter 2).

In German-speaking countries the most relevant studies testing Atkin-
son's model have employed procedures for measuring the avoidance of
failure motive that were better grounded in theory. These methods are the
TAT procedures of Heckhausen (1963a; see also Meyer *et al.,* 1965) and
Hoyos (1965), and the Achievement-Motive Grid by Schmalt (1973, 1976a,
1976b).

Controlling Expectancy of Success and Failure

Since the subjective probability of success is the only situational variable
represented in the model, it was necessary to examine the means of reliably
varying and controlling subjective probabilities of success. Various tech-
niques that had not yet been systematically tested were employed for this
purpose.

We can assume that differing expectancies of success will result from
objective characteristics of the task situation, such as differing distances from
the target in a ring-tossing task (McClelland, 1958a), or differing complexity
and length of problem-solving tasks (Smith, 1963). Yet it remains unclear
exactly how subjects make decisions about their own competence to perform
the various tasks (Kogan & Wallach, 1967).

The same is true of the technique of creating expectancies by informing
subjects of group or social norms (e.g., Feather, 1963a; Weiner, 1965a).
This technique is frequently used, apparently for economic reasons; it in-
volves telling subjects what percentage of a comparison group solved indi-
vidual tasks of varying difficulties. This information must also be trans-
formed into differing expectancies, depending on subjects' perceptions of
their own competence. Subjects apparently assign little validity to norm
information for the purpose of evaluating their own chances of success. If,
for example, subjects are informed of extremely high or low group norms,
they still estimate their chances as being close to the midpoint of the subjec-
tive difficulty dimension, as if they knew nothing about task difficulty and
were following the "principle of indifference" of older probability theory
(Feather, 1963b, 1966; Feather & Saville, 1967). This is especially true

when group norms are low. Better results are obtained from a combination of this method with a visually presented classification of difficulty (Schneider, 1973; Starke, 1975; Chapter 2, this volume).

The significance of the factor of perceived competence, or "consciousness of competence" (Fuchs, 1963), for the estimation of chances of success had not been entirely overlooked by achievement motivation researchers (see Atkinson, 1964, p. 255; Moulton, 1967, 1974). Yet initially this factor was not considered worth testing systematically, although a series of observations indicated that a positive concept of one's ability can be a component of a success-oriented achievement motive, and a negative concept can be a component of a failure-oriented achievement motive (Fuchs, 1965; Kukla, 1972a; Meyer, 1973a; Moulton, 1974; Schmalt, 1976b).

Systematic research on the ability concept did not begin until the attribution concept had been incorporated into the analysis of achievement-oriented behavior (see Chapter 5). Meyer and his colleagues (see Figure 3.1) showed that when alleged group achievement norms for hypothetical tasks were communicated to subjects, these norms were translated into subjective probabilities in a manner clearly dependent on the subjects' concept of ability (Meyer, Folkes, & Weiner, 1976; Meyer & Hallermann, 1977).

From the relationship of self-rated ability level to amount of intended effort, Kukla (1972a) and Meyer (1973a) inferred that expected investment of effort also influences subjective probability of success. Other things being equal, the more effort subjects expect to invest, the higher their expectancy of success should be. However, research has not yet shown to what extent expectancy of success can vary for a single task with variation of intended effort. Thus it is not yet possible to make definite statements about the effect of expected investment of effort on expectancy of success.

The only method that seems suitable for inducing expectancy of success throughout the entire range of difficulty is that of deCharms and Davé (1965). DeCharms and Davé introduced into achievement motivation research a technique by which subjects are first given adequate opportunity to determine their own success rates at various levels of task difficulty. This affords subjects the opportunity of obtaining indubitably valid information about their own performance at the various levels of difficulty. This technique can eliminate the significance of actual competence for the objective probability of success and diminish the significance of perceived competence for the formation of expectancies.

In a series of studies designed to test these and other techniques, Schneider and his colleagues (Schneider, 1971, 1973, 1974; Schneider & Posse, 1978a, 1978b, 1978c) measured (1) subjective probabilities of success, and (2) decision time and confidence with which subjects indicated whether they expected to hit the target or not (see Lee, 1971, pp. 62–63). The task was a

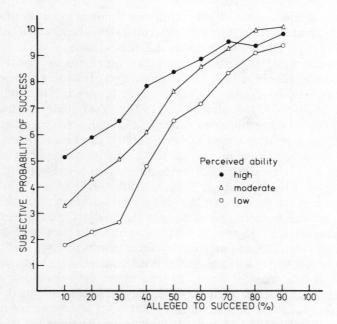

FIGURE 3.1   Subjective probability of success as a function of task difficulty (percentage alleged to succeed) and self-rated level of ability.   (From Meyer & Hallermann, 1977, p. 136.)

motor skill game in which a ball had to be hit through a goal, the size of which could be disguised.   The subjects were first given an opportunity to become familiar with the task in detail through ten games at each of the nine levels of difficulty.   Since decision time was measured without the knowledge of the subjects, it was expected to be less subject to motivationally conditioned distortions (Savage, 1954) and thus have greater validity as a behavioral indicator of expectancy or uncertainty than would any stated estimations of probability.   From considerations of plausibility (see Brim, 1955) as well as from calculations based on information theory (Shannon & Weaver, 1949), it was concluded that maximum subjective uncertainty should occur when expectancies of success and failure are equal.   According to the model (see Atkinson, 1957, p. 364), subjects should be motivated most highly toward seeking success, or else should be most highly inhibited, when they feel least certain about the outcome of achievement-oriented behavior.

Experiential observations communicated spontaneously or upon subsequent questioning by subjects in these studies also suggest that the internal states experienced during the pursuit of such achievement goals are states of insecurity or uncertainty.   These states can be measured—for example, by

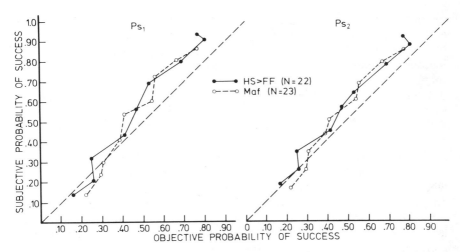

FIGURE 3.2   Relationship between objective probabilities of hits (relative frequencies of hits) and estimates of subjective probability of success for success-motivated ($HS > FF$) and failure-motivated (Maf) subjects. Estimates of subjective probability of success were determined in two ways: with respect to a single round of the game that was about to be played (Ps_1), and with respect to ten rounds that were about to be played (Ps_2). (Schneider, 1972; figure adapted from Schneider, 1973, p. 134.).

scales of subjective probability of success — but are manifested more directly in direct indicators such as decision time and confidence in answering (Schneider & Posse, 1978b; see also Wise, 1970).

After extensive acquaintance with the task, the subjective probabilities of success expressed by subjects deviated only in minor, though systematic, ways from the relative frequencies of hits (objective probabilities of success). Figure 3.2 reflects a typical outcome. The horizontal axis indicates the objective probabilities of success as determined from relative frequencies of hits; the vertical axis shows scaled subjective probabilities of success operationalized in two different ways.

In predicting events of chance, objectively slight chances are typically overestimated and objectively good chances are underestimated (Lee, 1971, pp. 61–62). With Schneider's task, which involved skill, in contrast, subjects tended to overestimate the probability of hits in the areas of low and moderate difficulty. A relative frequency of hits of .40 corresponds to an average subjective probability of .50. The relationship shown in Figure 3.2 was replicated several times with this task (Schneider, 1973, 1974; Schneider & Meise, 1973; Schneider & Posse, 1978a, 1978b) and has appeared with other tasks as well (see Howell, 1972).

For tasks of moderate difficulty, subjects tend to estimate subjective probability of success as rather high in comparison with the relative frequency of hits. The area of moderate expectancy of success or maximum subjective insecurity, delineated by the model as containing maximum achievement motive tendencies, is to be found somewhat closer to the difficult end of the difficulty continuum than one would expect from the relative frequency of hits.

Subjective uncertainty scores, which are based on direct indicators, suggest even higher expectancies of success. Figure 3.3 shows typical results of a study including these indicators (Schneider, 1974, Experiment I). The average decision time that subjects took in answering the question as to whether they expected to hit the target and their average confidence in answering this question were measured. At level of difficulty 5, the average estimate of probability of success was .50. At an even more difficult level, level 4, we find the extreme values for average decision time and average confidence. The 50% criterion for the distribution of "yes" answers as to whether subjects expected to hit the target confirms the results. The average relative frequency of hits (objective probability of success) at level 4 was .29; at level 5, with an average subjective probability of success close to .50, the objective probability was .37. Not until level 6 was the relative frequency of hits .50. These data on subjective probabilities and direct indicators of uncertainty suggest that subjective uncertainty occurs at a higher level of difficulty than the objective success probability of .50.

The results of this experiment (Schneider, 1974) are stable and have been replicated frequently (Schneider, 1973, 1974; Schneider & Posse, 1978a, 1978b, 1978c). They cannot be found in the prediction of chance events: The highest directly determined subjective uncertainty about chance events was found closer to the area of easy tasks (Schneider & Rieke, 1976). Apparently it is only in achievement-related tasks that such a future-oriented attitude, anticipating improvement in performance, manifests itself in optimistic expectations. This "hope bonus" (Schneider, 1971) is reflected more closely in behavioral measures such as decision time than in subjective probabilities of success, which are apparently more closely oriented toward relative frequencies of hits.

After such extensive acquaintance with the task there were no differences between success- and failure-motivated subjects in expectancy of success at the individual levels of difficulty. In contrast, other studies in which subjects had little or no experience with the task revealed differences between the two motive groups. Before, or at the beginning of an achievement-oriented activity, success-motivated subjects predict greater chances of success than do failure-motivated subjects (Brody, 1963; Feather, 1965; Schmalt, 1974; Schneider, 1972; Shrable & Moulton, 1968). These findings can be explained to the extent that success-motivated subjects can be said to believe,

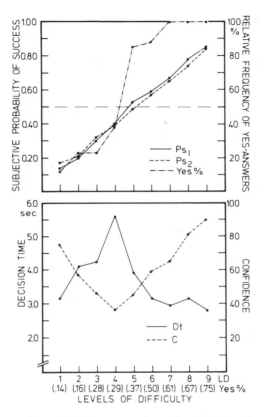

FIGURE 3.3 Average estimated probabilities of success (Ps_1 and Ps_2) and percentage frequencies of yes answers (yes %) in answering the question as to whether the subject expected to hit the target, as well as the related average decision times (Dt) and confidence of decision (C) at the nine levels of difficulty of the task. Below each level of difficulty its average objective probability of hits (P) appears in parentheses. (Adapted from Schneider, 1974, p. 154.)

more than do failure-fearing subjects, in their own ability to perform various achievement-related tasks (Meyer, 1973a, 1976; Schmalt, 1976a).

The Direct Examination of Some Propositions of Atkinson's Model

Up to now attention has been directed toward the examination of some propositions of Atkinson's model, such as the connections of success and failure valences with probability of success, or the twofold determination of the valences of success and failure through subjective probability of success and through achievement motives. The assumptions that probabilities of success and failure add up to 1 and that the factors in the model show a multiplicative association were not examined, or else were examined only superficially.

Relation between Valence and Probability of Success

On the basis of all available results we can assume the existence of a monotonically decreasing or increasing correlation between probability of success and valence of success or failure in the range of difficulty involved in the experiments (Feather, 1967; Jopt, 1970; Karabenick, 1972; Krug, 1971; Schneider, 1973). This range of difficulty extends no further than between .10 and .90 in the cases in which actual experience of levels of difficulty has been the basis of judgment. Research on level of aspiration (Lewin *et al.*, 1944) suggests that this range of difficulty cannot be extended at will. It seems that success- and failure-related affects can be experienced only in the range in which a task can actually succeed or fail.

With methods used so far, it has not been possible to determine whether the correlations among these variables are linear, concave in a downward direction, or S-shaped. When categorical scaling is used, linear correlations appear, at least for group scores (Feather, 1967; Jopt, 1970; Karabenick, 1972; Krug, 1971; Litwin, 1966; Schneider, 1973). With proportional scaling, the correlations are concave in a downward direction (Jopt, 1970; Schneider, 1973). When correlations of individual subjects are analyzed, categorically scaled valences also show downward concave and S-shaped correlations as well as linear correlations (Karabenick, 1972). The methods of scaling that have been used so far do not permit us to determine the true correlation; more progressive scaling techniques, such as the conjoint measurement procedure (see Tversky, 1967a, 1967b), cannot be used in this area because of the theoretical impossibility of freely combining probabilities and valences.

Valence as a Product of Motive and Incentive

The only study that documents the connection between motives and valences is by Litwin (1966). Litwin's success-motivated subjects showed a steeper climb through the levels of difficulty in their ratings of the attractiveness of success than did failure-fearing subjects. None of the other studies in which both achievement motives and the valences of success and failure were measured show any clear connections among these factors (Feather,

1967; Jopt, 1970; Karabenick, 1972; Krug, 1971; Schneider, 1973). Strodt-beck, McDonald, and Rosen (1957) observed that Jewish high school students (known from other studies as highly achievement motivated) made clearer evaluative distinctions among occupations than did students of Italian origin. This sociographic finding supports the general plausibility of the hypothesis, but cannot be used as direct documentation (Atkinson, 1964, p. 274).

Another finding that cannot be reconciled with Atkinson's assumption is pointed to by Feather (1967), Karabenick (1972), and Schneider (1973). In the studies to which they refer, a positive correlation is shown between the angles of ascendance of the scaled success and failure valences and subjective probabilities of success. If this finding is not a methodological artifact, then it indicates that, for the same person, success valence tends to become more positive as subjective difficulty increases, and failure valence tends to become more negative as subjective difficulty decreases. According to the model, however, the first tendency should be associated with a strong success motive, and the second tendency with a strong failure motive. Since the two motives are assumed to be mutually independent, the two tendencies should not be associated with each other more often than is statistically probable.

When the propositions of Atkinson's model were tested directly, they proved to be correct only in part. It is thus all the more surprising that the model has been used with some success to predict achievement-oriented behavior.

The Explanatory Value of Atkinson's Model

Phenomena in the area of risk taking and goal setting and in the area of achievement and persistence during task performance were chosen to test Atkinson's model.

Risk Taking and Goal Setting

In risk-taking experiments the subject chooses one or more tasks to perform from a series of qualitatively similar tasks of varying difficulty. According to the model, success-motivated subjects choose levels of difficulty at which their subjective probability of success is close to .50. Failure-motivated subjects, in contrast, are believed to avoid this range of difficulty most of all. In goal-setting experiments subjects performing a series of tasks choose their goal or level of aspiration for the next experiment. The task must be one that permits quantitatively graduated goal-setting with regard to quantity or quality. Success-motivated subjects are expected to set goals

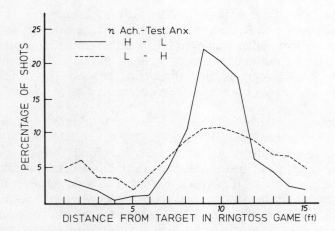

FIGURE 3.4 Percentage of shots taken from each line in a
ringtoss game by success-motivated (high *n* Ach, low test anxiety,
n = 13) and failure-motivated (low *n* Ach, high test anxiety, *n* =
13) subjects. (Adapted from Atkinson & Litwin, 1960, p. 55.)

that they have an equal chance of reaching or missing. Considering the
relationships described earlier between objective frequency of hits and ex-
pectancies, we must assume that these goals are attained in somewhat fewer
than half of all cases. Failure-motivated subjects, in turn, are expected to
avoid this area in particular, and to set goals that are either very difficult or
very easy to attain.

Risk Taking. The first study in this area (McClelland, 1958b) was de-
scribed in Chapter 2. Its results were available while the model was being
formulated, and thus cannot be used to test the model. However, McClel-
land's procedure was the basis for a whole series of subsequent experiments.
For example, Atkinson and Litwin (1960) repeated McClelland's experi-
ment with success- and failure-motivated students (*n* Ach/TAQ). Here too,
participants in a ringtoss game chose freely ten times the distance from which
they would throw a ring over a stake. Figure 3.4 shows relative frequencies
of choices of success- and failure-motivated subjects in relationship to objec-
tive task difficulty (distance from the goal).

In this experiment success-motivated subjects showed a clear preference
for an objectively moderate difficulty. Since subjects were not allowed to
play before they made their choice, their only basis for decision was the
apparent difficulty — that is, distance. However, the median distance of 9
feet was objectively a difficult task. Only 23% of all rings tossed from that
distance reached the goal.

Failure-motivated subjects did not choose the end regions of the continuum, as had been predicted by the model. Instead, they showed a flatter distribution, with somewhat stronger preference for very short and very long distances.

The observation that success-motivated subjects prefer an objectively difficult region, which also appeared in many other studies (summarized by Schneider, 1973, Chapter 1), led to suggestions that the model be revised by placing the maximal approach tendency in the difficult region (Heckhausen, 1968a; Schneider, 1973; Chapter 4, this volume). Atkinson (1957) himself viewed this phenomenon as the result of overestimation, by success-motivated subjects, of subjective probabilities of success in comparison with relative frequencies of hits. Studies in which choices were made on the basis of information about probabilities of success showed that, here too, levels of difficulty were chosen to which a probability of success of less than .50 was attributed (between .30 and .40) (see Figures 3.3 and 3.5). However, this preferred region of difficulty was also the one with the longest decision time for answering the question as to whether the subject expected to hit the target (Schneider, 1973; Schneider & Meise, 1973; Chapter 4, this volume). If we accept the assumption that decision time and confidence are more direct and more valid indicators of internal, behavior-determining expectations, then these findings do not contradict Atkinson's model.

Failure-Motivated Strategies of Task Choice. Atkinson and Litwin (1960) attributed to errors in the sample the finding that subjects who feared failure did not seek the ends of the continuum of difficulty. They suggested that none of the students was truly failure motivated — not a very convincing explanation, considering that the same observation was made with a less select sample.

We must also assume that risk preference in such a situation is also influenced by other motives. This is especially true of such studies as that of Atkinson and Litwin, in which not only the experimenter but also three other subjects were watching (Atkinson & Feather, 1966, Chapter 20). We can assume parallel connections between value orientation toward success and failure, and subjective task difficulty, for some of these other motives — such as the affiliation and approval motive (Atkinson & O'Connor, 1966; Schneider & Meise, 1973). The more success one has at an objectively difficult task, as opposed to an objectively easy task, the more pride a subject can be expected to feel at receiving approval from others. A subject attempting to obtain such approval could be expected to choose tasks in the middle range — assuming that the expectancy-value model is also valid for these motives.

Schneider and Meise (1973) examined the hypothesis and were not able to confirm it. Instead, failure-motivated subjects (*NH*) chose levels of extreme difficulty, regardless of whether they were highly affiliation motivated and whether the experimenter was present or not. Here, however, the subjects were students from a vocational school and the experimenter was a teacher known to the students. These findings suggest that extremely defensive risk-taking strategies, such as avoidance by moving to either end of the continuum of difficulty, appear only with tasks for which failure challenges central (ego-relevant) achievement goals, and thus affects self-confidence.

Jopt (1974) confirmed this assumption for the same motor skill task. Failure-motivated subjects (*NH*) chose tasks at the ends of the continuum of difficulty only when the task was presented as being a meaningful test of skills related to their occupation. This reveals one disadvantage of restricting the model exclusively to such direct affective action outcomes as pride and embarrassment. It is apparently impossible to explain this unstable phenomenon of failure-oriented risk preference without taking into account further behavioral consequences as suggested by the basic model of motivation presented in Figure 1.2, such as possible changes in concepts of self-esteem. Further consequences are weighted differently, depending on whether subjects believe themselves to be responsible for the consequences of their actions or not.

Meyer (1969) found that subjects who showed strong feelings of responsibility for success and failure in a questionnaire (Crandall, Katkovsky, & Crandall, 1965a) preferred moderate risks. Failure-motivated subjects tended somewhat more to choose easy and difficult tasks. Here too, the model offers no way of predicting these variances in behavior, which apparently differ only by phenotype. However, in a goal-setting experiment Heckhausen (1963a) found that failure-motivated subjects (*NH*) who had both high failure motives and high success motives tended to set higher goals. Schmalt (1976b; LMG) confirmed these results in a subsequent goal-setting experiment. Jopt (1974) and Schneider (1973) reported similar risk-taking results in the game of skill described earlier. Apparently failure-motivated subjects with high achievement motivation (*Tm*) tend more to solve the conflict between approach and avoidance by placing excessively high demands on themselves. Failure-motivated subjects with low achievement motivation tend instead to avoid challenging tasks. This assumption is supported by the results of some experiments that showed that higher goals were set when the task was presented in a highly achievement-oriented context than in relaxed situations (Feather, 1958; Raynor & Smith, 1966; Smith, 1963). A differentiated analysis of the various preferences of failure-motivated subjects cannot be performed until differing expectancies and differing consequences of actions are taken into account (see Heckhausen, 1977b). We will return to this topic in Chapter 6.

The decision between difficult or easy tasks for failure-motivated persons may also be influenced by other situationally aroused motives. A series of authors (Atkinson & O'Connor, 1966; Kogan & Wallach, 1967; Moulton, 1965) suggested that the social desirability of high versus low levels of aspiration, combined with certain personality dispositions, might result in higher goal setting in situations involving spectators. Schneider and Meise (1973) found that failure-motivated persons (*NH*) who were also positively motivated toward affiliation (affiliation – motivation TAT, Laufen, 1967) chose harder tasks in the presence of an experimenter. Jopt (1974) found with the same task that success- and failure-motivated subjects (*NH*) tend to choose harder tasks when they have a high need for social recognition (questionnaire by Marlowe & Crowne, 1960).

Additional Findings on Risk Taking. There are further sets of findings that confirm Atkinson and Litwin's results. For example, Atkinson, Bastian, Earl, and Litwin (1960), Litwin (1966), and Weiner (1965a) found that subjects with high achievement motivation (FTI, Atkinson *et al.*, 1960) and success motivation (*n* Ach > TAQ) chose objectively moderate levels of difficulty more than did subjects with low achievement motivation and failure motivation.

Kogan and Wallach (1967) showed quite clearly that, with respect to risk-taking studies in which expectancies are aroused solely by objective task characteristics, the model cannot be tested effectively. This can be explained by the different ways in which subjects with varying ability process this information. The same is true of studies in which the only information received by subjects is group norms.

Damm (1968), deCharms and Davé (1965), and Schneider (1973) found no differences between success-motivated and failure-motivated subjects (*n* Ach > TAQ and *NH*) when using an improved technique introduced by deCharms and Davé. This technique involved giving subjects the opportunity to become familiar with the task by trying it out a sufficient number of times at all levels of difficulty. On the other hand, when the choices are made on the basis of objective levels of difficulty or objective probabilities of success (Hamilton; *n* Ach/TAQ), Hamilton (1974), Jopt (1974), and Schneider and Meise (1973) find clear distinctions between success- and failure-motivated subjects. In the studies by Jopt, and by Schneider and Meise, failure-motivated subjects (*NH*) preferred the end regions of the objective continuum of difficulty. However, these were not identical with the end points of the scale of subjective probability. When the subjects' choices are compared with their subjective probabilities of success, which were obtained subsequently, the differences between success- and failure-motivated subjects are still significant, but the curves are no longer mirror images of each other (Figure 3.5).

The differences in risk preference of success- and failure-motivated sub-

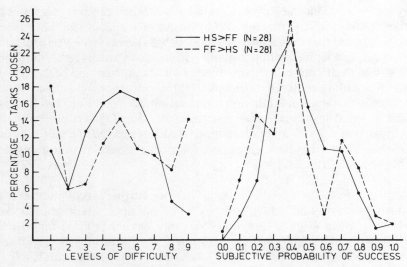

FIGURE 3.5   Percentage of tasks chosen by success-motivated ($HS > FF$) and failure-motivated ($FF > HS$) subjects by objective level of difficulty and by communicated subjective probability of success.   (Adapted from Schneider & Meise, 1973.)

jects predicted by the model were established—at least as relative differences—when suitable methods were used to determine subjective probabilities, though not in all published studies.   It appears that some important situational and personality factors have not yet been examined. The studies mentioned differ in many ways.   For example, not enough attention has been paid to the situational embedding of task choice; to the emphasis or lack of emphasis on the importance of the task; or to the social character of the situation.   A postexperimental analysis of the experimental studies with regard to such characteristics (Schmalt, 1974; Schneider, 1976) did not provide a conclusive explanation of the negative findings.

Finally, it is necessary to mention that initially the model was used with some success to predict risk taking in games of chance with varying odds (Atkinson *et al.,* 1960; Hancock & Teevan, 1964; Meyer, Walker, & Litwin, 1961).   This was somewhat surprising (Kogan & Wallach, 1967), since it was believed that achievement motivation could only be aroused when the result of an action could be attributed to the subject's own competence (McClelland *et al.,* 1953).   Indeed, subsequent experiments with better techniques did not confirm these findings (Littig, 1963; Raynor & Smith, 1966); thus we must conclude that the model is indeed applicable only to achievement situations.

Goal Setting (Level of Aspiration). Lewin *et al.* (1944) analyzed goal-setting studies on the basis of their own expectancy-value model. According to this model, subjects set their goals in that region where the sum of weighted valences of success and failure is maximal. According to Escalona's (1940) assumption of an S-shaped correlation between valences of success and failure and probability of success, this maximum occurs when the probability of success is less than .50. Thus, subjects would set goals that were a little higher than the last goal reached. If we accept the conservative assumption that the probability of reaching the goal attained in the last attempt is at least .50, then this strategy, applied to goal-setting scores, should lead to a slight positive goal discrepancy (difference between level of aspiration and last goal attained). Atkinson (1957) added to Lewin's analysis an explanation of this phenomenon. In terms of Atkinson's model positive goal discrepancy results when success-motivated subjects overestimate their objective chances of success. These subjects choose goals with less than .50 objective probability of success. Failure-motivated subjects are thought to avoid this area of difficulty, setting very high or very low goals. Moreover, they show what is referred to in goal-setting research as "atypical" goal-setting behavior. If these subjects approach the area of moderate expectancies — and thus maximal arousal of fear of failure — through unexpected success at very high goals or unexpected failure at very low goals, and if no other way out is available, they will move to the opposite end of the scale of difficulty.

Krug (1971) and Moulton (1965) showed that success-motivated subjects — compared with failure-motivated subjects (*NH* and *n* Ach > TAQ) — tend to set moderate goals. That is, their goal discrepancies are at zero or slightly positive. Heckhausen (1963a), Meyer *et al.* (1965), and Schmalt (1976b) found that subjects with moderate and moderately high goals (goal discrepancies of zero and somewhat over zero) have, on the average, higher scores for positively directed achievement motivation (*NH; NH*, LMG) than do subjects with negative and extremely positive goal discrepancies. Walter (1968) found the same relationship, but only for girls. Correspondingly, Thomas and Teevan (1964, cited by Birney *et al.,* 1969) found that highly failure-motivated subjects tend more to show negative and extremely positive goal discrepancies than do subjects with low failure motivation (hostile press). Along the same lines, Raynor and Smith (1966) found that failure-motivated subjects (TAQ > *n* Ach) show greater variation in their goal discrepancies than do success-motivated subjects.

An analysis of the so-called atypical reactions after success and failure in some of these studies showed in addition that failure-motivated subjects (TAQ > *n* Ach in English-language studies; *NH* or *NH*, LMG in German-language studies) have more atypical and rigid goal settings than do success-motivated subjects (i.e., no change after success or failure) (Feather, 1969; Heckhausen, 1963a; Krug, 1971; Moulton, 1965; Schmalt, 1976b).

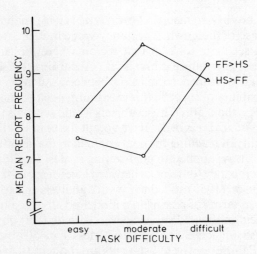

FIGURE 3.6   Median number of reports on per-
formance at an estimation task sought by success-
motivated   (*HS* > *FF*)   and   failure-motivated
(*FF* > *HS*) subjects (*NH*, LMG).   (Adapted from
Butzkamm, 1972, p. 76.)

Published studies on goal-setting behavior of success- and failure-moti-
vated subjects document differences in goal setting by these subject groups,
as the model predicts — at least, relative differences.

The Search for Feedback on Achievement.   According to McClelland
(1961), success-motivated and highly achievement-motivated subjects are
interested in concrete feedback on their level of achievement.   Therefore,
they tend to choose occupations in which such concrete feedback seems
possible.   This general hypothesis was confirmed in a study by Starke
(1975).   Success-motivated subjects (*NH*, LMG) request feedback on their
performance more frequently with an achievement-oriented task than with a
non-achievement-oriented task.   From Atkinson's model we can predict
that success-motivated subjects will seek feedback about their performance
primarily for tasks of moderate difficulty, while failure-motivated subjects
will avoid this level of difficulty.

On the other hand, Butzkamm (1972) observed a strong tendency to seek
performance feedback in both motive groups (in 86% of the possible cases),
but the predicted differences between motive groups were also present.
Success-motivated subjects (*NH*, LMG) sought considerably more feedback
on their performance in estimating numbers of points than did failure-moti-
vated subjects (see Figure 3.6) when the task was moderately difficult.   At

the higher and lower levels of difficulty for the same task, there were clear distinctions between the two groups in the expected direction, but the difference was not so great.

Heckhausen (1975c) reported that success-motivated subjects (*NH*) were more likely to ask for feedback on a hypothetically proposed task at subjectively moderate levels of difficulty, while failure-motivated subjects expressed the strongest wish for performance feedback with the subjectively easy task.

Halisch and Heckhausen (1977) measured the frequency with which feedback was sought during task performance, measured by the subject's eye contact with an assistant competing at the same task. Here there was no difference in feedback sought between success- and failure-motivated subjects (Aronson's doodle test), based on task difficulty. Both groups, however, sought eye contact most frequently for moderately difficult tasks (maximal insecurity about results). This sort of check on success during task performance serves directly to guide the subject's course of action by regulating effort. It should be distinguished from postexperimental feedback after task completion (reported in other studies), which apparently serves primarily the purpose of self-evaluation.

Performance and Persistence

So far relatively few studies have used the model to predict inter- and intraindividual differences in performance. Achievement-oriented behavior can be observed only externally, as it is performed; the preceding and accompanying mental operations can only be inferred. The tendencies to seek success and to avoid failure are said to have a natural affinity for particular plans of action, strategies of task processing, or operations (Dörner, 1976). In interaction with other personality factors (such as ability) and situational factors (such as task characteristics), these tendencies are manifested in measurable performance.

Researchers testing the predictive value of the risk-taking model for performance differences have not analyzed internal plans for action. This is not surprising, considering that behaviorist dogmas were dominant when achievement motivation research began. However, it is surprising that actual external achievement-oriented behavior was not the object of observation. Instead, researchers restricted themselves to an unfortunate procedure taken over from the testing movement: the analysis of already existing performance results. However, such results are always ambiguous, for similar results can be obtained with very different procedures (Brunswick, 1952). For example, Weiner (1965a) found that failure-motivated subjects improved their performance less after failing than after succeeding at a number–symbol task (time taken to record a particular number of symbols). This was interpreted as confirming the assumption that failure-motivated subjects are more inhibited after failure.

In a replication of this study (Schneider, 1973, Chapter 2) the same effect was observed; however, the experimenter also observed that the subjects discovered and corrected some of their own errors while performing this task. If these corrections are counted as additional entries, then the average processing time for failure-motivated subjects was no longer following failure than after success. These subjects merely made more errors, part of which they discovered and corrected. When the process is analyzed carefully, the assumption of a simple inhibition of performance is not tenable.

This example also makes it clear that it is scarcely productive to talk simply of performance in achievement situations. At the very least, we must distinguish between quantity and quality of performance. Since this distinction is not made in the risk-taking model, the hypotheses that can be derived from it apply to both aspects of performance equally, and to any task. This is not an advantage, though it may at first seem so.

Persistence is surely a less ambiguous indicator of achievement motivation than is performance. Subjects who are motivated primarily by hope of success stay at a task longer when they have moderate expectancies of success (and thus relatively strong motivation) than when they have very high or very low expectations of success. On the other hand, subjects who are motivated primarily by fear of failure show the least persistence when their expectancies of success are moderate.

The time spent on a task is a direct measure of persistence. However, while it does not seem problematic to attribute persistence to positive motivation, it is indeed questionable whether we can say that the more subjects fear failure, the less persistence they show. Great persistence at extremely difficult tasks seems to be one possible form of failure-avoiding achievement-motivated behavior (Feather, 1961; Nygard, 1977).

Persistence. Feather (1962) and Atkinson and Cartwright (1964) have pointed out that persistence can be analyzed only in connection with simultaneous analysis of alternative behaviors and the motivations attributed to them. Feather (1961, 1963a) conducted two persistence experiments in this manner to test the model. In the first study (Feather, 1961) the subjects were given insoluble puzzles to work. Half of the subjects were told that their task was difficult, with a group norm of 5% success; the other half were told that it was easy, with a group norm of 70% success. Since the tasks were actually insoluble, subjects in both groups experienced continuous failure. The experience of failure at the task that was supposedly easy was expected to bring about a moderate expectancy of success, and thereby also maximum arousal both of the success motive and of the failure motive. In contrast, failure at the supposedly difficult task was expected to cause both groups to move farther and farther away from the region of maximal motive arousal. Success-motivated subjects were thus expected to show relatively less persistence here than in the first condition, and failure-motivated subjects were expected to show greater persistence.

The experiment supported both theses. It also showed that failure-motivated subjects (n Ach $<$ TAQ) had greater persistence in an absolute sense at a task described from the beginning as difficult than did success-motivated subjects. Feather had predicted this effect. However, the hypothesis can be derived from the model only when we assume moderately high expectancies of success for the alternative task — that is, if failure-motivated subjects would have been forced to experience an even stronger arousal of fear of failure with the alternate task. With non-achievement-oriented alternative activities, the model predicts that failure-motivated subjects would never show greater persistence.

In Feather's second study (1963a) the level of difficulty of the alternative task — left open in the first study — was specified: Subjects were told that the group norm was 50% success. The first assigned task was described as very difficult, with a group norm of 5% success, and was indeed insoluble. Again, success-motivated subjects gave up earlier than did failure-motivated subjects, although the difference was not statistically significant. In addition, the author's prediction was confirmed: The higher the initial expectation of success for success-motivated subjects, the longer they stayed with the first task. Feather did not expect or find a complementary phenomenon occurring with failure-motivated subjects: that is, that the higher the initial expectation of success was, the sooner failure-motivated subjects would manifest a relatively stronger avoidance tendency and abandon the first task (see Nygard, 1977, p. 90). However, a postexperimental analysis by Nygard showed that the phenomenon was indeed present, though concealed. Atkinson and O'Connor (1966) replicated Feather's first experiment and found differences that pointed in the same direction. However, these differences were not significant.

In an ambitious study Nygard (1977) tested the hypotheses about persistence in success- and failure-motivated subjects, measuring success and failure with a questionnaire (Achievement Motive Scale, Gjesme & Nygard, 1970; see Rand, 1978). He found that the higher the success motive was, the longer subjects persisted at a task of medium difficulty, but the more subjects feared failure, the earlier they shifted to a task that had been described as easy. In contrast, when the task was presented as easy and the alternative task as moderately difficult, the result was as follows: The higher the failure motive was, the more both girls and boys showed persistence; the higher the success motive, the less persistence. The author expected the same results for a difficult task with an alternate task of moderate difficulty, but in fact, no connection could be discovered there between achievement motive and persistence. Difficulty was varied in these studies by informing the subjects of group norms and by the actual difficulty of the assigned task. Thus it was possible to confirm the model's predictions about inter- and intraindividual variation in persistence. Persistence has turned out to be unquestionably determined by the interaction of personality factors and situational factors and can only be analyzed when alternative courses of action are taken into account.

Performance. According to the model, when a human being processes qualitatively similar tasks of varying difficulty, success-motivated subjects should perform best with moderate expectations; in contrast, when expectations are moderate, the performance of failure-motivated subjects is most severely inhibited, if indeed other motivational factors can bring them to attempt the task at all.

Again, in a strict sense this prediction cannot be tested because Atkinson's achievement motivation theory does not permit statements to be made about what aspect of performance is being measured — for example, quantity or quality. However, psychologists have known since the beginning of the century (see Lobsien, 1914; Moede, 1920) that the same motivational incentive can have diametrically opposing effects on different aspects of performance. For example, an increase in quantity is often associated with a decrease in quality (summarized by Iseler, 1970). The number – symbol task mentioned earlier has been used frequently in achievement motivation experiments. With this task it was discovered (e.g., by Schneider & Kreuz, 1979) that direct variation of effort by means of instructions and goal-setting results in a simultaneous increase in number of tasks completed and decrease in quality at the level of greater effort. As a rule, quantity seems to be a more appropriate indicator of positive motivation than quality (Thurstone, 1937). Apparently it is easier for subjects to increase the speed at which they work than the quality of their performance (Adam, 1972).

Even early research in industrial psychology (see Poppelreuter, 1918, 1923) showed that a subject's natural achievement-directed tendency is more a matter of quantity than quality. Special measures and training procedures are necessary in order to increase quantity while simultaneously improving or at least maintaining quality. Whenever possible, if there are no serious consequences, subjects tend to substitute quantity for quality (see Bavelas & Lee, 1978).

As a rule subjects cannot follow dual instructions to attend to quantity as well as quality (Hunn, 1925). This is especially true when no direct feedback is given about both quality and quantity of performance. Strang, Lawrence, and Fowler (1978) found that subjects would substitute quantity for quality in the case of high goal-setting and dual instructions to aim at quantity and quality, but only when they did not receive feedback on both speed and correctness immediately after completing each task (simple arithmetic problems). In contrast, the promise of summary performance feedback at the end of the experiment did not prevent subjects from accepting the risk of an additional error in exchange for a faster work style.

To be sure, not all tasks are equally suited to substitution of quantity for quality. Frost and Mahoney (1976) offer support for the notion that this substitution occurs primarily in tasks with a prescribed sequence of steps. On the other hand, in tasks in which the course of problem solving can vary — i.e., the steps are not prescribed — increased effort cannot be translated directly into faster work, since individual operations involved in the task must first be discovered. Similar considerations had already been raised at the beginning of industrial psychology (Windmöller, 1930).

Finally, it is possible to emphasize the aspect of quality for subjects through the manner of giving instructions and the choice of task, so that subjects will direct their effort primarily toward improving quality. Terborg and Miller (1978) set higher goals for quantity for one subject group performing a manual construction task and a higher level for quality for the other subject group. Subjects followed instructions in the second condition as well as in the first; they achieved a relatively higher quality of performance than in the condition without goal setting by experimenters, or in the condition with a goal set for quantity.

Thus increased effort does not necessarily lead to increased quantity and simultaneously decreased quality. This happens only when (1) the sort of task chosen makes this exchange possible in the first place, and (2) quality is not emphasized in such a way by the nature of the task, the instructions, or feedback on performance, that the attention of the subjects is focused primarily on the avoidance of errors. Interestingly enough, in the study by Terborg and Miller (1978) the experience of making an effort correlated only with the quantity of effort, even in the condition in which quality was emphasized. Thus it seems that the experience of effort is determined primarily by the quantity of work experienced.

The only support for the correctness of the differential hypotheses of the Atkinson model was provided by Karabenick and Youssef (1968) on the basis of a verbal learning task. Success-motivated students (n Ach $>$ TAQ) learned word pairs of objectively equal difficulty fastest when the word pairs were presented as moderately difficult. Students who feared failure, on the other hand, learned the words more rapidly when the task was presented as easy or hard (see Figure 3.7). Success- and failure-motivated students per-

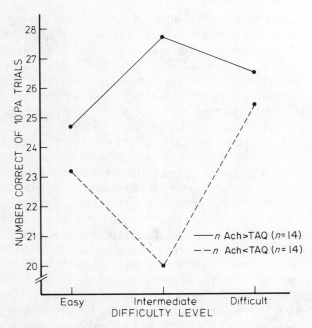

FIGURE 3.7 Number correct on 10 trials at learning easy,
moderately difficult, and difficult word pairs (paired association
trials) by success-motivated and failure-motivated subjects.
(Adapted from Karabenick & Youssef, 1968, p. 416.)

formed differently only on the task that was presented as moderately diffi-
cult.

Karabenick and Youssef's experiment measured quality of performance
of a skill that had not yet been completely mastered (number of correct
answers). However, it is possible that subjects also make more errors in
paired associations that have not yet been fully learned when motivation to
complete the task is strongest. As we have shown, quality of performance
cannot be seen as a suitable indicator of positive motivation or of inhibition,
since increased effort is not necessarily reflected in quality. Thus the per-
formance drop for success-motivated subjects between tasks of moderate
difficulty and difficult tasks cannot be interpreted unambiguously without
additional indications of effort.

Krug, Hage, and Hieber (1978) tested the model by predicting perform-
ance on a bicycle ergometer (revolutions per second) — surely a less ambigu-
ous achievement than remembering word pairs. Success-motivated stu-
dents (*NH*, LMG) performed best at a relatively difficult task, that of
covering a certain distance in 10 seconds (group norm 25% success). Fail-

ure-motivated students, in contrast, did best at the tasks represented as difficult or as very easy (group norms 0% and 100% success). However, the differences were not significant. Moreover, similar correlations (Mehrabian questionnaire) were found for success- and failure-motivated students. Both groups exerted maximal effort for the task described as moderately difficult (group norm 25% success); effort dropped for the tasks described as very difficult and very easy (group norm 0% and 100% success). In contrast with achievement in studies by Karabenick and Youssef, the sort of achievement measured by this task can be seen as a suitable indicator for effort exerted (see Borg, 1962; Schmale & Vukovich, 1961), and thus as a suitable indicator for positive motivation focused on carrying out the task. Assuming that student subjects had moderate expectancies of success for the task described as moderately difficult (group norm 25% success), as they reported at the time, then the findings at least do not contradict the hypothesis that can be derived from the model for success-motivated subjects.

The law of difficulty in motivation (Hillgruber, 1912; Ach, 1910, 1935) was rediscovered and introduced as a competing attempt at explaining the correlations between subjective task difficulty and achievement (Locke, 1968). According to this law, as long as the task is not too difficult and thus out of the question (Ach, 1935), the more difficult a task appears, the more subjects will exert themselves. The factor that guides and regulates effort is perceived task difficulty.

The results reported by Krug et al. (1978) refute this assumption only in appearance; in fact, they do not. In the hardest condition, which involved a drop in level of achievement, subjects had been told that no one had ever reached the goal set by the experimenter. Perhaps this "too difficult goal" was not accepted by the subjects (see Mento, Carteledge, & Locke, 1980).

On the basis of his own series of studies, Locke (1968) questioned the explanatory value of the risk-taking model for differences in performance. Locke's studies were inspired by the results of a study by Atkinson (1958) and their replication by McClelland (1961). Atkinson (1958) found originally that highly motivated female college students (n Ach) performed best on two tasks when they were competing with two other female students for a money prize. Subjects with low motivation, on the other hand, achieved most when they were competing with only one other subject (objective probabilities of success: .33 and .50). When only one of twenty subjects can win the prize, performance drops in both groups, even when the objective probability of success is .75 (3 of 4 can win). In this study achievement was measured by a combination of the raw scores on the two related tasks: (1) number correct on Düker arithmetic problems; (2) number of crosses drawn in circles by subjects. While the latter score measures quantity exclusively, the first score combines quantity and quality.

McClelland (1961) replicated part of this experiment using the Düker arithmetic problems with Japanese, Brazilian, and German male students. The larger the number of students with whom subjects believed they were competing — that is, the less the chance of success — the better the perform-ance among students with high as well as low motivation (n Ach). However, here too, when chances were low, highly motivated subjects performed bet-ter than subjects with low motivation. Moreover, in 12 studies summarized by Locke (1968) it turned out that on the average, achievement rose in a monotonic fashion as difficulty (defined by the height of the goal that was set) increased. To be sure, in almost all tasks assigned by Locke and his co-workers, only the quantitative aspect of performance was analyzed. In an experimental laboratory situation, it appears that the harder the task, the more subjects will exert themselves. Again, measures of quantity are the most suitable indicators of effort. In these experiments difficulty was raised to an objective probability of success of less than 10%.

Locke, Shaw, Saari, and Latham (1981) summarized a substantial num-ber of additional studies on the law of difficulty in motivation. The more recent studies have also tended to show that the law of difficulty in motiva-tion describes achievement-oriented behavior reliably. This is true not only of speed tasks, at which the quantitative aspect of performance is measured, but also of more complex tasks at which the quality of performance is measured to a greater degree.

For example, Masters, Furman, and Barden (1977) showed that the higher the goal, the more preschool children learn (number correct in a visual discrimination task). Campbell and Ilgen (1976) found that in chess prob-lems, performance was better when a higher goal was set, particularly when the number of correct solutions was measured (as opposed to the number of attempted problems).

Along with others (e.g., Rothkopf & Kaplan, 1972), LaPorte and Nath (1976) found more retention and understanding of a previously studied text when a higher goal was set for the test that was to follow. To some extent this effect can be explained by greater persistence and thus is not particularly surprising. When the amount of study time was left open, subjects with higher goals spent significantly more time with the texts; but the group with higher goals performed better even when study time was controlled. The authors attribute this to a difference in learning strategies. It is well docu-mented that adults and older children know and have considerable practice in strategies for learning material, such as increased rehearsal time and deeper forms of processing material through more associations. Thus the attribution to a difference in learning strategies is plausible and does not contradict our assertion that for many tasks subjects do not know how to improve the quality of their performance.

Other findings attest to the validity of both principles — the expectancy-value model and the law of difficulty in motivation. These findings suggest that the law of difficulty in motivation may be a subordinate regulatory principle of achievement-oriented behavior, having to do with the effort that is exerted once subjects have undertaken a task (goal). Mento, Carteledge, and Locke (1980) found that it is possible to explain by means of the expectancy-value model whether a goal will be accepted at all. The expectancy-value model describes and explains the choice of goals, or the acceptance of prescribed goals; the law of difficulty in motivation comes into play as a subordinate regulatory principle only when the subject is actually pursuing a goal.

We must conclude from the research summarized above that the explanatory value of the risk-taking model has not yet been convincingly demonstrated for actual achievement-oriented behavior. Only a few studies confirmed predictions that were made on the basis of the model; the majority of the studies tend instead to document the validity of the law of difficulty in motivation. As we have explained, a choice between these two explanations would not be meaningful, since it is not a matter of competing models.

On the whole, we can say that motivational research in general will not make any real progress in explaining achievement until it adds a theory of achievement to the existing models. Achievement research has produced highly ambiguous findings on effort, and thus on motivation. It seems useless to cite achievement data unless we have a concept of how task-related effort is translated into various strategies of task processing and thus into different measures of achievement for different tasks. Not even the Yerkes-Dodson Rule (Yerkes & Dodson, 1908), used by Atkinson (1967, 1974) as an additional means of analyzing achievement findings, compensates for the basic vagueness of the model. The findings that are described by the Yerkes-Dodson Rule are themselves in need of explanation (see Hockey, 1979). It will be necessary in this regard for motivational research to take advantage of cognitive psychology, with its modern investigatory approaches and the models that have developed from them.

Hardly any findings suggest that failure-motivated subjects are maximally inhibited when probability of success is moderate. Inhibition of performance, or rather, the absence of effort, is only one of many possible ways to avoid failure that might impair self-esteem. A far better way must be to attain success (Birney et al., 1969) by increasing effort. The assumption of simple inhibition of achievement-motivated behavior by fear of failure apparently prevented achievement-motivation researchers influenced by Atkinson from developing hypotheses and methods for research into additional defensive behaviors.

In other research contexts a series of defensive behaviors other than inhibition of action or blocking have been identified. Experimental animal research has already distinguished among three basic threat-avoidance reactions in the lower mammals (see Gray, 1971): freezing, like inhibition in Atkinson's sense; flight; and active struggle. It can be supposed that the number of available defensive behavioral strategies increases with development, rather than decreases. Only outside of the more strictly traditional research of the Atkinson school do we find approaches to a theoretical and experimental analysis of defensive behaviors in achievement situations (Birney *et al.*, 1969; Fuchs, 1976; Heckhausen, 1963a; Hoyos, 1969). Future research must concern itself more with these questions.

Applications

A few studies have tested the explanatory value of the model in predicting more important kinds of decisions and achievements than is feasible in an ordinary laboratory situation.

Decision Making

Walter (1968) showed that during free time, success-motivated elementary pupils in a Montessori school tended more than failure-motivated pupils to choose moderately difficult exercises from five levels of dictation exercises. Isaacson (1964) found that success-motivated college students tended more than failure-motivated students to choose major subjects of average objective difficulty.

In a series of studies the model was used to predict the occupational choices of success- and failure-motivated subjects (summarized by Kleinbeck, 1975). For example, Mahone (1960) found that failure-motivated students chose (from a list) unrealistic occupations more than did success-motivated students. The classification, made by two clinical psychologists, was based on students' intelligence and on their interests as expressed in questionnaires. Burnstein (1963) found similarly that although failure-motivated students did indeed tend to choose occupations with lower prestige value from the list, they simultaneously chose a few occupations with the highest prestige value and thus the least chance of success. Morris (1966) established that success-motivated schoolchildren, more than failure-motivated children, expressed a wish for occupations that would be classified as moderately difficult by objective criteria. Kleinbeck (1975) found, in a study involving German schoolchildren of approximately the same age, that success-motivated male subjects tended to choose careers of average and great difficulty (as classified by a comparable subject group), while failure-motivated subjects chose those that were somewhat easier.

School Achievement

O'Connor, Atkinson, and Horner (1966) examined school achievement in homogeneously and heterogeneously grouped classes. They predicted that the expectancy of success (in comparison with the class average) would be in a middle range for homogeneous classes more often than for heterogeneous classes. Success-motivated students were expected to perform relatively well in this middle range, and failure-motivated students to perform relatively poorly. The predicted relationship with respect to improvement in performance over a period of one to two years appeared only with success-motivated subjects, but not with the failure motivated. Weiner (1967) reported comparable effects with university students: Success-motivated subjects profited more from the homogeneity of abilities achieved by means of grouping.

Finally, Gjesme (1971) predicted that only in a group of average ability would the motives to seek success and to avoid failure be positively or negatively related to school performance, since in this group average expectancies and the maximum arousal of the motives could be assumed. This prediction was confirmed. A similar relationship appeared for the high-ability group in an experiment with girls of the same age (Gjesme, 1973).

All in all, the risk-taking model has turned out to be heuristically productive. It has inspired a series of studies on many different aspects of achievement-related behavior, enabling us to discover previously unknown phenomena. In all areas discussed it has been possible, in varying degrees, to verify the hypotheses derived from the model. The results have been surprisingly good for persistence, satisfactory for risk taking and goal setting, and quite unsatisfactory for performance. Since the heuristic potential of the model appeared earlier to be exhausted, this situation called for continued theoretical development in the mid-1960s.

4

Revisions and Extensions of the Risk-Taking Model

As Chapter 3 showed, success-motivated and to a lesser extent also failure-motivated subjects tend to choose tasks or set goals for which objective and stated subjective probabilities of success are less than .50.

If, as the findings of Schneider *et al.* suggest, we accept that the expectancies guiding behavior differ from stated expectancies (Schneider, 1973), then this body of results does not contradict the model. The expectancy guiding behavior contains a kind of "bonus of hope," while stated expectancies are closer to objective frequencies of success. Hamilton (1974) distinguishes in a similar fashion between the expected achievement and the achievement that is aimed at (which is usually higher).

Revision of the Original Model

Initially, however, this contradiction between observable achievement-related behavior and predictions from the model, which Atkinson had not explained adequately, had given rise to some suggestions for modifying the model. All suggestions involved shifting the maximum approach tendency to the more difficult area.

According to Heckhausen (1967b, 1968a), the success incentive Is can be defined as $.7 - Ps$. We can assume that for tasks with a probability of success greater than or equal to .7, success incentives have no effect at all. Correspondingly, the negative incentive of failure If can be defined as $.3 - If$. If the probability is less than or equal to .3, failure is no longer frightening. If the incentives thus defined are multiplied by the appropriate probabilities, the maximum for the approach tendency turns out to be between the probabilities .4 and .3; for the avoidance tendency, between .6 and .7.

The same is true of the assumption of concave downward-directed correlations between probabilities of success, and success and failure incentives (Wendt, 1967). This can be represented analytically as exponential functions (Schneider, 1973), or even better, as logarithmic functions (Fuchs, 1976). Even when we assume S-shaped correlations between these factors, as did Escalona (1940) and Festinger (1942), the steeper rise in the intermediate area of incentive functions causes an asymmetric shift in the products of incentives and probabilities (summarized by Schneider, 1973).

These revisions make the model better suited for explaining the empirical findings. From a purely empirical standpoint, the choices made by success-motivated subjects can be predicted in a similar manner either with one of these asymmetrical model revisions or with Atkinson's original model. In the latter case it is necessary to add a bonus of approximately 20% to objectively determined moderate probabilities of success, and a 10–15% bonus to stated subjective probabilities.

However, none of these revisions of the model solves the problem identified many years ago by Simon (1955). All of these model variations are algebraic. That is, when initial variables are known, the maximum resulting motivational tendency is already established as well. According to such models, when expectancies are stable — after extensive experience with a task, for example — success-motivated subjects will always choose tasks at which the success-oriented tendency reaches its theoretical maximum. However, subjects do not behave in this fashion. They do tend to prefer a certain level of difficulty; however, they also choose all other levels of difficulty, though with decreasing frequency.

In other areas of research, similar discrepancies between behavior and predictions by the model have led to extension of the models by allowing for error or reformulating them into stochastic models. Observation of behavior and analysis of individual choice sequences makes it seem probable that altogether different strategies of approaching a task appear in such choice situations. These strategies cannot be predicted by the model.

One example is the so-called choice series (see Heckhausen & Wagner, 1965; Jopt, 1974). Frequently subjects begin with the easiest version of a task, even if they already have extensive experience with the task. If they are successful, they go on to a more difficult task; if not, they stay at the same level of difficulty or change to an easier one. Schneider and Posse (1982) analyzed the probabilities of a shift from one level of difficulty to another after success and failure at a psychomotor skill task. When the choices of all subjects in a number of studies are summarized (total observations: 2735), we find that after success 53% of the subjects chose a more difficult task, 39% stayed at the same level, and only 8% of all cases chose an easier task. Naturally these probabilities of shift were different after failure. In 73% of

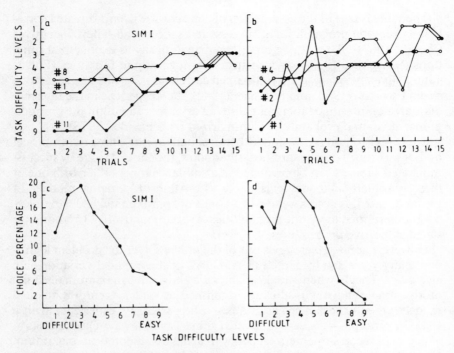

FIGURE 4.1   Choice sequences of the 9 gate widths in the motor skill game, beginning with the same levels of difficulty. (a) 3 simulated subjects; (b) 3 actual subjects (selected at random from the subjects of a study involving this task (Schneider, 1974, experiment II); (c) shows the sum of choices for the simulated sample; (d) shows the sum of choices for the real sample ($N = 32$ in both studies). As usual, moderate difficulty levels are preferred in both samples. (Adapted from Schneider & Posse, 1982, p. 267.)

all cases subjects stayed at the same level of difficulty after failure; in only 16% of the cases they chose an easier task, and in 11% they actually tried a more difficult task.

A computer model (SIM I) predicted individual choice sequences in a way quite comparable to that repeatedly observed with the psychomotor skill task.   The first choice was determined by chance; success and failure were determined on the basis of a probability function adapted for the actual objective probabilities of success at this task.   Shifts by one level of difficulty after success and failure were determined by empirically established probabilities.   When the choices of a group of 20 or 30 simulated subjects were summarized, the distribution of choices was the usual one, with a maximum in the area of moderate difficulty.

Figure 4.1 shows the choice sequences of three actual subjects from one of the studies using this psychomotor skill task (Schneider, 1974). All began with an easy task. These sequences are contrasted with those of three simulated subjects who began at the same levels of difficulty. This illustrates the similarity of the tasks chosen and of the summation curves from the actual individual trials (Figures 4.1b and 4.1d) or from the computer-determined choices (Figures 4.1a and 4.1c). The summation curves show the general trend toward increasingly difficult tasks.

Here task choice involved matching behavior. That is, all levels of difficulty were chosen, even those for which the motivational tendency was not maximal. This can be seen as the summary expression of a strategy that could be described as follows: "Start with an easy task and work your way up." Somewhat more time was spent on the tasks for which success and failure were equally probable; only this last phenomenon can be explained by the model. The first strategy mentioned does not involve irrational behavior; it permits subjects, though not in an optimal manner (see Schmidt, 1966), to test the tasks and their own competence.

The same phenomenon can also be explained in the context of the continued development of Atkinson's theory of achievement motivation into a dynamic theory (see Chapter 7, this volume). On the basis of this new approach Kuhl and Blankenship (1979a, 1979b) simulated choice behavior by means of a computer program; this resulted in the prediction, confirmed by an empirical study (see Figure 6.2), that even when expectancies are stable, subjects choose increasingly difficult tasks. In the context of the dynamic theory of achievement motivation, this prediction is based on the assumption that success reduces the tendency to choose any particular task more than failure does. Since success occurs more frequently at easy levels than at difficult levels, then as subjects become more familiar with a task, the tendency to choose easy tasks should become relatively weaker.

It is not yet possible to decide to use any particular one of these approaches in explaining achievement-related behavior. However, this discussion should show that it is not especially helpful to base the analysis and testing of theoretical models on the sum of choices by subjects. In such summation curves psychologically relevant decisions are unrecognizable. Not until individual choice sequences have been analyzed and compared with predictions made by the various models will continued progress in the theoretical analysis of choice behavior be possible.

The Introduction of Tendencies to Inertia

Living beings are constantly active while they are awake. In order to explain why an organism sometimes initiates a particular behavior in a particular situation and sometimes does not, given that its needs remain unchanged, we must analyze the factors that motivated the earlier behaviors and possibly also the factors that would motivate alternative behaviors. Feather's previously described experiments on persistence in achievement situations (1961, 1963a) met these methodological requirements. Atkinson and Cartwright (1964) made this important methodological principle for analyzing motivation into a "first theoretical principle" of motivational psychology: Once aroused, a goal-directed motivational tendency continues until it is satisfied or eliminated. This original concept of a tendency to inertia is that of a general continuing motivational tendency, to be added to all situationally aroused motivational tendencies for goals of similar functional value in such a way that preferences do not change. This makes the explanation of the change from one activity to another the primary goal of any motivational theory.

Freud (1915) and Lewin and his co-workers (Lewin, 1926, 1935) had already formed similar conceptions. Lewin's notion of a "system under tension" certainly proved to be heuristically stimulating. A series of classical studies showing the effectiveness of continuing motivations after interruption of an activity were based on these theories (see Ovsiankina, 1928; Zeigarnik, 1927).

Early achievement motivation researchers also dealt with this phenomenon, demonstrating that memory for unfinished tasks in Zeigarnik's sense is especially prominent in highly motivated and success-motivated subjects (e.g., Atkinson, 1953; Heckhausen, 1963a) and that these subjects are also more likely to resume an interrupted task (Weiner, 1965b).

Atkinson criticized the extent to which his own model (see Atkinson, 1964; Atkinson & Cartwright, 1964) was tied to stimuli. Behavior occurs only when a motivation or motivational tendency is aroused from among latent motives by an achievement goal, by the perception of an incentive and the expectancies associated with it. In contrast with the concepts of earlier physiology and of behaviorist research, however, organisms show spontaneous activity (von Holst, 1937). For example, instead of waiting for situations in which achievement incentives present themselves, humans seem to seek such situations actively or create them. Even if we assume that in this case achievement goals and thereby valences and expectancies are initially present only as thoughts, it is necessary to explain what gave rise to these thoughts.

Atkinson's model cannot offer such an explanation, since its explanation of the occurrence of motivational tendencies, which is supposed to determine the creation of goal thoughts (fantasy contents) as well, already assumes the existence of these factors, valences, and expectancies. Experimental animal research developed the concept of a "drive behavior" initiated by "internal" stimulus production to explain this phenomenon (see

Leyhausen, 1965). Periodically recurring organismic need states cause goal-directed or apparently goalless, exploratory searches through environmental situations in which these needs could be satisfied.

As the controversy about the concept of a spontaneous aggression drive (Lorenz, 1963) shows, however, this model from animal research can be applied productively only to those motives of which we can assume that a spontaneously occurring drive and corresponding drive behavior are adaptive (Wicker, 1970). Doubtless that is true of motives based on organismic needs. Of course the achievement motive is considered to be a learned human motive. However, Lewin (1926) suggests that learned motives, or "superordinate goals for the will," function similarly to organismic needs. Human motives that we assume are learned, such as affiliation and achievement, represent ubiquitous "recurring concerns" (Klinger, 1971), whose origin, however, must be attributed less to natural evolution than to the ubiquitous requirements of human social welfare. Thus we can assume that such learned motives — as classes of superordinate behavioral goals — cause the spontaneous occurrence of concrete behavioral goals even when no cues are present in the situation. After an action is interrupted, these motives cause "unfulfilled intentions," which are transformed back into actions at the appropriate opportunity (Lewin, 1926). While this concept is based on an organismic model, Atkinson and Cartwright (1964) use concepts and metaphors from Newton's mechanics in their own attempt to close this explanatory gap. Just as a body continues moving, once pushed, until it is stopped by external forces, motivational tendencies also show inertia. Once aroused, they continue until they are fulfilled or terminated. If they cannot be translated into goal-directed actions at the time, they join any other tendencies of functionally equivalent valence that may be aroused and reinforce them.

In the model this tendency to carry over is added to the multiplicatively connected components of achievement motivation as a tendency to inertia Ti. Applied to a general model of motivation (motive $\times$ expectancy $\times$ value model), the following algebraic expression results (Atkinson & Cartwright, 1964): avoidance = motive $\times$ expectancy $\times$ valence + tendency to inertia.

Weiner (1965a) applied this general concept to the two achievement motives. Both were expected to be satisfied (i.e., terminated) after success and to continue after failure. In the latter case two things happen: Success is not achieved and failure is not avoided. Atkinson's formula for achievement motivation, the resulting tendency Tr, is thereby extended as follows:

$$Tr = ([Ms \times Is \times Ps] + Tis) + ([Maf \times If \times Pf] + Tif).$$

The numerical strength of the tendency to inertia is determined by the strength of the previously aroused tendency to seek success or to avoid failure at a time when it was not possible to satisfy these tendencies. For example, when subjects with a dominant success motive fail, their success-seeking motivational components would increase when they undertake a new achievement-oriented activity; subjects with a dominant failure motive would undertake a new activity with increased motivation to avoid failure.

Empirical Documentation

In a series of experimental studies Weiner and his colleagues (summarized by Weiner, 1970) undertook to test the modified model. These studies were continued with research by Schneider *et al.*, described later in this section.

In order to use hypotheses that can be derived from the revised model in experiments, we must control a number of situational factors. In these studies, tendencies to inertia were induced by failure at achievement-oriented activities. Either a goal set by the experimenter was not reached, or if it was reached, it was compared with group norms and disqualified. However, these manipulations were effective only when the subjects accepted the goals that were set explicitly by the experimenter or implied in the social norms.

Moreover, according to the original model the only changes in approach and avoidance tendencies were based on change in probabilities of success after success and failure. Thus the studies designed to test the revised model had to attempt to separate the role of changed expectancies from the role of additional remaining motivation in the process of altering goal-directed motivation. This required (1) precise control of subjective expectancies and (2) familiarity with the maximally motivating region of the difficulty scale. The controversy about this was described in Chapter 3 (Heckhausen, 1968).

Thus in Weiner's first experiment (1965a) one subject group experienced continual failure at a number–symbol task described as difficult (group norm 30% success) and another group experienced continual success at a task described as easy (group norm 70% success). (The subjects either could or could not complete the worksheet in the allotted time.) We will assume that the experimenters succeeded in persuading subjects to internalize the announced norms and that success and failure led to similar alterations in subjective probabilities. In that case, according to Atkinson's symmetrical model, the situationally aroused achievement tendencies to attain success and avoid failure are similar in both conditions. In these conditions the experiences of total success or total failure create expectancies that are equally far from a moderate, maximally motivating expectancy of success. In the failure condition, however, we would expect two motivations to be added together as tendencies to inertia: the unsatisfied search for success and the unsatisfied avoidance of failure. Thus success-motivated subjects could be expected to show a relatively stronger motivation to seek success after failure than they would have after success, while correspondingly, the failure-motivated subjects would be more strongly motivated to avoid failure.

Results show that after feedback of failure, compared with feedback of success, failure-motivated subjects improved their performance relatively less and success-motivated subjects relatively more. Success-motivated subjects remained at their achievement-oriented task longer before going on to a non-achievement-oriented activity, while subjects who feared failure stopped work relatively earlier after failure. However, the differences in endurance that were also predicted did not appear unless the only subjects used for analysis were those who did go on to the non-achievement-oriented task in the time remaining at their disposal.

The following criticism must be made of this experiment: As mentioned earlier, it is generally not possible to use the announcement of social norms to persuade subjects to internalize extreme expectancies. Feather (1966) gave his subjects exactly the same norms and found that the subjects who had been given the difficult norm (30% success) began with expectancies of success between .50 and .60. After one failure, the average expectancy of success-motivated subjects was between .30 and .40: precisely the region in which maximum approach tendency would be expected, according to the asymmetric revisions of the model. Thus Weiner's findings can be explained with the asymmetric model revision that shifts the maximum approach tendency to the difficult region ($Ps < .50$). This offers no convincing support for the assumption of tendencies to inertia.

However, a replication of this study with an improved technique for determining subjective probabilities of success and with somewhat altered initial probabilities does confirm Weiner's findings on the whole (Schneider, 1973, Chapter 2). In this study the group experiencing continual success was told that the task was difficult and those who continually experienced failure were told that it was easy. Moreover, an additional variation of apparent task difficulty ensured that subjects would accept the stated norms (10% and 90% success). In a preliminary experiment these manipulations proved successful. Subjects who had not accepted the norms (as determined from their estimates of probability of success before carrying out the task) were not included in the analysis. In addition, the preliminary experiment revealed that using these procedures changed the probabilities of success after success and after failure to an approximately equal extent.

Between the first and second trials success-motivated subjects improved their speed at the number–symbol task more after failure than after success. It had also been predicted that the performance of failure-motivated subjects would worsen relatively more after failure than after success feedback. However, this was true only of quality of performance, not of quantity. In comparison with Weiner's experiment, this study employed a difficult number–symbol task with very similar symbols. After failure at this difficult task, failure-motivated subjects made relatively more mistakes than after success; to some extent they noticed and corrected these errors. When corrections were taken into account, the quantitative aspect of achievement showed greater improvement (though not at a significant level) after failure than after success, even with failure-motivated subjects.

It was not possible to predict the occurrence of these effects in failure-motivated subjects, either on the basis of Atkinson's original model or on the basis of the revision, for neither model made any statements about the aspect of performance that was being measured. The predicted drop in performance of failure-motivated subjects after failure consisted only in an increase in errors (a qualitative decrease), not a quantitative decrease. This fact, along with other observations, allows us to question the basic assumption that fear of failure has a purely inhibiting function. Apparently failure-motivated subjects do not exert less effort after failure than after success; they merely make more mistakes, for whatever reasons. This observation is supported by the results of an earlier study involving an easy number–symbol task (very dissimilar symbols, Schneider, 1973, Chapter 2). Here both success- and failure-motivated subjects increased the quantitative aspect of performance more after failure than after success.

Without doubt, quantity of performance, or speed in the processing of a task, is a better index of achievement motivation, including the avoidance-oriented inhibiting motivation described by Atkinson (Thurstone, 1937). A decrease in quality can also result from excessively high motivation, owing to interference with information processing (Hebb, 1955; Welford, 1962, 1976) or substitution of quantity for quality (Wickelgren, 1977).

Thus Schneider and Kreuz (1979) were able to show for the easy and difficult number–symbol tasks used in their experiments that with increased effort (induced by higher goal setting or direct instructions) quantity increased and quality of performance decreased. These results emphasize the necessity of distinguishing between measures of quantity and of quality in testing the predictive value of the original and extended models for achievement and alterations in achievement.

Three additional studies, summarized by Weiner (1970), fail to document the explanatory value of the model as extended by the concept of tendency to inertia. In the first study (Weiner & Rosenbaum, 1965), success-motivated subjects (n Ach > TAQ), more often than failure-motivated subjects, chose a difficult and a moderately difficult task from a series of puzzles. They tended not to choose the non-achievement-related task (evaluating pictures). Here tendencies to inertia were expected to accumulate, since failure was unavoidable. However, in general, the more difficult the puzzles became, the fewer puzzles were chosen by both motive groups. This behavior matches predictions of the revised model only for failure-motivated subjects.

In the second experiment (Weiner, 1970, Experiment II) the achievement-related puzzle tasks were described to subjects as varying in difficulty by announcing different social norms (5%, 30%, and 95% success). These figures corresponded to the actual number of solvable puzzles. According to the extended model, success-motivated subjects should choose more puzzles in the difficult condition (5% success) after failure than in the easy condition (95% success) after success. Failure-motivated subjects should do exactly the opposite. However, both motive groups chose more puzzles after success than after failure, although success-motivated subjects did choose significantly more puzzles in this condition than did failure-motivated subjects. It is easy to explain this difference, as well as that in the preceding study, by the difference in expectancies of success in the two motive groups and by the assumption that maximal arousal for success-motivated subjects and maximal inhibition for failure-motivated subjects occurs when subjective probability of success is .30. The design of the third experiment, described by Weiner in the same summary as the other two (1970), is not suitable for testing the extended model.

Another study by Weiner (1966) turned out to be important for continued theoretical development of research in achievement motivation and fear of achievement. On the basis of the extended model (and in contrast with the Hull–Spence approach to explaining performance differences between fearful and nonfearful persons; see Spence & Spence, 1966), Weiner predicted that in a verbal learning task poor performance is caused not by complexity per se, but by experiences of failure attributable to the complex tasks. Weiner (1966) did indeed find that in a complex learning task with success feedback, anxious subjects performed better than nonanxious subjects. Their performance was worse, relative to that of nonanxious subjects, at a less complex task for which they received failure feedback.

These results were conceptually replicated by Schneider and Gallitz (1973; see Weiner & Schneider, 1971) with a somewhat different learning task, for the motives "hope of success" and "fear of failure," as measured by Heckhausen's (1963a) technique. After failure, failure-motivated subjects performed worse than success-motivated subjects at a simple as well as a complex verbal learning task.

Unfortunately, these results led to a false conclusion in the field of achievement motivation. The results suggested, misleadingly, that objective task characteristics had nothing to do with the formation of motivationally determined intra- and interindividual performance differences.

In summary, Atkinson's model—as extended by the concept of a tendency to inertia—has not yet been convincingly validated by experimentation. All of the findings of Weiner and his colleagues can be explained by the assumption of initial differences in expectancies of success among success- and failure-motivated subjects and by differences in revision of these expectancies after success and failure. We must also assume that maximal approach or avoidance occurs in a region of objective difficulty. To be sure, the results of Schneider's follow-up investigation of Weiner's first experiment encourage us to assume motivational remnants after failure, at least for success-motivated subjects. However, a more precise analysis of changes in quantity and quality of performance showed that it was incorrect to assume that dominant fear of failure caused an inhibiting tendency to inertia, at least for the group of failure-motivated subjects determined according to Heckhausen's criteria.

In order to do justice to these findings, Schneider (1973, Chapter 2) returned to the original assumptions of Heckhausen (1963a) about achievement motivation and of Ach and his colleagues (see Ach, 1935) about achievement behavior in general. In achievement situations both success- and failure-motivated subjects attempt to perform in a way that fulfills individual or social norms. Success-motivated subjects are more concerned with attaining a possible success, and failure-motivated subjects are more concerned with avoiding a possible failure. Both goals are frustrated by failure. Some findings suggest that failure-motivated subjects are more likely than success-motivated subjects to give up their goals altogether after failure. If this does not happen, then upon a renewed attempt, subjects begin by exerting more effort (working faster or avoiding more errors). Failure shows subjects that the effort previously exerted was inadequate. The task is apparently more difficult than they originally thought, so correspondingly more effort must be exerted.

Here too, as in the analysis of the correlations between subjective task difficulty and achievement, the law of difficulty in motivation (Ach, 1935; Hillgruber, 1912) offers an alternative explanation. The law can be extended by two differential hypotheses derived from Heckhausen's "hypothetical system of effects" for achievement motivation (Heckhausen, 1963a). First, after failure, subjects with undirected high achievement motivation and subjects who fear failure tend to exert more effort; second, the latter find further failure far more threatening than do success-motivated subjects.

However, it is not easy to test these hypotheses in achievement experiments. Externally observable performance outcomes are always the result of interaction between task processing procedures determined by motivation and ability, on the one hand, and the concrete task on the other hand. Working faster has a positive effect on quantity with simple tasks that have already been mastered (Thurstone, 1937) and in individual cases even on quality (Schneider, 1978a). However, with other tasks, particularly with problem-solving tasks, effects of working faster are decidedly negative (see Bartmann, 1963).

As a rule, subsequent studies confirmed the general hypothesis but not the differential hypothesis. Compared with success feedback, knowledge of a single failure causes both success- and failure-motivated subjects (*NH*) to increase the quantitative aspect of performance. Depending on the kind of task, errors also increase (Depeweg, 1973; Schneider, 1979; Schneider & Eckelt, 1975; Schneider & Heggemeier, 1978; Susen, 1972). In only one study (Schneider, 1978a) did errors decrease, and in only one study (Schneider, 1978a) did both quantity and quality of performance increase after failure (see Figure 4.1). Failure-motivated subjects improved their performance after failure more than success-motivated subjects, but only in a simple vigilance task (Schneider & Eckelt, 1975).

These findings show clearly that task parameters are an important factor in the process by which motivational differences affect performance. They also show that without an achievement theory of at least rudimentary nature, achievement motivation research can make no contributions at all to the clarification of the differential effects of success and failure or of performance incentives on achievement. Depending on the measure of achievement and the task employed, with the same initial situation we can expect better performance at some times and worse performance at others. Thus the revised model cannot readily be tested by achievement-related experiments.

To be sure, it seemed at first that the importance of objective task parameters for the various effects of success and failure on the performance of success- and failure-motivated subjects was relatively low. Apparently this was misleading. It is true that the decisive motivational effects are caused by the experience of success or failure and not by task complexity per se. However, the measurable performance that results varies with type of task, as the reported findings have shown. Earlier German psychology of the will and applied psychology have speculated on which task characteristics stimulate or make objectively possible the various processing strategies (summarized by Schneider & Kreuz, 1979). It seems surprising that so little attention has been paid (Witte, 1976) in achievement motivation research, even by more recent cognitively oriented researchers, to these approaches and to such cognitively oriented explanations of achievement-oriented behavior as those of Ach and his colleagues (see Ach, 1935). This is especially surprising for research in the German language area, since Ach's approach was taken up again and extended after the war by his followers Düker (see Düker, 1963) and Mierke (see Mierke, 1955) and their colleagues. For example, Ach (1935) assumed that the harder the task, the more effort would be exerted ("law of difficulty in motivation," Hillgruber, 1912). Ach also discussed the concept of awareness of ability and the notion that increased effort would be exerted only to the point at which subjects believed they were able to solve the task. These are the three basic characteristics of the so-called Kukla model of achievement-related behavior (Kukla, 1972a); it would be far more appropriate to call it Ach's model.

Specific suggestions as to how motivation (effort) is transformed into performance of various tasks cannot readily be derived either from Atkinson's model (extended by the concept of inertia) nor from the basic model of motivation that was developed from Ach's and used by Schneider and his colleagues to explain performance changes after success and failure. The basic model of motivation may turn out to be heuristically more productive, since it encourages the search for task-processing strategies that are suggested by visible task characteristics in combination with approach or avoidance motivation (see Fuchs, 1976). But such a molar analysis of achievement-oriented behavior will not suffice to fully explain differences in achievement findings. For this purpose we will need an achievement theory based on a more molecular level of analysis, containing mechanisms whose function is independent of the sensory modalities.

We can see evidence for this conclusion in the results of a study by Schneider (1978). In contrast with many other experiments, both quantity (speed) and quality of performance improved following failure at a visual discrimination task (see Figure 4.2a, b). In this task a visual stimulus was presented briefly (< 175 msec) and then had to be classified into one of two categories. The improvement in both measures of performance is apparently the result of increased effort following failure, since the perception of exerting effort was categorized as higher following failure and there was also a relative rise in pulse rate (Figure 4.2c).

An analysis of the quantity–quality exchange in this task (see Pachella, 1974) showed that errors did not merely increase along with a decrease in response time, as usual, but also with an increase in response time. This was true of the first half of the experiment, before success and failure feedback, and also after feedback. The author assumed that longer hesitation caused the stimulus to disappear from visual short-term memory. Without a model that explains the way in which information-processing mechanisms work together to produce the required performance, this and many other achievement findings do not lend themselves to a motivational analysis.

Personal Standards: Determinants of Difficulty
Preference and Self-Evaluation

In Chapter 3 we explored a number of explanations for the left-skewed deviation of risk preference from the preference function of the risk-taking model. Schneider (1973) attributes this deviation to problems with the

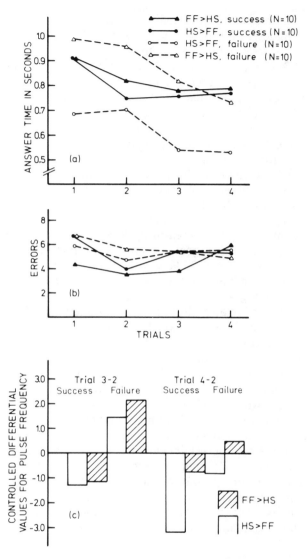

FIGURE 4.2 Alteration in quantity of performance (speed) (a), quality of performance (b), and pulse frequency (c) after feedback on success and failure between the third and fourth trials. (Adapted from Schneider, 1978a, pp. 77, 79.)

methodology of measuring probability of success (behavioral indexes vs. subjective estimates, degree of wishful thinking). Heckhausen (1968a) simply shifted the preference function on the abscissa ($Is = 0.7 - Ps$). Hamilton (1974) followed a similar procedure. In nonlinear functions as well, incentive is made dependent on probability of success. Festinger (1942) did this in an ogive function; Schneider (1973), following Wendt (1967), used an exponential function: $Is = (1 - Ps)^n$, assuming that the exponent is a function of the achievement motive. This modification is not as rigid as the additive modifications by Heckhausen and Hamilton, since the exponent can be different for each subject.

No matter which model revision was used, the purpose was always to explain individual differences in risk taking or goal setting with the aid of motive scores. Although it has been observed repeatedly that excessively high or low or balanced level of aspiration is a personal characteristic, for a long time no one thought of measuring level of aspiration directly, as a personal preference regarding goal discrepancy or a preference for a particular level of difficulty. Kuhl (1978a) was the first to do this, by inserting the so-called personal standard into the risk-taking model as an additional personality variable along with the motive scores. In contrast with Schneider (1973), Kuhl returned to an additive model, but like Schneider he individualized the relationship between probability of success and incentive. The personal standard S determines the point on the scale of difficulty that constitutes the midpoint of the incentive scales for success and failure. The standard is defined as a degree of difficulty that determines the extent of self-evaluation after success and failure. Anyone for whom positive self-evaluation occurs with a difficult task (i.e., when $Ps < .50$, for example, $Ps = .30$) must master a relatively difficult task ($Ps = .30$ instead of .50) in order to experience a moderate success incentive. If the standard is not difficult, the moderate success incentive shifts in the direction of easier tasks. With a standard of moderate difficulty ($Ps = .50$), the success incentive function corresponds to that of the original model. Accordingly, the success incentive Is that is defined by a personal standard for self-evaluation equals the success incentive of the original model minus the difference between moderate difficulty (.50) and actual standard for positive self-evaluation Ss:

$$Is = 1 - Ps - (.50 - Ss), \quad \text{or} \quad Is = (Ss + .50) - Ps.$$

With more difficult standards ($Ss < .50$) the success incentives of all regions of difficulty decrease; with easier standards ($Ss > .50$) they decrease. The same is true of the standard for negative self-evaluation Sf. Here the difference between the point of moderate difficulty and a subject's actual standard is subtracted from the model's original equation for failure incentive ($If = Ps$):

$$If = Ps - (.50 - Sf), \qquad \text{or} \qquad If = (Sf - .50) - Ps.$$

On all levels of difficulty a difficult standard results in an increase in failure incentive and an easy standard results in a decrease in failure incentive. Separate determination of the standards for positive and for negative self-evaluation is rather like an alteration in the measurement of level of aspiration that involves identifying a performance range below or above the point at which a person begins to feel negative or positive affect (confirmation interval; see Birney *et al.*, 1969). In contrast with the confirmation interval, however, a personal standard as defined by Kuhl is not a level of achievement according to which subjects evaluate themselves positively or negatively, but rather the point at which the success or failure incentive reaches average strength (.50). Even when subjects' performance remains somewhat below their standards for positive evaluation, a positive incentive for success remains ($< .50$). The same is true of the failure incentive. For the sake of simplicity, Kuhl's extension of the model allows standards for positive and negative self-evaluation to meet at a single point on the scale of probability of success.

The result of Kuhl's redefinition of success and failure incentive is that subjects with a difficult standard actually experience a negative success incentive with very easy tasks. To the extent that their incentive values for success are greater than their incentive values for failure—that is, to the extent that they are success motivated—subjects avoid very easy tasks. On the other hand, failure-motivated subjects with nonstringent standards would be expected to experience failure incentive with a very difficult task and to prefer such tasks. Only at first glance does this seem paradoxical. It is hardly possible that failure could threaten the self-esteem of such subjects throughout the entire range of difficulty; failure should be least threatening with tasks that seem unsolvable.

Figure 4.3 shows the resultant tendency strengths on the basis of Kuhl's elaboration of the model for success- and failure-motivated subjects with difficult ($S = .20$) and easy ($S = .80$) standards. As the figure indicates, success-motivated subjects with difficult standards tend to choose difficult tasks (approximate $Ps = .35$) and those with easy standards tend to choose easy tasks (approximate $Ps = .70$). If success-motivated subjects were not grouped by personal standard difficulty, and if the success motive NH and the standard were not correlated, we could say that the average success-motivated subject chooses tasks of moderate difficulty.

Failure-motivated subjects with difficult standards (right side of Figure

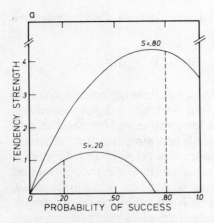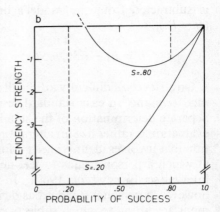

FIGURE 4.3   Resultant tendency strength as a function of subjective probability of success *Ps* for success-motivated (a) and failure-motivated (b) subjects who set difficult ($S = .20$) or easy ($S = .80$) standards. (Adapted from Kuhl, 1978a, "Standard setting and risk preference: An elaboration of the theory of achievement motivation on an empirical test," *Psychological Review, 85,* p. 242, by permission of The Journal Press.)

4.3), on the other hand, still prefer the easiest tasks of all (here *If* is close to zero) and avoid difficult tasks most of all.   Failure-motivated subjects with easy standards would be expected to choose the most difficult tasks ($Ps < .30$) because the incentive value of failure becomes positive here.   However, these subjects have another alternative: the easiest tasks, where the failure incentive approaches zero.   If failure-motivated subjects were not grouped by personal standard, and if the failure motive (negative *NH*) and the standard were not correlated, the average preference function would be that of the original risk-taking model — that is, preference extremes at both ends of the scale of difficulty.   However, Kuhl's elaboration of the model would make it possible to answer a question that had not yet been clarified — that is, which failure-motivated subjects prefer very difficult tasks and which very easy tasks? (see "An Extended Motivation Model" in Chapter 7).

Since risk-taking and goal-setting experiments have often shown that success-motivated subjects prefer tasks that are a little too difficult and failure-motivated subjects prefer tasks that are either too difficult or too easy, it would seem appropriate for an individual goal-setting norm (more precisely: goal-discrepancy norm)· to be a constitutive characteristic of the achievement motive (see Heckhausen, 1963a, 1967a).   Thereby difficulty preference and level of aspiration would become independent personality variables along with the motive scores.

Because of lack of evidence, Kuhl does not attempt to state whether the personal standard is a highly generalized or task-specific norm value. At any rate, it should be a more generalized value than actual risk taking or goal setting. The decisive question is to what extent the personal standard is correlated with the individual motive constellation. In one of the first studies that we reported, Kuhl tested the model and found only a weak but significant correlation of .36 between n Ach and the level of difficulty of the personal standard.

Kuhl's subjects worked on different versions of a problem (connecting points without letting the connecting lines cross) at various levels of difficulty. In a preliminary phase, Kuhl stabilized the subjective probability of success of the various task difficulties at .80, .60, .50, .30, and .10. Then subjects set their standard as the level of difficulty that would cause them a feeling of discontent if they did not master it. (The standard for positive self-evaluation was not measured separately, since it has a high correlation with that for negative self-evaluation; Kuhl, 1977.) Subsequently the main experiment began, in which each subject was allowed to choose a level of difficulty 50 times and work at it.

Table 4.1 contains choice frequencies for both motive groups, divided into easy and difficult standard-setting. Results correspond to the hypotheses derived from the model (see Figure 4.2). Success-motivated subjects with an easy standard chose tasks of moderate difficulty as well as somewhat easier tasks (*Ps* of .50 and .60); those with difficult standards, in contrast, chose difficult tasks (*Ps* = .30). Failure-motivated subjects with a difficult standard tended more to choose easy tasks, while those with an easy standard

TABLE 4.1

Average Number of Choices as a Function of Task Difficulty, Motive Type, and Standard-Setting[a]

	Task difficulty (*Ps*)				
Motive type	.10	.30	.50	.60	.80
Success-motivated					
Easy standard	3.7	5.2	19.0	16.0	6.0
Difficult standard	8.5	14.7	9.2	8.5	9.0
Failure-motivated					
Easy standard	6.0	13.0	14.2	9.7	6.0
Difficult standard	1.7	3.7	25.0	12.0	7.5

[a] Adapted from Kuhl, 1978a, "Standard setting and risk preference: An elaboration of the theory of achievement motivation on an empirical test," *Psychological Review, 85,* p. 245, by permission of The Journal Press.

tended to choose difficult tasks. These results suggest that various problems might be clarified by further testing of this model. Most of all it is necessary to determine whether personal standard is more of a motive parameter or a motivation parameter. That is, to what extent does it apply to all situations, and to what extent is it stable over time?

Butzkamm's (1981) study of self-reinforcement following expectancy-incongruent feedback suggests that personal standards should be seen as motive parameters. For Butzkamm's subjects positive or negative self-reinforcement depended clearly on the discrepancy between initially set level of aspiration and subsequently reported performance results. In most trials of the experiment this discrepancy explained 50–60% of the self-reinforcement variance. The achievement motive was also influential; after success, success-motivated subjects evaluated themselves more positively than did failure-motivated subjects. However, these motive effects were apparently mediated by motive-related differences in goal setting. That is, when the influence of various goal-setting discrepancies on self-reinforcement was factored out by means of a regression analysis, all connections between motive and self-reinforcement disappeared. We will return to this study in connection with self-reinforcement and self-concept.

Future Orientation

From the perspective of the risk-taking model, task activities are isolated events. After a task is completed and the subject has succeeded or failed, the only incentive-related consequences are feelings of success or failure, represented by the two incentive variables in the model. Such an absence of further consequences reflects the fact that the activity is performed in a laboratory, the usual setting for testing a model. However, by no means does this reflect the performance of tasks in actual everyday situations such as school or work. Here the completion of a task has further consequences, particularly in that it opens up new possibilities for action and brings the subject closer to a distant superordinate goal. Many researchers have suggested that attention be paid to future orientation (e.g., Heckhausen, 1963a, 1967a; Lewin, 1951; Murray, 1951; Nuttin, 1964, 1978). However, the first serious attempt at studying future orientation came from field research in industrial psychology, not from laboratory research.

In a theoretical integration of research in industrial psychology, Vroom (1964) added future orientation to the shortened version of the expectancy-value models, including the risk-taking model. This was done because the action outcome achieved has a certain instrumentality for the occurrence of further positive or negative consequences, which together constitute the

anticipated outcome valence and — along with the probability of a success-
ful outcome — determine the strength of motivation to act. We examine
this more closely in Chapter 6. The basic model of motivation described in
Chapter 1 of this book (Figure 1.2) already contains the addition from
Vroom's version of instrumentality theory; its "superordinate goal" repre-
sents the future orientation of motivation.

Prior to Raynor's model (1969), model revisions were designed to explain
why goals slightly beyond the reach of the subject were preferred. Corre-
spondingly, the model revisions were left-skewed, incorporating subjects'
difficulty preferences. Future perspective was based on aspired score (Ham-
ilton, 1974) or expected progress ("bonus"; Schneider, 1973). This always
involved improvement of outcome by repeated execution of similar tasks.
It is closer to everyday life to consider a sequence of different tasks instead of
the repetition of similar tasks, since the completion of a task is the prerequi-
site for progressing to another. Here future orientation assumes a chain of
tasks in sequence, with each task based on the successful completion of the
preceding task.

Raynor (1969) described this as a "contingent path," contrasting it with a
noncontingent path consisting of a series of actions that do not constitute
prerequisites for one another and do not lead to a superordinate goal. In
making this distinction, Raynor refers on the one hand to Vroom (1964) and
on the other hand to Nuttin (1964), who calls these "open" versus "closed"
tasks. The risk-taking model is concerned only with the simplest case of a
single task completion on a noncontingent path, the case of a closed task.

Raynor's Model Extension

In the simplest case of a contingent path — that success at the current task
is the prerequisite for success in a subsequent task — there are at least two
components. The success tendency for the current action includes the
strength of the success tendency for this current (first) action itself ("instru-
mental value"). In addition, it includes the strength of the success tendency
for the action to follow — the future (second) action ("intrinsic value") —
which leads to the goal and ends the path of action. Corresponding conclu-
sions can be drawn for the failure tendency.

A shortened formula for the resulting tendency Tr is

$$Tr = (Ms - Maf) \times \sum_{n=1}^{N} (Ps_{1,n} \times Is_n).$$

It is easy to see that the individual motivational strength based on the relative
strengths of the success and failure motives $Ms - Maf$ intensifies with the

number of steps of action and that individual differences increase under the influence of future orientation.

The subjective probability of success that a current action will lead to success at a future action n of the path $Ps_{1,n}$ is determined by the product of the probabilities of success of all subsequent actions: $Ps_{1,n} = Ps_1 \times Ps_2 \cdots Ps_n$. The combined probability of success determined in this fashion indicates how difficult or easy it appears at the beginning of a contingent path (i.e., before the first action) to complete the path with success after the last action n. Otherwise, however, we see the usual relationships of the risk-taking model, in which success and failure incentives depend entirely on the combined probability of success ($Is_n = 1 - Ps_{1,n}$; $If_n = -Ps_{1,n}$). This adherence to the old model is disappointing. The longer the contingent path and the farther the superordinate goal, the more we should expect incentive-related consequences beyond mere self-evaluative emotions.

A further difficulty in applying Raynor's model resides in the necessity of measuring the anticipated probabilities of success for each individual step of action in advance. Raynor measures them by means of a somewhat questionable simplification. He keeps all probabilities of success in the path constant and gives them the value for the Ps of the action about to be performed. Accordingly, two factors determine the addition of future-oriented components to motivation for the current task: the size of Ps for that task and the number of steps of action in the contingent path. As Figure 4.4 shows, some surprising predictions can be made from the combination and variation of these two determinants.

First, from Figure 4.4 we can see that—corresponding to the original risk-taking model—success-motivated subjects are always positively motivated and failure-motivated subjects are always negatively motivated, if no extrinsic tendencies intervene. Second, a task of moderate difficulty provides maximum motivation as long as the path consists of only one step—that is, the path is noncontingent. That is the special case—the only case—for which the original risk-taking model is valid. Third, when the current task has future-oriented significance and would open the way to further steps in the path, the strength of the (positive or negative) future-oriented motivational components for the current task increases steadily with the number of steps. The sum of the individual components of the successive steps is indicated in Figure 4.4 by the surface below the individual curves. Fourth, the preceding observations suggest that as the path grows longer the motivational differences between the two motive groups increase. Fifth, if the path consists of more than 6 or 7 steps, the strength of approach or avoidance motivation for success- and failure-motivated subjects increases more at each step with easy tasks ($Ps = .90$) than with tasks of moderate difficulty ($Ps = .50$). Motivation is lowest for very difficult tasks consisting of a path

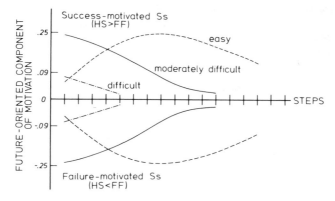

FIGURE 4.4 Future-oriented components of current task motivation for success- and failure-motivated subjects for individual tasks in a contingent path, with varying degrees of difficulty in the task series (easy: *Pnsn* = .90; moderately difficult: *Pnsn* = .50; difficult: *Pnsn* = .10). The strength of the resultant tendency to achieve for each individual step in the path is represented by the corresponding ordinate value; the strength of the total tendency to achieve is represented by the size of the area under the portion of the curve. (Adapted from Raynor, 1974, pp. 135–136.)

of more than two steps. Of all the successive steps in the path, the seventh introduces maximal additional motivational components into the comparison of the three initial probabilities of success. Corresponding conclusions can be drawn about failure motivation for failure-motivated subjects.

Empirical Check

Raynor and Entin (1972; see also Raynor, 1974, pp. 142–144) checked these predictions in a persistence experiment. Student subjects received three folders with a series of complex arithmetic tasks. They were told that the first and easiest folder was moderately difficult (*Ps* = .50), the second was more difficult, and the third most difficult of all. Each of the 35 problems in the first folder was solved successfully by all subjects. The dependent measure of persistence was how many problems they attempted to complete before going on to the next, more difficult folder. For half of the subjects a contingent path was created; for the other half, a noncontingent path. In the contingent condition subjects were told that they could attempt as many problems as they liked, as long as they had succeeded in completing each preceding problem; in the noncontingent condition they were told that they could go on working even if they were not able to solve all the problems.

TABLE 4.2

Choices of Major Area by Success- and Failure-Motivated Subjects, with Subjective
Estimate of Chances of Receiving the Degree[a]

	Level of difficulty			
Motive group	Most difficult[b]	Intermediate[c]	Easiest[d]	In between
Success-motivated	1	12	55	23
Failure-motivated	1	8	28	14

[a] Adapted from Wish, 1970, p. 88.
[b] Ps closest to .00.
[c] Ps closest to .50.
[d] Ps closest to 1.00.

For the most part, the results speak well for Raynor's derivations from the
model. In the first task series (initially described as moderately difficult)
subjects continually experienced success, and thus this type of task must
have been experienced as growing increasingly easy. In this series success-
motivated subjects completed more problems before going on to the next
type of task in a contingent path than in a noncontingent one. In a contin-
gent path they also worked longer than failure-motivated subjects. The
reverse was expected for failure-motivated subjects, but this was not the
case. They neither worked longer in a noncontingent than in a contingent
path, nor did they persist longer in a noncontingent path than success-moti-
vated subjects (as they should have according to the risk-taking model, since
the probability of success continued to increase beyond .50).

Not only persistence, but also risk taking should differ depending on
whether the path is contingent or noncontingent, contrary to the predictions
of the original model. Success-motivated subjects should be most drawn to
easy tasks, and failure-motivated subjects should be most repelled by them.
Wish (1970) explored this with students from a school of management who
actually found themselves in a contingent path. Their school awarded
degrees in major areas of varying difficulty. Wish used the students' actual
curricular choices as well as the students' probability ratings for their own
successful completion of the course of study. Table 4.2 contains the results
for both motive groups, divided into Ps of .00, .50, and 1.00, as well as the
other ratings. The results do not confirm the expectations, however. Both
success-motivated subjects and failure-motivated subjects chose the easiest
majors, not the most difficult. This effect corresponds to results already
mentioned — from Isaacson (1964) and Morris (1966) — and to results from
Kleinbeck and Schmidt (1979), in which instrumentality for superordinate
goals plays a role. These are discussed in Chapter 6 (see Figure 6.8).

In other studies achievement results were the dependent variable. Raynor and Rubin (1971) gave their subjects five series, each containing 25 complex arithmetic problems. They made it clear to all subjects that they had a 50% chance of solving 20 tasks in the allotted time. In the contingent condition subjects were told that they were allowed to continue only if this goal of 20 problems had been reached. In the noncontingent condition all the series could be worked even if the time criterion was not met. The number of problems correct in the first series was compared for both motive groups and both contingency conditions. The results corresponded to Raynor's elaboration of the model both in quantity and in quality. Success-motivated subjects (n Ach $>$ TAQ) are more likely to be superior to failure-motivated subjects with a contingent path than they are with a noncontingent path. Success-motivated subjects also achieve more and perform better with a contingent than with a noncontingent path, apart from the comparison with failure-motivated subjects. The reverse is true of failure-motivated subjects. Entin and Raynor (1973) found that this was equally true for a simple task (adding two-place numbers) and for a more complex task (Düker task).

Using the same experimental technique, Raynor and Sorrentino (1972) compared results for contingent and noncontingent paths of 4 to 7 steps, using Düker tasks with probabilities of success of .80, .50, and .20 (in a second study, .90, .50, and .10). The authors expected that as task difficulty increased, the performance difference between the two motive groups would decrease. They found the expected decrease for the easy task in favor of success-motivated subjects, as well as an unexpected improvement in performance of difficult tasks by failure-motivated subjects.

Finally, some studies show that future orientation moderates motive effects on performance by college students at their studies (Isaacson & Raynor, 1966; Raynor, 1970) and on the experience and evaluation of an imminent exam (Raynor, Atkinson, & Brown, 1974). For success-motivated subjects, in contrast with failure-motivated subjects, experiencing to a higher degree the instrumentality of top performance in their studies for success at exams and for professional success leads to improved performance in their studies.

In summary, Raynor's extension of the model attempts to account for the future orientation underlying achievement-oriented behavior. Of course, the extension does not solve all problems of the risk-taking model. For example, the incentive of superordinate goals is completely tied to probabilities of success. The motivating valences (motive $\times$ incentive) are reduced to mere self-evaluation, as in the risk-taking model, even though their effects are multiplied throughout the individual steps of action. Individual differences in incentive — based, for example, on variations in the personal importance of superordinate goals — are not taken into account. According to

Raynor, two equally long paths of action, of which the first steps have equal probability of success, would always arouse the same motivational strength in subjects with a similar motive pattern, even though the two superordinate goals might be quite different in importance to the person involved.

In addition, Raynor simplifies the future orientation of achievement-oriented behavior in two questionable ways. First of all, the instrumentality of each individual step for taking the next step in a contingent path is equated with the probability of success of the first step. Second, Raynor confused the instrumentality of the superordinate goal with its psychological distance in time. Both instrumentality and distance in time are determined simply by the number of steps in a contingent path. On the one hand, instrumentality $Ps_{1,n}$ is not a pure expectancy parameter, but is also determined by the number of steps in the path. On the other hand, temporal distance from a goal has a motivational effect for Raynor only with contingent paths, but not with noncontingent paths, even if they involve an incentive-related consequence delayed in time.

Raynor (1976) distinguished between the number of anticipated steps in a path, which he calls task hierarchy, and the experience of temporal length in the path, which he calls time hierarchy. As time hierarchy — that is, the distance from the superordinate goal — increases, motivational strength is thought to decrease; as task hierarchy increases, motivational strength is thought to increase.

Temporal Goal Distance and Achievement

The effect of a future superordinate goal on motivation to perform a current task is surely dependent not exclusively on the number of steps in the contingent path, but also on the extent to which the consecutive steps already seem structured — or at least on the perceived distance in time of the superordinate goal (Heckhausen, 1977a, p. 321). The latter concept, of psychologically perceived temporal distance from the goal, seems to be important, though it has been neglected (Heckhausen, 1967a, pp. 77, 80).

Gjesme (1974, 1975, 1976, 1981) attempted to resolve Raynor's confounding of instrumentality and temporal distance from the goal. A noncontingent path seems appropriate for this purpose, since it involves no instrumentality, and thus temporal distance from the goal can be varied independently.

In three studies Gjesme (1974, 1975, 1976) examined the effect of increasing goal distance on the results of easy anagrams and arithmetic problems about to be solved, by informing subjects that they would learn the results at one of four times: immediately afterwards, a week later, a month later, or a year later (and that this would be followed by another performance of the same task). If the announcement of the results is seen as a goal, this experiment can be said to involve a noncontingent path with varying distance from the goal.

Since it is a noncontingent path, we cannot assume, as Raynor does, that motivation increases in proportion to distance from the goal. Using Miller's (1944) conflict model, Gjesme assumes the opposite. When temporal distance from the goal event is greater, the approach tendency decreases in success-motivated subjects and the avoidance tendency decreases in failure-motivated subjects (motive classification by Gjesme & Nygard, 1970; Rand, 1978). If we assume a monotonic relationship between resulting motivational tendency and the achievement parameters for quantity and quality, the performance of success-motivated persons would worsen as distance from the goal increases, and the performance of failure-motivated persons would improve (because the inhibiting effect of failure motivation would decrease). Gjesme (1974) found this to be true of quality of performance, but true of quantity only for success-motivated persons.

In a second study Gjesme (1976) compared five subject groups with differing text anxiety scores (TAS). The results confirmed those of the 1974 study. As goal distance increased, highly anxious subjects improved the quality of their performance (again, quantity of performance remained constant), while with subjects having low anxiety, quantity rather than quality of performance tended to drop. However, these tendencies were not very pronounced.

In a third study Gjesme (1975) introduced still another personality factor in the experience of time. Within each of the two motive groups, he distinguished further between high and low future orientation with the aid of a questionnaire. Subjects with a high future orientation see the same events as closer in time than do subjects with low future orientation. Therefore, approach motivation should always be stronger for success-motivated persons with a high future orientation than for those with a low future orientation, given that objective distance from far-off goals is the same and disregarding borderline cases. Accordingly, when future orientation is high the drop in performance that begins as goal distance increases should be less than it is when future orientation is low. Gjesme expected the same to be true of the strength of avoidance motivation in failure-motivated subjects: With high future orientation, avoidance motivation was expected always to be stronger than with low future orientation, given that objective distance from far-off goals was the same. Accordingly, when future orientation was high, the improvement in performance that began as goal distance increased should have been less than it was when future orientation was low.

Gjesme's expectations were not confirmed with success-motivated subjects, neither for quantity nor for quality of performance. Their performance grew worse as goal distance increased, independent of future orientation. In contrast, the performance of failure-motivated subjects improved as expected in quantity and quality as goal distance increased, given that future orientation was low; but when future orientation was high, goal distance had no effect. Overall, we can conclude from the findings that high future orientation inhibits the performance of failure-motivated subjects. This is analogous to the experimentally manipulated increase in nearness of a goal event that threatens self-esteem. From a practical standpoint this means, for example, that schoolchildren fearing failure would perform more efficiently if the teacher emphasized the distance of the goal or of the critical test of current learning.

All of Gjesme's findings can be summarized by the statement that both achievement motives are more strongly aroused as the perception of temporal distance from the goal decreases. This improves the performance of success-motivated subjects and inhibits the performance of failure-motivated subjects. The perceived goal distance in time depends, on the one hand, on objective time distance, and on the other hand on the personality trait "future orientation."

In a theoretical analysis entitled "Is There Any Future in Achievement Motivation," Gjesme (1981) added a third determinant of perceived goal distance in time to the first two determinants (objective time distance and future orientation). The larger and more structured the anticipated goal — the more valence it has — the more its perceived distance decreases. Empirical confirmation of this determinant would be a further step toward overcoming Raynor's confounding of goal distance in time with instrumentality; moreover, it would give us the right to say that there is now "a future in achievement motivation."

Efficiency of Performance and Cumulative Achievement

The theoretical relationships between motivation and the results of performance are still largely unclarified and have not yet been empirically investigated in a systematic manner, as Chapters 3 and 4 have shown. What we need is a theory of achievement — that is, a theory about how performance originates in response to task assignments. The risk-taking model is useful only in that it prevents the crudest simplification — the notion that the achievement motive is a personality variable having a direct (specifically, a positive monotonic) relationship to parameters of task performance. This simplification confuses motive with motivation. It is a naive, pseudoscientific manner of explaining differences in achievement, based on the ability concept of traditional research on intelligence, and is almost impossible to eliminate.   It is still possible to find studies that explain individual differences in school achievement by motive differences (e.g., Wasna, 1972) or attempt to determine the validity of motive measurement on the basis of differences in performance (Entwisle, 1972).   In contrast, the risk-taking model shows that even schoolchildren with high achievement motives can have lower achievement motivation than children with low achievement motives in certain classroom situations.   Subjective probability of success (which is dependent on ability) determines the resultant motivational strength in the classroom (see Gjesme, 1971).   If the difficulty level of the instructional material as perceived by the individual child is not controlled, the correlations between motive strength and school achievement could be positive, zero, or negative and would not enable us to draw any conclusions about the influence of the achievement motive on achievement in school.

The theoretical relationship between motivation and achievement has not been clarified.   For a long time it was suggested that as (1) the resultant motivational strength grew, (2) the intensity and persistence of task-related effort would increase and thereby the (3) quality and quantity of performance results would also improve.   While the monotonic relationship of the first and second factors seems unproblematic and in the case of persistence is also well documented (see Feather, 1962, 1963a), the relationship between the second and third factors is questionable.   To be sure, greater persistence increases the quantity and (more often than not) the quality of performance, as reflected in the final outcome.   Certainly greater intensity of effort improves the quantitative aspect of performance at simple speed tasks (for example, see Locke, 1968).   But does it also improve the qualitative aspect of performance, especially with more complex tasks and difficult tasks?   The risk-taking model contains no special categories that would help us to answer this question.   For this case too, it predicts a positive monotonic function. Up to now only Karabenick and Youssef (1968) have been able to demonstrate for a more complex task (pair associations) a connection between motive strength and quality of performance such as the risk-taking model would suggest.   In a book edited jointly with Raynor (1974), *Motivation and Achievement,* Atkinson worked out in more detail the theoretical connection between motivation and quality of performance outcome.   Two factors are involved: the efficiency of task processing, as based on temporary strength of motivation to perform a particular task at a certain level of quality, and the amount of persistence at a certain average level of efficiency over an entire period of a person's life, as reflected in cumulative performance outcomes. Both points of view suggest a functional connection in developmental psychology between motive strength and quality of performance outcomes. We will now examine these concepts.

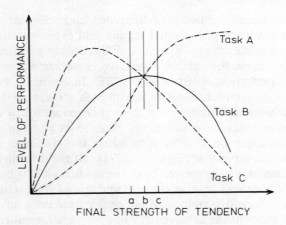

FIGURE 4.5 Dependence of efficiency of perform-
ance on motivational strength with three tasks of increas-
ing complexity: Task A, simple; Task B, moderately
complex; Task C, very complex. As strength of motiva-
tional tendency decreases (c, b, a), the efficiency of task
processing rises along with degree of complexity.
(Adapted from Atkinson, 1974a, p. 200.)

Efficiency

Following the old Yerkes–Dodson Rule (1908), Atkinson (1974a) as-
sumes that the relationship between motivational strength during task per-
formance and efficiency as reflected in quality of performance is not mono-
tonic, but is rather an inverse U curve. Earlier researchers pointed this out as
well—for example, Broadhurst (1959), Eysenck (1966), and Vroom
(1964). Maximal efficiency does not occur when motivational strength is
maximal, but rather when it is optimal. As a rule, optimal motivational
strength is submaximal. The more complex and difficult the task require-
ments, the lower the optimal motivational strength. "Undermotivation"
and "overmotivation" impair the efficiency of any task. Figure 4.5 illus-
trates the function of motivational strength and quality of performance as
regards efficiency for a simple task (A), a moderately complex task (B), and a
very complex task (C). The optimal motivational strength for Task B is
suboptimal for Tasks A and C. At optimal motivational strength for either
Task A or Task C the efficiency for the other task is nearly minimal.

Thus it is a question of the extent to which individuals are optimally
motivated for the specific requirements of a task, and not under- or overmo-

tivated. The resulting motivational tendency is determined by (1) motive strength, (2) subjective probability of success for the task, and (3) situational incentives (which are independent of the probability of success), such as personal importance of the task or its significance for the step-by-step approach to a superordinate goal. Motivational strength, and thus also the efficiency of task processing, results from the interaction of three independent factors: personality (motive), task (subjective probability of success), and situation (incentives consisting of further results and extrinsic results of success and failure, such as attaining superordinate goals or evaluation by strangers). When the situation also involves incentives consisting of extrinsic results, the strength of the extrinsic motives (e.g., affiliation in an achievement situation) also plays a role.

No systematic analysis of the connections among the individual determinants of motivational strength has been made. Atkinson's hypotheses in this regard are merely plausible assumptions. All other factors being equal, Atkinson suggests that as motive strength increases, the closer the probability of success is to $Ps = .50$ and the stronger the situational incentives are, the higher will be the resultant motivational strength. Since Atkinson sees the failure motive (TAQ) as an inhibiting factor, resultant motive strength (n Ach $-$ TAQ; $HS - FF$) is a matter of "net hope" NH. That can lead to the seemingly paradoxical prediction that a higher failure motive improves efficiency because otherwise—given the same success motive—a state of excessive motivation could occur, particularly with more complex task requirements and strong situational incentives.

Like the interactive effect of the three determinants on motivational strength, the efficiency functions of motivational strength that are dependent on the nature of the task have not yet been systematically analyzed. There has been little differentiation in the consideration of task requirements; researchers have distinguished crudely between less or more complex tasks. To be sure, for a long time researchers in achievement motivation (Atkinson, 1960, pp. 267–268; Weiner & Schneider, 1971) have taken into account the confounding of complexity of task requirements with subjective probability of success that is characteristic of anxiety research (Spence & Spence, 1966).

Documentation of the inverse U-curve efficiency function of motivational strength has been based on Atkinson's (1974a) reanalyses of earlier dissertations with multithematic incentive situations (Reitman, 1957 [published 1960]; and Smith, 1961 [published 1966]), as well as on dissertations by Entin (1968, published 1974) and Horner (1968, published 1974b).

Entin (1974) grouped his subjects by strength of resultant success motive (n Ach $-$ TAQ) and affiliation motive and created two conditions differing in incentive strength of affiliation themes: private versus public achievement feedback. In the first condition the results were posted on a bulletin board the next day, under an anonymous code number; in the second condition, results were posted with the subject's full name. Subjects were asked to work arithmetic problems, some simple and some complex (Düker arithmetic problems). When feedback was private, the conditions resembled those for which the risk-taking model was designed: The only possible consequence was self-evaluation, and evaluation by others was impossible. In this condition the quality of performance was better in the group with high success motive (n Ach > TAQ) than in the group with low success motive, for both simple and complex tasks. The monotonic relationship may be based on the fact that optimal motivational strength had not yet been attained in either condition. Thus we would expect the effect of public feedback to be particularly interesting, since in this condition subjects with equally high success and affiliation motives might increase their resultant motivational strength beyond the point of optimal efficiency and became overmotivated. There was indeed a tendency for the number of correctly solved problems to decrease in this condition: not only with the more complex problems, but also with the easy ones. Thus the findings hardly support the assumption of a curvilinear efficiency function of motivational strength.

Atkinson's (1974a) reanalysis of the studies by Atkinson and Reitman (1956) and Reitman (1960) was a little more convincing. In a multithematic incentive situation (group competition, pressure to achieve by the experimenter, and reward offered) subjects with high success motives performed worse at Düker arithmetic problems than they did in an individual situation. Subjects with low success motives improved. Atkinson (1974a) also reanalyzed Smith's dissertation (1961, published 1966). Smith differentiated more among situational incentive contents, labeling the situations "relaxed," "achievement-related," and "multithematic." In the group with high success motives the number of correctly solved Düker tasks rose from 53.0 (relaxed) to 78.8 (achievement-related) and fell to 55.3 (multithematic). In the group with low success motives a monotonic increase appeared from one condition to the next: 34.8–55.8–85.3. The assumption that the three situational conditions actually aroused motivation of differing strengths, as expected, was substantiated by average scores from an effort test.

Finally, Horner (1974b) assigned male students Düker problems and anagrams, either in an individual situation or in competition with a male or female partner. Again, subjects were cross-classified by motive strength. Table 4.3 contains the results. As expected, the groups with high and low success motives differed significantly only in the individual condition. When competition incentives were added, the picture became less clear. Apparently the affiliative incentive value of competition—depending on

TABLE 4.3

Performance of Men in Achievement-Oriented Situations[a]

	Conditions		
Motive pattern	Noncompetitive (alone)	Competition with female	Competition with male
High affiliation			
High resultant achievement	46.5	53.9	48.4
Low resultant achievement	41.8	53.6	56.1
Low affiliation			
High resultant achievement	48.4	53.4	53.7
Low resultant achievement	40.8	47.7	46.7

[a] Mean number of anagrams constructed by men in 10 minutes as a function of resultant achievement motivation, affiliative motivation, and experimental condition. Achievement motivation was measured by n Ach $-$ TAQ. Results are given in standard scores, derived from a motivationally matched sample of honors and nonhonors subjects. Each distribution has a mean of 50 and *SD* of 10. Adapted from Horner, 1974b, p. 249.

the strength of the affiliation motive — led to an increase in resultant motivational strength, particularly when the male subjects were competing with male rather than female partners. If the strength of both motives was high, the achievement level dropped during competition with male partners. This can be interpreted as excessive motivation, assuming the existence of the efficiency function described earlier. The same was true with the Düker tasks.

The findings suggest that the thesis of an inverse U-curve efficiency function, dependent on motivation, has a certain heuristic explanatory value. It would be desirable to investigate this efficiency function instead of continuing merely to show its plausibility by reanalyzing achievement findings that deviate from the model in multithematic incentive situations. For this purpose it would be necessary to differentiate more precisely among parameters of complexity, particularly with regard to task complexity, and to differentiate along a wider spectrum. With regard to situational incentives, results would be clearer if motivational strength were increased by means of gradual increments in incentive content of achievement themes (e.g., as it was done by Locke, 1968; or Mierke, 1955) rather than by means of extrinsic incentives. Finally, with regard to subjects, the two achievement motives should be measured with the greatest of care, in order to test Atkinson's questionable statement that the failure motive is nothing but a subtractive factor produced during measurement of the resultant motivational tendency.

In Chapter 3 we pointed out the important role of task parameters, which have tended to be neglected, in clarifying the correlation between motivational strength and achievement. For example, in the case of motor strength and endurance, excessive motivation does not reduce achievement, but increases it. Sorrentino and Sheppard (1978) demonstrated this on the basis of swimming competitions at three universities. The trainers allowed Sorrentino and Sheppard to control conditions in a field experiment in which motivational factors (achievement motive and affiliation motive) were combined with competition factors (individual versus group competition). Success-motivated subjects (n Ach > TAQ) with a high positive affiliation motive achieved more under group conditions than individual conditions. For these swimmers, during group competition the two maximally activated motives added up to a strength that can be described as "excessive motivation" in comparison with individual competition.

Cumulative Achievement Outcomes

First of all we must add that level of task performance is determined not only by the efficiency of motivational strength for specific task requirements, but naturally also by individual skill at performing the task. According to Atkinson (1974b), level of performance is the product of skill and efficiency. That means that only in the case of equal efficiency — for example, at taking an intelligence test — are actual skill differences revealed in results. In contrast, when efficiency varies, persons with equal "true" skill can produce quite different outcomes. In this sense we can say that all intelligence research up to the present has implicitly made the improbable assumption that from a motivational standpoint all subjects work with maximal (or at least with the same) efficiency. Since test and exam situations are multithematic incentive situations with high motivational arousal, especially when they determine whether superordinate goals will be reached, the efficiency of many subjects is presumably lowered by excessive motivation. These subjects will seem less competent than they actually are under everyday conditions. Thus achievement test results are a mixed product of true skill and motivation-dependent processing efficiency, and it is hard to disentangle these factors.

According to Atkinson, subjects with high motive strength are frequently trapped in highly arousing situations of excessive motivation and suffer a drop in level of performance. However, their high motive strength is useful to them under everyday working conditions, in which resulting motivational strength is lower than in a test situation. Here they find themselves operating at a level of optimal efficiency, which favors longer persistence during successive phases of daily work. Atkinson assumes a monotonic relationship between achievement motive strength and time employed for achievement-related activities. In the long run, high average efficiency and great persistence lead to high cumulative achievement. Atkinson (1974b) attempted to demystify the concepts of so-called overachievement and underachievement (see Heckhausen, 1980a; Thorndike, 1963; Wahl, 1975), which have been investigated extensively and discussed in the field of educational psychology. These concepts involve phenomena contrary to expectations in the relationship between school and college achievement on the one hand and measured level of ability on the other hand. In contrast with overachievers (described earlier), underachievers have low motive strength, so that they reach optimal efficiency only in achievement situations of strong arousal, such as during an intelligence test. Over a longer period and under everyday conditions, however, their work shows neither efficiency nor persistence, so that their cumulative achievement outcomes are lower.

Thus cumulative achievement depends not only on skill and efficiency, but also on the total length of time devoted to task performance. Since the level of performance is determined by skill and efficiency, we can say with Atkinson that cumulative achievement is the product of level of performance and time devoted to task performance. Work time is determined not only by the strength of the success motive ($HS - FF$), but also by the arousal of achievement themes in the everyday environment and the strength of competing motives (see Feather, 1962) that favor the occurrence of non-achievement-oriented alternative activities.

Achievement motivation plays a dual role in bringing about cumulative achievement. On the one hand, it influences the efficiency of current task processing, depending on task requirements and along with individual ability to perform the particular task involved. On the other hand, it influences the total length of time devoted to task performance, competing as it does with motivational strength for alternative activities. Figure 4.6 represents the connection of all these factors visually. The perspective here resembles that of developmental psychology. The multiplicative interaction of level of performance and time spent on the task has an influence not only on cumulative achievement, but also on the person involved, in the form of improvement in skills. As the proverb suggests, "Practice makes perfect."

Skill test results correlate at a level of .30 to .50 with cumulative grade point average. Thus the results explain about 10–25% of the variance. The overriding question is, "To what extent can variance be further explained by Atkinson's network of causes of cumulative achievement?" That would

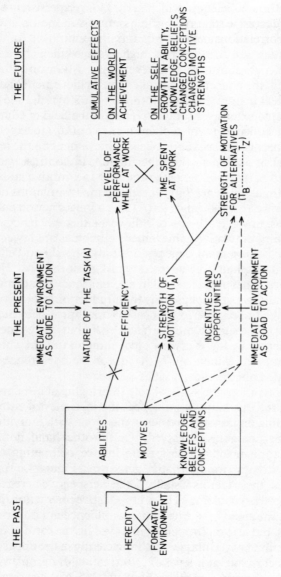

FIGURE 4.6 The dual role of motivation as a determinant of cumulative achievement. Along with individual skill at performing a given task (A), motivation (T_A)—depending on task requirements—influences the efficiency of current task processing. It also influences the length of total work time devoted to the task in question in relationship to motivational strength for alternative activities (T_B . . . T_Z). (Adapted from Atkinson, Lens, & O'Malley, 1976, p. 51.)

involve a complex investigation that would take into account separate measurement of motivationally determined efficiency in ability testing and of motivationally determined efficiency and persistence under everyday conditions. Then, in successive stages of development, we would expect to find increasingly close correlations between the achievement motive (*NH*) and cumulative achievement, as well as between motive and ability ("Practice makes perfect").

Detailed empirical analyses have not yet been made. Sawusch (1974) examined the implications of the network of causes using a computer simulation with a hypothetical sample of 80 subjects to whom scores for ability, achievement motive, and motive for alternative activity were randomly attributed. Considering the various assumptions that can be made on the basis of the model (i.e., that motivation during testing is higher than during normal work situations, that there are various correlations between motive and ability, that there is a curvilinear efficiency, etc.), it is not surprising that motive strength can be closely connected with cumulative achievement.

However, outcomes simulated on the basis of the model are not convincing. In order to be convinced, we need to see empirical outcomes resembling model predictions. Atkinson, Lens, and O'Malley (1976) were the first to produce such findings. They compared the resulting achievement motive (*n* Ach − TAQ) and intelligence test scores (California Test of Mental Maturity) of sixth- and ninth-grade students with the grade point average of the same students in the twelfth grade (3–6 years later). On the whole, more of the variance in final grade point average can be explained by the intelligence test differences than by the motive differences (which can be attributed entirely or in part to the varying measurement reliability of both predictors). Motive strength of the sixth- (or ninth-) graders covaried most clearly with grade point average in the twelfth grade for students with high intelligence test scores; there was no correlation at all in the lower range. In the middle range of intelligence, motive strength correlated with grade point average for the twelfth grade, but only starting with the ninth grade — not for sixth-graders.

This motivational effect on grade point average, which is moderated by ability level, corresponds to Atkinson's concept of cumulative achievement. Cumulative achievement, for Atkinson, is a product of achievement level during task performance (dependent on ability and efficiency) and persistence at the task (dependent on motivational strength). Thus, the motivational effect is naturally manifested most clearly in the upper range of intelligence. Since it is also apparent in the middle range for ninth-graders, perhaps we can say that by this time the ability of the older students has reached the critical level. Incidentally, we could predict the same outcomes on the basis of Raynor's concept of future orientation. In a contingent path of action, high initial probabilities of success lead to the highest (and thereby also most persistent) motivation. Schoolchildren with high ability have the highest probabilities of success in the classroom.

In addition, the covariation between motive strength and level of ability was greater in the ninth grade than in the sixth grade. Although Atkinson's study was not longitudinal, this suggests for developmental psychology that the more time is used for practicing skills, the more they develop. In other words, differences in motive strength lead to differential growth in ability. To be sure, this has not yet been documented convincingly; nor has it been shown in what way the many individual determinants in the network of factors determining cumulative achievement are connected with each other.

5

The Contribution of Attribution Theory

Various motivational theories, including those in the behaviorist tradition, are constructed partly of cognitive elements (e.g., Festinger, 1957; Hull, 1930; Tolman, 1932, 1959; Woodworth, 1958). These elements vary in their importance for theory. One example is the fragmentary anticipatory goal reaction (rG – sG mechanism) introduced early by Hull as an equivalent of Tolman's expectancy concept in stimulus – response theory in order to do justice to the phenomenon of latent learning. Atkinson's theory (1957, 1964) includes such a cognitive element, in the form of subjective probability of success. Together with the incentive variables, it determines the strength of achievement motivation.

In evaluating Atkinson's theory, Madsen (1974, p. 426) found the incentive variables to be more central than the expectancy variables and classified the theory as an incentive theory.

Incentive theories are those in which a dynamic effect is attributed to external stimulus-events. This effect consists of producing a state of activation in the organism that — certainly along with cognitive variables — determines behavior (Madsen, 1974, p. 422). In Atkinson's theory these external stimulus-events involve success and failure incentives that are conceived of as anticipated positive and negative affects following success or failure. The fact that the achievement motive is defined as a disposition to seek or avoid these affects (Atkinson, 1964, p. 241) indicates that these incentives have greater theoretical significance than subjective probability of success. This is true even though the construction of the model suggests the opposite, since incentives are defined as factors dependent on probability of success (see Chapter 3).

In motivation theories constructed exclusively of cognitive elements, the motivational process is directly dependent on cognitive factors, whether these factors guide and direct the motivational process or have a direct motivational effect (Madsen, 1974, p. 424). Bolles (1974) described the status of cognitive variables in these motivational theories in a similar fashion. Cognitive processes can initiate a variety of behaviors. It is neither necessary to make these cognitive processes dependent on external stimuli events, nor are superordinate goals toward which behavior is directed theoretically necessary (1974, p. 19).

In addition to the concept of expectancies (anticipatory goal reaction) mentioned earlier in this chapter, the principal cognitive elements recently introduced into achievement motivation theory are causal attributions made by individuals for their own action outcomes and those of other persons. Attribution theory is concerned with such causal attributions and with the principles according to which these attributions are made. Occasionally attribution theory has been seen as a "cognitive turning point" and distinguished from "mechanical" behavior theories (Heckhausen & Weiner, 1972; Weiner, 1972). Such a contrast is only relative, when examined more closely. The actual change is the increase in reference to various cognitions and the readiness to give cognitions a more prominent role in the explanation of behavior. Causal attributions seem appropriate as explanatory elements because individuals are generally not content simply to register events in their environment, but rather they attempt to trace back these events to particular causes. In fact, this tendency to attribute events to causes is often seen as the activating of central needs of the individual (Heider, 1958, p. 81; Kelley, 1967, p. 193). Causal connections make a substantial contribution to the orientation of individuals in their environment. They allow people to make precise predictions about future events and to adjust their behavior appropriately. Approaches based on attribution theory describe such networks of assumptions and the way in which they create order. Attributions, as components of these networks, have the function of giving meaning to environmental events, thus allowing individuals to predict and control their behavior (Meyer & Schmalt, 1978).

Causal Elements and Their Classification

Heider (1958) was the first to describe individual elements causing action outcomes. First he divided the individual causal elements into two different groups, (internal) personality factors and (external) situation factors. Personality factors include ability and motivation; ability is seen as stable over time, and motivation is seen as a variable causal element. The motivation factor itself can be divided into two components. On one hand, the term "motivation" refers to what individuals are trying to do (intention), but on the other hand it also refers to how hard they are trying to do it (effort). The situation factor can likewise be divided into a stable causal element (difficulty) and a variable element (luck). These individual causal elements are first of all components of "naive" behavioral theories such as the "man on

TABLE 5.1
Causes of Success and Failure, Classified by Locus of Control, Stability, and Controllability[a]

Controllability[b]	Internal		External	
	Stable	Unstable	Stable	Unstable
Uncontrollable	Ability	Mood	Task difficulty	Luck
Controllable	Typical effort	Immediate effort	Teacher bias	Unusual help
			Typical help from others	

[a] Adapted from Weiner, 1979, p. 7.
[b] The fields in boxes contain the causal factors from the original Heider–Weiner chart. As can be seen, it does not take into account the dimension of controllability (intentionality). Neither of the two stable causal factors—ability (internal) and task difficulty (external)—is controllable, whereas one of the unstable causal elements is controllable (effort; internal) and one uncontrollable (luck; external).

the street" uses. In attribution theory causal elements are the object of scientific behavioral theories and are represented as theoretical constructs.

Weiner and his colleagues (Weiner *et al.*, 1971; Weiner, Heckhausen, Meyer, & Cook, 1972; Weiner & Kukla, 1970) deserve credit for recognizing the significance of causal attribution for achievement motivation and formulating a theory of achievement-motivated behavior that is based largely on these causal attributions.

Weiner distinguishes among four causal factors, which he outlines with the help of the dimensions "stability" and "area of responsibility," much like Heider (see Table 5.1). Attempts to extend and supplement Weiner's theory began early. Rosenbaum (1972) proposed that a third dimension be added to the dimensions of stability and area of responsibility, which were already being used for classifying individual causal elements and explaining causes of action outcomes. This dimension was intentionality, which had already been described by Heider (1958) but was not included among Weiner's original dimensions. Thus it was possible to differentiate among eight different causal factors. The third dimension was originally intended to facilitate differentiation among such factors as mood and effort. Both are internal, variable causal elements, and yet basically different in nature. Effort is a matter of deliberate control; this is hardly the case with mood. Weiner (1979; Weiner & Litman-Adizes, 1980) chose to pursue the same line of differentiation. However, instead of the dimension of intentionality, Weiner inferred the presence or absence of controllability as a latent dimension behind the various causal elements (Table 5.1).

Abramson, Seligman, and Teasdale (1978) described an additional dimension for the "learned helplessness" paradigm—that is, globality versus specificity. Specific causal elements affect specific individual actions; in contrast, global causal elements affect entire fields of action. However, this extended paradigm has rarely been used to explain achievement-oriented behavior. The reason may be that it is not possible to imagine that the dimensions are mutually independent. Investigations of achievement-oriented behavior almost always concern the two original dimensions, locus and stability. A few studies also take into account the dimensions of controllability and globality.

Intentionality has not yet been taken into account. There are already some indications that it might be fruitful to distinguish between intentional and unintentional causal elements (Weiner & Litman-Adizes, 1980) in the analysis of motives other than achievement, such as aggression (Nickel, 1974), power (Schmalt, 1979b), and helping (Ickes & Kidd, 1976). In addition, the extended paradigm also enables us to distinguish between typical effort and immediate effort.

Various studies have revealed the need for this differentiation. It has been shown that effort cannot always be seen as a causal element that varies over time. Frequently effort is also treated as a dispositional characteristic (see Rest, Nierenberg, Weiner, & Heckhausen, 1973). When effort is considered as a disposition (trait), it is treated as an element that is even more stable than ability (Saxe, Greenberg, & Bar-Tal, 1974, p. 42).

Elig and Frieze (1975) report that all spontaneously occurring causal attributions in the area of achievement can be classified under one of the three dimensions in Table 5.1. Altogether the authors identified 19 different causal elements. Cooper and Burger (1980), Frieze (1973), Meyer and Butzkamm (1975), and Rheinberg (1975, 1977) investigated whether the four causal factors derived by Weiner from Heider's naive psychology actually are sufficient for an adequate description of the attributional process for success and failure. In these studies subjects were asked to make causal attributions for their own (fictitious) achievements, or teachers were asked to give causal explanations of their pupils' achievement. The studies showed that effort and talent—personality factors—were by far the most frequent and thus also the most important causal elements used by subjects to explain their own achievements and those of others. Some new causal elements also appeared—for example, home environment and general physical and emotional state. These elements were acquired characteristics and physiological processes that were not contained in the three-dimensional paradigm but could be incorporated into it without difficulty. However, these processes were relatively insignificant as causal explanatory factors.

Of course, the use of different causal elements for success and failure is also dependent on the social and cultural significance of achievement. We must expect to find different attributional elements in other societies. For example, Triandis (1972) reported that in Japan and Greece, patience was mentioned as a reason for successful results, and in India tact and unity (see also Chandler *et al.*, 1981). The individual causal elements are objects of naive psychology, but the dimensions by means of which they are classified are not. They are more or less intuitive extrapolations by scientists attempting to organize the elements by qualities that they have in common and qualities that distinguish them from each other. Therefore, a taxonomy of causal elements must be submitted to empirical examination.

An initial investigation by Passer, Kelley, and Michela (1978) explored the dimensionality of causal attributions for negative events in the interpersonal realm. They found no support for the dimensions proposed by Heider and Weiner. Moreover, the dimensioning of causal attributions differed depending on whether the subject's actions or the subject's partner's actions were being analyzed. Meyer (1980) analyzed causal attributions for the successes and failures of others. He presented his subjects with questionnaires describing 16 different situations and asked them to indicate for each situation to what extent each of nine given causal elements was responsible for the outcome. These causal elements were difficulty of exam, general intelligence, luck, mood, preparation for exam, study habits, teacher's ability, teacher's effort, and test-taking ability. The questionnaires were subjected to a three-mode factor analysis. The three factors represented in the nine causal elements and the 16 situations correspond to the dimensions of stability, locus, and controllability. Attributions for success and failure do reflect the dimensions of stability, locus, and control.

Explaining Achievement-Related Behavior

Attribution theory made its first contribution to the theory of achievement-related behavior when Weiner and Kukla (1970) proposed that success- and failure-motivated subjects used causal factors in clearly distinct ways. In comparison with failure-motivated subjects, success-motivated subjects attributed success more and failure less to themselves (Weiner & Kukla, 1970, pp. 8 – 9). As we will see, this hypothesis was refined later with respect to the relative preference for individual causal elements in attributions for success and failure by success- and failure-motivated subjects. Even at first, however, it was clear that many of the behavioral differences between success- and failure-motivated subjects can be explained by these asymmetries in causal attribution (Weiner *et al.*, 1971).

A few researchers had already attempted to show connections between achievement motivation and perceived causes for a person's own successes and failures. For example, Rotter (1966, p. 3) suggested that his concept of internal versus external reinforcement control might be connected with the achievement motive, although Rotter's concept does not pertain exclusively to the achievement domain. Close relationships have not yet been found between these constructs (Meyer, 1973a; Phares, 1976). There are, however, indications that locus of control might be a moderator variable mediating between the achievement motive and behavior. Wolk and DuCette (1973) reported that some of the predictions derived from Atkinson's (1957, 1964) risk-taking model were true only for internals.

The concept of "intellectual achievement responsibility" developed by Crandall, Katkovsky, and Preston (1962) and Crandall *et al.* (1965a) has turned out to be more successful. This concept shows a series of correlations with achievement-related behavior. Meyer (1973a), Schmalt (1976b), Weiner and Kukla (1970), and Weiner and Potepan (1970) also reported positive correlations for male subjects between success-oriented achievement motivation and responsibility for one's own success.

Earlier Feather (1967) attempted to incorporate the concept of responsibility for one's own success or failure into Atkinson's risk-taking model. He assumed that perceived responsibility has a moderating effect on the relationship between incentive and probability of success. However, the attempts to extend Atkinson's risk-taking model by adding a cognitive factor such as responsibility for one's own success or failure were unfruitful and soon abandoned.

Though on the one hand Weiner moved away from the risk-taking model, on the other hand his theory did remain within the expectancy-value framework as used by Atkinson. The model parameters — motives, incentives, and probabilities of success — were retained but were linked to causal attributions. Motives were conceived of as preferences for certain causal attributions. Furthermore it was postulated that expectancy change and affects (incentives) were partially determined by these same attributions. The dimension of stability was said to determine expectancies and changes in expectancies; the locus-of-control dimension of causal attribution was said to determine affects. And finally, achievement-related behavior is determined by expectancies and affects. Table 5.2 summarizes these relationships.

In addition to the achievement motive, a number of other factors are listed in this table as antecedents of attributions. These antecedents are not actually part of the attributional theory of achievement motivation, but they do nevertheless have a definite influence on causal explanations of success and failure. Such antecedents include specific situational cues, nature and structure of the available information, assumptions about the interaction of

TABLE 5.2

The Attributional Model of Achievement Motivation[a]

Antecedents	Causes of success and failure	Causal dimensions	Effects	Behavioral consequences
Specific situational cues	Ability	Stability ──────→	Expectancy shifts	Intensity
Success–failure	Effort	Locus of control ──→	Affective reactions	Choice
Pattern of outcome	Task difficulty	Controllability ╱		Persistence
Information patterns	Luck			Resistance to extinction
Causal patterns	Mood			Others
Individual differences (achievement motive)	Fatigue			
Observational perspective	Others			
Reinforcement schedules				
Others				

[a] Adapted from Weiner and Litman-Adizes, 1980, p. 37.

individual causal elements (causal schemata), observational perspective, reinforcement schedules, and various additional factors.

Causal Explanation of Success and Failure: Self-Serving Bias

Many investigations indicate that subjects tend to feel personally responsible for their positive outcomes but minimize or even deny responsibility for negative outcomes (summarized by Bradley, 1978; Kelley & Michela, 1980; Miller & Ross, 1975; Wetzel, 1982; Zuckerman, 1979). Results of this sort are generally attributed to the fact that individuals seek to establish a positive self-esteem and to maintain it to the greatest extent possible. The principle of such a "hedonistic bias" in causal explanations, which follows affective-dynamic rules more than rational rules, was first described by Heider: "The reason has to fit the wishes" (1958, p. 172).

Beckman (1970) conducted one of the first studies. She used female student teachers to teach children certain arithmetic concepts. The children were assumed to be working the entire time at the same high or low level, or improving their performance, or allowing their performance to drop. Subsequently the teachers analyzed the results for causes. Neutral observers did the same on the basis of a written transcript of the teacher–student interaction. The results showed that teachers tend to see themselves as personally responsible for improved performance to a greater extent than the observers. Low-level performance or a descending performance pattern, on the other hand, tends to be explained externally and attributed to the pupil's lack of motivation or situational factors. This difference in attribution between teachers and neutral observers suggests that a self-serving attribution might have been operative.

Results such as these have often been reported. Sometimes the opposite effects occur in the case of failure, which in the opinion of the authors suggests that ego-protective mechanisms, preventing self-devaluation, coexist with tendencies to increase self-esteem. Accordingly, the fact that in otherwise comparable situations success tends to be explained internally and failure externally is well documented. It remained an open question for a long time, however, whether this phenomenon could be interpreted as an attributional bias in the service of self-esteem.

Miller and Ross (1975) analyzed the relevant studies and concluded that the difference found between attributions for positive and negative outcomes is not due to ego-enhancing motivational factors, but could be explained as a rational procedure. That is, as a rule people perceive a covariation between their own actions and positive results more clearly than between their own actions and negative results. In addition, people tend to assume responsibility more readily for expected events than for unexpected events. Naturally — all else being equal — once people undertake an action they tend to expect success rather than failure. Moreover, the perception of covariation between one's own efforts to achieve and the results is said to be stronger in the case of desirable events (success) than in the case of undesirable events (failure) (Miller & Ross, 1975; but see also Miller, 1976, pp. 901–902). In every case people are tempted to assume responsibility for success, but to refuse responsibility for failure, without any recourse to motivated attributional errors. Miller and Ross interpret diverging attributions for success and failure by means of an information processing model in which a person's own intentions, expectancies, and perceived covariations between behavior and outcome play a role.

In order to test these hypotheses, it is necessary to expand and alter previously used experimental designs. The subjects' level of expectancy must be controlled. In addition, we must differentiate among attributions, at least with regard to their stability over time. And finally, new experimental paradigms are necessary. Attributions of one's own successes and failures and those of others, as in Beckman's study (1970), differ not only with regard to ego involvement, but also because of differences in information available to actors and observers. Thus such studies cannot be used to aid us in clearing up this controversy.

Feather (1969) reports an initial experiment in which level of expectation in relation to success and failure outcomes was controlled. He differentiated among attributions only with regard to the factors ability and luck. He found that unexpected successes and failures are attributed to luck; in contrast, expected successes and failures tend to be attributed to ability or lack of it. He concluded that unexpected events tend to be explained externally and expected events tend to be explained internally. This conclusion is not totally convincing, because ability is an internal but stable causal element and luck is an external but variable element. Two replication studies involving numerous methodological modifications included all four of Weiner's causal factors (Feather & Simon, 1971; Gilmor & Minton, 1974). These studies essentially confirmed the earlier results for ability and luck attributions. In addition, the studies showed that — independent of the level of expectation — success tends more than failure to be attributed to effort and ability. This can be interpreted as a motivated attributional error.

A study by Luginbuhl, Crowe, and Kahan (1975) also showed some significant differences in ability and effort attribution for a subject's own success and failure. Success was attributed primarily to a high degree of effort and failure primarily to a lack of ability, whether the events in question were expected or unexpected.

Schmalt (1978) also examined the attributions for successes and failures at tasks varying in apparent difficulty. This study showed that success tends more than failure to be made dependent on the internal factors ability and effort. Failure, on the other hand, tends more often than success to be explained by luck. This was true independent of the level of expectancy (task difficulty). These findings clearly support the assumption that attributions made after success tend to raise self-esteem and attributions after failure tend to be defensive. This is especially true of attributions to ability and luck. At the same time, the results reported for attributions to effort are compatible with the approach based on information theory, which involves perceptions of covariation. When effort is invested, failure is unlikely to be attributed to lack of effort, whereas success might very well be attributed to effort (see Nicholls, 1975, p. 380).

When attributions in this study are examined as to dimensions, taking level of expectancy into account, we see that unexpected successes and failures elicit more variable and internal attributions than do expected results. This contradicts Feather's (1969) notion that unexpected results tend to be explained externally.

Frieze and Weiner (1971) and McMahan (1973) report findings quite similar to Schmalt's (1978) for attributions to others as well as to the self. Thus it is not yet certain whether unexpected successes and failures are explained more frequently by external factors (luck) or by internal, variable factors. Perhaps the factors chosen to explain unexpected results depend on task and situational characteristics.

These last three studies also lend further, if indirect, support to the self-esteem interpretation of attribution asymmetries, for they show that it is precisely the unexpected results for which subjects assume responsibility, and not, as the information processing approach of Miller and Ross (1975) assumed, the expected results.

The assumption of motivated attributional errors is supported more directly by investigations in which the relevance of the situations to self-esteem is manipulated directly. In the first investigation Miller (1976) assumed that the asymmetries in the causal explanation of success and failure that are caused by motivated attributional errors would occur primarily in connection with pressure for self-evaluation. He assumed that in the absence of pressure for self-evaluation there would be no motivational basis for asymmetrical attributions of success and failure. His subjects first filled out a questionnaire (Social Perceptiveness Scale) designed to measure social competence, and then received feedback on success and failure. In one condition the questionnaire was described as a sensitive and highly valid instrument (strong concern for self-evaluation) and in the other condition it was introduced as a rather questionable instrument developed by a psychology student (little concern for self-evaluation).

On the one hand, the results confirm the earlier findings that attribution tends to be internal after success (social competence, effort) and external after failure (task difficulty, luck). However, this asymmetry is pronounced only when there is a strong concern for self-evaluation. This supports the interpretation of attributional asymmetries as motivated attributional errors. If we assume that achievement themes are always connected with self-evaluation, we must also assume that asymmetrical attribution will tend to occur when achievement themes are aroused.

Federoff and Harvey (1976) carried out another experiment in which the situation was varied with respect to evaluation by others. They assumed that self-esteem-related attributional asymmetries appear only when objective self-awareness (Duval & Wicklund, 1973) is increased by heightening the feeling of being evaluated by others. This effect was thought to be independent of the expectancy of a positive or negative outcome. Federoff and Harvey claimed to be investigating the competence of lay therapists in administering psychotherapy and induced different initial expectancies in their subjects as to the success of the undertaking. In this study success and

TABLE 5.3
Attributions for Success and Failure to Self and to an External Factor[a]

	Success		Failure	
	Internal	External	Internal	External
High self-awareness				
Positive expectancy	7.98[b]	5.28	4.46	8.27
Negative expectancy	8.01	6.65	4.28	6.10
Low self-awareness				
Positive expectancy	6.71	6.22	5.92	6.93
Negative expectancy	6.47	6.24	6.13	6.45

[a] Adapted from Federoff and Harvey, 1976, pp. 341–342.
[b] The higher the score, the greater the attribution to self (internal) or to the patient (external).

failure were determined by the extent to which the subjects were able to produce a state of relaxation in their "patients." The degree of relaxation was shown on an indicator. The feeling of being evaluated (objective self-awareness) was produced by telling the subjects in one condition that their efforts were being filmed by a camera that had been set up in the room.

The results of this investigation with respect to internal attribution (the subject's own ability) and external attribution (the patient's problem) are shown in Table 5.3. The familiar asymmetry with respect to internal (ability) attribution appeared under conditions of high objective self-awareness. Independent of the level of expectancy, positive results were attributed to the subject's own ability more than were negative results. This effect was not observed when objective self-awareness was low. The results for external attribution were more complex. Negative outcomes were attributed to external factors (task difficulty) more than positive outcomes, but only when objective self-awareness was high and at the same time a positive outcome was expected. The results partially contradict the hypotheses developed by Duval and Wicklund (1973), but they do confirm the expectancy of motivated attributional errors in connection with evaluation by others.

Weary (1980) reported quite analogous findings from a similar experiment in which the degree of publicness was varied instead of objective self-awareness. The familiar attributional asymmetries occurred here independent of the level of expectancy, particularly when the subjects performed publicly.

In general, these studies—especially the more recent investigations, which were better controlled—showed a pronounced confirmation of the assumption that motivational attributional asymmetries exist (see Bradley,

1978; Zuckerman, 1979).   These studies have shown clearly that in their cognitions and attributions subjects are frequently not concerned solely with optimal adjustment to reality through the most realistic possible attribution of past events; rather, attributions also serve other motives.   Kelley and Michela (1980, pp. 474–477) list three such motivations:

1.   motivation for self-enhancement and self-protection
2.   motivation for positive presentation of the self to others
3.   motivation for belief in effective control

The studies described here have given us information about the effectiveness of the first two types of motivation in particular.   Up to now the motivation to exercise effective control has been examined primarily in connection with attributions of responsibility for negative outcomes (e.g., a serious accident) (Lerner & Miller, 1978; Walster, 1966; Wortman, 1976). Pittmann and Pittmann (1980) showed that the experience of loss of control motivates subjects to increase their search for attributions.

The findings from a study by Bernstein, Stephan, and Davis (1979) suggest the simultaneous operation of motivational and rational tendencies in a cognitive process.   For a series of examinations Bernstein *et al.* (1979) measured expectancies of success, performance on the exams, and the attributions made for this performance.   Subjects tended to feel responsible for good grades on exams, but to give external explanations of poor performance.   Expectancies of success were formed primarily on the basis of considerations of effort (preparation).   Subjects whose expectancies were confirmed made more attributions to effort, the basis of their expectancies, than subjects who received unexpected grades.   This, however, seems quite rational.

The self-serving tendencies are further qualified by a series of personality traits such as locus of control (Rotter, 1966), helplessness (Diener & Dweck, 1978), social anxiety (Arkin, Appelman, & Burger, 1980), negative self-concept of ability (Meyer, 1973a, 1981; Schmalt, 1982), and depression (Alloy & Abramson, 1979).   Studies in which measures of interindividual differences were taken into account showed that external control, helplessness, negative self-concept, and anxiety are often correlated with an equally strong internal attribution for success and failure, while a low profile on these dimensions is associated with a definite tendency to an asymmetric pattern of attribution. Alloy and Abramson (1979) showed that depressive subjects can assess the effectiveness of their own actions very accurately, while nondepressives tend to overestimate their own possibilities of exerting influence when the desired outcome is very attractive.   The authors conclude that depressives are indeed "sadder but wiser"—thus more rational.

The achievement motive, as shown below, is another predictor for an asymmetric attribution pattern.

Sequence Effects

In addition to these general effects of success and failure on attribution, the sequence of success and failure experiences is also influential. Jones, Rock, Shaver, Goethals, and Ward (1968) examined attributions for various failure – success sequences. They measured ability attributions for steadily improving or worsening task performance with the total number of successes and failures remaining constant. The investigation showed a decided primacy effect, as did various replication studies. More ability was attributed to subjects who began with successes and whose performance steadily worsened than to subjects with initial failures whose performance later improved.

Jones, Goethals, Kennington, and Severance (1972) investigated the conditions under which this primacy effect occurs and found their assumption of assimilation confirmed. Assessments of ability are formed on the basis of initial impressions of success or failure. These assessments, which are remembered for a long time, influence the processing of subsequent information. Whenever subsequent information contradicts initial assessments of ability, it is assimilated to the initial assessment in such a way that it can be reconciled with it. Since situational factors remain invariant, variable personality factors (effort) are used to explain drops or rises in achievement, making it possible to retain the original assessment of ability.

Newson and Rindner (1979) countered the assimilation hypothesis by assuming a mechanism of subjective sufficiency. They interpreted their findings as meaning that the subjective impression of having enough information prevents a person from taking further information into account. Subsequent information that contradicts earlier information is disregarded.

Informational Patterns

Kelley (1967, 1973) was the first to describe a series of causal constellations in which behavior is linked to particular causal factors. He presented two models, one of which applies to information based on one single observation and one to information based on multiple observations of events. Attribution from a single observation is based on the configuration of those factors that are being considered as possible causes. Attribution from multiple observations is based on the covariation of effects with possible causes. According to the covariation principle, an effect is attributed to the cause with which it covaries over a period of time. Kelley sees the causal attribu-

TABLE 5.4

Information Patterns for the Three Attributions: Stimulus, Person, and Circumstance[a]

	Information pattern		
Attribution	Consensus	Distinctiveness	Consistency
Stimulus	High	High	High
Person	Low	Low	High
Circumstance	Low	High	Low

[a] From Orvis, Cunningham, and Kelley, 1975, p. 607.

tions of the "man on the street" as a parallel to the analysis of variance used by behavioral scientists (Kelley, 1973, pp. 109–110). The analysis-of-variance conception of attribution basically describes processes of information-acquisition and -processing. Information of three kinds is processed:

1. distinctiveness—the extent to which a response occurs exclusively in connection with a single entity (a particular thing or person)
2. consensus—the extent to which an entity leads to the same response in all participating persons
3. consistency—the extent to which an entity always leads to the same response

Information based on several observations can vary in all three ways. When information is categorized by whether it is high or low in distinctiveness, consensus, and consistency, three typical patterns of information result. These patterns lead either to person attributions, situation (stimulus) attributions, or circumstance (chance) attributions (Table 5.4).

This model has been tested by a series of experiments. McArthur (1972) conducted the first comprehensive study. She combined low and high degrees of the three types of information—distinctiveness, consensus, and consistency—to investigate whether an event was attributed to a person, a stimulus (situation), a specific circumstance (chance), or a combination of the three. The data clearly support Kelley's assumptions. An event tends to be attributed to the person when it occurs in connection with many entities (low distinctiveness) and in a consistent manner (high consistency), consensus being of minor importance in this case. On the other hand, an event tends to be attributed to the situation when it occurs in connection with only one entity (high distinctiveness), is temporally consistent (high consistency), and occurs for many individuals (high consensus) (see Table 5.4). Zuckerman (1978) repeated McArthur's (1972) experiment with some minor variations. He found a definite use of consensus information.

It was used primarily for inferring causes for occurrences, and not so much for deliberate actions. Support for Kelley's assumptions can also be found in the study by Meyer (1980), which was mentioned earlier. Meyer found that consistent success or failure was attributed to stable internal factors, while inconsistent outcomes were attributed to variable internal factors. High consensus performance was attributed to external causes, and low consensus performance was attributed to internal causes.

Stevens and Jones (1976) repeated McArthur's (1972) experiment once more, but this time self-attributions for actual successes and failures were analyzed for differences in kind of information (distinctiveness, consensus, and consistency), using the four causal factors described by Weiner *et al.* (1971). In contrast with McArthur's (1972) findings — which were based on fictive situations — this study indicated no basis for the rational attribution behavior implied in the analysis-of-variance procedure described by Kelley. Attribution, especially for failure, seemed to be influenced not by the kind of information used, but only by strategies relieving the person of responsibility.

Other studies have investigated individual factors of the informational pattern, particularly consensus. Taken as a whole they have considerably restricted the claim to general validity of Kelley's model. The studies by McArthur (1972) and Orvis *et al.* (1975) showed very little effect of consensus information on attribution. In a series of studies Nisbett, Borgida, Crandall, and Reed (1976) found no effect of consensus information on self-attributions; the same was reported by Feldman, Higgins, Karlovac, & Ruble (1976) for attributions to others, except when the persons making the attribution possessed direct information about their own experiences in a comparable situation (see Hansen & Donoghue, 1977).

Hansen and Stonner (1978) directly compared information processing by observers with that of actors. They found that observers did process consensus information, while the participants themselves showed no inclination to use consensus information in their causal attributions.

On the other hand, the significance of consensus information increased when it was made available after the event (Ruble & Feldman, 1976), not initially as in the earlier studies. Consensus information also receives more attention when special emphasis is placed on the representative nature of the subject group (Hansen & Donoghue, 1977; Wells & Harvey, 1977).

In contrast, information concerning distinctiveness and consistency retains the same significance for the attribution process regardless of its position. Enzle, Harvey, and Wright (1980) conducted a study in which subjects used distinctiveness information more than consistency or consensus information, both for self-attributions and for other-attributions.

Almost all studies in this area involved the survey technique developed by

McArthur (1972), in which subjects are confronted with empirical general-
izations of individual instances of behavior (e.g., "John laughs at almost
every other comedian") but are not confronted with the individual instances
of behavior themselves. Fischhoff (1976) criticized this, pointing out that
information about individual instances of behavior is normally more avail-
able than are the generalizations presented in the questionnaire. Investiga-
tions using this technique can thus uncover preferences in the utilization of
information, but not in the acquisition of information.

Major (1980) conducted a study in which subjects were able to acquire
discrete bits of information about individual segments of behavior in what-
ever sequence and quantity they liked. The results corresponded to those of
other investigations: Consensus information hardly influenced subsequent
attributions. Only distinctiveness information influenced subsequent attri-
butions in the manner predicted by Kelley (1967, 1973). In general, it
turned out that subjects undertook attributions on the basis of amazingly
little information. However, this information was acquired in a character-
istic sequence: first consistency information, then distinctiveness informa-
tion, and finally—if at all—consensus information.

The image of a seeker of information who is by no means thorough, but
rather, concerned with frugality, is substantiated by a study by Hansen
(1980) as well. Here we see that subjects are most likely to choose that
information which allows them to confirm an existing assumption about
possible causes (person or situation) in the simplest way possible. Some-
times this information involves consistency, and sometimes distinctive-
ness. Information that does not help the subject make a decision about
causes (in this case, consistency—see Table 5.4) is not retained; nor is
information that could refute the subject's original assumptions.

These studies call into question the image of a rational information-seeker
and information-processor, as suggested by the term "lay scientist."

Kelley's covariation concept assumes that data from several observations
are available. Orvis et al. (1975) suggested that covariation concepts might
often lie at the basis of inferences about possible causes, even when there was
only one opportunity for observation. On the basis of the available individ-
ual bits of information, the entire pattern of information that was appropri-
ate would be activated and would guide the attribution process: The avail-
able data about one of the three aspects of information (distinctiveness,
consistency, and consensus) would be compared with all three patterns of
information (for stimulus attribution, person attribution, or circumstance
attribution) (see Table 5.4). The attribution made would be the one corre-
sponding to the pattern of information with the closest fit to the available
information. For example, information about high consensus should lead
to comparatively strong stimulus (situation) attributions because the factor

"high consensus" appears only in the stimulus information pattern. Similarly, information about low distinctiveness should lead to relatively strong person attributions. This idea was confirmed by Orvis *et al.* (1975).

Causal Schemata

Assumptions about the association of individual causal elements — their configuration — are important when attributions are made on the basis of a single observation. Kelley (1972) described such configurations as causal schemata. Two schemata are particularly prominent. The first, a schema for "multiple sufficient causes," describes disjunctive relationships of at least two causal factors. The presence of a single causal factor is a sufficient explanation of the effect. The second schema is one for "multiple necessary causes" and describes conjunctive relationships of at least two causal factors. All causal factors — in the simplest case, two — are necessary for the explanation of the effect.

The significance of these causal schemata is that they allow the individual to predict effects on the basis of the presence or absence of particular causal elements or to infer the presence or absence of particular causal elements from the existence of particular effects. Causal schemata allow us to make hypothetical deductive statements about the causal structure of a given situation (Kun & Weiner, 1973, p. 198).

According to Kelley, schemata for multiple necessary causes are employed to account for extreme and unusual events, while common and expected events are explained by multiple sufficient causal schemata. Kun and Weiner (1973) examined such predictions in the attribution of achievement results, using certainty judgments about the presence or absence of ability and effort in the case of expected and unexpected successes and failures. This is based on a simple consideration. When one of two causal elements is known and a positive action outcome exists, we are extremely uncertain of the simultaneous presence of a second causal factor if we are using a multiple sufficient schema. After all, one causal element is sufficient to explain the effect. On the other hand, if we use a multiple necessary schema, we are relatively sure because in this case both causal elements are necessary for the explanation of the effect. The reverse is true when no action outcome has taken place and only one of the two causal elements is present. Here the uncertainty about the existence of the second factor is high when a multiple necessary schema is used, and low if a multiple sufficient schema is used.

In the study conducted by Kun and Weiner the subjects received information about the level of difficulty of the assigned task, about success and failure, and about the presence or absence of either ability or effort. Kun and Weiner expected that usual action outcomes — that is, success at an easy

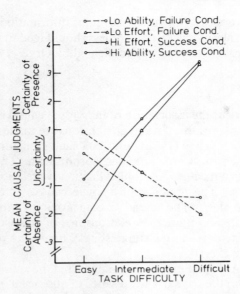

FIGURE 5.1 Mean certainty judgments of
high ability and effort (success condition) and
low ability and effort (failure condition), given
information concerning the complementary
cause (effort or ability), task outcome, and the
difficulty of the task. (From Kun & Weiner,
1973, p. 203.)

task and failure at a difficult task—would be explained by multiple suffi-
cient schemata (the presence or absence of ability or effort). Unusual
outcomes—that is, success at a difficult task and failure at an easy task—
would be explained by multiple necessary schemata (the presence or absence
of ability and effort).

The results of this study appear in Figure 5.1. They confirm the hypothe-
ses. Unusual outcomes tend to be explained by multiple necessary sche-
mata: high confidence about the presence (in the case of success) or absence
(in the case of failure) of the complementary causal factor when ability or
effort is present or absent. On the other hand, usual outcomes are explained
by multiple sufficient schemata in conformity with the hypothesis. The
absence of the complementary factor is assumed with high certainty. In
these cases Kun and Weiner (1973) had originally conjectured that subjects
would merely be less certain in their judgments. The authors explain this
unexpected effect with the assumption that their subjects do not think of
ability and effort as separate factors, as had been implicitly assumed.

Rather, subjects see ability and effort as negatively covarying factors: An able person does not need to exert so much effort, and a person who exerts effort cannot be very able. An epistemological warning is in order here. In Kun and Weiner (1973) and other studies, a causal schema is first inferred from the observed data. It then acquires the status of a hypothetical construct, which, in turn, is employed to explain the original data (see Fiedler, 1982).

Actor–Observer Perspective

The attribution of success and failure is also influenced by the observational perspective — that is, whether the causes of one's own action outcomes are being sought, or those of others' action outcomes. Jones and Nisbett (1971) postulated divergent attributions by actors and observers. They assumed that actors tend to see their actions as being caused by situational requirements, while observers tend to see stable dispositional characteristics of actors as the causes of action. Jones and Nisbett (1971) assumed three sources that give rise to these differential perceptions of causality. Actors and observers differ in their visual perspectives, their motivations, and in terms of available information. Actors have more information about their own behavioral history and about the internal and external conditions preceding the action. Thus they have information about consistency and distinctiveness. Observers, on the other hand, must rely primarily on consensus information: that is, information about the extent to which the observed behavior corresponds to that of other persons in the same situation.

In addition, actors and observers process information differently because different aspects of the available information are salient for them. For the observer, the actor's behavior takes place against the background of invariant surroundings; actors tend to be oriented toward their environment and to adjust their behavior to it.

The effect of divergent causal attributions has been documented in a series of studies (see Kassin, 1979). These studies showed that actors tend to make situational attributions while observers make dispositional attributions. Hansen and Lowe (1976) offer more direct proof for the hypothesis of differential information processing, particularly in the case of identical causal attribution by actors and observers. Even when an event is perceived in the same manner by two people, attribution by actors depends more on distinctiveness and consistency information and attribution by observers depends more on consensus information (see Hansen & Stonner, 1978). The question of the extent to which attributions — particularly those made by observers — are influenced by consensus information is a point of special interest. Many factors may be influential, among them: perceived similarity between actor, observer, and consensus groups; judged homogeneity of ingroup and outgroup members; and beliefs about response variability in a given situation (Higgins & Bryant, 1982; Quattrone & Jones, 1980).

Additionally, a number of studies compared attributions for one's own and others' successes and failures in actual situations. Feather and Simon (1971) assigned anagram tasks to pairs of subjects and afterward gave success and failure feedback. The subjects were to make attributions for their own and their partner's performance. Results showed that in attribution for others, success is attributed more internally and failure more externally, relative to attribution for oneself. Medway and Lowe (1976) produced analogous results by measuring success and failure attributions with a self-responsibility questionnaire (Crandall et al., 1965a). This study also measured the achievement motive, which, however, had no effect on attribution.

These results correspond to the effects hypothesized by Jones and Nisbett (1971) on general attribution differences between actors and observers, but only with respect to the success condition.

It is questionable whether differences in information processing are sufficient explanations for these findings, since actors and observers were working on the same tasks and thus were able to avail themselves of the same information for their attributions. Possibly, motivational factors are responsible for those differences. However, results of a study by Bar-Tal and Frieze (1976), in which the different perspectives of actors and observers were induced according to theory, were as expected. Actors, compared with observers, tended to attribute their successes and failures more externally (to task difficulty), while observers saw these results more often as dependent on internal factors. In contrast, Cunningham, Starr and Kanouse (1979) concluded from their study that the actor–observer hypothesis may hold only for undesirable events. Their actor-subjects tended to deny responsibility for negative events but not for positive ones.

A study by Eisen (1979) had more direct bearing on the issue of informational versus motivational factors underlying the commonly found actor–observer differences. She found that actors attribute desirable events more often internally, and undesirable events less often internally, than observers.

Taken as a whole, these studies reveal a series of meaningful differences between causal explanations of success and failure by actors themselves and by observers. These differences have been well documented empirically (Jones, 1979; Kelley & Michela, 1980; Ross, 1977; Watson, 1982). However, the extent to which motivational, as compared to informational, factors must be utilized to explain the differences is still an open question (Harvey, Town & Yarkin, 1981; Kelley & Michela, 1980). Two studies by Miller increase the plausibility of motivational influences. Miller, Norman, and Wright (1978) found that observers gave more dispositional explanations for actions when they expected to enter into competition with the person performing the actions. The authors explained this as activation of the motivation to control — that is, the need to make the future behavior of a partner predictable. This interpretation was confirmed in another study. Miller and Porter (1980) showed that a person's own responsibility (internal attribution) for a social interaction decreases with temporal distance; initially diverging attributions by actors and observers come to resemble each other. However, attributions remain the same when further interaction is expected — that is, when a need for effective control arises.

Differences in causal attributions for action outcomes such as those described here are certain to influence motivation in complex achievement situations, since they have consequences for self-evaluation as well as for evaluation of others. Divergent attributions for one's own successes and failures and those of others are particularly influential in school settings, in which evaluations of performance by others are central. Since performance evaluations and subsequent sanctions of success and failure depend on attributions, it is clear that attributions are very important for motivation in a pupil – teacher interaction.

More recent programs designed to increase achievement motivation in schoolchildren thus tend to begin with the teacher's attributional tendencies. The attribution of success and failure to stable personality traits (here, differences in students' ability), so typical in attributions for action outcomes of others, frequently leads to undesirable motivational consequences for students. Such programs attempt to challenge and alter teacher attributions (see Chapter 6).

Achievement Motive and Causal Attribution

In earlier sections we explored the determinants of attributions from a rather universalistic perspective. As we mentioned, a number of interindividual differences contribute to divergences in attribution. The elaboration of achievement motivation theory in accordance with attribution theory had as its focal point biases in attribution. The hypothesis was that success-motivated subjects feel responsible primarily for their successes, while failure-motivated subjects tend to feel responsible for their failures (Weiner & Kukla, 1970). Later these assumptions were made more specific with regard to individual causal elements, which led to more differentiated statements. Success was said to be attributed by success-motivated subjects to internal factors (primarily effort), while failure-motivated subjects attributed success to external factors. In contrast, failure was said to be attributed by success-motivated subjects to lack of effort and by failure-motivated subjects to lack of ability.

Weiner and Kukla (1970, Experiment 5) reported the first relevant findings. They showed that in comparison with failure-motivated subjects, success-motivated subjects tend to attribute relatively good performance (success) to ability. When their performance is relatively poor (failure), they tend to believe that they did not exert enough effort. In addition, success-motivated subjects perceive a definite covariation of the quality of their performance with the effort they have invested (see Kukla, 1972b).

Jopt and Ermshaus (1977) gave their subjects two different tasks to perform: one corresponding more closely to intellectual competence (a digit–symbol substitution) and one that required more manual dexterity (a pegboard). The subjects performed these tasks, rated their performance, and indicated the significance of each of the four causal factors for their achievement. The authors reported that no motive differences appeared in connection with causal attributions for the manual task. The task that placed demands on intellectual competence produced results in conformity with the theory only when subjects rated their performance as a failure. Failure-motivated subjects tended to attribute failure more to stable factors (low ability and high task difficulty) than did success-motivated subjects.

Meyer (1973a) conducted a series of investigations in which he studied the relationship between achievement motive and preferences for causal factors. Using a digit–symbol task he induced failure on five consecutive trials and asked subjects to explain their failure with the aid of the four causal factors in such a way that the weights of the individual factors added up to 100%. In comparison with failure-motivated subjects, success-motivated subjects tended to attribute their failures more to variable factors (bad luck and insufficient effort) and comparatively less to low ability. Krug (1972) reported similar findings concerning ability and effort attributions, using a slightly modified method (independent scaling of the four causal factors).

Patten and White (1977) tried to replicate Meyer's experiment, using both Meyer's scaling technique, which leads to interdependent measurements, and independent scaling of the four causal factors. However, unlike Meyer (1973a) and Krug (1972), they were unable to confirm any differences in attribution preference between the motive groups.

In two other studies Meyer (1973a) induced failure and success at a cognitive task: once using fictitious group norms and once using the subject's individual level of expectancy as points of reference for the feedback manipulation. The first investigation involved as causal factors only ability and luck. In comparison with failure-motivated subjects, success-motivated subjects tended to experience success as attributable more to ability than to luck, and failure as attributable more to luck than to ability.

In the second study success and failure were induced for the same task relative to the subjects' own level of expectancy for their individual performance. The experimenter added a certain number to the number of correct

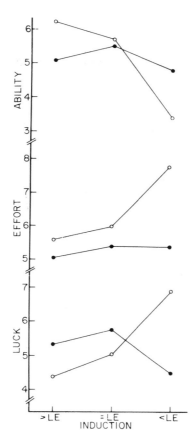

FIGURE 5.2 Average scalings of the causal factors ability, effort, and luck in success- (O) and failure-motivated (●) subjects. The fictitious number of correct answers was either above the level of expectancy (>LE), equal to the level of expectancy (=LE), or less than the level of expectancy (<LE). (Adapted from Meyer, 1973a, pp. 81–82.)

answers predicted by the individual (inducing success) or subtracted it (inducing failure). These results constitute the clearest proof so far for the concept of divergent attributions of success- and failure-motivated subjects (see Figure 5.2).

Success-motivated subjects attributed success more (and failure less) to their own ability than did failure-motivated subjects. The exact opposite was true of attribution to luck: Success-motivated subjects attributed success less to luck and failure more to luck. For effort attribution, a significant difference appeared only in the failure condition. Success-motivated subjects tended to attribute failure more to lack of effort than did failure-motivated subjects.

Schmalt (in preparation) explored the question of diverging attribution biases, focusing on the failure motive. He introduced a pseudodiscrimination task to some subjects as difficult and to some as less difficult. The experience of failure or success was induced by reporting a performance level that lay above or below a previously agreed-upon criterion. Subsequently subjects scaled the importance of each of the four causal factors for their performance. This study showed that highly failure-motivated subjects (characterized in this case by a self-concept of low ability) attribute their failure to lack of ability more than do subjects with low failure motivation, regardless of the induced task difficulty. Attribution to lack of effort is less prominent in highly failure-motivated subjects than in subjects with low failure motivation. On the other hand, highly failure-motivated subjects tend to attribute success to favorable circumstances more than do subjects with low failure motivation (see Figure 5.3). This pattern of results corresponds to the expectancies formulated for the failure motive.

Still another aspect deserves consideration. We have already described a rather universalistic tendency to feel responsible for successes and to deny responsibility for failures. This asymmetry in the attribution of responsibility for success and failure, which is said to be based on motivational factors, appeared primarily in attributions to ability and luck. If we examine the results from this standpoint, we see that the asymmetries in attribution to ability and luck are characteristic only of subjects with low failure motives. Only subjects with little fear of failure are able to profit from the comparatively favorable consequences of self-evaluation provided by this form of attribution asymmetry.

Schneider and his colleagues (Schneider, 1977) tried to substantiate the assumed correlations between achievement motivation and causal attributions in a series of studies. In none of these studies did they find the correlations predicted by attribution theory; in some cases, the opposite seemed to hold (but see below, Chapter 6).

In a study employing path analysis Covington and Omelich (1979) established positive correlations only between motive disposition (MARPS, TAT) and ability attribution; the other correlations that had been predicted turned out to be either negative or nonexistent (see Figure 5.9).

We must still exercise caution in claiming validity for the assumption of divergent attributions by success- and failure-motivated persons, even though there is much support for this claim. Yet in comparison with the

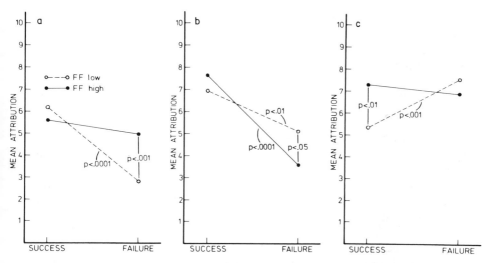

FIGURE 5.3 Causal attribution to the factors ability (a), effort (b), and luck (c), after success and failure, for subjects with high and low failure motivation (FF_1, LMG). (Figures for ability and luck adapted from Schmalt, 1982, p. 49; the figure for effort from Schmalt, in preparation.)

theoretical significance of the hypothesis the degree of empirical confirmation still leaves much to be desired. Weiner (1980b, p. 338) has stated that the enthusiasm concerning the influence of individual predispositions — particularly the achievement motive — on causal attributions must be tempered in the light of its empirical support. One reason for this may be that existing knowledge about the general conditions under which asymmetrical attributional patterns appear did not receive the attention it deserved. Earlier we pointed out a number of situational and personality factors that tend to encourage or prevent attributional asymmetries.

An experiment by Alloy and Abramson (1979) demonstrates in an impressive manner the importance of situational and personality factors for attribution. When chance outcomes are made very attractive, nondepressed persons overestimate their own influence on the situation, and when the results are unwanted, they underestimate their influence. Both attributions are self-serving. Thus it is imperative (see Wong & Weiner, 1981) that we take into account moderating situational variables such as the extent to which achievement is stressed as important, the extent of self-reference, and the extent to which the situation is public. Such variables encourage the development of self-referential motivations such as self-enhancement, positive self-presentation, and control motivation. Along with the achievement motive, these variables help determine the kind of asymmetry found in an attribution pattern.

For example, it is important to make a strict conceptual distinction between studies carried out in real-life situations and those carried out only with the aid of fictitious situations (e.g., situation descriptions). The difference in reality reference influences attributional asymmetry to differing extents (see Fontaine, 1975). In analyzing the results of attribution experiments, researchers fail all too often to distinguish between attributions from the perspective of an observer and attributions about the subject's own performance results. Hardly any findings can be replicated so easily as the observation that naive observers normally tend to overestimate personality factors (Jones, 1979, p. 107), while subjects themselves are more likely to draw upon situational explanations. The undifferentiated equal treatment of both experimental approaches inevitably leads to confusion among findings. The neglect of antecedent conditions, such as informational patterns, causal schemata, or sequence effects (except by Frieze & Weiner, 1971), has turned out to be a serious disadvantage. As we showed above, attributions are quite clearly dependent on the nature of the available information, how it is used, and how it is processed. Studies involving these types of variables could, on the one hand, clarify the conditions under which the asymmetries discussed here occur, and on the other hand, also the question as to which phase of information processing introduces asymmetries (see Heckhausen, 1980b).

This is all the more important because Weiner sees the divergent attribution tendencies as the actual distinction between the two motive groups. According to Weiner, the achievement motive (i.e., the success motive) is not characterized by the disposition to feel pride in one's own achievement, as Atkinson had assumed, but rather by "the capacity for perceiving success as caused by internal factors, particularly effort" (Weiner et al., 1971, p. 18). This implies that Weiner sees the achievement motive as a cognitive disposition rather than as an affective disposition, as Atkinson had assumed. The reason is that affect is partially dependent on the preferred attributional pattern. However, this does not yet answer the question as to whether it is the mediator (the preferred attribution pattern) or its affective effects that are the "actual" motivating factor. In fact, the contrast between cognitive and affective may only appear to be a problem. It is also difficult to see how the individual form of the disposition (if "capacity" is understood as a dispositional tendency) to use a particular interpretive pattern can influence behavior directly by giving rise to approach or avoidance behavior (Weiner et al., 1971, p. 10).

Additionally, the conclusions that can be made from Weiner's statements lead us into a dilemma. If success-motivated persons behave in such a way that they can explain success as the result of effort expenditure, then it makes sense for them to exert themselves. On the other hand, if failure-motivated persons behave in such a way that they need not link failure to lack of effort, then it also makes sense for them to exert themselves. That is the most certain way to exclude the necessity of attributing failure to lack of effort. The logical conclusion is that everyone would have to exert effort all the time — a conclusion that corresponds neither to everyday experience nor to empirical data.

In keeping with Weiner's ideas — but basing his proposal on his own divergent findings — Meyer (1973a) has proposed that the achievement motive (i.e., the success-related motive component) should not be defined by effort attribution, but rather "as the disposition to attribute successes to one's own ability" (1973a, p. 152). We consider this proposal in Chapter 6.

Effects on Expectancies and Affects

As we stated earlier, the essence of the attributional elaboration of achievement motivation theory is to define the cognitive determinants of the expectancy and value parameters. These formulations can rely to some extent on tradition. For example, Rotter (1954, 1966) based his theory of social learning on the central assumption that expectancies and expectancy changes depend basically on cognized causes of behavior. To be sure, Rotter made expectancies dependent on the extent of internal versus external control of reinforcement. Expectancies were assumed to be maximal when the action outcome was subject to internal control; in contrast, they were assumed to be minimal when the action outcome was subject to external control. There is still no conclusive empirical evidence for this (see Meyer & Schmalt, 1978).

On the other hand, there is good empirical support for the assumption that affective reactions to particular events are substantially dependent on the evaluation of the affect-arousing event (Folkman, Schaefer, & Lazarus, 1979; Lazarus, 1968; Schachter, 1964; Weiner, 1982).

Weiner *et al.* (1972) associated this tradition with the dimensions of causal attribution. In contrast with Rotter's theory, Weiner saw the dimension of stability as determining the extent of expectancy change after success and failure, while locus of control determined the extent of affective reactions (see Table 5.2).

Causal Attribution and Expectancy

According to Atkinson's theory, only the effect of success and failure and the strength of the achievement motive have been investigated as possible determinants of divergent changes in expectancies. The results show that, as a rule, expectancies increase after success and decrease after failure ("typical" changes) and that revisions following success and failure are dependent on the strength of the achievement motive (Feather, 1968; Schneider, 1972). Attribution theory describes the cognitive determinants of these changes in expectancies, stating that amount of typical expectancy change is especially great when success or failure is attributed to stable causal elements (ability and task difficulty). In contrast, changes of expectancies are minimal when variable elements (effort and luck) are called upon to explain results.

These predictions are based on the plausible assumption that when subjects tend to attribute their own failures to lack of ability or to excessive task difficulty, expectancies of success will be more noticeably revised downward than when failures are attributed to insufficient effort or bad luck. Short-term increases in effort are possible, and one can hope for more fortunate circumstances, thus maintaining expectancies at an approximately equal high level despite failure. On the other hand, in the case of stable attributions such alteration in causal determinants cannot be expected, so that eventually expectancies of success must decrease. Analogous statements can be made with regard to attributions of success.

Meyer (1973a), the first to investigate this question, pointed the way for later studies. In two quite similarly designed experiments he induced success or failure on five consecutive tasks. After each trial he asked subjects to what extent the result could be attributed to ability, effort, task difficulty, and luck, and how high the probability of success was for the next trial. No significant effects appeared after induction of success, but only after induction of failure. However, not all of these effects corresponded to theory. When the decrease in subjective probabilities of success that occurred after failure was examined in relation to attributions to individual causal elements (Weiner et al., 1972, p. 244), no significant differences turned out to be associated with ability. Subjects who attributed their failures primarily to task difficulty indicated without exception relatively lower probabilities of success. Those who attributed their failures primarily to the variable elements (effort and luck) reported without exception relatively higher probabilities of success (see Figure 5.4).

Taken as a whole, subjective probabilities of success dropped unmistakably after failure. However, the hypothesized diverging of expectancies of success associated with individual causal elements could not be established. Probability disparities were noticeable only when all factors were considered at the same time. It turned out that when failure was attributed relatively clearly to stable as opposed to variable factors, the subsequent subjective probabilities of success sank more pronouncedly and were also lower overall.

Three further studies continued Meyer's exploration of the connection

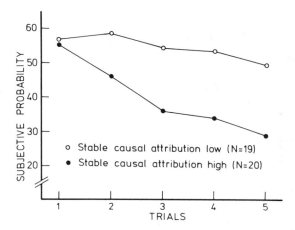

FIGURE 5.4   Median extent of expectancies of success
with high or low attribution to stable factors. (Adapted
from Meyer, 1973a, p. 105.)

between causal attributions and subsequent expectancies (Fontaine, 1974; McMahan, 1973; Valle & Frieze, 1976). They examined attributions of the subject's own outcomes and of others' outcomes and operationalized actual or fictitious successes and failures. In all of the studies, correlations were found only between absolute height of expectancies and stability of causal attributions, but not between changes of expectancies and stability. In a study by Riemer (1975) no correlations appeared at all.

In another study Weiner, Nierenberg, and Goldstein (1976) investigated again the question of the determinants of differences in expectancies and changes of expectancies. They designed a decision experiment such that their own theoretical position was opposite to that of Rotter (1966). For Rotter, the locus of control of reinforcement influenced expectancy changes, while Weiner saw these changes as dependent on the stability dimension.

The authors gave their subjects a modification of the block design test to work and induced zero, one, two, three, four, or five successes for the subjects in a between-subjects experimental design. After the last trial, probabilities of success and causal attributions were obtained from the subjects. The authors employed a new technique for measuring causal attributions. They developed a measure consisting of four scales, each of which resembled another with respect to one of the two causal dimensions but varied with respect to the alternative dimension. For example, one question was whether the subjects were successful at the task because they were always good at that sort of task or because they exerted especially great effort for that

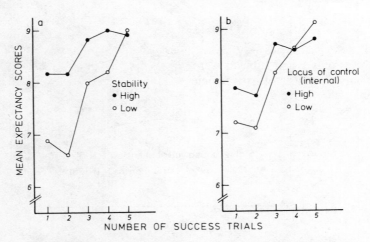

FIGURE 5.5   Expectancies of subjects with either strong or weak attributions of their successes to stable (a) or person-dependent (b) causes. (From Weiner, Nierenberg, & Goldstein, 1976, "Social learning versus attributional interpretations of expectancy of success," *Journal of Personality, 44,* p. 67. Copyright 1976 by Duke University Press, Durham, NC.)

particular task.   Two internal causal elements were contrasted with one another in this question; they differed with regard to the alternative causal dimension — that is, stability.   Thus each decision had to be made within a single dimension, which permitted direct examination of the two controversial approaches (see Figure 5.5).

As expected, no correlations existed between locus of control and the extent of changes of expectancies.   However, the differences that were found for the stability dimension did not conform with theory, contrary to the statements of the authors.   A preference for stable causal factors was associated with higher expectancies — a difference that already existed at the beginning of the experiment.   In contrast, the clearest changes of expectancies occurred in connection with rather low attribution to the stable causal factors.   This can be interpreted in the following manner: A low attribution to stable factors is associated with low expectancies of success; thus, success is an unexpected event.   This leads to the subsequent revision of the "can" concept (relation of one's own estimated ability to task difficulty) and then to a rise in expectancies of success.   Thus changes in expectancies would tend to occur particularly in the case of destabilized "can" concepts (Heckhausen, 1980b).

Wollert (1979) pointed out an additional determinant of changes of expectancies that had not yet been taken into account.   In his study he assumed that the extent of changes of expectancies was not dependent on content aspects of preceding cognitions, but rather on the confidence with which the expectancies were held. Wollert found definite changes in expectancies only when subjects were not yet sure of the outcome. On the other hand, changes of expectancies were not influenced by whether the influence factors manipulated by the instructions were subject to internal or external control.

In summary, then, we can say that the relationship between level of expectancy and stability of causal attribution is well documented. However, the extent of the influence of the various causal dimensions on changes in expectancies has not yet been satisfactorily explained.

Causal Attribution and Affect

In Atkinson's (1957, 1964) theory of motivation an important function was ascribed to achievement-related affects, because their anticipation is seen as the actual motivating agent. The model presented these anticipated affects as completely dependent on subjective probabilities; in multiplicative association with subjective probabilities, anticipated affects help to determine achievement-oriented behavior (see Chapter 3).

Weiner releases the affect variable from its condition of being completely determined by the expectancy variable. He suggests that the affective value of an achievement-related goal is dependent primarily on the kind of causal attribution made by the subject. It seems intuitively plausible to assume that the extent of experienced pride in an achievement depends on the extent to which one feels responsible for this achievement (Weiner *et al.,* 1971, p. 10). The assumption was supported by the previously mentioned studies by Lazarus (1968) and Schachter (1964), which suggested that the extent of internal versus external attribution distinctly influences subsequent affective reactions. For this reason Weiner (1972, p. 374; 1977, p. 183; 1982; Weiner *et al.,* 1972, p. 240) based affect in achievement-related situations (i.e., pride and shame) on the locus-of-control dimension of the attribution, proposing that attribution to internal factors leads to the relatively clearer pride and shame affects (see Table 5.2). Weiner (1972, pp. 374–375) refined this assumption still further, suggesting that effort attribution has a greater influence on affect than does ability attribution.

In comparison with Atkinson's assumption, Weiner's assumption involved totally different model variables and led to predictions that agreed only in part with those derived from Atkinson's (1957, 1964) model. Indeed, Atkinson had assumed an inverse linear relationship between the subjective probabilities and the incentive value of success and failure. This assumption led to the prediction that especially intense achievement-related affects would be experienced after success at difficult tasks and failure at easy tasks. Weiner also took into account that success at difficult tasks and failure at easy tasks were attributed to an especially great extent to internal factors (Kun & Weiner, 1973; Schmalt, 1978). From this came the statement, based on attribution theory, that attribution to internal factors maximizes affective consequences (see Weiner, Russel & Lerman, 1978, 1979).

Weiner (1974a, 1974b) has consistently argued that attribution to effort generates more affect than does ability attribution, using findings from experiments on attribution for others' performance results. These experiments were designed in a manner similar to a paradigmatic study by Lanzetta and Hannah (1969). In one of the first of these studies Weiner and Kukla (1970) asked their subjects to imagine that they were teachers and needed to give their students feedback about their performance in the form of plus and minus points. The "teachers" received information about whether the students were gifted or not, whether they had exerted effort or not, and what the performance results were.

An important finding was that overcoming a personal handicap through great effort received the highest positive evaluation, while insufficient effort by able students was censured most strongly. These general findings have been replicated frequently (e.g., by Rest et al., 1973).

As a whole, the investigations that were conducted along these lines have provided us with considerable insight into the various ways of evaluating the achievement of others, as dependent on the perceived causes of this achievement. Nevertheless, it is doubtful whether these findings can also be generalized to the case of experienced and anticipated affects after one's own success and failure. It is also doubtful whether the findings can be used to support Weiner's position, as he attempted (e.g., Weiner, 1974a, 1974b).

At least three points cause such a generalization to seem unacceptable:

1. The dependent variables in all the investigations are evaluative sanctions (praise and blame). These reactions must be distinguished conceptually from affects.
    Sanctions involve regulation of behavior by others; affects, in contrast, are directly related to self-regulatory processes (see Halisch, 1976).
2. In almost all studies the subjects were confronted with fictitious situations in which it was hardly possible for achievement-related affects, as envisioned by achievement motivation theory, to be aroused.
3. Finally, evaluation of oneself is performed from a completely different perspective than that of evaluation of others. The two perspectives emphasize different causal factors and correspondingly also lead to differences in evaluative behavior.

The results are far less consistent if, in line with theory, we consider only affects that are actually experienced after success and failure in real situations. As a rule it appears that affective reactions are more pronounced when attributions are made to internal causes. However, this relationship is sometimes true of effort attribution and sometimes of ability attribution. In rare cases it is equally true after success and after failure. Thus Meyer (1973a) and Nicholls (1975) reported significant correlations between ability attribution and affect following success, but not following failure. Quite contrary to Weiner's assumptions, effort attribution had no correlation with affective reactions following success and failure. These findings are entirely supportive of an alternative hypothesis formulated by Heckhausen (1972c), in which ability attributions have a particularly strong effect on affect. In contrast with most studies, however, Riemer (1975) manipulated the four causal elements as independent variables and found both internal causal elements associated with stronger affective reactions following success.

Schneider and his colleagues (in summary, Schneider, 1977) found in a series of investigations only very weak, unstable correlations between attributions to individual causal factors and the reported affects following success and failure. If all these studies are taken into account, however, there is indeed the suggestion of a relationship between internal causal attribution and the experience of affect after success. In a more recent experiment Schneider (1977) reported correlations between affect and both internal factors following success. After failure, in contrast, the effort attribution alone determined affect. In summary, the studies reported so far have shown that the causal factors ability and effort have no general, decisive effect on the experience of affect following success and failure.

An important factor that may have a moderating effect on the relationships between causal attributions and subsequent affect was described by Luginbuhl *et al.* (1975) and Nicholls (1975, 1976). They suggest that the effect of causal attribution on affect depends largely on the extent to which the task in question seems to have long-term consequences or relevance for self-esteem. If a task is unrelated to self-esteem, or if the relationship is uncertain, and if current performance results have no recognizable instrumentality for future activities, an effort attribution might influence affect. When society is to evaluate performance, the extent of effort invested affects sanctions. It is almost a moral obligation to exert oneself when effort would ensure positive results (see Weiner, 1973).

On the other hand, in our society sanctions are also based on concrete performance results; outstanding achievement is evaluated as particularly positive (see Chapter 7). From a long-range perspective, however, outstanding achievement must depend primarily on ability and not so much on effort. Thus with tasks that are relevant to self-esteem and instrumental for future goals, there is a closer relationship between ability attribution and subsequent affect (Nicholls, 1976).

Nicholls (1976) attempted to support his hypothesis with an experiment based on the method used by Weiner and Kukla, in which, however, subjects made attributions and reported affects in relation to their own performance. In a second phase subjects were asked to indicate whether they would rather be someone with high ability who exerts low effort or someone who exerts high effort but has low ability. In the first part of the experiment pride in success was associated slightly more with effort attribution than with ability attribution, while shame about failure tended more to be associated with low effort attribution and high ability attribution. In the second part of the experiment the subjects indicated that they would rather be very able than exert considerable effort. This effect was independent of the results of the task performance. These results support the author's central statement: "Effort is virtuous, but it's better to have ability" (Nicholls, 1976, p. 306).

The findings of Ames, Ames, and Felker (1977) can be interpreted in a similar manner. In this investigation groups of two subjects worked together in one condition and competed with each other in another condition. The satisfaction experienced at the completion of the task was associated with ability attribution under competitive conditions and with effort attribution under cooperative conditions.

Obviously, it is doubly stressful to be forced to attribute failure to lack of ability. On the one hand, it is unpleasant to be publicly exposed as simply stupid; on the other hand, this also means that in the future, as well, one must always expect failure and must admit to oneself that one cannot control an important person-environment area. In an experiment by Berglas and Jones (1978) male subjects who experienced a sequence of chance successes tended to handicap themselves when they expected to fail in an additional test, in order to make it impossible to attribute the failure to lack of ability. In this case self-handicapping involved taking a drug that interfered with performance. In this manner they were able to retain their belief in their own competence.

Heckhausen (1972c, 1978a) had pointed out that ability attribution generates more affect than does effort. He proposed that the affective consequences of success and failure are particularly pronounced when causal attribution suggests the need for a revision of the subject's self-concept of ability. Such conditions prevail when success and failure are unexpected and are attributed primarily to the subject's own ability. We return to this approach later.

A problematic point in the studies described so far is the concretization of the affects measured. This may explain some of the inconsistent findings. Weiner hypothesized that causal attribution was correlated with achieve-

TABLE 5.5

Correlations Between Causal Attribution and Affect[a]

	Ability		Effort		Task difficulty		Luck	
	Easy	Difficult	Easy	Difficult	Easy	Difficult	Easy	Difficult
After third success								
Joy	.20	.01	.12	.06	−.06	−.05	−.14	.45*
Pride	.16	−.05	.42*	−.03	−.02	.01	.20	.11
After third failure								
Anger	.20	.13	−.01	−.11	.31*	−.04	.09	−.07
Shame	.35*	.14	−.18	.11	.19	.17	−.25	−.12

[a] Adapted from Schmalt, 1979, p. 522.

* $p < .01$

ment-related affects such as pride and shame (Atkinson, 1964; McClelland *et al.,* 1953). These affects also contain aspects of moral evaluation (Heckhausen, 1980b; Sohn, 1977).

Schmalt (1979a) analyzed the correlations between causal attribution and affect in relation to expected and unexpected success and failure. One analysis was made for pride and shame, and one for the affects joy and anger. In this experiment, which was described briefly above, subjects worked on pseudodiscrimination tasks that were described to them as easy or difficult. They received consistent success or failure feedback in three successive stages. The relationship between attribution and affect following the third success (or, respectively, failure) is described in Table 5.5. Definite correlations can be seen between the internal causal factors and pride and shame, on the one hand, and between the external factors and joy and anger, on the other hand.

Pride was experienced when a series of successes that conform to expectancies were attributed to high effort. In contrast, shame was experienced when a series of unexpected failures was attributed to low ability. Joy was experienced when a series of unexpected successes was attributed to chance, and anger was experienced when a series of unexpected failures was attributed to high task difficulty.

These findings indicate that there are no generally valid relationships between attribution and affect. Apparently performance results and the degree to which they confirm preexisting expectancies moderate the correlation between attribution and affect.

If we assume that attribution to ability in the case of unexpected failures suggests the need for revision of the concept of ability (Heckhausen, 1972a, 1978a), then a number of findings can be interpreted according to Heckhausen's hypotheses. The correlation between effort attribution and pride in the case of expected success, on the other hand, tends to speak for Weiner's assumption. The correlations between joy and anger and causal attribution show that even external attributions of performance outcomes can lead to affects such as joy and anger (see Weiner, 1974b, p. 61). In general, these findings — together with others — confirm that causal attribution to internal factors determines achievement-related affect, but that external factors can also influence affect in achievement situations (anger, annoyance, frustration).

Sohn (1977) also examined — in fictitious situations — the relative influence that ability and effort attributions have on different types of affect. In contrast to Weiner's assumption, ability attributions had at least as much influence on what Sohn saw as "morally neutral" affects, such as happiness and unhappiness, as effort attributions did. When performance outcomes were negative, ability attribution led not to shame, but rather to clearer unhappiness affects. Effort attribution, in contrast, led to more pride and shame affects than did ability attribution, and these pride and shame affects were more pronounced than happiness and unhappiness.

Weiner et al. (1978) examined affects aroused in an achievement situation, attempting to find out which affect types are actually associated with which causal factors. They first searched dictionaries for descriptions of positive and negative affects and made comprehensive lists of affective reactions to success and failure. Then they appended these lists to a short success-and-failure story that included a definite attribution to a particular causal factor. The subjects were to choose from the list the affect that seemed appropriate. Finally, the experimenters identified those dominant affects that were most clearly and exclusively connected with a particular causal factor. Table 5.6 contains these dominant affects. As we can see, the affects that were experienced after success and failure varied considerably, depending on the causal factor chosen for the attribution.

This experiment by Weiner et al. (1978) was based on a very broad concept of affect. It is surely not possible to see all concepts listed as pure affects (e.g., incompetence or aggression). It is interesting that pride and shame are not even included among the dominant discriminating affects. However, their ability to discriminate is greater with internal than with external factors. That means that we can feel relatively safe in categorizing pride and shame as associated with internal factors.

Weiner, Russell, and Lerman (1979) essentially replicated these investigations, using somewhat different techniques. Additionally, their results en-

TABLE 5.6

Attributions and Dominant Discriminating Affects for Success and Failure[a]

Attribution	Affect
Success	
Unstable effort	Activation, augmentation
Stable effort	Relaxation
Own personality	Self enhancement
Other's effort and personality	Gratitude
Luck	Surprise
Ability versus task difficulty (ease)	Competence versus safety
Failure	
Ability	Incompetence
Unstable effort; stable effort	Guilt
Personality; intrinsic motivation	Resignation
Other's efforts; other's motivation and personality	Aggression
Luck	Surprise

[a] Adapted from Weiner, Russel, and Lerman, 1978, pp. 76 and 81. Some causal factors were taken from the study by Elig and Frieze (1975).

couraged them to formulate an extended three-stage model of affect determination. In this model performance outcomes are initially evaluated as to whether they constitute success or failure, which leads to certain short-lived affects (happy, disappointed). Immediately afterwards causes for the outcomes are sought, and affects that are specific to the attributed causes appear. Finally, in the third stage attributions are assigned to causal dimensions (such as internal–external), initiating self-esteem cognitions; these self-esteem cognitions initiate further affective processes. Such self-evaluation affects probably last longer than any other affects associated with the experience of success and failure. They also have a stabilizing effect on the entire motivational system (see Chapter 6). Some of these assumptions were examined in a study conducted by McFarland and Ross (1982). They differentiated between outcome-related affects (such as happiness and disappointment) and attribution-related affects (such as pride and competence). They found that affects closely related to self-esteem were influenced by attributions after success and failure. General positive and negative affects were determined by outcome, but contrary to the model these affects were also influenced by attributions. The temporal sequence of events hypothesized by Weiner et al. (1978, 1979) was not examined in this study. In sum, this experiment adds further evidence to the notion that affective responses are clearly determined by cognitive processes.

The Achievement Motive as a Self-Reinforcing Motive System

It is hard to overestimate the importance of the correlation of causal attributions and affects in achievement situations for the theory of achievement motivation. In the model of motivation developed by Heckhausen (1972a, 1975a, 1977a), which is described as a self-reinforcement or self-evaluation model, causal attributions and the associated affective reactions play a decisive role. Self-evaluation is seen in this model as a process in which — prospectively and retrospectively — task outcomes are compared with self-set standards and classified as success or failure. The task outcome is then attributed to particular causal factors, which leads to various kinds of self-evaluation processes and subsequently to the familiar effects on expectancies, changes of expectancies, and affects. The latter are assigned self-reinforcing qualities in the model.

The main idea behind the construction of such a model was that the achievement motive was no longer believed to be a single "summary" concept, but was now divided into a series of processlike components; an attempt was made to identify those parameters that represent individual (motive-determined) differences that appear under otherwise equal arousal conditions (see Chapter 6). Such a model can show how various subprocesses are interrelated and stabilize the entire motive system, like a self-regulatory mechanism. These subprocesses make the motive system independent of actual experiences of success and failure, and even make it resistant to change, in the case of long-lasting experiences that "cannot be reconciled" with the motive tendency (e.g., a series of failures by a success-motivated subject). Causal attributions for success and failure play a key role in this process. On one hand, they are subject to a differential motive influence, and on the other hand, these attributions constitute an important link to the affects, which are seen as self-reinforcing.

Success-motivated subjects tend to explain their successes internally, especially by attributing them to ability; as a rule they attribute their failures to insufficient effort. In contrast, failure-motivated subjects believe that their successes depend on external factors, particularly chance, and their failures are primarily caused by low ability. These differences in attribution tendency should lead to asymmetries in self-reinforcement as well. Thus the same task outcomes have different self-reinforcement consequences for success- and failure-motivated persons. Success-motivated subjects possess the overall "happier" self-reinforcement strategy. They give themselves relatively stronger positive self-reinforcement after success and relatively less negative self-reinforcement after failure than failure-motivated subjects.

From the perspective of theory construction we must now ask whether we should conceive of the processes of self-evaluation and self-reinforcement as separate but related processes, or whether instead we should assume one single process — the self-evaluation process — and assign affective reactions the status of linked ancillary processes. The actual behavior-guiding effect would then come from the cognitive–affective self-evaluation processes. However, the distinction between these two processes has not yet been made in a satisfactory manner, neither theoretically nor operationally (Halisch, Butzkamm, & Posse, 1976). Thus only the principle of economy would be served by assuming that there is only one process (self-evaluation) and subsuming the process of self-reinforcement under this category. In the extended model of achievement motivation (Heckhausen, 1977a) this step has been taken.

No matter how this question is ultimately decided, it should be possible to discover an asymmetry in the affect balance between success- and failure-motivated subjects contingent upon success or failure experiences. In a study already cited several times Meyer (1973a) was the first to report such an asymmetry — but it was documented only as a tendency. According to Meyer, success-motivated subjects show more positive affect after success than failure-motivated subjects because of internal attribution. On the other hand, after failure, success-motivated subjects show comparatively less negative affect because of external attribution.

A study by Jopt and Ermshaus (1977) revealed that success-motivated subjects were less hard on themselves in evaluating their failures than were failure-motivated subjects. In this study failure-motivated subjects also attributed failure more to stable causal factors (low ability, high task difficulty). This effect applied to intellectually challenging tasks only. The same correlations did not appear with another task, which called for manual skills.

Heckhausen (1978a) investigated this question in a study in which subjects experienced unexpected successes or failures at a pseudodetection task, after having first reached a learning plateau. Before and after performing the task subjects were asked how able they believed themselves to be for that sort of task and how much effort they had exerted. Their answers were interpreted as ability and effort attributions. As an affective reaction the subjects indicated the extent to which they were satisfied with themselves by means of a pointer that they set between $+10$ and -10.

As for the correlation between motive constellation and self-evaluation, success-motivated subjects in the failure condition rated themselves less negatively, as expected. No significant differences appeared in the success condition. If attribution is taken into account, in the success condition the extent of effort attribution was not associated with any differential affects, but the extent of ability attribution did turn out to be associated with differ-

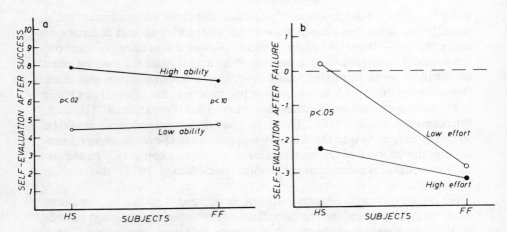

FIGURE 5.6   Self-evaluation after a series of successes (a) and a series of failures (b) by success-moti-vated (*HS*) and failure-motivated (*FF*) subjects with low or high ability attribution and low or high effort attribution. (Adapted from Heckhausen, 1978a.)

ential affective reactions.   This effect was more pronounced for success-mo-tivated subjects than for failure-motivated subjects (see Figure 5.6).   Success was more obviously pleasurable when it was attributed to ability.

In the failure condition it was primarily the effort attribution that deter-mined affect; affective reactions to failure were more negative, the more subjects believed that they had exerted effort.   Again, this effect was more pronounced with success-motivated subjects than with failure-motivated subjects (see Figure 5.6).   These results contradict Weiner's postulate of the positive effect of high effort attribution on affect.   The results can be ex-plained by the simple conclusion drawn by the "man on the street," that one's own ability must be low if one continues to fail after increasing the effort exerted.   The higher subjects believed their effort to be — and, corre-spondingly, the lower subjects believed their ability to be — the greater would be the negative affect after failure.   In addition to this attribution effect, there was another motive effect that was independent of it.   After the same failures, success-motivated subjects evaluated themselves less nega-tively than did the failure-motivated subjects.   The revision of ability esti-mates has an especially strong influence on affect.   Success-motivated sub-jects reported particularly strong negative affects when they had to revise their estimates of their own ability after a series of failures.

In a second experiment with the same design (Heckhausen, 1978a) in-volving 10–13-year-old subjects, however, the expected findings were only partially present.   The motive-related asymmetry in self-evaluation could not be established.   In the success condition the ability attribution had a greater impact on affect.   A high ability attribution was associated with positive self-evaluation, which was also higher for success-motivated subjects. After failure the effort attribution turned out to have an influence on affect, in interaction with motive. Success-motivated subjects were less dissatisfied with failure that they attributed to low effort than they were when they had exerted great effort. This effect corresponds to the results of the first study.

However, failure-motivated subjects behaved in exactly the opposite fashion. The more they attributed failure to low effort, the more negative were their self-evaluations. These results with failure-motivated subjects corresponded to Weiner's assumptions and were parallel to the findings of the other-evaluation studies (see p. 156).

Developmental psychology offers some suggestions for the explanation of the divergent results for failure-motivated children. Perhaps these children have not yet relinquished sufficiently the perspective of observation by others. On the other hand, they may lack the formal syllogistic skills necessary to conclude from lack of effort and from failure that one's own estimate of ability need not be called into question.

Touhey and Villemez (1980) conducted a study that shows how subjects' estimates of their own ability are derived syllogistically from the desired performance outcome and the extent of effort invested. Their subjects worked on arithmetic and word-association tasks, once with instructions to invest as much effort as possible and once with instructions to relax instead of exerting effort during task performance. After performing the first task the subjects received feedback on their performance (mediocre or superior). They were then asked to estimate their ability to perform the next task well. Those subjects who received feedback about a superior performance differed in their estimate of their ability, depending on the effort invested and on their achievement motive. Failure-motivated subjects, applying the syllogism described above, assessed their ability as highest when they had exerted almost no effort and nevertheless had succeeded. Success-motivated subjects behaved exactly opposite: They rated their ability higher when they had also exerted very great effort and received a superior performance rating. In summary, the question of when formal logical operations are used to infer ability estimates from effort and performance data deserves further study.

Effects on Behavior

Theoretical Concepts

The last element in the model of achievement-motivated behavior is the behavior itself (see Table 5.2). In McClelland's and Atkinson's achievement motivation theories it was possible to make stringent predictions about achievement-oriented behavior. These predictions were derived directly from strength of the motivational tendency, which itself was derived from the familiar model parameters (see Chapters 3 and 4).

Such a notion, in which some sort of interaction of expectancy and affect is assumed (not necessarily a multiplicative one, as with Atkinson) is absent from Weiner's theory. Instead, Weiner presented a series of suggestions that would distinctly limit the significance of expectancy and affect in behavioral determination, although in the attributional model of achievement-motivated behavior (Table 5.2) they immediately precede behavior. According to Weiner, that model merely describes the temporal order of events, while actual behavioral determination occurs through attribution. Thoughts (causal attributions) determine behavior; they precede expectancy change and affect (Weiner *et al.,* 1972, p. 241).

With this, the behavior-determining function would be completely removed from expectancies and affects and would depend on causal attributions themselves. Weiner supported his statement in explanations in which he defined the construct status of causal attributions more clearly. According to him, attributions mediate between antecedent conditions and subsequent achievement-related behavior (Weiner *et al.,* 1972, p. 247) instead of mediating between antecedent conditions on the one hand and affects and expectancies on the other hand. This concept corresponds well to the motive definition in which the achievement motive (the success motive) is seen as the disposition to attribute success to internal factors, particularly effort. Of course, it is hard to understand what is actually motivating about the effort attribution (see above).

Perhaps Weiner also saw this difficulty, since he formulated yet another motivation model (Weiner *et al.,* 1972, p. 247; Weiner & Sierad, 1975). In this model he brought expectancies and affects into play again as the motivating goal states toward which behavior is directed, after having spirited them away earlier. Quite different behavioral principles were formulated for the different types of achievement-related behavior, and these were in part differentiated further by motive group. In the first place, the free approach to achievement-related activities was said to be mediated by internal attributions of success (primarily effort), because it increases positive affect (Weiner *et al.,* 1971). In the second place, persistence in the face of failure was said to be mediated by unstable failure attributions (lack of effort, bad luck). This attributional tendency leads to the maintenance of relatively high subjective probabilities of success, long-lasting persistence at the task, and finally, improved performance. However, the two unstable causal factors not only have a similar relationship to expectancies of success, but also differ considerably in their influence on affects. A relatively high expectancy of success in the face of failure is sometimes associated with strong negative affect (if effort is insufficient) and sometimes with weak negative affect (if luck is bad). This leads to the formulation of different behavioral principles for success- and failure-motivated subjects. Success-motivated subjects weigh probability of success higher than affect, while failure-motivated subjects give greater weight to the negative affect that follows failure (Weiner & Sierad, 1975, p. 416).

Finally, success-motivated subjects choose tasks of intermediate difficulty, as in the risk-taking model, because it is at that level of difficulty that success and failure suggest effort attributions most convincingly — and such attribution increases motivation. In this sense, success and failure at tasks of intermediate difficulty provide definitive information about the person's own ability. Weiner derived an additional behavioral principle from this fact. Success-motivated persons choose tasks of intermediate difficulty because they receive the most information about their own ability from such tasks. In contrast, the choice of extremely easy or difficult tasks by failure-motivated persons leads to external attributions — and these offer no information about the person's own competence. Success-motivated subjects seek such information pertaining to their own ability, while failure-motivated persons attempt to avoid it (Weiner *et al.*, 1971, pp. 15 – 19; Weiner *et al.*, 1972, p. 247; Weiner & Sierad, 1975, p. 416).

Weiner presented three different behavioral principles to explain the three classical forms of achievement-motivated behavior (maximizing positive affects, preserving a high expectancy of success, and maximizing information). These behavioral principles have no obvious connection to Weiner's general motive definition, in which an internal causal attribution (particularly effort) constitutes the actual motivating motive goal.

Thus a motive definition that anchors the actual motive goal of achievement-oriented behavior in internal causal attributions, implicitly assuming the existence of a single universal achievement motive, has to coexist with the formulation of three behavior-specific motivational principles. This unresolved coexistence of several motivational principles introduces a significant lack of clarity into the theory. This is all the more true because no coordinating assumptions relate type of behavior and motivational principle to one another, and because a motivational principle (maximizing information) that was neither represented nor explained in the theory was introduced as an explanatory construct.

Calling the acquisition of information a motivational principle is not new. Schneider (1971, 1973) had already attempted to explain achievement-motivated behavior with such a principle. Controversy does exist, however, about whether the maximization of information about one's own ability can be a motivational principle that explains behavior, and whether the maximization of information in this explanatory function is more influential than the hedonistic principle of the maximization of affect (see Chapter 6, "Search for Information or for Affective Satisfaction?").

Attribution and Achievement

Enough has been said about problems inherent in the theory. We now turn to the question of empirical support for the assumed relationships between motive disposition, attribution, and behavior. Again Meyer (1973a) was the first to perform the relevant studies in this field. In this study, in which a series of failures was induced, Meyer measured increments in speed of performance as well as attributions and changes of expectancies.

Figure 5.7 shows increments in speed of performance from Trial 1 to Trial 2 as a function of the causal attribution for failure at the first trial. According to these findings, a relatively clear tendency to make attributions to stable factors leads to slower performance, while high attribution to unstable factors leads to increased speed of performance. These findings agree with Weiner's statements about the role of effort attribution, in that effort attribution determines motivational strength and thereby also the level of performance. Unfortunately, however, luck attribution had similar effects. Weiner *et al.* (1972) interpreted these findings as meaning that every attribution that makes it possible to keep expectancies at a high level will lead to improved performance. Thus the factor determining behavior is not the effort attribution, as could be expected from the general motive definition, but rather the expectancy of success that is mediated by variable causal attributions.

Meyer (1973a) also took motive groups into account in analyzing his data. He found that success-motivated subjects worked faster after failure than did failure-motivated subjects. When the data were simultaneously classified by motivation and by attribution, it turned out that failure-motivated subjects performed worse after failure only when their attribution to stable factors was high. Moreover, success-motivated subjects improved their performance more when they attributed failure more to unstable than to stable factors.

Patten and White (1977) attempted to replicate this experiment with identical and with slightly altered methods. When attributions were measured, as in Meyer's (1973a) study, no effects appeared, but effects did appear when attributions were measured independently of each other. But even these effects, which corresponded to those of Meyer, disappeared when initial differences in speed of performance were factored out. Performance speed for subjects with unstable causal attribution climbed more pronouncedly than for subjects with stable causal attribution. This relationship is independent of the achievement motive. Likewise, success-motivated

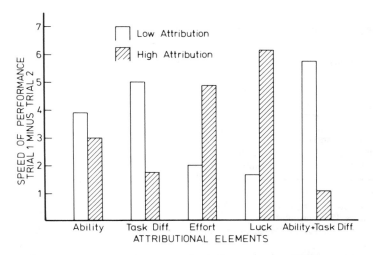

FIGURE 5.7   Increase in speed at a number–symbol task between the first and second trials as a function of high and low attributions to the individual causal factors and a combination of the two stable factors. (Adapted from Meyer, 1973a.)

subjects (MARPS) showed a more pronounced improvement in perform-ance than failure-motivated subjects, an effect that is also independent of attribution. The finding that motive disposition and causal attribution have independent effects on performance can hardly be reconciled with the attri-butional elaboration of achievement motivation theory.

Kukla (1972b, Experiment II) explored the relationships between attribu-tion and performance (anagram tasks) in a situation without previous expe-rience of failure. In contrast with the studies by Meyer (1973a) and Patten and White (1977), Kukla treated attributions as independent variables. He told subjects working in two independent groups that solving anagrams depended primarily on ability, or on effort (along with ability). These two different attributions had no general effect on performance by themselves, but only in interaction with the achievement motive. It turned out that success-motivated subjects (MARPS) performed better than failure-moti-vated subjects when the importance of effort for level of performance re-ceived special emphasis. That finding corresponds to theory, unlike the finding that differences between the two conditions were found only with success-motivated subjects.

Weiner and Sierad (1975) investigated the linkages between motive, attri-bution, and performance in an experiment in which they created various attributions by means of experimental manipulations. Subjects were given

TABLE 5.7
Attributional Sequence and Hypothesized Behavioral Consequences[a]

	Experimental condition[b]			
	Low		High	
Thought action sequence	Control	Experimental	Control	Experimental
Failure attribution	Low ability	Drug	Low effort	Drug
Expectancy of success	Low	Low	High	Low
Negative affect	High	Low	High	Low
Performance	Low[c]	High	High	Low

[a] Adapted from Weiner & Sierad, 1975, "Misattribution for failure and enhancement of achievement strivings," *Journal of Personality and Social Psychology, 31,* p. 417, by permission of The Journal Press.
[b] For subjects high and low in achievement motivation in the control and experimental (drug) conditions.
[c] Indicates performance relative to same-motive subjects in the alternate condition.

four trials of repeated failure at a digit–symbol substitution task. Prior to the failure experience, experimenters had given half the subjects a placebo that would purportedly interfere with hand–eye coordination. This group was expected to attribute its failures to the drug (experimental condition). In the other group the attributions were not changed (control condition). In this condition the failure attributions were expected to be those typical of success- and failure-motivated subjects: attributions to low effort or low ability.

Table 5.7 shows the behavioral effects that were expected and the processes that were assumed to mediate them. Failure-motivated subjects were expected to attribute failure to low ability in the control condition and to the effects of medication in the experimental condition. Both were stable factors for the duration of the experiment, so that the expectancy of success would be very low in both groups. The ability attribution was expected to lead to more negative affect than the drug attribution. The drug attribution, however, was expected to reduce the aversive consequences of failure and to increase motivation to solve the problem, which was expected to result in relatively better performance.

Predictions for behavior of success-motivated subjects were more complex. Success-motivated subjects attributed failure in the control condition to low effort and were thus expected to have high expectancies of success. In the experimental condition this attribution was changed in favor of the drug attribution, which led to low expectancies of success, like those of the failure-motivated subjects. In the control condition, just as among failure-motivated subjects, negative affect was expected to be stronger than in the experimental condition.

While it was easy to predict high performance for the success-motivated subjects in the control condition, it was harder to predict the behavior of success-motivated subjects in the experimental condition. One behavioral determinant (expectancy) was changed in such a way as to lower performance, while the other one (affect) was changed in such a way as to increase performance. Assuming that the behavior of success-motivated subjects would be influenced more by expectancy than by affect, Weiner and Sierad (1975) predicted relatively low performance in this condition.

In summary, then, the drug attribution was expected to lead to a relative improvement in performance by failure-motivated subjects and to a relative decline in performance by success-motivated subjects. This seemed reasonable, building on the assumption that the relatively low level of negative affect would improve the performance of the failure-motivated students, while the relatively low expectancies would interfere with the performance of the success-motivated subjects. In this case behavior was determined by two different motive-linked motivational principles.

The findings of this study, presented in Figure 5.8, clearly correspond to the predictions. In the control condition success-motivated subjects improved their performance more distinctly than failure-motivated subjects. This replicated the differences in performance after failure that are normally expected from success- and failure-motivated subjects. With the attribution manipulation the relationship was reversed, as expected.

Comparing the data of each motive group in the two conditions, we can see that success-motivated subjects performed better in the control condition than in the experimental condition, since they were able to retain their preferred effort attribution. On the other hand, failure-motivated subjects worked better in the experimental condition than in the control condition, since they were not bound to the detrimental ability attribution.

Attribution and Risk Taking

Weiner's assumption that different risk-taking propensities can be explained by whether or not risk taking provides information is indirectly supported by two studies by Meyer et al. (1976) and Weiner et al. (1972). In the latter experiment subjects were asked about the importance of effort as a factor in achievement, with regard to tasks of varying degrees of difficulty. These subjects found effort to be a particularly important determinant for outcomes at intermediate difficulty. Whether this also explains behavior is an altogether different question.

In Meyer's experiment subjects were asked to imagine that they had

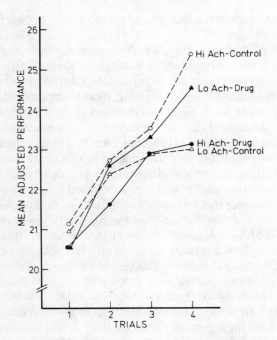

FIGURE 5.8   Mean speed of performance (number
of digit–symbol substitutions), adjusted for pretest
performance, for the test trials as a function of level of
achievement needs (high vs. low) and the experimental
condition (control vs. drug attribution).   (Adapted
from Weiner & Sierad, 1975, "Misattribution for fail-
ure and enhancement of achievement strivings," *Jour-
nal of Personality and Social Psychology, 31,* p. 419, by
permission of The Journal Press.)

worked on achievement-related tasks at various levels of difficulty but had
received no information about results.   They were to indicate for which task
they would like to receive feedback.   As expected, the subjects wanted infor-
mation about success and failure for the task at which their subjective proba-
bility of success was close to .50 (but see Heckhausen, 1975c).   Since, how-
ever, feedback about success and failure has affective as well as informative
consequences, this investigation too offered no conclusive support for
Weiner's position.

   In several experiments Schneider and Posse (1978a, 1978b, 1978c) ob-
tained causal attributions for success and failure from subjects working on a
skill task where difficulty could be varied at nine levels; they also obtained
individual preference patterns for the choice of tasks varying in difficulty.

Results were quite similar in the various experiments: Internal causal factors did not allow for prediction of individual preference patterns for tasks of graduated difficulty. That is, subjects did not choose the tasks that would have encouraged them to attribute performance outcomes predominantly to effort or ability. At most, we could say that attribution to ease of performance allows us to predict task choice: Subjects chose tasks at which they did not need to attribute success primarily to the easiness of the task. These results call for serious limitations on the use of the approach based on attribution theory.

Starke (1975) tested the approach based on information theory more directly. His subjects performed a total of six achievement-related tasks (intelligence tests) and non-achievement-related tasks (evaluation of preliminary sketches for advertisements, etc.). He emphasized that the first type of task had something to do with ability, while the second type of task did not. Immediately after performing the tasks, subjects were allowed to choose one of two tasks for evaluation, thus deciding whether or not to obtain information about their ability. In addition, they were allowed to receive more precise feedback about their performance from the experimenter three days later. Success-motivated subjects (LMG) chose to have the achievement-related task evaluated more than did failure-motivated subjects. Success-motivated subjects also showed a greater tendency to request information about their ability from the experimenter.

This study supports Weiner's hypothesis that success-motivated subjects are more interested in obtaining information about their own ability, while failure-motivated subjects tend to avoid such information. It is not possible, however, to determine whether this is particularly the case with tasks of intermediate difficulty, since task difficulty (subjective probability of success) was not controlled in this experiment. However, Butzkamm (1972) found this to be the case, as reported in Chapter 3.

Kukla (1972b, Experiment III) reported an experiment in which risk taking was analyzed in connection with the achievement motive and causal attribution. He had his subjects work on a task that was fully dependent on chance, but he made them believe that the results depended only on ability in one condition, and primarily on effort (along with ability) in the other condition. Kukla expected that preference for intermediate risks would be particularly pronounced after the induction of an attribution pattern that was supposed to be typical of success-motivated persons (attribution to effort and ability). This tendency did indeed appear, but only with success-motivated persons, as in Kukla's first investigation (1972b, Experiment II). Success-motivated subjects (MARPS) also exhibited a stronger tendency for moderate risks, independent of their attributions. These results too were congruent only in part with the notion that the difference in behavior of success- and failure-motivated subjects must be mediated by different attributions.

Attribution and Persistence

Schmalt and Oltersdorf (in preparation) are the only researchers so far to have studied motive-related differences in persistence, using actual persistence indicators like those employed by Feather (1961, 1963a) — that is, continued interaction with the task — instead of achievement measures such as Meyer (1973a) and Patten and White (1977) used. This is particularly interesting because it is here that Weiner's and Atkinson's theories lead to predictions that in part contradict each other. If we applied the principles of attribution theory, we would predict that success-motivated persons would persist for a long time and failure-motivated persons for a relatively short time, independent of the level of difficulty of the task to be processed.

This conclusion is based on motive-related differences in attribution: Success-motivated persons attribute their failures to lack of effort, while failure-motivated persons attribute theirs to lack of ability. The differences in expectancy change constitute the mediating motivational principle. Such a general effect of motive groups on persistence does not fit Atkinson's theory, where persistence is conceptualized as an interaction effect of motive group and task difficulty (see Chapter 3).

In the study by Schmalt and Oltersdorf (in preparation), predictions based on Atkinson's model were directly compared with those of attribution theory. The results of this study (LMG) confirm Atkinson's theory and replicate Feather's findings (1961, see above). In contrast, there are no motive-related differences in persistence mediated by attributions.

Andrews and Debus (1978), however, do show the importance of attributions for the study of persistence. This study demonstrates that persistence is low when attribution is made both to ability and to task difficulty, and high when attribution is made to effort. The task was a novel task with an unspecified degree of difficulty. Since no motive differences were taken into account in this study, a test of the entire model is not possible.

In addition to persistence there is still another area in which Weiner's theory of achievement-oriented behavior leads to predictions that differ from those based on Atkinson's theory: goal-setting behavior. On the basis of Atkinson's model it was predicted correctly that the relatively rare phenomenon of atypical and rigid goal setting would appear in particular among failure-motivated subjects (see Chapter 3). However, in attribution theory (Weiner et al., 1971, p. 3) atypical and rigid goal setting would appear primarily with effort attributions. According to Weiner, it is precisely the success-motivated subjects who could be expected to manifest this behavior in the face of failure.   Research so far indicates (e.g., Moulton, 1965) that the hypotheses derived from attribution theory do not hold (see Chapter 3).

Examination of the Entire Model

Most of the studies presented here so far have been restricted to individual elements of the whole structure of behavior-determining variables, neglecting other variables that were represented in the model.   Weiner and Sierad (1975) took into account all variables described in the model when deriving their hypotheses; these variables were not directly measured, but only inferred.

Covington and Omelich (1979) conducted a study that measured all factors of the model in a real-life setting.   They obtained causal attributions, affects, and probabilities of success from students who regarded their initial test results in an introductory psychology course as a failure and thus wanted to take a second test.   In addition, Covington and Omelich (1979) had access to data about motive dispositions and about the results of the second test.

Figure 5.9 presents the result of the subsequent path analysis of the data. We can see that the correlation of motive (MARPS, AAT) with attribution to low ability and to bad luck is significant.   The first effect conforms to theory, but the second does not.   The absence of a correlation between n Ach and effort attribution is equally unexpected.

The shame affect is basically determined by the internal factors effort and ability.   Failure attribution to lack of effort diminishes shame, while ability attribution increases it.   These results indicate the presence of the compensatory causal schema (see above) and the primacy of ability attribution for the arousal of affect (see above).   The relationship between n Ach and the shame affect ($-.194$) can be broken down into a nearly significant direct effect and a nonsignificant effect mediated by attributions.   Motive dispositions and attributions, then, are affect determinants, important but independent of each other.

Expectancies are correlated only with effort attribution in this study, but in a direction that was not predicted.   Tracing back failure to low effort leads to the lowering of subsequent probabilities of success.   The relationship between motive and expectancy of success (.209) can be broken down into a significant direct effect and a nonsignificant indirect effect, mediated by all four attribution elements.

Performance on the second test was determined by various factors.   First of all, there is a correlation of .145 between motive and test performance, which can be separated into a nonsignificant direct effect and a nonsignificant indirect effect for all of the mediating variables.   Significant direct paths exist only between expectancy and performance (.333) and between shame

ANTECEDENTS   CAUSAL ATTRIBUTIONS   CAUSAL EFFECTS   BEHAVIORAL
                                                                              CONSEQUENCES

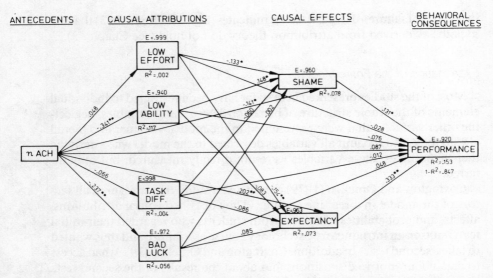

FIGURE 5.9 Path diagram of effects of *n* Ach, causal attributions, expectancy, and shame on subsequent performance following failure. *$p < .06$; **$p < .05$. (From Covington & Omelich, 1979, p. 1493.)

and performance (.131). None of the direct or indirect path coefficients for the four causal elements is significant. This does not support the central assumption of cognitive theory—that is, that behavioral differences (here performance differences) between the motive groups are mediated by attributional differences. The achievement motive has turned out to be the most influential factor in the system. It influences the shame affect directly, as well as indirectly through ability attribution. *N* Ach also exerts a direct impact on expectancy and is the ultimate determinant of achievement-related behavior, both directly and indirectly (mediated by expectancy). The authors explained their findings by ascribing to the attributions that they obtained after the fact the status of subsequent justifications and not of causes of performance. These findings have provided almost no support for the attributional approach to achievement motivation theory.

However, the results may also indicate that those attempting to theorize on the basis of assumed rigidly deterministic linkages between the various model parameters (see Table 5.2) have gone too far. Perhaps the individual elements should not be separated so rigidly, with the result that we could then take into account additional possibilities of situational or personal factors beyond the achievement motive (see Kelley & Michela, 1980).

In its present form the model has the status of a pure trait theory in which cognitive, affective, and behavioral processes are made dependent on a single variable. Thus it would seem that the model based on attribution theory is less advanced than Atkinson's (1957, 1964) interactionist approach.

In summary, we can say that the inclusion of cognitive elements in a theory of achievement-motivated behavior has been most fruitful and has provided many new ideas for applied research (see later sections in this chapter, and Chapter 6). To be sure, we are still far from a unified, integrated theory with noncontradictory statements. Moreover, we cannot claim that this theory is merely an expectancy-value theory supplemented by cognitive determinants. The extent to which expectancies and affective reactions and their interaction determines behavior has not yet been clarified; at the present, a number of behavioral principles coexist, without any coordinating definitions. What the theory lacks is a single behavioral principle that applies to all areas of behavior, a kind of motivating incentive. The ultimate goal of achievement-related activity has been lost during the search for diverse cognitive and affective behavioral determinants.

When Do Attributions Occur?

The attribution of particular events to causal factors—especially to stable causal factors—facilitates orientation in the world and helps us predict our own behavior and that of others. We should be able to assume that causal attributions play a pervasive role in experiential processes. On the other hand, in many situations the search for causal attributions is unusually disturbing. Their implications for self-evaluation can distract us from the action being carried out, leading to preoccupation with problems of self-evaluation and finally to the inability to act (Heckhausen, 1982a; Kuhl, 1982c).

Finally, in many situations we can use ready-made systems in which events are already closely tied to particular causes (Kelley & Michela, 1980). It is likely that they are scarcely represented in the experiential process. It is not necessary to analyze the causes of those experiences that do not call into question the basis of our hopes and expectations. Accordingly, it is primarily the unexpected and frustrating events (e.g., failure) that initiate causal analyses (Weiner, 1982).

Wong and Weiner (1981) have investigated this assumption in a number of studies. They confronted their subjects with four hypothetical situations (expected and unexpected successes and failures) and had the subjects indicate in free response what kinds of questions they thought they would ask themselves in such a situation. The analysis of these questions showed that "why" questions were particularly likely to occur after failures and unexpected action outcomes. These findings were confirmed in a number of studies employing different methods, in fictive situations as well as real-life situations.

The search for causes is not based on accidental points of view. Rather, it follows a heuristic logic in which the various causal dimensions are worked through one after the other, in order of importance. Attention is first directed to the locus of control (internal – external); then to the individual's ability to control the causal factor (controllable – uncontrollable); and finally to the question of whether the causal element is stable or unstable (see Table 5.1). No concrete assumptions were made about when attention might be turned to the dimensions of intentionality and globality.

Wong and Weiner (1981) explored this question in several experiments in which frame stories were imbedded in various thematic contexts. Subjects were asked to assign the individual causal elements to the five dimensions themselves; or, without the detour involved in stating the individual elements, subjects rated the importance of the five dimensions directly, on a scale. Regardless of whether successes or failures were involved and regardless of whether expected or unexpected events were involved, the dimensions of locus of control and controllability had high priority over the other three dimensions. They occurred earlier, and overall more frequently, in causal analysis. For individual causal elements distinct differences between the success and failure conditions appeared. Effort attributions were made more frequently after failure than after success, while task difficulty attributions were made more after success than after failure. These findings contradict the usual egotistic distortions, which we have already described.

In a final experiment Wong and Weiner (1981) investigated the information-acquisition process in a real-life situation. Students taking a midterm exam were asked to evaluate their previous performance on exams and assess the extent to which this level of achievement met their expectancies. Then the subjects were offered information that supposedly would help them determine the factors responsible for their performance. The information was in five envelopes, one for each of the causal dimensions. As expected, the subjects were primarily interested in information about the dimensions of locus of control and controllability, regardless of how they had assessed their test performance and of the extent to which this had corresponded to their expectancies.

Lau and Russell (1980) reported an interesting attempt to analyze the occurrence of attributions under life-like conditions. They analyzed sports stories about baseball and football games from daily newspapers for their attributional content, in four categories: games that were won, games that were lost, results that were expected, and results that were unexpected (i.e., a clear favorite loses a game). Causal analyses occurred primarily after unexpected game outcomes, independent of whether the outcome was a win or a loss.

Taken together, the findings from these two studies show that attributions occur primarily following unexpected and frustrating action outcomes. The search for causal factors follows a heuristic logic that is oriented toward the criterion of the greatest possible efficiency of action. If unexpected results are to be understood correctly, or if failure is to be made good, it is important first of all to know whether one is at all personally responsible for it, and whether the factors in question can be controlled.

Wong and Weiner (1981) also analyzed additional cognitive processes during performance. The questions concerned not only causal attributions, but also the action itself and the subject's self-esteem and reevaluation processes (i.e., cognitions about ability). Again, in a number of studies performance-oriented questions—generally about various possible performance outcomes for the future—tended to be asked after failure, especially after an expected failure. This suggests why causal attribution following failure tends to focus on the internal, controllable factor of effort. Wong and Weiner (1981) see that focus as an adaptive function of causal attributions, facilitating effective planning of instrumental actions for the overcoming of an aversive situation.

Data on cognitions concerning reevaluation of one's own ability show that people tend to subject their ability to a reevaluation more after success than after failure. However, this effect is hard to interpret. It appears in subjects focusing on their own actions as well as in subjects focusing on the actions of others, but only in fictitious situations, not in real-life situations. Thus these findings can hardly be explained as egotistic tendencies.

Differences in the kind and extent of spontaneously occurring cognitions are dependent not only on situational factors but also on personality factors. Interindividual differences in various personality parameters are also associated with different cognition patterns. Diener and Dweck (1978) described the first such difference. They divided their subjects into two groups on the basis of the "Intellectual Achievement Responsibility Scale" (IAR; Crandall et al., 1965b). The first group was characterized by "helplessness"; the second was "mastery oriented." Both groups were assigned a series of discrimination problems, in eight training trials and a subsequent failure phase. In two separate studies the subjects were to make attributions for their failure, or simply to verbalize their reactions.

The two studies showed distinct performance differences between the two subject groups. Moreover, subjects who had been described as helpless justified their failure with uncontrollable factors (low ability) and thought about things that were irrelevant to the task; the mastery-oriented subjects never even undertook such attributions. Instead, their cognitive activities were focused on solving the problem and concerned instructions to themselves and processes for controlling their own solution strategies.

Kuhl (1982c) pointed out a personality variable similar to Diener and

Dweck's, which he described as action versus state orientation. According to Kuhl (1982c), the two orientations are characterized by different cognitive processes. The cognitive activities of action-oriented persons are said to refer primarily to effective control and execution of actions. State-oriented persons, on the other hand, focus more on the situation that has been created, with its implications for self-evaluation and evaluation of others, including the associated causal analyses. Thus it seems that search for causal attributions is most evident when an outcome is unexpected and when desires have not been fulfilled (Weiner, 1982). Causal analysis seems to be a prerequisite for using appropriate behavioral strategies and for overcoming frustrating situations.

Attributions as a Component of Commonsense Theories?

In general, the studies reported here indicate that causal attributions have two primary functions. First, they facilitate a more or less efficient control of behavior; second, they make it possible to keep the subject's self-esteem relatively free from stresses, to varying degrees. In this regard success-motivated persons seem to be more fortunate. Their attribution strategies enable them to perform efficiently, while preserving their self-esteem. These effects are also moderated by situational variables. Here we have a complete and conclusive picture of cognitive and motivational processes in action. There can be no doubt, then, that taking into account introspective data has considerably increased the explanatory value of psychological theories about achievement-oriented behavior. At the same time, this approach also contradicts the assumption by Nisbett and Wilson (1977) that subjects are unable to attain insight into the causal structures on which their behavior is based and to report on them.

The findings of many studies show that introspective data must be considered as meaningful determinants of behavior and should not be relegated to implicit theories, public theories, or very general notions of the extent to which individual causal factors determine behavior, as Nisbett and Wilson (1977) have assumed. This is especially true of the experiments in which subjects were able to reconstruct their causal attributions through free response, as in the study by Wong and Weiner (1981).

Meanwhile, findings from other fields already show the validity of subjects' statements about their assessment of the causes behind their decision. These findings make it clear that subjects actually do rely on their own memories in describing causal elements, with very little tendency to fall back on general and public theories about the origin of behavioral effects (Sabini & Silver, 1981; Wright & Rip, 1981).

Learned Helplessness

The paradigm for research on learned helplessness is an experiment involving animals. After dogs were subjected to uncontrollable aversive stimuli, they showed certain behavioral deficits. It was necessary to alter the experimental procedure when the theory was applied to research with humans. As a rule, subjects in learned helplessness experiments are confronted with problems to be solved; they are to discover a hidden solution pattern. In a noncontingent fashion the subjects receive feedback that their work is correct or false; however, in every case this feedback is designed to give them the impression that they have not yet found the correct solution pattern and have failed at their task.

The theory of learned helplessness describes a general performance deficit that depends on noncontingent performance feedback. Objective noncontingence is said to lead to a feeling of lack of control and finally to the expectancy that events are uncontrollable in general. This, in turn, is said to have a negative influence on motivation, on the learning of new contingencies, and even on affective processes (Seligman, 1975).

Empirical investigation of this theory with human beings has led to divergent results. The predicted effects appeared in some studies, but not in others; a third group of studies even reported a reverse helplessness effect (summarized by Roth, 1980).

One reason for the divergence of these findings may be that the motivational effects of failure induction have not yet received adequate theoretical consideration. The phenomenon of learned helplessness is particularly interesting for achievement motivation researchers, who have been exploring the motivational effects of failure for a long time with quite similar experimental paradigms. Recently such research has led to an increased convergence of explanatory approaches and has been reflected to an especially great extent in the growing importance of cognitive processes for explaining the helplessness effect (Dweck & Wortman, 1982; Roth, 1980).

Causal attribution has turned out to be the most important moderating variable (Abramson, Seligman, & Teasdale, 1978; Miller & Norman, 1979; Wortman & Brehm, 1975). The expected helplessness effects are especially likely to occur when failure (subjective noncontingency) is explained by internal and stable factors—that is, by low ability. As long as subjects believe that it is possible to solve a problem, they are not likely to experience noncontrollability when objective noncontingency mediates doubts about their ability. If the impression of their own low ability that was induced in this manner is general and global enough, ability attribution is said to lead subjects to expect difficulties in other task situations as well. Finally, then, we come to the motivational and cognitive deficits described by the theory.

This is exactly what is predicted by the attributional interpretation of achievement motivation theory for cases when failures are explained by low ability.

The findings of Tennen and Eller (1977) speak for this view. The authors induced either a task difficulty attribution or an ability attribution for the lack of controllability. Attribution to task difficulty tended to have a positive influence on subsequent learning, while the expected deficits were observed with ability attribution.

According to these results, helplessness effects should be particularly prominent with tasks that do not suggest difficulty attribution — that is, with easy tasks and tasks of intermediate difficulty. Frankel and Snyder (1978) explored this assumption. After a training phase with noncontingent performance feedback for discrimination tasks, subjects were particularly inhibited in performing an anagram task when the task was described as moderately difficult, but not when it was described as difficult. The authors explained this as a result of egotistical attributional strategies.

When task difficulty is high, a failure need not be linked to low ability, even when effort invested was high; the same is not true of tasks of intermediate difficulty. Similar statements are made about the reasoning of failure-motivated subjects by the risk-taking model of achievement motivation.

If helplessness effects are mediated by causal attributions — especially attributions to low ability — it is to be expected that interindividual differences in the use of such causal elements produce different helplessness effects. Individuals who tend toward a high degree of self-esteem-centered thoughts after failure, which Kuhl (1982b) assumes is particularly true of state-oriented persons, must be just as much affected by helplessness as failure-motivated subjects, who link failure primarily to low ability.

The possibility of transfer effects from the training phase to new performance situations poses a particular problem for helplessness research. Abramson, Seligman, and Teasdale (1978) and Miller and Norman (1979) have attempted to solve this problem by identifying varying degrees of generalization for attributions. They assume that transfer effects are most pronounced when the causal attributions tend to be general and global and involve similarly generalized expectancies. There is still no definite empirical support for this assumption.

Kuhl (1981) contrasted the assumption of a motivational deficit mediated by global attributions and expectancies with the hypothesis of a functional deficit. Functional helplessness occurs when a person's ability to function cognitively is hampered by a massive bombardment of cognitions that are irrelevant to the task at hand and concern the person's own state. Noncontingent performance feedback that is perceived as failure is said to bring about an increase in state-oriented cognitions, other things being equal. In two experiments Kuhl (1981) confirmed his assumptions. Helplessness effects are especially likely to occur when state-oriented cognitions are aroused by the situation or when subjects have a habitual tendency to state-oriented cognitions.

This notion is reminiscent of the attentiveness hypothesis from anxiety research (Sarason, 1972, 1975; Wine, 1971, 1980). According to this hypothesis, the impaired performance that is often found in subjects with high anxiety can be explained by the increased occurrence of self-esteem-related and task-irrelevant cognitions. Some studies have already investigated the assumption of differential effects of helplessness training in success- and failure-motivated subjects. The first study (Jardine & Winefield, 1981), predicted a helplessness effect only for failure-motivated subjects, while reactance effects were predicted for success-motivated subjects. The results of the study confirm only the second part of the predictions.

A more complex analysis, in which the level of difficulty of the training task was taken into account along with the achievement motive, was conducted by Winefield and Jardine (1982). This study made it possible to compare the integrative helplessness – reactance model (Wortman & Brehm, 1975) directly with the risk-taking model (Atkinson, 1964). The integrative model predicts that helplessness effects (performance deficits) are especially likely to be found when control expectancies (success expectancies) are low. In contrast, the risk-taking model predicts that when persons with low probabilities of success experience failure, motivation does not sink; rather, these persons persist for a long time (Feather, 1961, 1963a) — but only if they are also failure-motivated persons.

How, then, do failure-motivated persons with low expectancies of success behave? They show no signs of helplessness; quite the contrary, they show the most unmistakable reactance effects of all experimental groups. These findings, which cannot be explained by any of the helplessness theories, emphasize the significance of motivational processes like those that are investigated from the perspective of motive differences by achievement motivation theorists.

Applications: Motive Modification Programs

We have already described the first attempts to modify motives of entrepreneurs and schoolchildren through training courses (Chapter 2). Theoretical and pragmatic eclecticism have characterized the procedures of McClelland and his Harvard group. Since then, others have taken these ideas and developed them further. They have focused on the essential elements of the manifold procedures, especially on the practicing of realistic goal setting. At the same time they have based the modification programs more and more on currently developed theory. The attribution theory version of achievement motivation was especially helpful for these programs. Heckhausen and Krug (1982) have described how the motive modification programs developed under the influence of theory, and with what results.

Causal Attribution as Implicit Program Content

Mehta's modification programs in India (1968, 1969; Mehta & Kanade, 1969) occupy a transitional position. They were still closely connected to the Harvard programs and were not influenced by attribution theory, but they did integrate the program into school instruction and involved teachers in a preprogram training session. Two programs were used: one for increasing the achievement motive and another for learning to set more challenging goals. The preprogram training sessions for teachers lasted 10 days for the first program and 2 days for the second program. Both programs were integrated into the school instructional program for 4 hours a week for 4 months, either together or separately. The goal-setting program contained an implicit attributional element. In order to give the schoolchildren a more positive image of their ability to achieve, they were asked to set goals for their monthly achievement tests and received encouraging feedback. The combination of the two programs brought about the most noticeable effects, both in increased motive scores and in greater improvement in school performance (dramatic only in science courses). The findings are not uniform, and moreover, the improvements in school performance did not last long.

Sports instruction is a particularly promising arena for improving motive scores because it is possible to see the level of difficulty being raised and to see performance improve in many kinds of exercises. Hecker (1971, 1974) and his colleagues (Kleine, 1976; Kleine & Hecker, 1977; summarized by Hecker, Kleine, Wessling-Lünemann, & Beier, 1979) found in 1-year and several-year sport instruction programs that free choice of task difficulty (e.g., on a "jump-trainer" machine that was especially designed for the purpose) and encouraging realistic goal setting increased concentrated persistence at sports activities as well as success orientation in achievement-motive scores (*NH*, LMG) in comparison with control classes. The "principle of the match" (Heckhausen, 1968b; Hunt, 1964) is central in the modification programs — that is, a close correspondence between individual level of ability and task demands (see individual reference norms, Chapter 6). In an instructional experiment with third graders Hecker and his associates explored the question of whether causal attributions, which had not been directly influenced, had also changed in the course of the school year (1975 – 1976). Attribution of success had indeed changed, but not failure attribution. In addition, the success motive increased and goal setting became more realistic. Experimental group subjects ascribed success more to their own ability and less to luck. These findings confirm the reasonable prediction that as goal setting becomes more realistic, internal factors are more likely to be used for a causal explanation than external factors. The reason is that ability and effort are more important in determining success at tasks of moderate difficulty than they are for easy or difficult tasks.

Similarly, Stamps (1973) obtained favorable modifications in fourth–sixth-grade students with high fear of failure, in comparison with a control group. This involved two intervention strategies: self-reinforcement and group therapy. In the self-reinforcement procedure students received ten arithmetic problems at each of 10 half-hour sessions during a 2-week period. They were asked to indicate how many problems they expected to solve correctly and to identify the level of aspiration above or below which a success or failure, respectively, would surprise them. Each time they attained their goal they were allowed to take a token in the absence of the experimenter. At the end of the experiment the students exchanged their tokens for prizes. (Incidentally, the students often took tokens even when they had not reached their goal.) This procedure forced the students to orient themselves toward their own earlier performance, not those of other students (see Chapter 6); moreover, they were forced to set goals that they could reach with some effort. In the group-therapy intervention, students competed in various party games. Thus their own success and failure depended on the performance of the others (social reference norm). The experimenter praised those who succeeded and reacted neutrally to failure. Intensive efforts received special praise; feelings of success and failure were reflected and explained in an understanding manner, as in nondirective therapy.

After each of the two interventions, fear of failure decreased considerably (Hostile Press; however, *n* Ach did not increase). But goal setting became more realistic and the area of aspiration narrower only after self-reinforcement, not after group-therapy intervention. In the self-reinforcement condition the students not only lowered their level of aspiration in order to take more tokens, but they also improved their performance considerably. Giving students an opportunity for self-reinforcement through an individual reference norm (without outside influence from group therapy) was sufficient to reduce fear of failure and to make the level of aspiration more realistic and (presumably along with stronger internal attribution) more precise.

Personal Causation

Let us now turn to those who have explicitly aimed at modifying causal attribution. Without being an adherent of Heider's attribution theory, deCharms (1968, 1976) identified a central experiential phenomenon of motivation, developed a motive modification program that could be integrated with classroom instruction, and carried out the program (de Charms, 1968, 1972, 1976). The experiential phenomenon consists of the feeling that one is an origin. This point of view can be traced back to various philosophical and psychological sources, for example, White's "effectance motivation" (1959; see Heckhausen, 1976b) and "intrinsic motivation" (see Chapter 6). From the standpoint of attribution theory the phenomenon involves the intentionality of actions and personal responsibility for their results. DeCharms posits "personal causation" as the desired goal of motive modification. In detail, this means (1) to set demanding but realistic goals for oneself, (2) to know one's own strengths and weaknesses, (3) to have self-confidence in the effectiveness of one's own actions, (4) to determine concrete behavioral strategies for reaching one's own goals, (5) to seek feedback on whether the goal has been reached, and (6) to take responsibility for one's own actions and their consequences, as well as taking responsibility for others.

Based on this description, resembling that of a person with a high success-oriented achievement motive, deCharms (1968, 1972) developed two diagnostic procedures. One, similar to the achievement-motive TAT, was designed to identify those schoolchildren who perceive themselves as origins. The other was a questionnaire for schoolchildren designed to determine the "origin climate" in their class (i.e., the extent to which their teacher created an instructional atmosphere that gave them opportunities to use their own initiative and to take responsibility). As expected, good students in the fifth through seventh grades had higher scores than poor students even when intelligence test scores were taken into account. In a sample of 23 classes the origin climate correlated with the average rate of learning.

The results of various modification programs were even more impressive (summarized by deCharms, 1976). In a 1-week preprogram training session the teachers were able to experience "personal causation" and created instructional units with the aid of the psychologists in a manner that gave students opportunities to make their own decisions, to take responsibility, to set binding goals—in short, to experience themselves as origins. Direct experiential exercises, such as "My True Self," "Stories of Success and Achievement," and written descriptions of how an origin feels and thinks occupied one half hour on each of 3 or 4 weekdays. Various parts of the program occupied a 3- or 4-week period; altogether individual classes were trained for a total of up to 1 or 2 years. The desired effects were observed not only in higher scores for personal causation and "origin-class-climate," but also in the increased realism of goal setting and in improved school performance (in comparison with national norms for that school year). When compared with the rest of the many different school improvement programs that have been developed and applied since the mid-1960s in the United States, deCharms' can be considered remarkably effective (see McClelland, 1978).

"Pygmalion in the Classroom" as a Motive-Modifying Attribution Effect

Rosenthal and Jacobson (1968) predicted that a "Pygmalion effect" would appear in school motive modification programs. While this was questioned by many (see Elashoff & Snow, 1971), the prediction brought about a focus on attribution theory in motive modification programs for schoolchildren. Is the teacher's belief in good faith in the students' supposedly high ability sufficient to raise their IQ scores? A mere expectancy effect (self-fulfilling prophecy) has neither been demonstrated empirically in a convincing manner nor explained theoretically in a conclusive manner. The viewpoint of attribution theory can be productive both empirically and theoretically in this regard. According to attribution theory, those schoolchildren who change their unfavorable attribution system for success and failure under the influence of altered teacher behavior, and thus exert more effort, could be expected to improve their school performance (if not their IQ scores) if they have not yet fully realized their potential for achievement. A Pygmalion effect would occur under the following conditions: Teachers would revise upward their assessment of weak students' ability and thus tend to attribute these students' failures to lack of effort rather than to ability. The students would then perceive the alteration of teacher attribution, come gradually to internalize it, and attribute success to their own ability and failure to inadequate effort. Accordingly, the students would exert more effort and persist longer, using their potential for achievement more than before. Their school performance would improve and eventually confirm the teacher's altered attribution.

This interpretation of the Pygmalion effect from the point of view of attribution theory was confirmed by a modification study (Scherer, 1972; see Heckhausen, 1976a, pp. 119–121). Schoolchildren who tended to attribute their failures more to lack of ability than to effort and who appeared from their intelligence test scores to be able to make better grades were selected from each of 12 fourth-grade classes. The teachers were given the names of these students and were informed about the criteria for selection. They also received a brief explanation of the Pygmalion effect from the point of view of causal attribution theory. They were asked to point out to the selected students that they would be able to perform better if they exerted more effort. Four months before and after the induction of expectancy of improvement the experimenters gathered data for experimental and control subjects on achievement motive (TAT), causal attribution for success and failure, intelligence test scores, anxiety, school performance in arithmetic, and school grades. In the posttest, the effects of the encouraging causal attribution by the teacher appeared not only in the target students, but also appeared unexpectedly in most of the other students in the class. However, in comparison with the control group experimental students tended now more to attribute failure to insufficient effort. They lowered their goals less often, achieved higher scores on individual intelligence test problems, and were less anxious.

Practicing Attribution Patterns for More Favorable Self-Evaluation

Intervention studies have involved alteration of causal explanations of success and failure in order to improve motivation, through experience and practice by the subjects themselves. Vorwerg (1977) administered 10 practice units of $1\frac{1}{2}$ hours each over a 3-week period to an extremely failure-motivated group of students $(HS < FF)$ who had volunteered for a training course. The trainer was the students' psychology instructor. First the subjects received an explanation of their failure-motivated experience and behavior, including the data from the motive diagnosis. Their experience and behavior were contrasted with a success-motivated approach, with special emphasis on differences in causal attribution. The subjects then practiced success-motivated behaviors and stabilized them through role playing. In contrast with a control group that had equally high failure motivation, the motive-trained students showed improvement in the following variables: decisiveness and confidence about decisions, expectancy of success, balanced level of aspiration, and lower scores for neuroticism and rigidity. The author claims that the training brought about a more realistic self-evaluation of their own competence by the course participants, along with a higher consistency of performance evaluation and causal attribution. Vorwerg stresses the importance of this consistency as a precondition for success-motivated behavior in achievement situations (Vorwerg, 1977, p. 235).

If the achievement motive is seen as a self-reinforcing system (Heckhausen, 1972a, 1975a), then three determining components of the motive system need corrective influence — either individually or together — in a modification program: goal setting, causal attribution, and self-evaluation (self-reinforcement).

In an instructional improvement program consisting of 16 sessions spread out over 4½ months, Krug and Hanel (1976) tried to correct all three determining components rather directly: through repeated practice of the desired mode of behavior, through praise and recognition by the trainer, and through learning from the model provided by the trainer, as well as through self-observation, recording, and verbalizing (internal speech) of all modes of behavior and cognitions relevant to the motive. The subjects were a selected sample of failure-motivated fourth graders, low in performance but not in intelligence. They were divided into an experimental group, an expectancy control group, and a control group. The program progressed from attractive tasks unrelated to school (e.g., ringtoss games) to arithmetic and spelling exercises closely related to the instructional program.

The connections between goal setting, causal attribution, and self-evaluation were explained concretely for each task; they were also demonstrated by the trainer, and students were shown how to work on each individual task. The trainer expressed out loud thoughts about goal setting, causal attribution, and self-evaluation. After this the subjects had their turn; in between, individual conferences took place (for details see Krug & Hanel, 1976; or Heckhausen & Krug, 1982).

At the end, in comparison with the expectancy control group and the control group, experimental group subjects showed more realistic goal setting, more favorable causal attribution after failure, and stronger positive self-reinforcement after success. They also showed considerably stronger confidence of success on the achievement motive tests (*NH*, LMG) and higher intelligence test scores. However, during the school semester no improvement in school grades or school achievement test scores appeared. It remains open whether the time available was too short for modifications in achievement, or whether the instructional program did not offer the students enough stimulus for actualization of the achievement motive in the everyday school routine. Such a possibility requires special consideration, since motive modifications can hardly take root without opportunities for realization in the everyday routine — as shown by McClelland and Winter's (1969) motive modification courses with Indian entrepreneurs (see Chapter 2).

In a more recent study involving fifth- and sixth-grade special education students with learning difficulties (and an IQ of at least 70), Krug, Peters, and Quinkert (1977) also examined the desired motive modification a half year after training in a second posttest. The program resembled that of Krug and Hanel (1976), adapted for students with learning difficulties. Of the three training areas, only goal-setting behavior showed the expected modification in the posttest in comparison with a control group. During training causal attribution and self-reinforcement also showed the desired modifications; however, the effects could not be shown statistically in the posttest. In contrast, all of the more global personality measures had improved signifi-

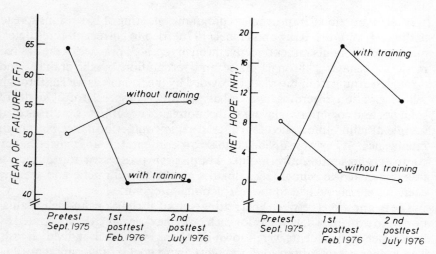

FIGURE 5.10 Stability of motive modification in fifth- and sixth-grade students with learning difficulties with and without a motive improvement program, divided into Fear of Failure (FF_1) and Net Hope (NH_1, LMG). (Adapted from Krug, Peters, & Quinkert, 1977, p. 673.)

cantly. Subjects now had a higher opinion of their own competence (self-concept of ability); test anxiety, manifest anxiety, and dislike of school had decreased. Above all, the motive change in the desired direction was pronounced and long-lasting. In a second posttest a half year later the reduction of the failure motive (*FF*, LMG) was still preserved, with the achievement motive showing hope of success (see Figure 5.10). At the end of Chapter 6 we discuss another aspect of motive-modification programs: reference-norm orientation.

Since the study by Krug *et al.* (1977), training programs have appeared in which participants are drilled in effort attribution. Andrews and Debus (1978) first discovered in a group of sixth graders a correlation between persistence and resistance to extinction on the one hand, and attribution of failure to insufficient effort on the other hand. Those students who tended least to attribute failure to insufficient effort were assigned either to a control group, to a group that received social reinforcement, or to a group that received both social and token reinforcement. Reinforcement (or a combination of reinforcements) was given when the subjects made the field "effort" light up after success and the field "insufficient effort" light up after failure on an "attribution box" with two 4-field panels showing Weiner's four causal factors. Immediately afterwards, as well as 4 months later, posttests were administered on the training task and on two transfer tasks.

In both reinforcement groups, in comparison with a pretest, a significant increase in persistence after failure appeared, as well as an increase in effort attribution.

Practicing Attribution Patterns to Overcome Learned Helplessness

Apart from achievement motivation research, Dweck's intervention study of learned helplessness (1975) demonstrated impressively the effectiveness of altering the attribution of failure. Dweck was one of a group of researchers concerned with "learned helplessness" (Seligman, 1975). Dweck and Repucci (1973) had already demonstrated that children who visibly worsen in performance or give up entirely after failure attribute their successes and failures to the presence or absence of ability and not to the effort exerted. In situations with failure-related cues (such as a particular experimenter with whom they had always experienced failure), they failed even at problems that they solved easily in other situations (with experimenters with whom they had always succeeded).

Dweck (1975) selected 8–13-year-old schoolchildren with extreme learned helplessness and placed them in one of two 25-session intervention programs. In one program the children occasionally experienced failure. They were encouraged to feel responsible for failure and to attribute it to insufficient effort. The other program followed a strategy that is customary in clinical psychology: positive reinforcement. The children always succeeded. With this treatment no improvement in achievement-related behavior or in performance outcomes appeared following subsequent failures. With the "attribution therapy" (see Valins & Nisbett, 1971), in contrast, the children improved their performance following failure and tended more than before to attribute the failure to inadequate effort.

6

Self-Concepts and Reference Norms

As analysis of any individual motive progresses past the initial reduction of persons in terms of summary trait construct labels such as success-motivated and failure-motivated, we typically come to realize that the original concept of the motive was too narrow. This has been especially true of achievement motivation research, in three respects. First of all, the subject's achievement-related behavior is partially determined by other motives as well. For example, the affiliation motive influences task choice (see Jopt, 1974; Schneider & Meise, 1973), and competing motives play a role in cumulative achievement (Atkinson, 1974b). As a rule, performance outcomes have side effects that affect other motives. In Chapter 7 we return to the role played by other motives, in connection with the discussion of extended motivation models.

Second — and it is this that is of interest here — we must occasionally take into account that which has been described by personality researchers as the "self." More central than a motive construct, the self is also a part of many compound constructs: self-image, self-concept, self-evaluation, self-reinforcement, self-regulation, self-control, self-awareness, self-efficacy, self-serving bias, and more.

Third, and last, norms by which actions and their outcomes are evaluated play a role in every kind of human activity. The concern with such norms is central to a standard of excellence (see Chapter 2) — a concept that was originally part of the definition of achievement motivation. Standards of excellence can be distinguished from each other in many respects. For our purposes here, the question is: On what are these standards based? There are various data bases for standards, called reference norms. These have considerable influence on achievement-related behavior, as research in the 1970s has demonstrated convincingly.

For three reasons achievement motivation research has found it necessary to take the self into account. First, it would have been hard to overlook the self-imposed commitment associated with goal setting and with the evaluation of the resulting performance in a way that affects a person's self-esteem. Some researchers see the achievement motive as a self-evaluative system (Halisch *et al.*, 1976; Heckhausen, 1972a); others focus on self-reinforcement as the consequence of an action outcome or — in anticipation — as a motivating incentive; or they focus on personal standards (Kuhl, 1978a). The productivity of these constructs and processes involving the self was already shown in part in Chapter 5.

Second, it would have been hard to overlook those self-image-like personality traits that take the form of "self-concept of ability." Such a self-concept was used as a decisive determinant of the subjective probability of success (e.g., by Meyer, 1976) and of intended and exerted effort. Researchers even attempted to replace the achievement motive with a self-concept of ability (Kukla, 1972a, 1978; Meyer, 1973a, 1973b).

Finally, the third reason for taking the self into account has nothing to do with trait theory: Some researchers have attempted to do more justice to the reflexive nature of human activity and experience (see Groeben & Scheele, 1977; Smedslund, 1972). The questions are: Under what conditions does the attention of persons performing an action redirect itself from the outside world to themselves? What self-centered cognitions appear in that context, and what are the effects? Not until recently have such questions been asked explicitly, although the attribution biases following success and failure that were described in Chapter 5 do call to mind the conditions and effects of self-centered cognitions. Apart from achievement motivation research, self-awareness theory (see Duval & Wicklund, 1972; Wicklund, 1975) has investigated the conditions under which self-awareness occurs and its effects. Carver and Scheier (1981) designed a control theory of behavior based on processes of directing attention and of self-regulation. We should also mention the more recent motive modification programs based on achievement motivation research (Krug & Hanel, 1976). Self-centered cognitions, which incidentally also include awareness of emotions (affects) relevant to self-esteem, are apparently aroused by conflicts, action outcomes contrary to expectancies (especially failures), and evaluation by others.

In the following pages we restrict ourselves to achievement motivation. First of all, we examine the perspective of trait theory, in which self-concepts are relatively long-lasting personality constructs. Then we take a look at the perspective of actual processes, which explores the conditions under which self-centered cognitions actually occur and their effects. The distinction between these two theories is not sharp, especially when we consider temporary alterations of the self-concept — that is, not only traits, but also states; or when we assume the automatic activation of regulatory mechanisms for the preservation of self-esteem, as with attribution bias in the face of failure.

Self-Concept Variables

In comparison with self-concept research, achievement motivation research has generally formulated self-concept variables in a relatively narrow and precise manner. These variables resemble that which McClelland (1951a) and recently Markus (1977) have described as self-schemata. Like motives, self-concept variables are seen as personality variables in the context of trait theory. They can aid in the further differentiation of motive groups. Some of them have a correlative relationship to a motive variable and to some extent can represent the motive variable with respect to certain behavioral correlates. There are no recent studies that, like Markus (1977), examine the influence of achievement-related self-schemata (e.g., self-concept of ability) on the processing of achievement-related information.

It is not surprising that the self was already considered at an early stage of research in connection with failure. Failure blocks action, contradicts expectancies of success, and attracts critical attention; all of these cause subjects to focus on themselves and to be confronted with their image of their own competence and a possible need for revision. Birney *et al.* (1969) distinguished phenomenologically three kinds of fear of failure and related defense mechanisms: (1) fear of self-devaluation, (2) fear of social devaluation, and (3) fear of non-ego punishments (e.g., material loss). Somewhat later Schmalt (1976a) used the grid technique (LMG) and factor analysis to distinguish between two kinds of failure motive, of which the first FF_1 consists of a self-concept of low ability and thus is closely related to the fear of self-devaluation.

Another variable, introduced early on, involved the distinction between internal and external control (Rotter, 1966): self-imposed responsibility for the outcomes of one's own actions. Feather (1967) introduced this variable C into the risk-taking model as a moderator of the dependence of success and failure incentive on subjective probability of success:

$$Is = C(1 - Ps) \quad \text{and} \quad If = -CPs.$$

The results were not encouraging, presumably because the Rotter questionnaire that was used measures responsibility for oneself quite globally, using situations with various themes. Apparently internal awareness of the consequences of one's own actions is not as generalized a self-concept as the Rotter school has always assumed. The self-responsibility questionnaire by Crandall, Katkovsky, and Crandall (1965b) has turned out to be more appropriate. This questionnaire is limited to successful and unsuccessful performance outcomes. Meyer (1969) was able to clarify goal setting to some

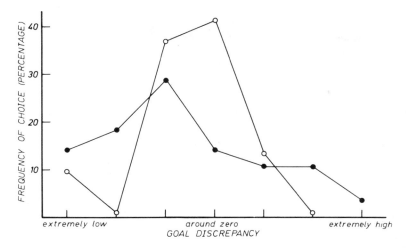

FIGURE 6.1   Preference for various goal-discrepancy ranges by fourth graders with high (O) or low (●) sense of responsibility for their own successes and failures. (Adapted from Meyer, 1969, p. 344.)

extent with two variables: responsibility for one's own success and responsibility for one's own failure.   As Figure 6.1 shows, subjects high in responsibility for themselves chose tasks of moderate difficulty, as did success-motivated subjects.   Krug (1971; see Meyer, 1973a, pp. 57–58) found that the subjects' responsibility for their own success does not allow us to predict realistic goal setting for them any more than does the motive score *NH*.

A personal standard for action outcomes is a special kind of self variable. It represents "demands on oneself that are anchored in self-concepts of varying degrees of generalizability" (Halisch *et al.,* 1976, p. 156).   Standards determine what the persons in question will see as success or failure of their efforts and thereby constitute an important basis for self-regulation of activity.   This point of view is primarily reflected in the concept of the achievement motive as a self-reinforcement system (Halisch *et al.,* 1976; Heckhausen, 1972a).   It was clearly inspired by a model of self-regulation that Kanfer (1971) suggested from the perspective of stimulus-response theory as a basis for therapeutic techniques of behavior modification.   Diggory (1966) demonstrated that generalized standards are far more resistant than are intentions or actual goals to revisions on the basis of performance outcomes contrary to expectancies.   Here Diggory agrees with Kuhl's construct of the personal standard (1978a), which we discussed in Chapter 4.

With the emergence of attribution theory around 1970 responsibility for oneself disappeared again from the standard repertoire of variables and was replaced by assessments of ability attribution and effort attribution.

Self-Concept of Ability

The "self-concept of one's own ability" (or competence; see Meyer, 1973a) replaced the sense of responsibility for oneself as a variable. After all, it was ability attributions that had originally attracted attention, for the two motive groups appeared to differ only on this dimension in explaining success and failure. In comparison with failure-motivated subjects, success-motivated subjects attributed success more to their own high ability, and failure less to their lack of ability. This fact gave rise to three considerations, along with a fourth that consisted of seeing the two motive groups as equipped with different attribution biases and seeing the achievement motive as a self-reinforcement system. We discussed the research that stemmed from this fourth consideration in Chapter 5.

All three considerations were necessary for the postulation of a self-concept of ability and for the research that was based on it. The first of these (Meyer, 1973a, p. 160) was basically not new — indeed, it was obvious. The subjective assessment of one's own ability was thought to determine the level of subjective probability of success in relation to perceived objective difficulty. This had already been mentioned by Atkinson (1964, p. 254), Fuchs (1963, p. 633), and Moulton (1967, in Moulton, 1974). The self-concept of ability, incidentally, would have to determine subjective probability of success if task difficulty were communicated to the subjects as a social comparison norm. In such a case all subjects would have to rank themselves in the achievement hierarchy of the reference group in question, on the basis of their assessment of their own ability (see Meyer & Hallermann, 1977; see Figure 3.1).

One aspect of this first consideration was new: The subjective probability of success would depend on the level of intended effort, as well as on self-concept of ability and perceived task difficulty. Intended effort, in turn, should be maximal at that degree of task difficulty that can just barely be mastered, according to subjects' estimate of their own ability. Effort would be minimal at the degree of difficulty that entirely overtaxes or underutilizes subjects' ability.

Independently of each other, Kukla (1972a, 1978) and Meyer (1973a, b, 1976) developed similar models: one describing effort calculation (Meyer, see below) and one describing rational expectancy-utility calculation (Kukla). Intended exertion of effort suggested itself in this context to both researchers as a dependent variable to be placed alongside of familiar variables in achievement motivation research, such as task choice, persistence, and performance.

The models of effort calculation (or intended effort) suggest the following: Subjects do not intent to exert more effort than seems necessary for the level of task difficulty in question. Beyond an upper level of difficulty after which even maximal effort seems unlikely to produce any benefit, the strength of intended effort drops (according to Kukla, the drop is abrupt). The higher one's own ability is believed to be, the lower is the subjective difficulty of a task. Thus, when the objective level of difficulty is the same for all involved, individuals who consider themselves more competent intend to exert less effort than those who consider themselves less competent. However, there is an upper region of objective difficulty that begins where those who consider themselves less competent regard even maximal effort as useless. In this region those who consider themselves more competent continue to increase their effort until they too have reached their upper level of difficulty. Thus it is only in this upper region of difficulty that those who consider themselves more competent intend to exert more effort than those who consider themselves less competent.

These plausible hypotheses about intended effort, already developed by Heider (1958, p. 11), have been confirmed in a series of studies (Meyer, 1973b, 1976; Meyer & Hallermann, 1974, 1977). However, one of Kukla's hypotheses was not confirmed: that of an abrupt decline in intended effort when task difficulty is too high. Both models of calculation of effort for success-motivated persons come to the same conclusion as the risk-taking model. Thus it is failure-motivated persons who provide the decisive test case for the usefulness of these two models and their superiority over the risk-taking model. However, neither of the two authors has yet attempted a demonstration of the superiority of their models over the risk-taking model, apparently for reasons related to the second of these three considerations about self-concept of ability.

The asymmetry of the attribution to ability following success and failure by the two motive groups suggested a second consideration — both to Kukla (1972a, 1972b, 1978) and to Meyer (1973a). The consideration is the assumption that success-motivated persons perceive themselves as being more able than do failure-motivated persons. It remains open whether the motive-related differences in self-concept of ability correspond to actual differences in ability. Both authors were so convinced by this assumption that they (apparently for this reason) neglected to test the assumption directly — that is, to test success- and failure-motivated persons for a difference in self-concept of ability.

Kukla did examine two aspects of self-concept of ability. In a digit-guessing task depending on chance, subjects who were highly motivated, as assessed by the Mehrabian questionnaire, considered themselves somewhat more able than did subjects with low motivation (Kukla, 1972b, p. 168). In a replication study, however, Touhey and Villemez (1975) found no difference between the two motive groups. In addition, Kukla (1977) found that highly motivated subjects (Mehrabian questonnaire) had a higher self-perception of ability to perform unspecified "intellectual" and "artistic" tasks than did subjects with low motivation. These findings correspond to the frequent observation that success-motivated subjects have more optimistic expectancies of success than failure-motivated subjects before beginning a new task. However, the difference disappears as soon as task processing begins (Atkinson *et al.,* 1960; Feather, 1965; McClelland *et al.,* 1953; Pottharst, 1955). Accordingly, we can assume a difference between the two motive groups in a very generalized and global assessment of ability. It has not yet been possible to demonstrate any effect of this difference on behavior. On the other hand, when subjects assessed their ability to perform concrete tasks, it was no longer possible to find any difference between the two motive groups. The issue is, however, still unsettled. Studies have failed to take into account subject pool characteristics of the samples drawn (see Cooper, 1983). Needless to say, within the two motive groups differences in self-perception of one's ability do affect behavior (see below).

Studies by Meyer (1973b, 1976; Meyer & Hallermann, 1974, 1977; Meyer *et al.,* 1976, Experiments III and IV) did not differentiate among his subjects with respect to achievement motive, but only in regard to self-concept of ability. Meyer's findings in these studies offer no explanatory advantages over the risk-taking model. If assessments of ability and task difficulty are transformed into subjective probabilities of success, then on the average, moderate probabilities of success have more effect on motivation than lower or higher probabilities of success.

In a study of task choice for the purpose of performance feedback (Meyer, 1976, p. 125; Experiment III in Meyer *et al.,* 1976) it was precisely the group with the lowest estimate of their own ability to perform the task in question (pistol shooting) that showed the strongest preference for moderate probability of success. If this group had consisted of failure-motivated subjects, we could have expected the reverse. Since motive data were also available for this study, Heckhausen (1975c) reanalyzed the findings. He found no correlation between motive and self-concept of ability. Task choice was explainable only by motive differences as described in the risk-taking model, not by differences in self-concept of ability (see Figure 6.2). Accordingly, these and other findings (Butzkamm, 1981, see below; Heckhausen, 1975b, 1975c; Jopt & Ermshaus, 1977) suggest that the achievement motive and self-concept of ability are not two sides of the same coin, but are independent of each other and must be considered separately.

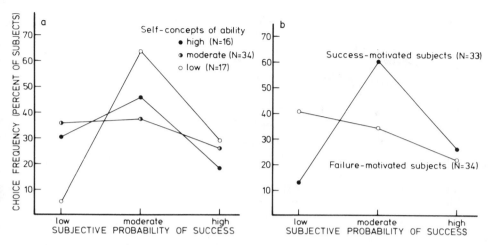

FIGURE 6.2 Choice frequencies (percentage of subjects) for success feedback on a task of low, moderate, or high subjective probability of success as a function (a) of differences in self-concepts of ability to perform the tasks, and (b) of the achievement motive score (positive *NH* vs. negative *NH*). (From Heckhausen, 1975c, pp. 7–8).

While Meyer investigated differences in self-estimated ability instead of motive differences, Kukla (1972b, 1974) continued exploring motive differences (based on Mehrabian) in his experimental studies. Curiously enough, however, he treated them only as differences in self-estimated ability, describing success-motivated subjects as high achievers and failure-motivated subjects as low achievers. Likewise, in Kukla's results as well, both risk-taking outcomes and performance outcomes can be explained equally well by the risk-taking model.

Touhey and Villemez (1975) replicated Kukla's (1972b) risk-taking study, adding a dimension that Kukla had neglected: distinguishing among subjects not only by motive, but also by self-concept of ability for the task in question. The two motive groups did not differ in their concepts of ability. Independent of their achievement motive, subjects with a self-concept of low ability chose a moderate risk more often than did subjects with a high estimate of their ability. Among success-motivated subjects, those with low estimates of ability chose moderate risks far more frequently than did those with perceived high ability, as long as the task had been presented as dependent not only on ability but also on effort. The same polarization appeared among failure-motivated subjects, given that the task had been presented as dependent only on ability.

Thus we must conclude that, on the whole, replacing the motive parameter with a parameter of self-concept of ability would indeed help clarify the determination of subjective probability of success. However, equating motive differences with differences in self-concept of ability has not been productive (Meyer, 1976). Only the combination of both personality parameters is productive, as shown by the replication by Touhey and Villemez (1975). The two effort-calculation models cannot replace the risk-taking model as an alternative model. Meyer's model has turned out to be inferior to the risk-taking model, if motivation is also taken into account; and if we call upon motive differences instead of assessments of ability, as in Kukla's model, the effort-calculation models are so similar to the risk-taking model that the findings do not permit us to decide among the models.

Meyer's original idea was to reduce motive differences between the two motive groups to a difference between self-concepts of ability, on the basis of the disparity in their ability attributions. This idea was plausible, but not compelling. It could just as well be a matter of motive-related attributional bias that is independent of subjects' estimates of their own ability. From the beginning the assumption was implausible for another reason, as well: In order to covary with a summary personality construct such as motive, the self-concept would have to involve a highly generalized notion of ability. However, that is unlikely, since people generally perceive themselves as varying in ability for various kinds of tasks. There are no correlations worth mentioning between questionnaire scores for a general self-concept of ability and self-estimated abilities for various kinds of tasks (Meyer, 1972; Starke, 1975). Meyer abandoned the assumption of a self-concept of generalized ability in favor of "task-specific ability perceptions" (1976, p. 133). That assumption does the most justice to the present state of research. We have already pointed out that motive-related differences in globally estimated ability (Kukla, 1977) have not been shown to have any motivational effect on the processing of any concrete task.

Jopt and Ermshaus (1977) found that failure-motivated students in non-college-preparatory junior high schools assessed their ability for a manual task (putting pins in a board) higher than for an intellectual task (digit–symbol test), after they had had some practice in both types of task in an individual experiment. Success-motivated students ranked themselves in the middle of this range of ability for both kinds of tasks. In addition, there is no close connection between perceived and actual ability (i.e., proven performance competence) (Arsenian, 1942; Hallermann, 1975; Starke, 1975; Wylie, 1968). Those relationships that were found were closer in the case of assessments of ability for a specific school subject than in the case of general self-concepts of ability, as Brookover, Thomas, and Paterson (1966) found with over a thousand seventh graders.

The third notion about self-concept of ability is that its very estimation is the actual motive goal. Meyer (1973a), like Weiner and Kukla (1970), saw achievement-oriented behavior as motivated by the desire to obtain new information about one's own ability. This contrasts with the "hedonistic" risk-taking model, in which the affective consequences of success and failure act as motivating incentives. In the attributional elaboration of the risk-taking model moderate probabilities of success have the greatest informational value. At that level success and failure can be attributed most easily to internal causal factors; thus, they have the greatest effect on motivation here. Since Meyer postulates the same desire for information for both motive groups, his predictions differ from those of the risk-taking model only for failure-motivated subjects. He is unable to account for evidence that failure-motivated subjects do not have maximal motivation for seeking success in the moderate range of probability of success (for goal setting alone, see Heckhausen, 1977a). On the other hand, the postulated motivating function can unfortunately be explained cognitively (as maximizing information) just as well as hedonistically (as maximizing a positive affective balance). Thus it seems futile to seek a decision in this fashion (but see Cooper, 1983; and below, "Diagnosticity").

The significance of the self-concept of ability to perform a specific task for various motivational parameters has been documented most thoroughly of all by Butzkamm (1981; Butzkamm, Halisch, & Posse, 1978). The task involved complex reactions. After the subjects had reached a plateau in the exercises they assessed their ability by both individual and social reference norms. The two assessments of ability correlated only weakly ($r = .32$), as Heckhausen (1975b) had already discovered. After a series of unexpected successes or failures, the self-concept proved to be more stable with a social reference norm ($r = .89$) than with an individual reference norm ($r = .56$). The two motive groups did not differ in their assessment of ability. Each had an equally wide variation in perceived ability. Moreover, the concept of ability was not rigid. In the subsequent series of unexpected successes or failures, subjects' estimation of their own ability both rose and fell.

And what is more, self-concept of task-specific ability turned out, partly in connection with motive, to be a decisive moderating variable of self-reinforcement and its two determinants, goal setting and causal attribution. That had been predicted, since attribution of ability had turned out to have the greatest impact on affect in self-evaluation following unexpected success and failure (see Chapter 5; Heckhausen, 1978a). Within each motive group the subjects with a high concept of ability (on the basis of individual as well as social reference norms) evaluated themselves more positively after success and less negatively after failure than did subjects with a low concept of ability. In addition, success-motivated subjects evaluated themselves more positively in every way after success than did failure-motivated subjects. Following failure the less favorable self-evaluation of failure-motivated sub-

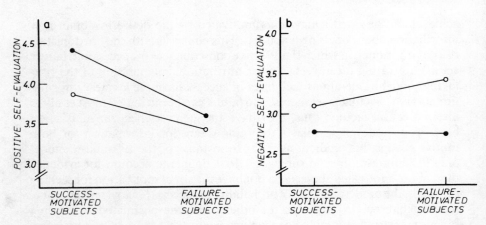

FIGURE 6.3   Strength of positive and negative self-reinforcement by success- and failure-motivated subjects following success (a) or failure (b) as dependent on high (●), or low (○) self-concept of task-specific ability.   (Adapted from Butzkamm, 1981.)

jects appeared only among those who also had a low self-concept.   Figure 6.3 shows the range in self-reinforcement scores for the two motive groups as a function of whether their concept of ability (measured by a social reference norm) was high or low.

The influence of the ability concept on self-evaluation becomes even clearer when we factor out statistically the overlay of goal-setting effects. The goal-attainment discrepancies alone determine about 50–60% of the self-evaluation variance.   Figure 6.4 shows this through a contrast within the group of failure-motivated subjects for the series of failures.   The subjects with a self-concept of low task-specific ability became increasingly dissatisfied with themselves — more than did subjects having a self-concept of high ability — as the series of failures, which were contrary to expectancies, continued.

One final point deserves more attention than it has received so far: that is, how naive an understanding of the concept of ability most persons have. For example, ability can be understood "statically" as an inalterable disposition, or "dynamically" as the cumulative result of learning.   It is a matter of "metaattributions" of a concept; these metaattributions are by no means limited to mere differences of opinion, but also influence the behavior of the person making the attribution.   Jopt and Sprute (1978) derived behavioral consequences for each hypothetical metaattribution and suggested an initial way of confirming them.   For example, the difficulty of the subject mathematics is considered lower by those schoolchildren in a high-level course who have a static instead of a dynamic concept of ability.   Likewise, the "static"

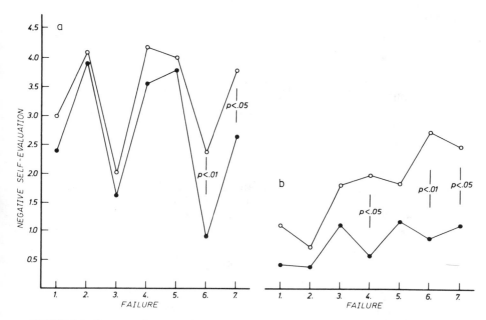

FIGURE 6.4   Strength of the negative self-evaluation of failure-motivated subjects with high (●), and low (○) self-concept of task-specific ability (social reference norm) for the series of failures, when goal-setting effects are not factored out (a) and when they are factored out (b). (Adapted from Butzkamm, 1981.)

participants in a low-level course consider mathematics to be harder than the "dynamic" participants in the same course.

Factors Influencing the Formation of Self-Concepts of Ability

As we have seen, self-concepts of ability (competence) are specific to a task area and capable of change.   The change is especially likely to occur in task areas in which subjects have not yet had many opportunities to experience how able they actually are.   Here a number of factors are influential.   In the case of an individual reference norm with repeated task performance, both the relative frequency of successes and failures and the order in which they occur are important (see Jones *et al.,* 1968).   Classroom behavior by the teacher that is guided by the progress of the individual child rather than by a social comparison of performance ("individual" instead of "social" reference norm — see below) encourages the positive development of a self-concept of ability in the children (Krug, Peters, & Quinkert, 1977; see also

Meichenbaum, 1972; and the end of this chapter). When the reference norm is social, the self-concept depends on the comparison of one's own performance outcomes with those of other persons (see Festinger, 1954; Kelley, 1973). Reference group effects are particularly influential. These effects are created, for example, by the extent of performance heterogeneity in the grouping of pupils, or by transfer to another kind of school (see Rheinberg & Enstrup, 1977). We discuss this in more detail at the end of the chapter. Naturally, direct estimation of ability by others such as teachers and parents is influential.

Such estimation by others does not even need to be communicated directly. Instead, it can be gradually recognized by the person being evaluated, through praise and criticism (and this probably happens more often than direct assessment). Although this seems paradoxical, praise signals a low estimate of ability and criticism signals a high estimate. The more often the successful completion of easier tasks is praised, the more the persons being praised have reason to assume that their ability is considered low by the person making the estimation; and the more often the failure to successfully complete relatively difficult tasks is criticized, the more likely it is that the persons being criticized will conclude that their ability is considered to be high. Meyer (1978, 1982; Meyer et al., 1979; Meyer & Plöger, 1979) demonstrated this in a series of studies. Two premises lie at the basis of these conclusions that are made by most persons about evaluation by others, and after the first 10 or 12 years of life everyone seems to share these premises (see Heckhausen, 1978c). The first premise is that when outsiders are evaluating performance, differences in effort exerted count more than differences in ability (Rest et al., 1973; Weiner & Kukla, 1970). The second premise has to do with attribution theory: In performing a task, increased effort can compensate for low ability within certain limits, and low effort can be compensated for by higher ability.

Conclusions about an evaluator's estimate of one's ability are especially likely to be made when the evaluator reacts differently to the same performance outcomes—that is, when the teacher praises or criticizes only one of two students. Naturally the praised or criticized persons need not internalize the perception that someone has assessed their ability as low or high. However, they are more likely to do so, the more valid the evaluator's competence to evaluate seems to them and the less valid their own competence to evaluate seems to them. Meyer and Plöger (1979; Meyer et al., 1979) examined the effect of perceived competence to evaluate by comparing a teacher who was familiar with the schoolchildren's performance with a teacher who was teaching the class for the first time and was not familiar with their performance. The subjects were asked to imagine that they were schoolchildren who were being either praised or criticized for moderate

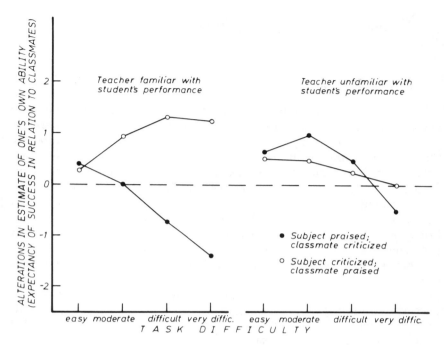

FIGURE 6.5   Alteration in the estimate of one's own ability for tasks of varying difficulty after praise or criticism of one's own performance of an easy task — in contrast to a classmate whose performance was similar — by a teacher who was or was not familiar with one's own performance. (Adapted from Meyer & Plöger, 1979, p. 231.)

success at an easy task in comparison with a fellow classmate whose performance was similar. As an indicator of alteration in estimation of their own ability, subjects were then asked to indicate their expectancy of success (in relation to that of a fellow classmate) for performing tasks at various levels of difficulty and to indicate how much the teacher seemed to like them and their fellow classmate.

As we can see from Figure 6.5, praise for performing an easy task led to a distinct drop in expectancies of success at more difficult tasks — that is, to a drop in subjects' estimates of their own ability — but only when the teacher giving the praise was the one more competent to evaluate ("familiar with students' work"). Correspondingly, criticism led to an increase in self-concept of ability. In contrast, praise and criticism by a teacher less competent to evaluate ("unfamiliar with students' work") was perceived as evidence of the teacher's like or dislike for them. It seems that the described alterations of self-concept on the basis of perceived evaluation of one's own ability by another person influence the choice of level of difficulty and the intensity and persistence at task performance.

Self-Centered Cognitions

Motivation research has tended increasingly since the early 1970s to view cognitions as intervening processes. This assumption enables us to explain many findings more simply, more "naturally," or at least more smoothly than does the stimulus-response approach, which banned cognitions from behavior analysis, calling them subjective secondary phenomena (see Heckhausen, 1973; Heckhausen & Weiner, 1972). The most prominent example is in attribution research, which — to overstate a bit — presents human beings as constantly involved in trying to explain the causes of phenomena. For a long time attribution researchers did not even explore whether such processes actually — that is, spontaneously — existed. Not until the 1980s did they begin to demonstrate the factual existence of attribution processes (see Wong & Weiner, 1981; Chapter 5). Instead, as a rule, the presumed processes have always been explored after the fact, so that we must join Nisbett and Wilson (1977) in asking to what extent mere everyday plausibilities about the matter in question have been offered instead of introspective data on actual observed events (see Chapter 5).

In contrast, the findings of Meyer and Plöger (1979; Meyer *et al.,* 1979), for example, represent methodological progress in relation to cognitions obtained directly, after an experiment. To be sure, Meyer and Plöger did not measure the subjects' deductive processes (two premises and a conclusion) directly. However, they did narrowly circumscribe the antecedent conditions and measured the predicted effect indirectly through behavioral consequences. To this extent these findings could also have been classified as self-centered cognitions.

Disregarding motive modification programs, there have been only a few sporadic attempts to produce self-centered cognitions or explore the different sorts of self-centered cognitions, as opposed to merely assuming that they were present. In this regard applied research has achieved more up to now than theoretical research. In some modification programs, such as those of Krug and Hanel (1976), self-centered cognitions about goal setting, causal attribution, and self-evaluation are practiced explicitly during task performance, even to the point of "internal speech" (see Chapter 5; as well as Heckhausen & Krug, 1982).

In an older laboratory study (Reiss, 1968) self-centered cognitions were deliberately induced. Unfortunately, no other researchers have yet followed up on this study. Reiss (1968; see Heckhausen, 1968a, pp. 140–144), used the technique of directed daydreams to place success- and failure-motivated subjects in one of three feeling states: a feeling of success (brilliant lecture to an auditorium full of people), a feeling of failure (embarrassing failure during a lecture), and an idyllic mood (strolling through a spring meadow and picking flowers). A content analysis of the induced dream-fantasies for hope of success and fear of failure showed a completely success-ful induction of each of the feeling states, regardless of motive group. The feeling induction was imbedded in a Zeigarnik experiment, after task per-formance and before reproduction of the tasks that had been performed. Subjects with an induced feeling of success showed a clear Zeigarnik effect: Far more incomplete than completed tasks were recalled. Subjects with an induced feeling of failure remembered the completed tasks somewhat bet-ter. The results for the idyllic mood lay between these extremes. Two conclusions can be drawn from these findings. First, the Zeigarnik effect does not take place during acquisition of information, but instead, not until the later phases of information storage or recall. And second, during these later phases current self-centered cognitions such as feelings of success and failure are the determining factors, rather than latent motive dispositions.

Achievement motivation researchers have tended to treat emotions as a stepchild and to take into account only pride and shame as motivating incentives, as Atkinson suggested. Weiner *et al.* (1978) were the first to go beyond this stage by attempting to identify the individual kinds of affect that are aroused by various kinds of successes and failures. Their results were already described in Chapter 5.

Basing his work on the extended model of motivation (see Chapter 7), Heckhausen (1982a) classified self-centered cognitions that occur during task performance, most of which contribute nothing to task solution. For example, these cognitions revolve around such matters as possible causes of possible action outcomes, the incentive value of the possible consequences of action outcomes, the current performance level, action-outcome expectan-cies, or the subject's own affective condition. To the extent that these cognitions are dominated by failure-related contents, we can speak of self-doubt cognitions. University students indicated anonymously immedi-ately after completing an oral exam how often contents from individual cognition categories had occurred to them during the exam. They estimated how disruptive the individual kinds of cognition had been for them. More-over, the subjects' achievement-motivational state (see Chapter 7) was de-termined from a questionnaire, in order to divide them into two groups: those with a hope-of-success motivational state during the exam, and those with a fear-of-failure motivational state during the exam. The question-naire items were based on the categories of the TAT scoring key for *HS* and *FF*, made concrete for an exam situation (as in Spielberger's procedure [1966] for measuring state anxiety).

During the exam self-centered cognitions that did not at all serve to improve task performance occurred in surprising variety and frequency. With most, but not all kinds of cognitions, disturbing influence increased along with frequency, particularly when cognition contents were failure oriented and centered around self-doubts. Their frequency and disturbing influence were subject to considerable individual differences, depending on motivational state. The self-centered cognitions were more frequent and more disturbing to those fearing failure than to those hoping for success (see Figure 6.6). The following cognitions were especially disturbing: causal analyses (their own lack of ability and preparation for the exam), expectancies of failure, anticipated incentive value of possible consequences, and awareness of nervous tension. But independent of their frequency, self-doubt cognitions had a more disturbing effect on subjects in the motivational state of fear of failure than on those who expected success. In the latter state mild self-doubts even improved performance.

The findings confirmed Wine's (1971, 1982) hypothesis of the role of attentiveness in test anxiety. In this theory it is not an overactivated state that leads to a drop in achievement by persons with test anxiety; rather, it is the excessive attention required by self-centered cognitions that distracts these persons from actual task performance. On the basis of the available findings, Wine's attention hypothesis can be delimited and differentiated as to different kinds of cognitions.

As expected, the exam grades did not correlate with the affective factors of the motivational state, such as nervousness, but rather with the cognitive factors (experience of incompetence, negative self-evaluation, and expectancy of failure). This corresponds to a two-component theory of test anxiety by Morris and Liebert (1970). Table 6.1 contains the individual correlation coefficients for cognitive and affective factors in Heckhausen's

TABLE 6.1
Correlation of Poor Exam Grades with Cognitive and Affective Factors of the Motivation State[a]

Cognitive factors			Affective factors		
Experiencing incompetency	Negative self-evaluation	Failure expectancy	Nervousness	Feeling overtaxed	Lack of reaction contro
.41**	.37**	.33**	.23ns	.16ns	.13ns
	.48**			.25*	

[a] $N = 65$. (Adapted from Heckhausen, 1982a, "Task-irrelevant cognitions during an exam: Incidence and effects," in H. W. Krohne & L. Laux (Eds.), *Achievement, Stress, and Anxiety,* p. 268, with permission of Hemisphere Publishing Corp.)
* $p < .05$; ** $p < .01$.

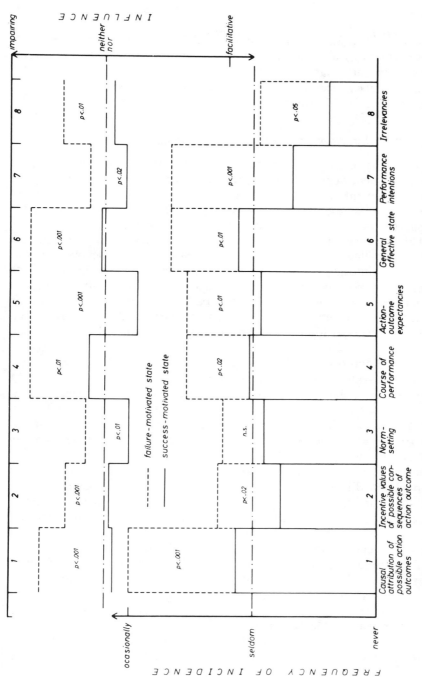

FIGURE 6.6 Frequency of incidence (below) and influence (above) of various kinds of cognitions during an oral test, for two groups of students (those hoping for success and those fearing failure). (Adapted from Heckhausen, 1982, "Task-irrelevant cognitions during an exam: Incidence and effects," in H. W. Krohne & L. Laux (Eds.), *Achievement, Stress, and Anxiety,* p. 261, with permission of Hemisphere Publishing Corp.)

experiment (1982a). Relationships were discovered in this experiment between emotions and various kinds of cognitions involved in analyzing causes. In particular, considerations of one's own ability were correlated with motivating incentive emotions that anticipate the consequences of the test outcome for self-evaluation and evaluation by others.

Search for Information or for Affective Satisfaction?

According to the first theorists of achievement-motivated behavior, the central behavior-controlling functions in achievement-related activity are (1) achievement affects — that is, pride and joy following success, and annoyance and shame after failure — and (2) the anticipatory emotions related to success and failure, hope and fear (Chapters 2 and 3).

This affective approach to explaining achievement-motivated behavior has been called into question in recent years by two concepts that were introduced into achievement motivation research from other fields. In both approaches, persons in achievement-related situations seek information about their own ability. The first approach links information acquisition with causal explanation for action outcomes; the second approach connects information acquisition to the experience of uncertainty about action outcomes.

The first approach is a reformulation, based on attribution theory, of the expectancy-value model of achievement-motivated behavior (Chapter 5). This approach presents persons in achievement situations as wanting to get to know more about their ability to achieve, instead of seeking affects or attempting to avoid them (Meyer, 1973a; Weiner & Kukla, 1970; Weiner et al., 1971). Moderate task difficulty is preferred, because here the outcomes can be attributed primarily to internal factors. Trope (1975) and Trope and Brickman (1975) have demonstrated that under normal circumstances tasks of moderate difficulty are also those tasks with the highest diagnostic value for the estimation of one's own ability. However, both informational aspects of tasks can be separated. According to Trope (1975) the diagnostic value seems to be more important as a causal factor for choice behavior than norm-referenced difficulty of tasks (pp. 479–485).

The second approach is a purely informational approach (see the findings presented in Chapter 3 on the correlation between subjective uncertainty and risk preference). It suggests an assumption first proposed by Berlyne (1960), according to which subjects prefer tasks for which their subjective uncertainty about the outcome is maximal. The action outcome reduces maximal uncertainty and, according to information theory, thus provides maximal information on achievement ability (Schneider, 1971, 1973, 1974; summarized by Schneider & Heckhausen, 1981).

*The Attributional Approach and Its Incomplete
Specification*

What is provided, then, by these cognitive interpretations of the incentives for achievement-related behavior? Initially the only support for attribution theory's explanation of task choice and goal setting was a study by Weiner *et al.* (1972) that is of doubtful relevance to achievement-oriented behavior. In this study subjects were asked to indicate which causal factor was most significant when evaluating others at norm-referenced tasks of intermediate difficulty; they ranked effort, one of the two internal causal factors, as most significant. However, it is doubtful whether such a social comparison paradigm covers the most relevant aspects of achievement-oriented situations in real life. In contrast to the scenario given by Weiner *et al.* (1972), the following factors would seem to be fundamentally relevant for achievement-motivated behavior: (1) the perspective of self-evaluation, not of evaluation by others; (2) an evaluation of task difficulty on the basis of individual (and not social) reference norms. This is particularly true for the achievement-oriented behavior of children in preschool years (see Heckhausen, 1982b). In addition, only individual reference norms make it certain that it is primarily achievement motivation that is being aroused rather than socially directed motivation, such as a motivation to seek approval. As a matter of fact, causal attribution for success and failure are quite different in situations where no social norms are provided: When subjects were asked to evaluate their own performance outcomes on the basis of individual reference norms they made no clear distinctions among various levels of task difficulty with regard to the significance of the internal factors effort and ability, especially the latter (Krug, 1971; Schneider and Posse, 1978a, 1978b, 1978c). Only with respect to perceived task easiness and difficulty as perceived causes for success and failure did subjects distinguish clearly among various levels of task difficulty.

In Weiner's reformulation of achievement motivation theory from the perspective of attribution theory, subjects in the middle range of difficulty would be expected to attribute success and failure more clearly to internal causal factors. Apparently they do this only when they are provided with social norms for task performance. Weiner did not take into account sufficiently Kelley's attribution model with its three covariation dimensions for inferring a situation-based versus person-based causation of an event (Kelley, 1967; see Chapter 5). In the experiments by Schneider and Posse, and by Krug, subjects working alone performed tasks that were new to them. This gave them the following information on Kelley's three dimensions: (1) distinctiveness (various levels of difficulty of the same task), (2) consistency (sequences of success and failure in different but stable degrees at each level of difficulty) but (3) no consensus information, since they learned nothing about the performance of other subjects. In Kelley's model (see Table 5.4) this would be an information pattern in which effects are attributed primarily to situational entities (here, task difficulty).

In contrast, a different experimental information pattern that is generally used to support attribution theory's version of achievement motivation theory offers (1) frequently no information about distinctiveness (only one level of task difficulty), (2) generally consistency information, and almost always (3) information about lack of consensus (indications that other persons have performed better or less well). With such an information pattern, according to Kelley, subjects could be expected to attribute the effects that have to be explained primarily to internal factors.

Weiner does not make this distinction. Apparently, however, Weiner's approach can only be applied to situations in which information about lack of consensus (social reference norms) is available. Not all, and probably not even the most important achievement-oriented situations, provide such information. The need to test the range of application of the attribution theory approach to achievement motivation systematically and experimentally has not yet been recognized and seems to be urgent. Until that is accomplished, it is not appropriate to claim that the attributional version of the achievement motivation theory explains all existing findings better than did the earlier theoretical approaches.

The Informational Approach

Schneider and his associates (Schneider, 1971, 1973, 1974; Schneider & Posse, 1978a, 1978b, 1978c) assume that individuals search for competence information in achievement situations. However, these authors distinguish between this ultimate goal for exploring different task difficulty levels and the immediate reason for choice behavior. Following Berlyne (1960), they assume that actual behavior is controlled by states of subjective uncertainty. In achievement situations individuals prefer tasks with an outcome that is maximally uncertain. According to information theory (Attneave, 1959), each outcome reduces a maximum amount of uncertainty, and thus provides a maximum of competence information (in summary, Schneider & Heckhausen, 1981).

Subjective uncertainty was assessed in these studies (1) directly by measuring decision time while predicting a success or a failure at different difficulty levels and by asking for subjects' confidence in this prediction, using a 20-point bipolar rating scale, and (2) from subjects' judgments of success probability, transformed into information theory's measure "H." These H-scores are for all practical purposes identical with the expectancy-value products (expected success and failure incentives) based on probability judgments in Atkinson's risk-taking model. Thus the only way to demonstrate that the concept of subjective uncertainty has greater explanatory value is to show that predictions of risk preference are more accurate when derived from direct measures of subjective uncertainty, decision time, and confidence, as compared to expected success incentive. In 11 of 12 studies, group preference for levels of difficulty of a given task was predicted more successfully from average decision time than from the expected incentive of success. However, it was not possible to demonstrate in these studies that the concept of subjective uncertainty does a better job of explaining individual risk-taking behavior. The percentage of individual preferred task difficulty levels that could be predicted, beyond chance, on the basis of scores of subjective uncertainty, was not significantly higher than the proportion predictable from Atkinson's original model (Schneider, 1974; Schneider & Posse, 1978a, 1978b, 1978c; summarized in Schneider & Heckhausen, 1981).

Moreover, the predicting of individuals' preferred series of levels of difficulty from scaled competence information, obtained from task performance at individual levels of difficulty, was relatively unsuccessful. Prediction was better with the original model, or with subjective uncertainty scores (Schneider & Posse, 1978a). This may not be surprising, since competence information was assumed to be the ultimate goal of achievement-oriented choice behavior. Only for part of the subjects did the evaluated competence information show the expected reverse U-shaped correlation with subjective, individually defined probability of success. For these subjects, results involving tasks with the greatest degree of subjective uncertainty also provided maximum competence information. For another part of the subjects the evaluated competence information rose monotonically with increasing difficulty (Schneider & Posse, 1978a). The latter group of subjects apparently did not base their judgment of competence information on the experience of subjective uncertainty, but rather on the experience of difficulty in achieving success. Information theory assumes that the informational value of an event is inversely proportional to the probability of that event (Shannon & Weaver, 1949). In addition, naive psychology supports this assumption. In many tasks success at the more difficult stages necessarily also means success at all easier stages as well, without there having been any qualitative change in the structure or requirements of the task. With such tasks, the higher the level of difficulty, the more information a success gives about a person's ability to perform the task (Schneider, 1973). This is a plausible conclusion, and may be the reasoning of some of the subjects, as scaling of competence information for some of the subjects indicates.

Competence information is therefore not a simple subjective quantity capable of being measured consistently. Correspondingly, the consistency coefficients determined through analysis of variance are lower than those of subjective probabilities of success and also lower than those of anticipated performance affects such as Atkinson described (Schneider & Heckhausen, 1981; Schneider & Posse, 1978a). When subjects are provided with social norms of achievement their average rating of competence information shows the assumed inverted U relation with norm-referenced difficulty (Cooper, 1983; Meyer *et al.,* 1976). In the study by Meyer *et al.* the averaged information rating peaked at a difficulty level of 40%. Yet in a hypothetical choice situation subjects preferred tasks with a norm-defined difficulty of 50%. Thus maximal competence information does not coincide with the preferred difficulty level. However, as the authors did not report the internal consistency of their ratings, the peak of rated information at a difficulty level below 50% might be an artifact, caused by averaging scores from groups with inverted U relationships together with scores from groups with linear relationships. The relationship which we refer to here is, of course, that between rated information and difficulty found by Schneider and Posse (1978c).

In Cooper's study maximal competence information was judged at a norm-referenced difficulty of 50%. Here subjects with high and intermediate resultant achievement motive scores (MARPS) evaluated the information value of the difficult task ($Ps = .10$) appreciably higher than the information value of an easy task ($Ps = .90$). Subjects low in achievement tendency evidenced no differences in ratings. In this study the evaluation of information from the difficult task correlated with the preference for the most difficult task.

General metapsychological considerations might lead us to assume that the ultimate goals of achievement-oriented activity are not the realization of affects, but rather the obtaining of competence information or its avoidance, since living creatures need information for orientation in the world as much as they need food (see Lorenz, 1969). Yet even so, anticipated competence information might not in itself control behavior. Achievement-related behavior may be guided by factors that are connected with anticipated competence information, such as subjective uncertainty; and also by anticipated affects, such as those that Atkinson had in mind.

Diagnosticity

Trope (1975) and Trope and Brickman (1975) argued that the information value for the self-assessment of ability at a given difficulty level can be separated from its norm-referenced difficulty. The diagnostic value is assumed to increase with its power to discriminate between persons high and low in a relevant ability.   For subjects with intermediate ability this is normally the case at a normative difficulty of 50%.   However, although performance feedback at such an intermediate difficulty level reduces maximal uncertainty about outcomes, it might not reduce maximal uncertainty about the relevant ability (Trope, 1975).

In order to distinguish between these two kinds of uncertainty and related competence information, the subjects in these studies were provided with the following pieces of information: (1) norm-referenced difficulty information and (2) the conditioned probabilities that persons low and high in the relevant ability will succeed at each task difficulty level.   For instance, even a normatively easy task might have a high or low diagnostic value.   In the first case the percentages of subjects low and high in ability succeeding at this task were given as 90.17% and 49.83%, in the latter case as 73.44% and 66.56% (Trope, 1975; Trope & Brickman, 1975).

Given such manipulated information about the diagnosticity of a task, subjects did indeed tend to choose tasks with high diagnosticity, rather than tasks of moderate difficulty as defined by the norm.   Trope predicted and found, in addition, that the magnitude of the preference for tasks of high diagnosticity increased with success-oriented achievement motive (MARPS).

In both studies there was a preference for easy tasks over difficult tasks. This effect contrasts with the results of all other risk-taking studies in achievement situations in which a preference for difficult over easy tasks had usually been observed (see Chapter 3).   Probably the hypothetical character of risk taking in the diagnosticity studies is not comparable to risk taking in real situations as, for instance, in studies by Atkinson and Litwin (1960), deCharms and Davé (1965), and Schneider (1973) — to mention only a few.

Apparently, under the highly restricted information given to the subjects in these and subsequent studies the importance of the so-defined diagnosticity was demonstrated successfully (Buckert, Meyer, & Schmalt, 1979; Trope, 1979, 1980; Unger, 1980; Zuckerman, Brown, Fischler, Fox, Lathin, & Minasian, 1979).   Therefore, diagnosticity information, when it is provided in the way described in these studies, does in fact influence task selection.   The question remains, however, does the notion of diagnosticity have any salience for subjects, or does it even make any sense outside the social psychologist's laboratory (see critique by Sohn, 1984).   Normally, people make their own inferences about tasks, particularly in school and other settings, where they observe peers trying the same tasks and succeeding or failing.   One would like to know whether individuals are able to assess the diagnostic value of tasks under everyday conditions containing minimal information.   As this has not been demonstrated so far, the external value of diagnosticity for achievement-oriented choice behavior appears to be insignificant. Finally, diagnosticity can hardly play an important role in a person's achievement-related behavior if that person performs the task in isolation, without knowledge about the performance of others. After all, the diagnosticity of a task, as defined by Trope and Brickman, is tied to information about other persons' performance of the task. Many studies indicate that in situations where no norms are provided subjects tend to choose moderate levels of difficulty (for a summary see Schneider, 1976). In this case task difficulty is defined only by one's own experience and the objective task characteristics. Such norms without social comparison for the task difficulty are, incidentally, the only decisive ones for preschoolers (Veroff, 1969; see below, next section). Here, diagnosticity would be an inapplicable predictor of task choice.

Considering all available results, we must conclude that it is difficult to decide whether the incentive value of achievement-motivated behavior consists of expected achievement-related information or expected achievement-related affects. Of course, this need not be an either-or question. It may depend on situational cues indicating to what extent an achievement-related action is motivated more by a desire for gain of self-diagnostic information or by the anticipation of self-evaluative emotions. Cooper (1983) has tried to answer this question by examining whether the resultant valence data (Atkinson, 1957) or the diagnosticity data (Trope, 1975) are better predicted by the initial task choice. The results favored diagnosticity positions. However, strong caution is in order for two reasons. First, the author himself points to the fact that the instructions given prior to task choice stressed that it might be self-diagnostic of one's ability. Second, the resultant valence data appear to be unfairly assessed, since subjective probability of success was induced by norm-referenced instructions (so that the individual subjects' estimates were in different parts of the probability range).

Very probably the question of a hedonistic versus cognitive motivation base is heuristically unproductive, since it cannot be answered. Psychological methods — analysis of behavior and experience — do not enable us to discover the ultimate goals of animal and human behavior. Information about this can come only from biological (phylogenetic) and sociological analysis.

As far as phylogenetic analysis is concerned, it is certainly true that there is no achievement-motivated behavior in the sense of attempting to meet performance standards among nonhuman primates. However, we can assume that there are preliminary versions of such behavior. One is the behavioral system "curiosity behavior," in which even infrahuman beings aim at discovering their own behavioral possibilities through "self-exploration" (Lorenz, 1969). The other is the behavioral system "social dominance" (Weisfeld & Beresford, 1982). The authors point out the parallels between the expansive erect movements of dominant animals among their own species (especially among anthropoids) and human expression of pride in success, which is also primarily characterized by erect position. They have also demonstrated experimentally that intraindividual alterations in the degree of erectedness are direct (and perhaps also unnoticed) reactions to the news of success and failure.

By no means do affects lack functional meaning in achievement-related behavior, any more than they do in human and animal behavior in general. We must assume two ways in which affect has an impact in the area of achievement:

1. A guiding function through arousing a behavior — by means of anticipated affects — and maintaining it by positive affective consequences, or ceasing a behavior if affective consequences are negative;
2. The long-term stabilizing of behavioral dispositions as suggested by learning theory's self-reinforcement paradigm (Halisch, 1976; Heckhausen, 1972a).

Achievement motivation researchers oriented toward attribution theory claim that achievement-related affects are (1) completely different from achievement-related cognitions, and (2) entirely determined by these cognitions (Weiner *et al.,* 1971, 1979). Such distinctions, if thought to hold absolutely, cannot be supported either by descriptive or by experimental analyses (Fuchs, 1963, 1965; Heckhausen, 1955; Zajonc, 1980). Perceived task difficulty is always the decisive variable before a task is performed. It is the basis of the affective interpretation of incentive in Atkinson's sense as well as the basis of the two interpretations we have described in information psychology. After a task has been performed and the outcome is known, there are relationships between causal attributions and emotions (e.g., between attribution to luck and surprise, see Weiner *et al.,* 1979). However, it would be premature to conclude that these are causal relationships. Instead of assuming, for example, that emotions are merely a consequence of causal attributions, we could see both as independent products or parallel information processing that differs in speed and explicitness. Alternatively, emotions could even precede attributions.

Through the feedback we receive about success and failure, performing tasks of varying difficulty allows us to form conclusions about our own performance ability. Simultaneously, achievement-related affects are aroused. Affects also provide us with information about the value content of environmental events (Arnold, 1960). This information may be less differentiated than an elaborate cognitive assessment; however, it can be quite adequate for a first reaction. When people need to act quickly in emergencies, this information should be adequate, and even superior to a cognitive assessment.

Reference Norm for the Evaluation of Achievement

In order to evaluate our own or someone else's performance outcome, we need a standard. Without a standard, we could only describe an action outcome; we would be unable to evaluate it as more or less successful or unsuccessful. Standards belong to the manifold classes of reference systems that are necessary in order for an event to receive its value and importance. Indeed, often the event might not take place without the reference system. Reference systems usually are not visible; rather, they form the inconspicuous background in front of which the event takes place in a particular manner that can change completely if the reference system changes. The same is true of standards. The scalelike quality of standards (level of measurement, polarity, extent of area covered, cutting-off points, etc.) is less interesting than the basis or origin of the standards. Heckhausen (1974a) proposed that standards be called "reference norms" because an outcome is referred to a particular comparison norm for evaluation. Rheinberg (in summary, 1980, 1982, 1983) used Heckhausen's distinction among various kinds of reference norms as the basis of a varied research program to show how motivation is dependent on the reference norm on which performance evaluation is based.

Kinds of Reference Norms

A performance outcome can be referred to earlier performance outcomes by the same person in order to determine whether the outcome has remained the same or is better or worse; that is an "individual" reference norm. The perspective for comparison is the longitudinal examination of individual development over time. A person's performance outcome can also be compared with corresponding performance outcomes of other persons, in order to rank it; that is a "social" reference norm. The perspective for comparison is performance distribution within a social reference group, often in a cross section over time. Performance outcomes can also be measured by criteria that lie in the nature of the task. A solution can be correct or incorrect, and the effect that is sought can be achieved to a greater or lesser degree; here we can speak of an "objective" or "task-inherent" reference norm. The task criterion can also be imposed from outside; we are confronting either a reference norm imposed by others or a "self-imposed" reference norm.

Each kind of reference norm is based on the processing of information about the covariation of success and failure on the three dimensions of Kelley's (1976) covariance model. The individual reference norm is based on consistency information — that is, on sequences of success and failure of an individual at various times with the same task. The objective reference norm uses distinctiveness information about success and failure at various tasks or at various levels of difficulty of the same task (entities).

Individual and objective reference norms (consistency and distinctiveness information) are easily integrated with each other. This was shown by Brackhane's experiments (1976; second study by Brackhane). The subjects performed a dart-throwing exercise individually (that is, without any social comparison information) and evaluated their series of outcomes. Initially they based their evaluation on objective, inherent structural task characteristics — that is, on the rings of the targets with the points entered on them (distinctiveness information, objective reference norm). As their experience with the distribution of their own achievements increased (consistency information, individual reference norm) they released themselves from their attachment to concrete task characteristics and constructed a reference system of three to five evaluation classes, in order to evaluate their individual performance by the standard of deviation from their own average score. If performance improved with increasing practice, the base point at which performance was evaluated as neither good nor bad shifted correspondingly — and with it, the entire reference system of three to five classes for evaluating the quality of their own performance. Finally, some subjects also inquired about the performance of other subjects, thus seeking additional information for social comparison (social reference norm).

A social reference norm is based on consensus information — that is, on the distribution of success and failure at a task in a social reference group. Findings on the development of individual reference norms and on the earliest use and integration of the various kinds of covariation information are described by Heckhausen (1980b, 1982b) and Nicholls (1975, 1978, 1979, 1980). Reference norms can also be interconnected with each other — that is, various kinds of covariation information can be integrated with each other. Thus an individual reference norm alone is not enough to determine the extent to which one has improved or grown worse. That is possible only when an individual reference norm is referred to an objective reference norm or to a social reference norm — that is, when the difference between previous and current performance is determined on the basis of task-inherent criteria or on the basis of a shift in rank. Every reference norm also has its blind spot. When it is not supplemented by a social reference norm, an individual reference norm disregards the extent to which others have improved their performance in the meantime and the extent to which one's own competence is comparable to that of others. A social reference norm disregards absolute progress in the mastery of task requirements as long as no objective reference norm is used. An objective reference norm, or one that has been set by some authority, does not necessarily reflect progress and individual differences in performance appropriately if it does not include anything resembling an individual or social reference norm.

No one has yet conducted a systematic investigation of the interconnection, coexistence, or conflict of reference norms. Every reference norm has its justification and advantages from certain practical points of view. That is particularly true of individual and social reference norms, for example, in evaluating the performance of schoolchildren. Should children learn about their progress in the form of their current rank in the class, or in the form of the progress they themselves have made in recent months? Such a question is not new: One and a half centuries ago Herbart concerned himself with it (1831, p. 210).

Various reference norms set the standards for achievement-oriented behavior in the development of the child. Veroff (1969) developed a three-stage theory of the genesis of the achievement motive and even distinguished among various kinds of achievement motive. According to Veroff, preschoolers are almost exclusively confronted with individual reference norms, so that an "autonomous" achievement motive can develop. When they enter school the social reference norm appears; the "social" or "normative" achievement motive is at its height between the ages of seven and nine. Gradually, however, the individual reference norm regains importance, so that in a third stage the two reference norms are combined into an "integrated" achievement motive. (We are not told what this "integration" involves.) (See on Veroff's three-stage theory Heckhausen, 1972a, pp. 962–963; Nicholls, 1980; Rheinberg, Lührmann, & Wagner, 1977; Schmalt, 1975.)

The Motivational Primacy of the Individual Reference Norm

In addition to developmental primacy, the individual reference norm also has motivational primacy. If subjects evaluate the success or failure of their performance outcome on the basis of whether they have improved, not improved, or even performed worse than their previous level, then they are sensitizing themselves for differentiated conclusions about level of ability and effort exerted. The covariation between ability and effort on the one hand and success on the other hand becomes clear. This covariation can lead to five ways in which motivation can become stronger with an individual norm than with a social reference norm.

1. Identical or similar performance outcomes can be experienced with more variation as to whether they are interpreted as success or as failure than

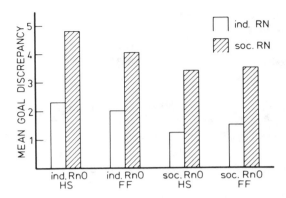

FIGURE 6.7   Mean goal-discrepancy scores of ring-
tossing as a function of (situationally stimulated) individ-
ual versus social reference norm (RN), personal orienta-
tion to individual versus social reference norm (RnO),
and the preponderance of the hope-of-success motive *HS*
or the fear of failure motive *FF*. (Adapted from Rhein-
berg, Duscha, & Michels, 1980, p. 182.)

is possible with a social reference norm.   A schoolchild with below-average
performance need not experience consistent failure, as would happen with a
social reference norm.   Even the below-average schoolchild can experience
success just as frequently as failure on the basis of individual progress,
whether progress is defined by task-inherent criteria or by the shifting of a
social rank.   And correspondingly, the above-average schoolchild can expe-
rience failure just as frequently as success.

2.   This independence of the experience of success and failure from social
comparison encourages realistic goal setting.   Neither is it necessary for the
below-average schoolchild to be constantly overchallenged, nor is it neces-
sary for the above-average schoolchild always to be underchallenged
(Rheinberg, Duscha, & Michels, 1980).   Figure 6.7 shows how much the
goal discrepancy in a ringtoss game decreases for 11- to 13-year-olds when
an individual reference norm is suggested instead of a social reference
norm.   This decrease occurs independent of the achievement motive and of
the individual orientation toward one of the two reference norms.

3.   Since goal setting is more realistic with an individual reference norm,
success and failure expectancies can be found in the middle range of subjec-
tive difficulty, which — according to the risk-taking model — is the area of
maximum motivation.

4.   The middle range of subjective difficulty provides the best conditions
for causal attribution, in that failure and success can be attributed to the
person's effort, rather than to external causes.   Moreover, subjects can dis-

criminate among differences in their own ability and in their own exertion of effort (Rheinberg *et al.,* 1980).

5. Finally, such attribution and discrimination makes it possible to maximize positive or negative self-evaluation, and thus — through an anticipatory self-evaluation incentive — to maximize motivational strength.

The motivational primacy of the individual reference norm has not yet been the object of laboratory experiments, except for studies of teacher–pupil interaction (Rheinberg, 1980) and for applied research in improving motivation. Unfortunately, the distinction between individual and social reference norms has not yet been investigated explicitly for differential effects on goal setting, risk taking, intention to exert effort, persistence, or response to success and failure (for example, see Meyer, 1976). In Chapter 4 we criticized the practice of automatically basing the induction of success and failure on social reference norms. The effect of an induction such as "*X* percent of the so-and-so subjects fail at this task" depends in part on how relevant the reference group is believed to be and how credible the experimenter's information is. The decisive factor is the rank that students assign themselves within the social hierarchy on the basis of their evaluation of their ability.

Our evaluation of our own ability to perform a particular task can vary considerably, depending on whether we base it on an individual or a social reference norm. The same variance is presumably true for subjective probability of success, although this has not yet been investigated. After all, subjective probability of success depends on the relationship of perceived objective task difficulty and assessment of one's own ability for the task in question. Heckhausen (1975b) found that self-evaluation of ability to perform a task presented as important for the subject's profession (a visual detection task for policemen) that was based on an individual reference norm differed from assessment based on a social reference norm (what percentage of colleagues were more able than the subject), even to the extent of showing no correlation. With a social reference norm one's own ability is compared with the distribution of the same ability within the social reference group; with an individual reference norm the ability in question is presumably compared with one's other abilities. Of course, assessment of the position of the various abilities is itself based on social comparisons, but it could also be oriented toward task-inherent criteria. Instead of an intraindividual comparison of various abilities, however, in some cases the evaluation of ability could be based on the continuum of task-inherent levels of difficulty. No analyses have been made of the origin of assessments of ability with an individual reference norm.

Regardless of the details of its origin, the assessment of ability with an individual reference norm does not have the same consequences for motivation as an estimation of ability according to a social reference norm. One example is intended effort or "calculation of effort," for which Kukla (1972a) and Meyer (1973a) have developed models (see below). Heckhausen (1972b) found that subjects intended to exert more effort when estimation of ability according to individual reference norm made it questionable whether they could master the task. Such rational calculation of intended effort corresponds to the law of difficulty in motivation (Hillgruber, 1912) and to the models designed by Kukla (1972a) and Meyer (1973a). In contrast, the opposite is true of the social reference norm for estimation of ability. The more subjects considered themselves well qualified for the task in comparison with their colleagues, the more effort they intended to exert. Instead of the law of difficulty, a special incentive effect is apparently at work here — the desire to preserve or upgrade one's own position of excellence through increased effort at a task at which one feels oneself superior to most others. Moulton (1974) had already pointed out this motivational effect of individual differences in competence.

As we saw in Chapter 5, success tends more to be attributed to one's own ability than failure tends to be attributed to one's own lack of ability. Correspondingly, we could be expected to estimate our own ability as higher after success to a greater extent than we would assess our ability as lower after failure. Heckhausen (1975b) found an upward evaluation effect after success for estimation of ability by an individual reference norm. However, the extent of upward evaluation by failure-motivated subjects depended on their estimate of their ability by a social reference norm. If they felt superior to their colleagues, they increased their estimate of their ability by individual reference norms considerably after success. On the other hand, if they considered themselves inferior they scarcely increased their estimate of their ability by individual reference norms at all after success. These findings indicate that the extent of dependence of individual reference norms on social reference norms is related to the achievement motive. Failure-motivated subjects are more dependent on social comparison in self-estimation of their abilities than are success-motivated subjects.

Reference-Norm Orientation in Self-Evaluation: Individual, Developmental, and Situational Differences

The last finding mentioned indicates a tendency toward individual preference for one of the two reference norms: that is, toward a reference-norm orientation. Rheinberg (1977, 1980) measured this tendency with a simple test, the "Minor Evaluation Task." Figure 6.8 shows the procedure for determining reference-norm orientation for evaluation of others' perform-

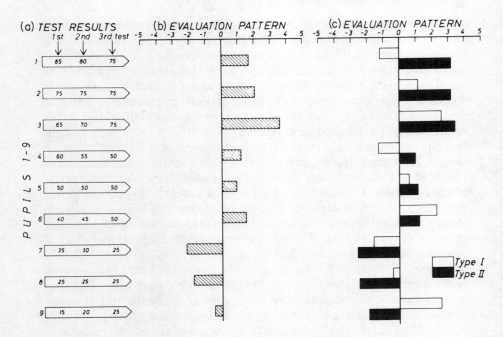

FIGURE 6.8   Various performance sequences of schoolchildren as test material for the "Minor Evaluation Task" (a) and the average pattern of positive or negative evaluation by teachers of the most recent performance of a pupil, for all subjects (b) and for two partial groups (c), divided with the aid of a hierarchical cluster analysis into two types.   Type I tends to use an individual reference norm; Type II tends to use a social reference norm.   (From Rheinberg, 1980, pp. 29 and 33.)

ance.   Performance sequences for nine schoolchildren on the basis of three test results per child increase, decrease, or remain stable (100-point maximum).   The class average is shown as around 50 points.   The most recent outcome is to be evaluated by subjects taking the test, with up to 5 plus points or minus points.   For example, subjects with a social reference norm orientation would evaluate the sequence 85–80–75 more positively than the sequence 15–20–25.   The reverse would be true of subjects with an individual reference norm orientation.   For them, the rise and fall in performance is more important than the position attained in the performance distribution within the class.   A hierarchical cluster analysis made it possible to divide the standardized evaluation profile of a sample of teachers into two opposing types of evaluation profiles, shown in Figure 6.8 (right).   The first type tends toward an individual reference norm; the second type tends toward a social reference norm.

After appropriate alterations it is possible to determine reference-norm orientation for self-evaluation as well as evaluation of others, by means of the

"Minor Evaluation Task." Rheinberg *et al.* (1977) demonstrated this with fifth- to thirteenth-grade students in college-preparatory schools and comprehensive schools. This was not a longitudinal analysis, but rather a cross-section analysis. Yet Figure 6.9 shows that between the fifth and thirteenth grades — that is, from the eleventh to the nineteenth year of life — individual reference norms become increasingly important. Toward the end of school they become dominant over social reference norms. That effect corresponds roughly to Veroff's (1969) postulate of an "integrated achievement motive": After dominance by individual, then by social reference norms comes a third stage in which both reference norms are connected, with the individual norm dominant. The "Minor Evaluation Task" suggests an integration, at least in that the test scores given are norm-oriented from an individual point of view as well (i.e., in individual longitudinal section). In other words, the individual reference norm is anchored within a social reference norm.

As can be seen from Figure 6.9, the trend toward an individual reference norm is apparently reversed temporarily in the ninth and tenth grades in favor of the social reference norm. Postexperimental analyses showed that in these grades students perceive a social reference norm more strongly than

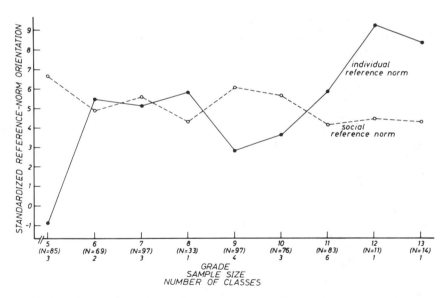

FIGURE 6.9 Average preference for individual and social reference norms in self-evaluation by fifth- to thirteenth-grade students in college-preparatory and comprehensive schools. (Adapted from Rheinberg, Lührmann, & Wagner, 1977, p. 91.)

usual in their teachers' behavior. This makes it clear that general develop-
ment in reference norm orientation is also subject to situational influences.
The importance of situational influences is also supported by the differences
between college-preparatory schools and comprehensive schools: In every
grade, especially the fifth, ninth, and tenth, comprehensive-school students
had a higher social reference-norm orientation than college-preparatory
school students. This is not surprising, when we consider that in compre-
hensive schools differences in ability are greater and more noticeable than in
college-preparatory schools. Students are subjected more often to perform-
ance comparison through evaluation procedures in the comprehensive
school, in order to differentiate college-bound from non-college-bound stu-
dents.

The extent to which individual differences in reference-norm orientation
are determinants of the achievement-motive system has hardly been investi-
gated at all. Some findings by Schmalt (1975) are indirectly related. He
separated picture situations (LMG) into those that suggest an individual
reference norm and those that suggest a social reference norm for perform-
ance evaluation. The external criterion was the earliness of the mother's
independence training of the subject, which can of course only be guided by
an individual reference norm. As expected, motive scores correlate with
earliness of the mother's independence training only for achievement situa-
tions in which an individual reference norm is suggested. A reasonable
conclusion is that motive scores split up according to reference-norm orien-
tation could explain performance in corresponding situations better than the
summary score. This idea has not yet been confirmed experimentally.

The first findings on correlation of reference-norm bias with motive scores
came from Rheinberg (1980). An individual reference-norm orientation
among sixth graders correlated positively with a success-oriented achieve-
ment motive (NH_1, LMG — i.e., if only FF_1, "self-concept of low ability," is
considered to be the tendency to avoid failure). However, the correlation
was weak ($r[124] = .29$). The correlation increases if we dichotomize the
reference-norm orientation scores, which do not have a normal distribution
($r_{bis} = .59; p < .001$). An individual reference norm was correlated less with
HS ($r_{bis} = .13$, ns) than with the absence of a self-concept of low ability (FF_1)
($r_{bis} = -.39; p < .001$). FF_2 (fear of failure) showed the same correlation.

Reference-Norm Orientation in Evaluation by Others: Individual and Situational Differences

Reference-norm orientation in the evaluation of others' performance has
been studied almost exclusively for members of one occupational group
whose everyday work involves evaluation: teachers. Rheinberg (in sum-

mary, 1977, 1979, 1980) is responsible for almost all the findings reported in this section. Within various teacher samples considerable individual differences in reference-norm orientation have generally been found, even when the situational evaluation context was the same for all. Naturally an individual alters reference-norm orientation depending on the nature and purpose of the current evaluation. But teachers with a primarily individual reference-norm orientation have turned out to be much more flexible than teachers with a primarily social reference-norm orientation.

In order to determine individual differences in reference-norm orientation for evaluation of others, a group of teachers was first asked to complete the "Minor Evaluation Task" and then to fill it out again in a particular evaluative situation (such as assigning grades, determining promotion to the next grade, conversing with parents or with the pupil alone or in class, etc.). All teachers assigned distinct functions to the individual evaluation situations. For example, grades and promotion were seen as having the function of certification and selection, and conversing with pupils or with the class as a whole was seen as having a motivational function. Teachers with social reference-norm orientation tended to prefer a social reference norm without exception to almost the same extent. In contrast, teachers with an individual reference-norm orientation adjusted to the current evaluative situation. When the function was certification and selection (grades, promotion) they based their evaluation on a social reference norm; when the function was motivational (conversation with the pupil or the class as a whole) they used an individual reference norm. Apparently the first teacher group expected to be able to motivate the students by social comparisons, while the second group expected to motivate by giving feedback about improvement in performance.

The suggestion of a comparative perspective is a particularly influential situational factor. Liebhart (1977) had his subjects evaluate four tests by each of four schoolchildren from an intraindividual comparative perspective (the four tests of each child in turn) and from an interindividual comparative perspective (one test by all four children in turn) to determine various causes of achievement. The intraindividual perspective — that is, the individual reference norm — favored attributions to effort. In contrast, the interindividual perspective — that is, the social reference norm — favored ability attributions.

Teacher Reference-Norm Orientation: Effects on Student Motivation

We have already pointed out the motivational effectiveness of the individual reference norm, which encourages a more balanced distribution of success and failure, balanced goal setting, realistic expectancies of success, primarily internal causal attribution, and pronounced self-evaluation. With reference-norm orientation a teacher can influence pupils' motivation both directly and indirectly: directly in that pupils take over the teacher's reference-norm orientation, and indirectly in that the teacher's reference-norm orientation structures the teacher's classroom behavior in such a way that the pupil can react adequately to the situation only by using the same reference norm. In the fifth grade, at the latest, children can describe accurately (Lührmann, 1977) their teachers' more prominent reference-norm orientations. Classroom behavior of teachers such as causal attribution, reinforcement, controlling the level of difficulty, and checking performance must be derived from the teacher's reference norm, as Heckhausen (1972b) postulated. Rheinberg and his colleagues (Rheinberg, 1977; Rheinberg & Krug, 1978a) have confirmed some of Heckhausen's hypotheses and some additional ones.

As for preferred causal attribution for the performance of schoolchildren, teachers with a social reference-norm orientation tended to choose factors that were internal and stable over time — that is, student traits such as ability and industriousness. Teachers with an individual reference-norm orientation tended more often to include factors that were variable over time, such as external factors in the learning and testing situations (see also Elke, 1978). Correspondingly, teachers with a social reference-norm orientation tended more to believe that student performance was predictable over a longer time span. With regard to reinforcement, the two teacher types showed the expected opposite reactions: Those with social reference-norm orientation expressed approval of above-average students even when their performance had declined, but teachers with individual reference-norm orientation tended to disapprove. Only those teachers with an individual reference-norm orientation showed approval of a below-average student whose performance was improving. These teachers also tended to give positive reinforcement and aid in solving the problem while students were still working on it. In contrast, teachers with a social reference norm tended not to praise or criticize until the correct or false answer had already been produced (Wagner, 1977). Finally, Rheinberg (1977) also found the expected difference between the two teacher types in the extent of individualization in their presentation of material. Teachers with an individual reference norm varied the level of difficulty of their questions more, including over time. They controlled the level of difficulty by offering aids to formulating the answer or reformulating the question after the student had already been called on and was trying to produce an answer (Wagner, 1977).

Rheinberg (1977) constructed a "Questionnaire for Determining Reference-Norm Orientation" from aspects of concrete instructional behavior that are indicative for reference norms. The questionnaire is more differentiated than Rheinberg's "Minor Evaluation Task," correlates moderately with the latter ($.30 < r < .50$), and is used in intervention studies (see below) as a diagnostic tool for the motivation-inducing impact of teacher personalities and for the success of training programs.

We can expect a positive influence on schoolchildren from all these correlates of individual reference-norm orientation, as reflected in instructional behavior. Positive effects should include actual achievement motivation in class, success in learning, and perhaps even the development of an anxiety-free achievement motive, coupled with confident expectation of success. Indeed, all of the evidence points in this direction. For 16 classroom teachers with a total of 492 third-grade students Brauckmann (1976) reported a correlation of $r(16) = +.54$ between the teacher's individual reference-norm orientation and the success motive determined for the class as a whole (HS, LMG). Rheinberg, Schmalt, and Wasser (1978) expected that, in 8 fourth-grade classes (196 students) whose teachers preferred social reference norms, the failure motive (FF_2 and NH_2, LMG) would be more pronounced than in 3 fourth-grade classes (76 students) that were used for comparison. Their expectancies were confirmed with respect to the failure motive data, and there were also corresponding differences in test anxiety (anxiety scale by Wieczerkowski, Nickel, Janowski, Fittkau, & Rauer, 1974) and in dislike of school.

These correlational studies have definite implications for motive development, as illustrated in a one-year longitudinal investigation of eight German high school classes (Peter, 1978; Rheinberg, 1979). The students were redistributed into classes at the beginning of the school year. Four of the classes were led by a teacher with individual reference-norm orientation, and four by a teacher with social reference-norm orientation ("Questionnaire for Determining Reference-Norm Orientation" and "Minor Evaluation Task"). Within each class the students were divided into terciles by intelligence test scores. The researchers expected to find the most dramatic effects of individual reference-norm orientation among students in the lowest third, no matter whether the measure was motivation or the students' self-concepts of ability. Where the teacher used individual reference norms the initial failure motive score (FF_1, LMG) decreased in the course of one school year, and this decrease was strongest in the low intelligence group (see Figure 6.10). Thus after a year a significant interaction resulted between reference-norm orientation and intelligence test scores. Corresponding results appeared for test anxiety and manifest anxiety as well (Wieczerkowski et al., 1974, AFS). Moreover, students in all three intelligence groups reported an increase in their own perceived ability (an increase that is less likely to be perceived with a social reference norm). At the end of the school year these students attributed their failures less often to a basic lack of ability than did students in the social reference-norm condition.

Trudewind and Kohne (1982) conducted an even longer-term investiga-

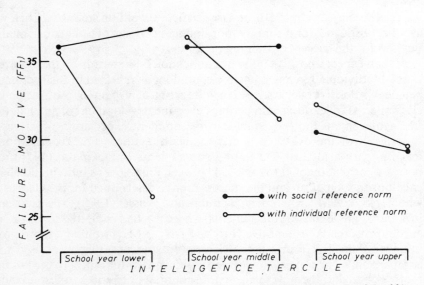

FIGURE 6.10   Change in failure motive (FF_1, LMG) in the course of the fifth grade by each of four high-school classes whose teachers had an individual or a social reference norm, divided into terciles in each class by intelligence test scores. (Adapted from Rheinberg, 1979.)

tion of the influence of the teacher's reference-norm orientation on the development of the achievement motive from the first day of school to the end of the fourth grade.   In a longitudinal study (see Trudewind, 1982) 13 school classes that had the same teacher with social reference-norm orientation for all four years were compared with 13 other classes having teachers with individual reference norms.   In Figure 6.11 we see that by the end of the first grade the success-seeking component of the achievement motive showed a relative increase in students whose teachers had an individual reference norm; for students whose teachers had a social reference norm, it decreased.

Moreover, a closer analysis showed that a general modification of the failure-avoidance component of the achievement motive in interaction with quality of performance was not noticeable until the fourth grade.   Fear of failure was rather low when school achievement was high and the teacher had an individual reference-norm orientation; when school achievement was low and the teacher's reference-norm orientation was social, fear of failure was rather high.   According to Trudewind and Kohne, the differential effect of the teacher's reference-norm orientation on development of the

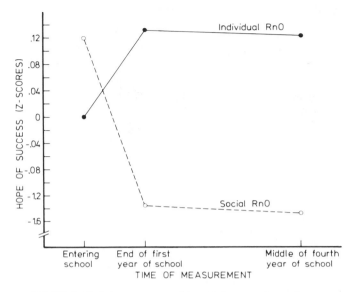

FIGURE 6.11 Mean *z*-scores of hope of success from elementary
school pupils at three measurement times as a function of their teachers'
reference-norm orientation (RnO) (13 teachers in each RnO condition
and a total of 311 pupils). (Adapted from Trudewind & Kohne, 1982.)

motive is primarily that individual reference norms further the development
of a variety of standards of excellence by which students can evaluate their
own efforts realistically.

Taken as a whole, the findings confirm the idea that reference norms for
the evaluation of achievement moderate motivation decisively; in fact, the
norms can even influence the development of the motive. The influence of
situational or individual differences in reference norm on the various param-
eters of achievement-related behavior have rarely been isolated experimen-
tally. Yet research on teacher-student interaction has indeed documented
that individual reference norms are important not only in developmental,
but also in motivational respects. In the next section we describe motive
improvement programs for students that begin with attempts to alter the
reference-norm orientation of the teacher.

Applications

Self-concepts, self-centered cognitions, and reference norms offer numer-
ous possible approaches to influencing motivation in an actual situation and
to altering a motive system permanently. As for self-concepts and self-cen-

tered cognitions — especially with attribution patterns — we described their applications at the end of Chapter 5. Now we show how fruitful the study of reference norms and their effects has been, especially for pedagogical and psychological applications. Above all, findings on the effect of reference-norm orientations have provided suggestions for planning instruction and organizing schools for better learning motivation. Heckhausen and Krug (1982) have written an overview of the development and the current state of procedures and programs for improving motivation to learn and modifying unfavorable achievement motives.

Individual Reference-Norm Orientation and Motive
Change in the Classroom

Programs for modifying motives have changed as achievement motivation theory has progressed. Their development was described in Chapters 2 and 5. Viewing the achievement motive as a self-reinforcing system (Heckhausen, 1972a, 1975a) has led to three starting points: goal setting, causal attribution, and self-evaluation. The motivational primacy of the individual reference norm, already described, includes these three determining factors. If the learning situation in the classroom encourages an individual reference norm, the basic prerequisite is already present for (1) an individual standard of excellence that makes realistic demands on one's competence, (2) causal attribution that raises the sense of responsibility for one's actions, and (3) self-evaluation that makes subjects more autonomous and does not encourage them to resign themselves quickly after failure.

Figure 6.12 illustrates the above point. On the left side appear four ways in which instruction can be designed to raise motivation: (1) the teacher's individual reference norm for evaluating performance and giving feedback, (2) individualization of task difficulty and leaving possibilities of choice open, (3) causal attribution to internal variables in the teacher's evaluation of performance, and (4) reinforcement by others on the basis of individual reference norms. Each of these four aspects furthers student motivation at individual process stages, as shown on the right side of Figure 6.12. On the instructional side, everything is apparently set in motion by the first aspect, an individual reference norm for performance evaluation and feedback. Rheinberg, Schmalt, and Wasser (1978) have shown that teachers with individual reference-norm orientation are already carrying out all four points on the instructional side wherever possible. These teachers also have classes with more positive achievement motive scores. It would seem appropriate to conduct a motive modification program with no intervention except to modify the teacher's reference-norm orientation in the direction of an individual reference norm. To the extent that such a change could be made

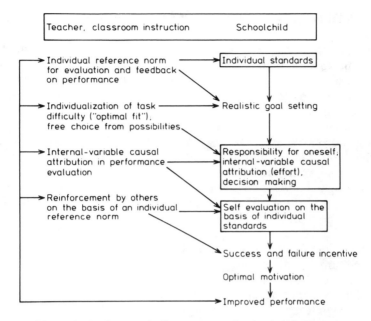

FIGURE 6.12 Cause-and-effect structure of optimal achievement motivation in schoolchildren when the teacher and classroom instruction are oriented toward an individual reference norm. (From Heckhausen, 1980b, *Motivation und Handeln*, p. 705, by permission of Springer-Verlag.)

permanent, the cause-and-effect structure shown in Figure 6.12 could be expected to develop "on its own" and take its course.

Krug and his co-workers published the first findings on this subject, from a study of 9 third-grade teachers and classes (Kraeft & Krug, 1979). The pretest showed that the teachers already had an above-average orientation toward individual reference norms, even before training began. The teachers were trained for eight weeks to follow an individual reference-norm orientation with their failure-motivated, low-achieving students. In the foreground were individual aspects of behavior, rather than the central cognitive element (the intraindividual performance comparison). Alterations in reference-norm orientation were determined through direct observation of teachers' classroom behavior and through questionnaires (Questionnaire for Determining Reference-Norm Orientation; Rheinberg, 1977). During the training course the frequency of the desired behaviors increased, without simultaneous corresponding alterations in questionnaire scores. However, both a behavioral index and a questionnaire index were associated with declines in failure motive among target pupils ($r[9] = -.71$ and $-.90$, respectively).

After training there was a surprisingly high correlation between social reference-norm orientation and strength of the success motive. It seems that "overtraining" — that is, strong accentuation of the individual reference norm at the expense of the social reference norm — reduces not only the failure motive, but also the success motive. This was especially true in this teacher sample, which even at the start was scarcely oriented toward social reference norms. Apparently social reference-norm orientation also strengthens the success motive in success-motivated schoolchildren. Instead of training teachers exclusively for an individual reference-norm orientation, it might be wiser to train them for flexibility in reference-norm orientation. In this regard many questions must still be clarified (what strengthens the motive for whom under what conditions?).

The initial reference norm before training can also be a determining factor. Rheinberg, Krug, Lübbermann, and Landscheid (1980) demonstrated in a 6-week intervention, during which teachers were constantly urged to encourage more intraindividual performance comparisons from their pupils, that overtraining toward individual reference-norm orientation is less likely when teachers have a pronounced social reference-norm orientation. Teachers who were already oriented toward an individual reference norm in their classroom instruction were much more successful in increasing intraindividual comparison than were teachers with a social reference norm. However, the increased frequency of intraindividual performance comparisons had a dual and conflicting overtraining effect. On the one hand, the students' participation in class, measured by frequency of hand-raising, increased considerably; on the other hand, the students' very high preference for an individual reference norm dropped. In contrast, classroom behavior of students whose teachers were oriented toward a social reference norm was in no way affected by the more frequent intraindividual performance comparisons. Only the students' tendency to favor an individual reference norm was strengthened.

Effects of Reference Groups

Since every educational system groups students into types of school and into classes on the basis of ability, a social comparison is inevitable, from teachers as well as students — particularly within a given class. Organizing instruction by grouping together students of the same age suggests a social reference norm. Social comparison is the most important source of information for evaluating one's own ability and that of others (see Festinger, 1954; Meyer, 1973a). The more the performance of same-age students within a single class varies, the more strongly a social reference norm suggests ability attributions. How students' ability is perceived by the students themselves, by fellow students in their class, and by the teacher depends on the approximate place that the student occupies in the achievement distribution of the class. If we compare students of objectively equal ability from classes with differing achievement distributions, or if we observe them when they change from one class to another, we find that their assessment of their own ability — and thus perhaps also the hope-of-success component of their achievement motive — is controlled by a reference group effect (on the general theory behind such effects, see Pettigrew, 1967).

Accordingly, ability grouping of students into classes could influence not only motivation, but also — in the long run — motive development. An initial example for this, which has already been mentioned, is the development of the preference for individual over social reference norm for self-evaluation. Rheinberg found that in heterogeneous groups of schoolchildren in comprehensive schools this development took place between the fifth and thirteenth grades, later than with homogeneously grouped students in college-preparatory schools (Rheinberg *et al.,* 1977).

Rheinberg and Enstrup (1977; Krug, Rheinberg, & Peters, 1977) found a reference-group effect among students of similar intelligence in different forms of schools. They compared fourth- to ninth-grade students with the same moderately low intelligence test scores ($70 < IQ < 86$) in special schools or comprehensive schools, for differences in self-concept of ability, test anxiety, and achievement motive. As could be expected with a reference-group effect, the special-school students demonstrated a better self-concept of ability and less test anxiety than the students in the general schools. The differences diminished from the fourth through the ninth grade. The special-school students showed only a tendency toward an achievement motive with higher hope of success (NH_2, LMG) than the other students. However, in all schools it was clear that the success motive (HS, NH_1, NH_2) became weaker from one grade to the next.

The reference-group effect can be tested even more directly by observing students who change from one type of school to another. Krug and Peters (1977) compared students with an average IQ of 86 who were transferred to special schools from the third and fourth grades in a comprehensive elementary school with students having similar intelligence test scores who stayed in the comprehensive school. The transferred students were expected to feel that they were performing at a much higher level in their new class environment, relative to their earlier one, and correspondingly to improve their self-concept of ability significantly, lose some of their test anxiety, and experience a decrease in the failure motive (FF_1) and an increase in the success motive (NH_1). All these effects were demonstrated at three times — directly after transfer, a half year later, and at the end of the school year — and were also confirmed in comparison with those children who remained in the comprehensive school (as an interaction between form of school and time of measurement). In comparison with students who had been in the special schools longer, the transferred pupils were less affected by a motive improvement program (Krug *et al.,* 1977) because the personalities of those recently transferred were already developing favorably on the basis of the reference-group effect.

The relevance and application of the effects reported for reference groups are obvious. They contradict a simple stigmatization theory (Goffman, 1967; Lösel, 1975) in which the members of a reference group that is evaluated negatively by society (such as students in special schools) are thought to be stigmatized in a socially negative way. Rheinberg and Krug (1978a, 1978b) analyzed why stigmatization is a special form of reference-group effect and under what conditions favorable or unfavorable consequences can be expected for personality development. "Integrated" school systems are often encouraged because it is hoped that they will prevent stigmatization effects. It is easy to overlook the fact that precisely the integration of heterogeneous reference groups of varying abilities can suggest discriminating social comparisons and decrease self-esteem, whereas self-esteem could have been developed with appropriate reference groups.

7

Broadened Perspectives:
Methods and Models

New Procedures for Measuring Motives and Motivation

The achievement motive cannot be measured directly, but rather must be measured indirectly in its actualization in a specific situation. Thematic situational variables have always been especially important for measuring the achievement motive by content analysis. The picture – situation arousal parameters in TAT research have generally been considered only from the standpoint of the general validity of the procedure; researchers have tended to lose sight of individual differences in reaction to situational parameters. And yet McClelland *et al.* (1953) have pointed out this problem and proposed that motive strength be determined on the basis of intensity as well as extensity, defined as follows: Motive intensity was supposed to be tied to specific, thematically narrowly defined situations (deCharms, 1968, p. 209), while motive extensity was supposed to depend on the number of different stimulus cues that can arouse achievement-motivated behavior.

Grid Test of the Achievement Motive

Schmalt (1973, 1976a, 1976b) developed a semiprojective procedure for children and teenagers up to the age of 14, the so-called grid test of the achievement motive (LMG). This procedure measures the intensity and extensity of various components of the achievement motive separately. It consists of 18 picture situations in which achievement could play a role. The 18 pictures are grouped into six different domains: manual, musical, scholastic, asserting independence, giving help, and sports (test form for children) (see Figure 7.1).

Under each picture the same 18 statements are listed. These statements represent some of the most important empirically documented aspects of theory. They pertain to the anticipations of success and failure that are typical for success- and failure-motivated persons and on the related differences in level of expectancy, or on different preference patterns for tasks of intermediate difficulty, or on actions instrumental in preventing failure or avoiding achievement-oriented situations. Moreover, different concepts of the subject's own ability were taken into account. Some items were conceived originally as fillers. The theoretical importance of these statements is underlined by the fact that they can equally well be seen as representative of the content categories of the TAT scoring key (see Table 7.1).

The subjects need only mark the statements that would apply for them in a given situation. This produces an answer matrix for each subject that consists of two dimensions: statements and situations. It is easier to construct individual patterns of person–environment relationships in this way than with traditional questionnaire techniques. The analysis of these answer

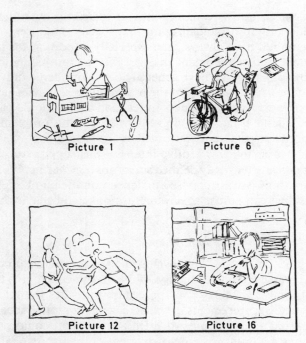

FIGURE 7.1 Picture situations from the grid test of the achievement motive, from the following areas: manual activities (Picture 1); independence and self-assertion (Picture 6); sports (Picture 12); and school (Picture 16). (From Schmalt, 1976a.)

TABLE 7.1

Statements Used in the Grid Test of the Achievement Motive[a]

Original diagnostic purpose	Content category[b]		Statement	Motive tendency
Filler	— — —	1.	He feels good doing this.	— — —
FF	If	2.	He thinks: "If that is difficult, I'd rather finish some other time."	FF_1
HS	E	3.	He believes he will be able to do that.	HS vs. FF_1
HS	G+	4.	He thinks: "I'm proud of myself because I can do that."	HS
FF	Ef	5.	He thinks: "I wonder if anything is wrong?"	FF_2
FF	G−	6.	He is not satisfied with what he can do.	FF_1
Filler	— — —	7.	He is getting tired doing this.	FF_2
FF	If	8.	He thinks: "I'd rather ask someone to help me."	FF_1
HS	N	9.	He thinks: "I want to be able to do that some day."	HS
HS	E	10.	He believes he did everything right.	HS vs. FF_1
FF	Ef	11.	He's afraid he could do something wrong.	FF_2
Filler	— — —	12.	He doesn't like that.	FF_1
FF	Nf	13.	He doesn't want to do anything wrong.	FF_2
HS	N	14.	He wants to be able to accomplish more than all the others.	HS
HS	N	15.	He thinks: "Most of all I want to do something that is a little bit difficult."	HS
Filler	— — —	16.	He prefers to do nothing at all.	FF_1
HS	I	17.	He thinks: "If that's very hard I'll surely try longer than others."	HS
FF	Ef	18.	He thinks he can't do that.	FF_1

[a] Adapted from Schmalt, 1976a.

[b] The TAT scoring key used here is that of Heckhausen, 1963a; compare above Chapter 2, p. 21.

matrices from the standpoint of behavior prediction has not yet been attempted. Behavior predictions are made primarily from an index in which the statements attributed to the success or failure motive (Table 7.1) are added up from the entire set of pictures. This index includes intensity and extensity aspects of the achievement motive, which are examined at the same time. In some studies situation-specific intensity or extensity measures of individual motive components were also examined (Schmalt, 1976a).

Table 7.1 contains the 18 statements from the grid test along with the original diagnostic purpose for which they were chosen (HS, FF), the relevant content category from the TAT scoring key, and the motive tendencies determined by factor analysis. The following three factors resulted from factor analyses that showed stable results across various samples:

HS_1 scale: concept of high ability; initiation of actions designed to master difficult tasks.

FF_1 scale: concept of low ability; initiation of actions to prevent failure.

FF_2 scale: fear of failure.

As in the corresponding analyses of the TAT scoring key and of questionnaires of test anxiety, two separate FF factors appear here along with a HS factor. Further studies involving a total of over 4000 subjects fully confirmed the original factor structure (Halisch, 1982; Schmalt & Schab, 1984). The confirmation applies to factor analysis of the 18 statements, to cluster analysis, and to three-mode factor analysis of the entire 18×18 answer matrix (Smits & Schmalt, 1978; Rösler, Besse, Manzey, & Grau, 1982). Median retest reliability was .80 after 2 weeks and .73 after 8 weeks. Split-half reliability was .88. Response tendencies such as acquiescence and social desirability were almost nonexistent. Validity studies that document the validity of the motive scores on the grid test have been conducted in nearly all areas of behavior to which the achievement motive construct applies (see Chapter 2, Chapter 3, Chapter 5).

The construct validity of the two FF components of the grid test is an especially interesting question because this bipartition was not originally expected. It has turned out that the two components have quite different effects on behavior. The FF_1 measure is connected with the choice of extremely high levels of difficulty in goal-setting experiments—that is, to one extreme of the difficulty continuum. In contrast, the FF_2 measure shows the deviation to both extremes of the difficulty continuum (high and low levels) that is generally expected from failure-motivated subjects (Schmalt, 1976b). Attributions of success and failure also show a pronounced difference. Subjects with high FF_1 attributed failure more to low ability and less to low effort, while subjects with high FF_2 attributed failure more to low effort (Schmalt, 1976a, 1982; see Chapter 5).

Correlations with performance measures also show a pronounced difference for the two motive scores. While FF_1 tends to have a detrimental effect on performance (grade-point average, digit–symbol test), FF_2 tends to facilitate it. In addition, when failure continues over an extended period the two factors show different correlations with persistence. While FF_1 is connected with distinctly low persistence, FF_2 is connected with rather high persistence, but only when FF_1 is low (Schmalt, 1982).

Thus the two failure-avoidance motive components show a consistent pattern. FF_1-motivated subjects have an unfavorable attribution pattern and tend to connect failure primarily with low ability. This leads them to abandon achievement-related activities quickly and to show low performance efficiency. In contrast, FF_2-motivated subjects tend to connect failure with low effort. They persist longer and eventually perform better (Schmalt, 1982).

Motivational State

Heckhausen (1982a) investigated the effects of various self-esteem–related cognitions on test taking and performance on examinations, using a new procedure designed to measure whether a motivational state tends toward hope of success or toward fear of failure. Directly after their exams students indicated on a questionnaire whether they tended more to expect success or to fear failure during the exam. The individual items were, again, oriented toward the content categories of the TAT scoring key, which had already been validated. Heckhausen's procedure (1982a) is a dispositional measure of situation-specific actualized motivational states—here during a test—unlike traditional dispositional motive measures, which are generalized for a variety of situations. Spielberger (1966; Spielberger, Gorsuch, & Lushene, 1970) proposed a similar procedure for the fear construct. For Spielberger state anxiety is an individual state characterized by subjective feelings of tension and arousal, while trait anxiety describes a general tendency to react with state anxiety (which is inappropriate in many situations).

Heckhausen's questionnaire on motivational states in a critical achievement situation involved a total of six factors, of which three were primarily cognitive and three primarily affective. They corresponded to a large extent to the distinction between self-doubt and nervousness (Morris & Liebert, 1969). The three cognitive components can be described as experiencing incompetence, negative self-evaluation, and failure expectancy (or the opposite of these states). The three affective components are nervousness, feeling overtaxed, and lack of reaction control. In Heckhausen's study (1982a) the motivational states "hope of success" and "fear of failure" were associated with different frequencies of various kinds of self-cognitions and different amounts of disturbing influence from these cognitions, as described in Chapter 6 (see Figure 6.6).

Action versus State Orientation

Finally, another procedure involving states in which individuals find themselves was developed in the attempt to measure the achievement motive. These dispositions are not motives such as the hope of achieving

success or the avoidance of failure; instead, they are two opposed motiva-
tional states of action control: action orientation versus state orientation
(Kuhl, 1982a). They could also be called two directives. We tend toward
one or the other directive, but different situations also call more for one than
the other.

The action-oriented directive favors all cognitions and activities that pre-
pare an intention for execution and transform it into actual behavior. In
contrast, the state-oriented directive is directed so much toward an analysis
of situational conditions and the person's own feelings that action is post-
poned, if indeed it is ever carried out. We can describe both directives as
metamotivational. They are neither directed toward the contents of the
behavioral goals nor toward the activities that are instrumental in attaining
them, but only toward motivational processes that favor or inhibit the trans-
formation of intentions into actions.

The necessity of distinguishing between the two metamotivational orien-
tations first arose in connection with Kuhl's analysis (1972, 1978b) of the
content categories for determining the failure motive with Heckhausen's
TAT key (1963a). This was discussed in Chapter 2. In analyzing over 1000
TAT stories with Rasch's (1960) stochastic test model, the FF content cate-
gories turned out to be two-dimensional. One of the groups of content
categories represented active confrontation with impending or actual failure,
in order to prevent or overcome it. Such contents frequently appeared in
success-motivated subjects. The other group of content categories accepted
failure and concentrated on the feelings, thoughts, and consequences stem-
ming from the failure. Schmalt (1976a) discovered a similar division with
factor analysis—that is, the FF_2/FF_1 scale.

Later—primarily influenced by Ach's (1910, 1935) analysis of the psy-
chology of will—Kuhl developed the distinction between action and state
orientation into a theory of "action control." This theory was designed to
explain whether and how an intention to act becomes action. We discuss
this in more detail in the last section of this chapter. Here it should suffice to
mention Kuhl's assumption that an intention can be transformed into ac-
tion when the action that is to be carried out is represented cognitively in four
different respects:

1.   the aspired-to state
2.   the present state
3.   the discrepancy between the two states
4.   at least one step of action that could help remove the discrepancy.

If one of these elements is missing, the intention "degenerates"—that is, it
cannot be carried out and thus also cannot be cancelled. In this manner a
tendency to persevere is created. This leads to state orientation and inter-

feres with action control. Kuhl (1982a) distinguishes among four aspects of state orientation. Each involves excessive centering on something that in itself needs to be considered for action control:

1. plan centering (fixation on the consideration of possible actions before an intention is formed)
2. goal centering while the activity is being carried out
3. failure centering as a fixation on the outcome of an action and its consequences
4. success centering as a fixation on the outcome of a completed action and its consequences.

Persons in stressful situations differ in their tendency to state-oriented motivation. In order to measure differences in this tendency, 20-item questionnaires have been developed for each of the four aspects of state versus action orientation. A sample item from each of the four scales follows.

1. Plan-oriented action versus state orientation: "When I stand in front of a movie theater in which a film that I would like to see is shown and I have enough time and money to go in,
   a. I buy a ticket right away.
   b. I consider whether I shouldn't be doing something else instead."
2. Action centering versus goal centering (at present available only in a version for children): "When my mother promises me a reward for going shopping for her,
   a. I keep thinking about the reward while I'm shopping.
   b. I usually forget the reward until I get back."
3. Action versus state orientation following failure: "If I've already tried in vain several times to solve a problem,
   a. I can't forget it for a long time.
   b. I don't think about it any more and turn to other things."
4. Action versus state orientation following success: "If I've solved a difficult problem,
   a. I keep on thinking for quite a long time about the experience of success.
   b. I'm soon concerned with quite different matters again."

The scales show adequate internal consistency (Cronbach's alpha) and — with the exception of the goal-centering scale — have been checked for validity by comparison with other personality scales (Kuhl, in press b). The subjects in the study by Kuhl and Grosse were 120 male and female eighth graders. Table 7.2 contains correlations of action orientation and state orientation with various dispositions, all of which — plausibly enough — could overlap to a certain limited extent with the two metamotivational

TABLE 7.2

Correlations between the Action and State Orientation Scales with Various Personality Dispositions[a]

Other personality traits	Action orientation (AO) versus state orientation (SO)					
	In planning		After failure		After success	
	AO	SO	AO	SO	AO	SO
Achievement motive (NH)	.17	−.29**	.26**	−.22*	−.17	.11
Future orientation	.01	−.20*	.18*	−.21*	−.18*	−.08
Test anxiety	−.11	.33**	−.19*	.36**	.03	−.01
Extraversion	.21*	.07	.19*	−.07	−.05	.21*
Self-consciousness	.03	.22*	.15	.24*	.04	.15
Cognitive complexity	−.10	.03	−.26*	.09	.06	−.14

[a] Adapted from Kuhl, 1984, p. 151.
* $p < .05$; ** $p < .01$. $N = 120$.

orientations. Thus the success motive (Gjesme & Nygard, 1970) and future orientation (Gjesme, 1975) show negative correlations with state orientation during planning and after failure, and positive correlations with action orientation after failure. Exactly the opposite is true of test anxiety (Wieczer-kowski *et al.,* 1974). Extraversion (Buggle & Baumgärtl, 1972) tends more to be associated with action orientation, and self-consciousness tends more to be associated with state orientation (Fenigstein, Scheier, & Buss, 1975). Finally, cognitive complexity (Bieri, 1961) is connected with low action orientation following failure. The scales for action versus state orientation have been validated with various behavioral data in a number of experiments (e.g., Kuhl, 1982b). These are described in the last section of this chapter.

Instrumentality Theory

One strength of Atkinson's risk-taking model is its radical simplification to the "pure case." No motives other than the achievement motives are aroused, and the actual motivating incentives exhaust themselves in affective self-evaluation following success and failure — that is, in the anticipation of pride or shame. This strength is at the same time a weakness of the model. Achievement-oriented behavior does not generally occur merely for the sake of self-evaluation. A performance goal that is attained or not attained can have many other incentive-laden consequences — for example, social, material, or instrumental consequences for the attainment of general educational and vocational goals (see Chapter 4, Future Orientation).

Quite different motives — that is, evaluative dispositions — can be expressed in the incentive values of these other consequences.

How can we do justice to these facts? At least in its formalization, an answer to this question involves an attempt to extend and differentiate the expectancy-value model, a model that is basic to all motivational phenomena (Feather, 1981). The refinement of the distinctions among various kinds of expectancy and value parameters has gone so far that summary constructs such as motive seem dispensable (Heckhausen, 1977a, 1977b). This means that the effort involved in measuring separately numerous individual parameters (with all of the measurement problems involved) has increased extraordinarily, along with the questionable nature of the interconnections among the parameters. For example, instead of measuring a few highly generalized motive constructs, we must determine the incentive values of a variety of anticipated behavioral consequences that constitute the individual differences of the expectancy horizon in a particular situation.

Simple behavioral models following the expectancy-value pattern, such as those that Atkinson (1957), Edwards (1954), and Lewin *et al.* (1944) formulated, had already been expanded in the mid-1950s, yet the expansions initially had minimal influence. Rotter (1955) extended the reinforcement value of an action to include all additional reinforcements that the first reinforcement brings about, in the form of further consequences weighted with the expectancy that such subsequent reinforcements would occur. Basing her work on similar considerations, and in the same year, Peak (1955) introduced the concept of instrumentality for the expectancy of reinforcing consequences.

The industrial psychologists Georgopolous, Mahoney, and Jones (1957) were the first to give serious attention to the possibility that a single action outcome can be instrumental for quite different goals. It is no accident that the instrumentality aspect of multiple action consequences is easier to observe in businesses and organizations, where every activity has further consequences, than in the laboratory. Georgopolous *et al.* (1957) asked workers in a household article factory to what extent their own work productivity seemed to them to be instrumental for the attainment of various goals such as earning a lot of money in the long run, getting along well with colleagues, or getting a better-paying position. The more personal importance (valence) assigned to the goals, the more strongly workers experienced the instrumentality connection. At the same time, work productivity was also above average when high personal importance was assigned to the goals.

Vroom's Model of Incentive Value

Not until the next decade did Vroom (1964) condense these new approaches to the so-called instrumentality theory into an incentive value model, thereby facilitating an overview of the current state of research in industrial psychology on choice of occupation, job satisfaction, and occupational success. Vroom linked the basic expectancy-value model with a supplementary model for determining the value variable. The basic model is the usual action model — that is, the product of the subjective probability of success and the incentive value of the corresponding action outcome. This incentive value is not dependent on probability of success, as in the risk-taking model, but rather on the incentive values of all further and indirect outcomes that can be more or less expected after the action outcome. That is, instrumentalities for the occurrence of certain further outcomes with certain incentive values are ascribed to the action outcome. The product of instrumentality and incentive value is calculated for each of these further outcomes, and the sum of these products is the incentive value of the action outcome.

Such an incentive-value model is more an evaluation model than an action model. It explicates the evaluation of a situation when an individual is already active in a particular direction and intensity or when an action outcome has already occurred. Thus it is reasonable to use this incentive-value model to examine job satisfaction (see Mitchell & Albright, 1972; Mitchell & Biglan, 1971). However, it cannot explain which of various possible alternative actions will be preferred and executed in a given situation. Nor can it explain the degree of intensity or persistence with which these actions will be preferred and executed. For that purpose, as in all expectancy-value theories, it is necessary to take into account the probability that the action will lead to the desired action outcome. Thus the summary value of the instrumentality-weighted incentives of all further outcomes is inserted as the value variable (incentive of action outcome x) into the basic formula of the action model. Multiplied by the subjective probability of success for action outcome x, it produces the strength of the action tendency for outcome x. This action model has been used extensively in industrial psychology for research into job performance and productivity (Dunnette, 1976; Heneman & Schwab, 1972; Hoyos, 1974; Kleinbeck, 1977; Wahba & House, 1974).

Vroom's work has led to quite a bit of further research, but also to a number of difficulties. The least of these difficulties is the use of the term *valence* when the term *incentive* or *weighted incentive* should have been used (as we did, above).

Action Outcome and Outcome Consequences

Still greater confusion was caused by the failure to distinguish between the action outcome and further outcomes (better, and more precisely: action outcome consequences) that are mediated by instrumentality connections, all of which Vroom called outcomes. Later certain authors (e.g., Galbraith & Cummings, 1967) distinguished between primary and secondary outcomes. Secondary outcomes are outcomes with incentive value for which a primary outcome could be instrumental. The next question was just as necessary as it was productive: What sort of secondary outcomes could result from the attainment of a primary outcome, and what sorts of questions should be asked of the subjects? Mitchell and Albright (1972) identified seven action consequences with extrinsic incentive value that are mediated by outside institutions on the basis of work outcomes: (1) authority, (2) prestige, (3) security, (4) opportunity to win close friends, (5) salary, (6) promotion, and (7) recognition. Additionally, they distinguished among no fewer than five intrinsic kinds of incentives that result from job performance and have significance for self-esteem: (1) feelings of self-esteem, (2) opportunity for independent feelings and thoughts, (3) possibilities for individual development, (4) feelings of self-fulfillment, and (5) feeling that a task has been completed appropriately. This differentiation is surely more realistic and more appropriate than the succinct contrast of two self-evaluation affects (pride and shame) that forms the basis of Atkinson's achievement motivation theory. Unfortunately, hardly any achievement motivation researchers have attempted a comparable differentiation of incentive parameters.

Instrumentality

Finally, the concept of instrumentality has caused great difficulties because it can easily be confused with the probability that an event will occur. While probabilities can have values between 0 and 1, instrumentalities vary between $+1$ and -1. Vroom intended to express in this way the expected causal connection between two successive events — that is, the extent to which the existence of an action outcome is a necessary and sufficient, or at least sufficient, condition for the occurrence (positive instrumentality) or nonoccurrence (negative instrumentality) of the consequences. If, for example, students do not expect to be promoted to the next grade on the basis of their previous grades, the nonimprovement of grades has a positive instrumentality for negative consequences — that is, nonpromotion. The resulting product (positive $\times$ negative) is negative. In contrast, improvement of grades has a negative instrumentality for negative consequences. The resulting product (negative $\times$ negative) is positive. In the latter case, fear-related incentive motivation leads to increased effort in schoolwork as long as students believe that their grades can be improved. If instrumentality did not vary between $+1$ and -1, but only — like expectancy — between $+1$

and 0, our student would become inactive through fear of nonpromotion, since the product of expectancy and negative consequences would always be negative or 0.

Inactivity is also the theoretical consequence of the risk-taking model, in which the resulting action tendency would always have to be negative or 0 if the failure valence (failure motive times failure incentive) were greater than the success valence. Since this is irreconcilable with everyday observations and empirical findings (Chapter 3 and Chapter 4), instrumentality theory has turned out to be superior to the risk-taking model because of the instrumentality concept alone (quite apart from the fact that it enables us to take into account a number of different incentive values that are independent of subjective probability of success). Moreover, as our example shows, the instrumentality concept already contains everything that has been formalized in the last few years in any model of so-called effort calculation (Kukla, 1972a; Meyer, 1973a; see Chapter 6).

Even the research in industrial psychology inspired by Vroom has generally not implemented the instrumentality concept as prescribed by the model. For example, the degree of connection between effort and consequences was investigated instead of the degree of connection between action outcome and further consequences (e.g., Hackmann & Porter, 1968). On occasion the investigation of the connection between effort and consequences was combined with the investigation of the connection between outcome and consequences (e.g., Gavin, 1970; Lawler & Porter, 1967). Sometimes only indirect estimates of perceived instrumentality were used (e.g., Galbraith & Cummings, 1967; Goodman, Rose, & Furcom, 1970). Above all, negative instrumentalities were not explored seriously, but rather, only estimates of probability were taken (e.g., Pritchard & Sanders, 1973). Examinations of the parameters postulated by the model and their connections suffered from the failure to implement the instrumentality concept as prescribed by the model. Thus the instrumentality values of the latter two authors contributed almost nothing to the explanation of variance.

Instrumentality Theory and Achievement Motivation Research

Researchers in achievement motivation have rarely taken advantage of the productive perspectives of instrumentality theory. Elements are found in Raynor's concept of future orientation: The contingent path is based on instrumentality relationships between successive problem solutions, though Raynor connects them only through probabilities of success. In Atkinson and Raynor's achievement theory (1974; see Chapter 4) the efficiency of

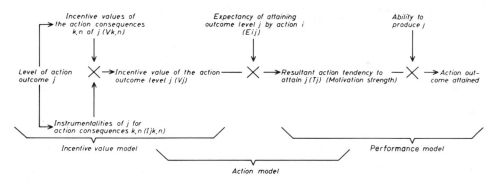

FIGURE 7.2   Process model of Vroom's instrumentality theory, combining the incentive value model, the action model, and the performance model. Vroom's terminology (Vroom, 1964) has been altered in part: *incentive value* instead of *valence, resultant action tendency* instead of *psychological force*.

current and cumulative achievement depends on the number and kind of situational incentive values, since these can lead to overmotivation or undermotivation.   But the influence of multithematic incentives on resultant motivational strength also awaits thorough investigation based on instrumentality theory.   In addition, Atkinson (1974b) was influenced by Vroom's so-called performance model in tracing back attainment of a certain performance level to the product of ability and efficiency.   The performance model is a third model, in addition to the incentive value model and the action model.   The action outcome attained is seen as a product of resulting action tendency and ability to perform the task in question.   This simple version of the performance model has not contributed anything worth mentioning to the explanation of variance in individual performance differences (see Heneman & Schwab, 1972; and Chapter 4).

Undoubtedly instrumentality theory can assist achievement motivation researchers in refining their formulation of questions, their experimental designs, and their explanation of cause and effect.   The next section reports some initial work in that area.   The basic concepts of instrumentality theory are illustrated by a process model that combines all three of Vroom's models: the incentive value, action, and performance models (see Figure 7.2).   The process model begins with the weighting (multiplication) of the incentive value of every action consequence by the instrumentality of the level of action outcome for the individual incentive values, resulting in the sum of the weighted incentive values for the level of action outcome.   In the action model the resulting incentive value is then weighted by the expectancy (subjective probability of success) that subjects will be able to attain their desired action outcome level through their own activity. This produces the resultant action tendency (motivation) to carry out the appropriate action — that is, the readiness to use an appropriate amount of effort. Finally, in the performance model the product of resultant action tendency and ability determines the action outcome.

An Extended Motivation Model: Splitting up the Summary Motive Concept

Since the early 1970s, researchers have differentiated and broken down the three principal factors of motivation — the personality factor (motive) and the two situational factors (subjective probability of success and incentive) — so much that we are now surprised that so much significant research could be accomplished with these summary concepts.

Let us first consider "motive" as an individual difference variable for weighting incentive. Initially the achievement motive was split into two motive tendencies: the success and failure motives. However, the failure motive was still too heterogeneous and was broken down into fear of failure based on a self-concept of low ability versus fear of failure based on fear of social consequences. In addition, certain individual personality parameters specify the individual motive system beyond typological assignment to a motive class. For example, there is considerable variance in the extent of goal discrepancy preferred and in whether the preferred discrepancy is positive or negative, especially among failure-motivated subjects. Kuhl (1978a) added goal discrepancy to motive as an additional personality parameter for individual generalized standard setting. Other personality parameters include such factors as attribution patterns, extent of future time perspective, reference-norm orientation, and strength of competing motives. These parameters all covary to some extent with summary motive classes. However, it does seem possible that if the parameters were all measured and considered separately, they might replace a summary motive construct and at the same time explain more variance in behavior — assuming that it is possible to measure all the individual parameters appropriately.

As for the incentive variable, it must be freed from its exclusive ties to subjective probability of success. Action consequences consist of more than self-evaluation. There are also other incentives — such as evaluation by others, superordinate goals, and extrinsic secondary effects — that motivate us to achievement-oriented behavior. As an individual evaluation of the situation is based on considering various kinds of possible action consequences, the incentive variable is a product of the interaction of personality and situational factors. Individual differences in anticipated incentives from an objectively similar situation are apparently the most likely variables to replace the present motive classification.

Finally, a number of situational factors must be added to subjective probability of success. The perceived instrumentalities of an action outcome for various action consequences are important. We must also take into account the perceived nature of the task, its requirements, the reference norms defined for the evaluation of the outcome, and the task-inherent causal structure for success and failure. Self-evaluation is affected by whether the task seems too easy or too hard, and whether it seems primarily dependent on ability, on effort, or on chance. We can ask ourselves to what extent any of these situational variables is purely situational — that is, lacking individual differences. Since it is always a matter of individual evaluation of situational conditions, individual prejudices can easily lead to accentuations and distortions. As reflected in debates on the interaction of personality and situation (see Olweus, 1977), the neat distinction between situational and personality factors and the question (perhaps inadmissable) as to which of the two determines behavior more decisively are at best oversimplifications.

Heckhausen (1977a, 1978b) has developed an extended model of motivation that contains most of the previously isolated motivational parameters. Its formalization is presented later, illustrated by a sample study. Although the model omits summary motive variables in favor of motivational variables that actually affect behavior, the necessity of motive constructs for explaining individual differences in behavior under otherwise equal situational conditions is not denied. To what extent is each individual motivational parameter also motive related — that is, to what extent is it dependent on personality characteristics as well as situational characteristics? This remains an open question. Heckhausen takes the opposite approach to previous explanatory strategies. He does not begin with a summary motive concept of individual differences (achievement motive) and then add one situational determinant after the other. Instead, he starts at the other end, with the many situation-dependent determinants that have been identified, seeking to find the extent of individual variation in each of them. This should eventually lead to a new motive concept with multidimensional differentiation. It remains to be seen how productive this approach will be and whether the investment in research on all these determinants will prove practicable. One can see that motivation theory has reached a state in which summary motive constructs are gradually taking on the character of fossils.

The extended motivation model is intended for goal-directed behavior and thus is not restricted to individual goal areas such as achievement-moti-

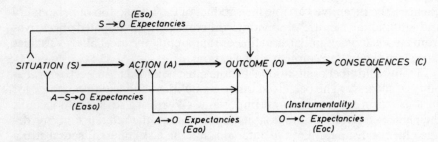

FIGURE 7.3 Four kinds of expectancies that are based on various event-stages in the motivational process. (From Heckhausen, 1977a, p. 287.)

vated behavior (for references to other motive areas, see Heckhausen, 1977b). It is a rationalistic model that assimilates and uses several approaches: the expectancy-value connection, instrumentality theory, achievement motivation theory, and causal attribution theory. The model also includes Bolles' (1972) "psychological syllogism": that is, the distinction between situation-outcome expectancies ($S - S^*$) and action-outcome expectancies ($R - S^*$; S^* signifies an incentive-laden outcome) from which the action to be performed results in the form of a syllogism.

The basis of the extended model is the product of expectancy and value. This product, which has previously not been described by any single word, can be called valence. Unlike traditional expectancy-value theories, the extended model identifies three kinds of related valences: situation, action, and outcome valences. The motivational process consists initially of determining the outcome to which the given situation will lead if one does not act on it (situation valence). Then one determines what actions on the person's own part might lead to an outcome involving desirable consequences or excluding undesirable consequences (action valence). The outcome valence is inserted into both the situation valence and the action valence as a value variable; it is the sum of all instrumentality-weighted incentive values of the consequences that will presumably result from a situation outcome or an action outcome.

The model is divided into four event-stages in the motivational process: situation, action, outcome, and consequences (see Figure 7.3). The action outcome is a kind of pivotal point. In itself it has no incentive; instead, it receives value from its consequences. Such a distinction between outcome and consequences is meaningful for at least three reasons. First, the subject is able to produce directly only action outcomes, but not their consequences. An outcome causes or facilitates the occurrence or nonoccurrence of a particular consequence without the subject's being able to intervene directly in the connection between outcome and consequences. Second, as a rule, an action outcome has a number of consequences. Some may not be intended, and one can either accept them or not. And third, the same action outcome has different consequences for different individuals, depending on their evaluative dispositions.

Expectancies

The structure of the model is clearest when we examine the distinction among four kinds of expectancies (see Figure 7.3). The situation-outcome expectancy (S → O) describes the subjective degree of probability that a current situation will lead to a future outcome state without one's own action. This expectancy contains a conditional base rate for the occurrence of future events. Along with the incentive values of the events — that is, the situation valences — everyone has built up from past experiences a large repertoire of such expectancies, on the basis of which all situations are evaluated (see Mischel, 1973). This kind of expectancy has always been neglected or confounded with action-outcome expectancies. In contrast, action-outcome expectancies (A → O) are almost the only expectancies that have been taken into account. They represent the subjective degree of probability that the situation can be altered by one's own actions in the desired manner.

A third kind of expectancy is the action-in-situation-outcome expectancy (A-S → O). It describes the subjective degree of probability with which external, variable circumstances will increase or diminish the action-outcome expectancy and thus lead to a resultant action-outcome expectancy. Finally, the outcome-consequence expectancy (O → C) describes the degree to which an outcome is instrumental for the occurrence of a consequence with particular incentive value. As in instrumentality theory, it is not expressed as a probability, but rather as an instrumentality that can vary between $+1$ and -1. In contrast with the action-outcome expectancy, this expectancy cannot be influenced by one's own actions — at least not directly.

Each of the four kinds of expectancy is based on a particular causal attribution of the event. The situation-outcome expectancy and the action-in-situation-outcome expectancy are based on the conviction that external causal factors are at work; in the case of achievement-related behavior these are — with the exception of task difficulty — relatively variable external factors such as support or interference by others or chance. Internal causal factors such as ability and effort appear in the action-outcome expectancy; they are seen in relation to task difficulty, which must be overcome by one's own ability and effort. The effort factor is not only variable, but also can be controlled by the persons who are exerting effort; thus these persons can even raise or lower the action-outcome expectancy in effort-dependent tasks if they intend to increase or reduce expenditure of effort. This intention is apparently based on a calculation of effort (see Chapter 6) that connects one's own ability with the degree of difficulty that is to be mastered. Alterations of the action-outcome expectancy after success and failure depend on the relative weight of the stable causal factors in comparison with the variable causal factors, as we explained in Chapter 5. The more that unexpected success and failure are attributed to ability and task difficulty, and the less they are attributed to momentary effort and chance, the more one tends to alter an action-outcome expectancy.

As for the outcome-consequence expectancies, the causal factors that create the instrumentality relationship have hardly been examined. The principal question is surely, "Which consequences are involved?" The instrumentality of the action outcomes for a superordinate goal might lie in the nature of the desired superordinate goal. Evaluation by outsiders and extrinsic secondary consequences (such as grades, titles, or payment) are provided by others, in part by institutions created for the purpose and on the basis of definite rules. The influence of arbitrary elements such as preferential treatment or discrimination can also be expected.

So far, the only role that causal attribution has played in achievement motivation theory is in the instrumentality of the action outcome for self-evaluation. Tasks that the acting person perceives as neither too easy nor too difficult, but rather as moderately difficult, have the highest instrumentality for self-evaluation affects. At such tasks success and failure can be maximally attributed to one's own ability and effort rather than to excessively low or high task difficulty or to good or bad luck (see Chapter 5). In this range of moderate difficulty slight differences in ability and effort have the greatest influence on the attainment of the goal. Thus the instrumentality function of difficulty for self-evaluation can be described as an inverted U function. When the action-outcome expectancy (probability of success) is 0 or 1.00, the value of the function is 0; when the action-outcome expectancy is .50, the function is $+1$.

Incentives

The consequences of action outcomes have incentive value. Not until instrumentality theory was formulated was a more detailed differentiation of consequences and their incentive values undertaken, since they, in sum, determine the outcome valence. Heckhausen (1977a) made a rough classification of various kinds of consequences for the extended model: self-evaluation, approaching a superordinate goal, evaluation by others, and side effects. As we saw in Chapter 3, the incentive values of self-evaluation following a successful action outcome have been described as monotonically inverse functions (Lewin *et al.,* 1944) or linear inverse functions (Atkinson, 1957; risk-taking model) of the action-outcome expectancy. This description has been confirmed to some extent. (Following failure, the self-evaluation incentive is, of course, not an inverse function, but rather a direct function of the action-outcome expectancy.)

The traditional position of achievement motivation researchers is that individual motive differences can be reflected directly in a differential weighting of the self-evaluation incentive for success and failure. As we reported in Chapter 3, the motive-dependent weighting of the success and failure incentives has hardly been documented convincingly. The studies cited in Chapter 3 did not restrict themselves explicitly to self-evaluation when measuring incentive values. Heckhausen (1978a) did, however, limit himself to self-evaluation incentive in one study. He found that in comparison with success-motivated subjects, failure-motivated subjects did not evaluate themselves less positively after success, but they did evaluate themselves more negatively after failure. This difference in self-evaluation was not based on a motive-related difference in failure attribution. Cooper (1983) has reported a motive-dependent weighting of success incentives, but not of failure incentives.

As a rule, action outcomes do not stand alone; instead, they facilitate our approaching a superordinate goal with high incentive value. This approach is a further consequence that receives its incentive value from the superordinate goal. Numerous laboratory studies have presented the tasks used to determine level of aspiration or achievement as personally important, without actually having determined whether and to what extent superordinate goal incentives were operative. The studies on the motivating influence of future orientation in a contingent path (Raynor, 1974) and of induced high goal setting (Locke, 1968; Mierke, 1955), which we have already described, are more convincing; but here too the superordinate goal incentive was not measured individually and in isolation.

In borderline cases the incentive value of evaluation by others can resemble the incentive value of self-evaluation, if we ascribe to the outside evaluator the same standards, reference norms, and causal attributions that we apply to our own performance outcomes. As a rule, however, evaluation by others probably arouses additional incentive values — for example, when subjects are seen by experimenters as cooperative and are respected by them. Seeing oneself as having risen (or as not having dropped) in value in the eyes of another person after a possible success or failure are motivating incentives. We can speak of self-serving attributional biases when people feel more responsible for their successes than they do for their failures (see Miller, 1976; Snyder, Stephan, & Rosenfield, 1976; summarized by Bradley,

1978). Failure-motivated subjects seem to be particularly receptive to the incentives of evaluation by others. When their affiliation motive is strong and tends toward hope of affiliation they set their goals excessively high in the presence of the experimenter. When their affiliation motive is weak or is determined by fear of rejection, their level of aspiration is low (Jopt, 1974; Schneider & Meise, 1973). Other examples are explicitly multithematic incentive studies that also include the incentive of competition, as we mentioned in the discussion of performance efficiency in Chapter 4 (e.g., Atkinson, 1974a; Horner, 1974a).

The incentives of evaluation by others certainly overlap considerably with the incentives of side effects of an action outcome. One good example is French's arousal study (1958b). When subjects with a high affiliation motive were working for the group rather than for themselves, and when the experimenter gave feedback during task processing about how well the group was working together, performance outcomes for these subjects showed the highest motivational strength. A further example is found in Heckhausen (1968a, p. 166), which examines the receptivity of subjects to anticipated side effects, given that the workings of such side effects conflict with those of the self-evaluative consequences of task difficulty. Subjects were allowed to choose tasks of varying difficulty, but for each task that they solved, regardless of difficulty, they received the same number of points on a test that they believed to be important. Under such conditions the easiest tasks were chosen most frequently. However, the linear preference function was significantly steeper (i.e., favored the easiest tasks more) with failure-motivated than with success-motivated subjects. Thus they were more receptive to the reward that contradicted intrinsic self-evaluation incentives.

Parameters for Anchoring Motive Constructs

If we do not want to proceed from a summary motive construct, then the question becomes, on which parameters of the extended model can motive-like constructs — that is, individual difference variables — be anchored most productively? A theoretical analysis by Heckhausen (1977a) has identified six parameter areas.

1. The first parameter area is the incentive weights of superordinate goals. Individuals differ according to which content classes of events and activities tend most to lead them to "concern with a standard of excellence" (McClelland *et al.,* 1953).

2. The second parameter area is the incentive weights of success and failure in self-evaluation. They apparently depend on the individual goal-

setting standard, which is a neglected variable, since goal setting has been treated only as a dependent variable up to now; however, see Kuhl (1978a).

3. The third parameter area is the degree to which action-outcome expectancies are revised in view of failure and success. Here individual differences are based on biases toward stable versus variable causal attribution. Self-concepts of one's own abilities play a central role here.

4. The fourth parameter area is the instrumentality of the outcome for self-evaluation. On the one hand, the extent of instrumentality (i.e., of internal causal attribution) for outcome levels of the same subjective probability of success can differ from one individual to the next. On the other hand, the instrumentality can be negative if the subject is hoping to avoid certain outcome feedback that is relevant to self-esteem. In such a case, outcome feedback has negative instrumentality for the avoidance of information that is relevant to self-esteem, especially when the incentive value of the outcome is negative. (In this case, the extended model predicts that the preference function for task difficulty will be reversed. When instrumentality is negative, areas of difficulty that would normally have negative self-evaluation valence receive positive valence.)

5. The fifth parameter area is the instrumentality of the outcome for the attainment of superordinate goals, which is expressed by individual differences in future orientation. Some individuals are more inclined or more able than others to anticipate the structure of the path of action and to extend its time perspective farther.

6. Finally, the sixth parameter area is susceptibility to incentives consisting of extrinsic side effects of an action outcome. Susceptibility to side effects depends on the individual's hierarchy of incentive weights for various motivational classes.

Five of these six parameter areas (leaving out the fifth area) were used by Ludwig (1982) in a structured interview with university students. When the answers were scaled, the correlations among these five parameters of the achievement motive were between .45 and .84. Two parameters showed especially close relationships: incentive weights of success and failure (i.e., whether the subject approaches or avoids achievement-related situations), and favorable versus unfavorable causal attribution pattern for success and failure. Both parameters were considered to be a single directional component of the achievement motive. Another compound component consisted of two other parameters: the level of personal standards, and the importance of the achievement motive (the preference for achievement-oriented situations over situations calling for affiliation, and the diversity of situations that are considered to be achievement-related). These two parameters are

TABLE 7.3

Significant Correlations (τ) between Five Model Parameters and Life-Span Data[a]

| | Model parameters of the achievement motive | | | | |
| | Importance | | Direction | | |
Achievement-related life-span data[b]	Importance of achievement	Personal standards	Incentive weight	Attribution pattern	Intrinsic vs. extrinsic
Cognitive competence		.49	.32		
Parents' reaction to failure in school					
Calm, encouragement	.23	.20	.44	.26	.27
External control	−.35	−.32	−.47	−.36	−.40
5th grade					
Fear of failure			−.34	−.32	
10–13th grades					
Fear of failure			−.53	−.35	−.25
Importance of performance	.47	.36	.22	.23	
Work invested	.45	.39	.20	.28	
School-leaving certificate	.35	.40	.39	.37	.41
Studies					
Amount of work	.65	.65	.47	.40	.36
Regularity	.55	.55	.33	.40	.38
Work intensity	.60	.66	.52	.50	.46
Test grades	.41	.50	.21	.21	.20
Cooperation with others	−.21				

[a] Adapted from Ludwig, 1982, p. 155.

[b] Biographical data cover the time from the middle of the period spent in school through the middle of university study. $N = 49$, of which 23 were male.

viewed as a single component representing the importance of the achievement motive.

In addition, the author measured a number of achievement-related life-span variables in her student subjects. Besides a test score for cognitive ability, the variables ranged from parents' reactions to failure in school and fear of failure in the middle and upper grades to study habits and performance in studies in the fourth and higher semesters at the university. Table 7.3 contains the significant correlations of these variables with the five model parameters of the achievement motive. The two boxes in the correlation matrix enclose those achievement-related life-span variables that are most closely correlated with the importance component and the directional component of the achievement motive. Parents' reactions to failure in school and the subject's own fear of failure in school are closely associated with the directional component; work behavior in school and at the university as well as grades are closely related to the importance component of the achievement motive. The findings are suggestive, encouraging us to develop model parameters for the achievement motive and to use them in analysis of everyday achievement-oriented behavior and of its development and outcomes.

In the past the extended model has been used as a heuristic model for further theory building, for the discovery of new research approaches, and for the explanation of findings that had been difficult to understand. In the latter sense Heckhausen (1977a) examined the results of 22 studies of task difficulty preference for their compatibility with the extended model. While the preference profile of success-motivated subjects was uniform in all studies and culminated in moderately high levels of difficulty, the preference profiles of failure-motivated subjects in the individual studies varied considerably. Four preference profiles were identified: high difficulty, low difficulty, high and low difficulty, and relative preference for the extreme ranges of difficulty. The risk-taking model cannot explain this variance. A post-experimental analysis of the respective experimental conditions for their demand characteristics suggested post hoc explanations of the individual preference profiles. For example, failure-motivated subjects preferred very high levels of difficulty when the situation offered more incentives for self-evaluation than for evaluation by others or when they had a high hope-of-affiliation motive. When incentives for evaluation by others dominated or when the affiliation motive was dominated by fear of rejection, failure-motivated subjects preferred low difficulty.

Choice of Tasks with Superordinate Goal Valences

Another study examined the conclusions derived from the extended model and contrasted them with Atkinson's risk-taking model and Raynor's elaboration of future orientation. Kleinbeck and Schmidt (1979) asked apprentices to choose from 11 levels of difficulty in producing a workpiece (social reference norm). Task processing was evaluated for time invested and for quality—by points, as usual—by the foremen in an automobile factory's workshop for apprentices. Along with evaluation of other tasks, evaluation of this task contributed to the decision as to whether the apprentice's training had been successfully completed. Before beginning work, the apprentices had familiarized themselves with the task of making a certain piece from a metal slug. They also predicted their subjective probability of success for each of the 11 levels of difficulty; indicated how important they considered success at this task to be for future success in their training (instrumentality of the action outcome for the superordinate goal); and chose one of the 11 levels of difficulty for the task to be performed. The subjects were divided into groups of success- and failure-motivated persons (according to Mehrabian, 1968) and were divided within the two motive groups by low and high subjective instrumentality of the task outcome for success in the overall training process.

Individual parameters were determined in order to derive hypotheses from the extended model. The incentive of the superordinate goal was twice as high as the maximum self-evaluation incentive. Low and high instrumentality was standardized at $+.20$ and $+.80$, respectively. For the success-motivated group the success incentive of self-evaluation was weighted twice as heavily as the failure incentive; correspondingly, the failure incentive was weighted double for failure-motivated subjects. The instrumentality for negative consequences of self-evaluation (failure incentive) received a minus sign for failure-motivated subjects, since they are supposed to pursue the motive goal of avoiding dissatisfaction with their own low ability, and a failure does not contribute toward the attainment of such a goal. And finally, the task difficulties chosen were divided into three groups of low, moderate, and high subjective probability of success (Ps of .20, .50, or .80).

The derivation of hypotheses from the formulas of the extended model (Heckhausen, 1977a) was as follows. First, it was necessary to determine the outcome valence, which in this case was composed of self-evaluation valence and superordinate goal valence. The instrumentality U of the self-evaluation consequences was defined as follows:

$$U = (Ps \times [1 - Ps]) \times 4.$$

That is, it varies between 0 and $+1$ and, like the resultant tendency in the risk-taking model, reaches its positive or negative maximum when $Ps = .50$. It decreases more and more rapidly in both directions as it approaches the two end points. The incentive value of the self-evaluation consequences following success Is and failure If is—in contrast with the risk-taking model—not a linear, but instead a quadratic function of the probability of success:

$$Is = (1 - Ps)^2, \qquad If = -Ps^2.$$

The valences of self-evaluation for success Vs and failure Vf are the product of the success or failure incentive and the instrumentality U for the relevant self-evaluation consequence:

$$Vs = (1 - Ps)^2 \times U, \qquad Vf = -Ps^2 \times U.$$

The average of the success and failure valences is the resultant self-evaluation valence V_{C1}:

$$V_{C1} = \frac{(Vs - Vf)}{2}.$$

TABLE 7.4

Action Valences Derived from the Model[a]

Ps^b	Success and failure motives equally strong (1/1)		Success motive stronger (2/1)		Failure motive stronger (1/2)	
	$Ins_{C2} = +.20$	$Ins_{C2} = +.80$	$Ins_{C2} = +.20$	$Ins_{C2} = +.80$	$Ins_{C2} = +.20$	$Ins_{C2} = +.80$
.20	0.12	0.36	0.16	0.40	0.13	0.37
.50	0.20	0.80	0.26	0.86	0.38	0.99
.80	0.17	1.13	0.18	1.14	0.65	1.62

[a] From Kleinbeck and Schmidt, 1979, p. 4.

[b] Ps = probability of success of the action outcome. Ins_{C2} = instrumentality of the action outcome for the superordinate goal. For the self-evaluation valence, success and failure incentives are either unweighted (success and failure motive equally strong); or the success incentive receives double weight (success motive stronger than failure motive); or the failure incentive receives double weight and the relevant instrumentality is negative (failure motive stronger than success motive). The incentive of the superordinate goal is twice as strong as the maximal incentive of self-evaluation.

In addition to the valence of self-evaluation consequences V_{C1}, another consequence that must be taken into account is the superordinate goal with its valence V_{C2}, since it contributes to the total valence of the action outcome V_O:

$$V_O = V_{C1} + V_{C2}.$$

The valence of the superordinate goal (like any other consequence) is, in turn, a product of incentive I_{C2} and the instrumentality Ins_{C2} of the action outcome for the superordinate goal:

$$V_{C2} = I_{C2} \times Ins_{C2}.$$

(Instrumentality must, of course, be determined separately for each outcome.) Finally we can determine the action valence V_A, which corresponds to the motivational strength aroused for a particular action outcome. The action valence is the product of the subjective probability of success of the action outcome in question and the outcome valence:

$$V_A = Ps \times V_O$$
$$= Ps \times \left[\frac{(Is \times U) + (If \times U)}{2} + (I_{C2} \times Ins_{C2}) \right].$$

When the parameter specifications given above are inserted into this formula, the action valences shown in Table 7.4 appear. These are the valences that can be expected for tasks with low, middle, and high probabilities of success and with perceived high or low instrumentality of task success for the attainment of the superordinate goal when the success and failure motives

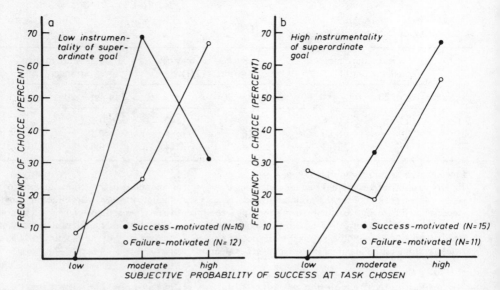

FIGURE 7.4   Task choice by success- and failure-motivated subjects, as a function of low (a) and high (b) instrumentality of the action outcome for a superordinate goal (success in job training).   (Adapted from Kleinbeck & Schmidt, 1979, pp. 8, 9).

are equally strong or one of the two is stronger.   According to the model, success-motivated subjects prefer moderate subjective levels of difficulty when instrumentality for the superordinate goal is low.   It is here — as in the risk-taking model — that the self-evaluation valence carries more weight than the superordinate goal valence.   In contrast, when instrumentality for the superordinate goal is high, its outcome valence is dominant and leads to a preference for the easiest tasks.   On the other hand, for failure-motivated subjects the self-evaluation valence and the superordinate goal valence do not contradict each other under either instrumentality condition, since their self-evaluation valence is always maximal with the easiest tasks.   Thus these subjects should always prefer the easiest tasks, regardless of their instrumentality for the superordinate goals.   In addition, we should note that for failure-motivated subjects action valences are positive under all conditions specified (and — unlike the corresponding resulting tendencies in the risk-taking model — not negative).

The results (see Figure 7.4) confirm the derived hypotheses fully.   The frequencies of task preference correspond to the ranks of action valence strengths in Table 7.4 under both instrumentality conditions.   (The only exception is that the choice frequencies for easy and moderately difficult tasks are slightly reversed in the case of failure-motivated subjects and high instrumentality.)

The findings show, as do Wish's results (Wish, 1970, mentioned in Chapter 4; see Table 4.2), that the risk-taking model is restricted to self-evaluation valences and is not adequate when superordinate goals on which something really depends come into play. Nor can Raynor's revision of the model explain these findings. His revision shows success-motivated subjects with a contingent path of action as preferring the easiest tasks, without any distinction being made among graduated instrumentalities for a superordinate goal. However, failure-motivated subjects would always have to choose the most difficult tasks. The extended model is apparently in a better position to represent the complexity of achievement motivation outside an experimental laboratory, because of the differentiation of the outcome valence into various incentive values and instrumentalities.

The extended model has also proved satisfactory in answering such questions as which schoolchildren in a class will prepare themselves sufficiently for an anticipated test. One of these studies involved a tenth-grade English test four weeks before final grades were assigned (Heckhausen & Rheinberg, 1980). All of the students had previously had ample opportunity to experience, as stressed by their English teacher, that studying at home would pay off in better test grades. But according to the extended model, a high action-outcome expectancy would not be a sufficient reason for students to prepare for the test. The students would also need outcome consequences with positive incentive value, as well as sufficiently high outcome-consequence expectancies (instrumentalities); that is, the amount of preparation must appear to be sufficient to ensure the attainment of the test grade that the student seeks. As for outcome consequences, 16 possible consequences of the test outcome were measured. All students indicated how many "weeks without allowance" each consequence would be worth for them. The instrumentalities were scaled. Incentive values and instrumentalities were averaged over all 16 consequences for each student.

Even this crude procedure, in which both variables are divided into three categories — high, medium, and low — shows (see Table 7.5) that as instrumentality (from left to right) and incentive value (from above to below) increase, the time used in preparation for the test turns out more frequently to be sufficient. Only 2 of the 26 students are not represented in the prediction frame of the model (sufficient preparation in the cells at lower left and upper right). Additionally, it is possible to determine which valences of the 16 consequences were particularly decisive. A factor analysis showed three kinds of consequences: (1) self-evaluative emotions (e.g., "I'll be somewhat proud of my ability."), (2) task-related incentive (e.g., "I'll know that I can communicate better when traveling in foreign countries."), and (3) superordinate goal of a satisfactory end to the school year. The incentive value of this superordinate goal alone did not correlate significantly with sufficiency of preparation ($\rho = .33$), but the corresponding instrumentality (.46) did,

TABLE 7.5

Test Preparation and Outcome-Consequence
Expectancy[a]

Median incentive value	Median outcome-consequence expectancy (instrumentality)		
	Low	Moderate	High
Low	$---\pm$[b]	$-\pm$	$-+$
Moderate	$-\pm\pm$	$-\pm\pm+$	$\pm+$
High	$\pm+$	$\pm++$	$++++$

[a] Adapted from Heckhausen and Rheinberg, 1980, p. 38.

[b] Students who claimed to have prepared sufficiently (+), insufficiently (−), or not quite sufficiently (±) for a test. $N = 26$.

along with the valence (the product of these two) (.57). In contrast, the incentive values of the two other kinds of consequences (self-evaluative emotions and task-related incentive) did correlate with sufficiency of preparation.

Further analysis showed that most students found all three kinds of consequences to be valuable. Those to whom evaluative emotions were important were also interested in the task itself, and those who were interested in one or the other of these two kinds of consequences also considered final grades to be an important superordinate goal. One or the other type of incentive could be missing without preventing preparation. That was the case for approximately every fourth student. Nevertheless, it looks as if self-centered incentive values were able to compensate for task-related ones, and task-related values for self-centered values; self-centered incentive values could also replace superordinate goal incentives, and the superordinate goal incentives could replace self-centered incentive values.

In other analyses of similar questions the extended motivation model also proved productive (e.g., Krampen, 1979). Its many individual determinants suggest a departure from group (i.e., regression) statistics in favor of analyses of logically structured propositions for each individual case. Rheinberg (1982) conducted such studies. He found students whose studying at home could not be explained by "utility-centered" motivation with the usual incentives as in the extended model, but only through "task-inherent stimulation" (Heckhausen & Rheinberg, 1980). That is, task performance was intrinsically motivating, pursued for its own sake.

Model Testing by Computer Simulation of the Individual Case

In all motivation models previously mentioned, sample-dependent parameters were used, linked deterministically in a mathematical formalization. From various points of view it seems more appropriate to create parameters that are not dependent on samples, in order to free the analysis from characteristics of the particular subject and task samples. This would also free the analysis from the assumptions made when data are evaluated using correlational or inferential statistics, such as assumptions about a normal distribution of scores. For this purpose stochastic test models like the one designed by Rasch (1960; see Fischer, 1974), in which each personality parameter is related to a task parameter (or, more generally, a situation parameter), are appropriate. For example, the perceived ability to perform a type of task and the experienced difficulty (solubility) of each individual problem can be derived from a matrix of the answers of all subjects to a question about the subjective probabilities of solving each problem. Latent personality parameters and latent task parameters can be estimated. Moreover, we can determine whether there is a specific objective correlation between the latent personality or item parameter and the response behavior —that is, a correlation that remains invariant when parameters obtained from different samples are compared.

And as for the connections among the model parameters, computer simulation enables us to combine the formulation of logical propositions with a stochastic test model. We can check the scores for each individual subject in a sample against the model, in order to determine the extent to which a simulated action parameter (dependent variable) in the model corresponds to a parameter that was actually measured. It is important to note that a motivation model need not apply to each subject. The behavior of different groups of subjects can correspond to different process models (see Bem & Allen, 1974). Not until we stop attempting to test models only for universal applicability can we overcome the onesidedness of traditional personality psychology, which dissolves subjects nomothetically into a collection of separate explanatory constructs and ignores situations or merely records them idiographically. In contrast, those who seek motivational models that claim validity only for specifically described personality groups tend to treat subjects more idiographically and situations more nomothetically—that is, to treat both sides in a more balanced fashion than before (see Heckhausen, 1977a, p. 311).

Guided by this principle, Kuhl (1977) analyzed some personality and situation parameters of achievement motivation models from the perspectives of measurement theory and process theory. His subjects performed

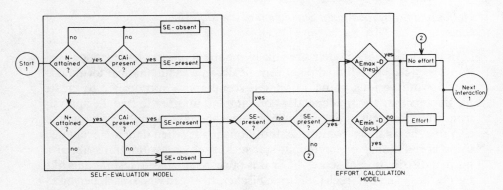

FIGURE 7.5 Model variant to explain intended effort, on the basis of anticipated self-evaluation as well as effort calculation. Legend: $N+$ and $N-$, norm values of the outcomes starting with which the experience of success or failure begins; CAi, internal causal attribution: $SE+$ and $SE-$, positive and negative self-evaluation; A_{Emax} and A_{Emin}, experience of one's own ability at maximal and minimal effort; D, experienced task difficulty on the basis of task-inherent reference norm. (Adapted from Kuhl, 1977, p. 278.)

variants of a task (connecting points in a net of coordinates) at 20 different levels of difficulty. Besides the performance outcomes, three additional dependent variables were measured subsequently as anticipation of repeated task processing: positive self-evaluation, negative self-evaluation, and intended effort. In addition, a number of personality and corresponding situational parameters with achievement themes were measured for each individual task with the aid of questionnaires. For example, for establishment of positive or negative norms subjects were asked: "Would you be able to speak of a good (bad) performance if you had (not) solved this problem?" This corresponds to the personal standard, as defined by Kuhl (1978a; see above). Other parameters included causal attribution (extent to which achievement is influenced by controllable causes such as effort and ability that can be acquired, rather than external causes); perception of one's own ability; solubility of the problem (with maximal and minimal effort); and others.

Figure 7.5 displays three model variants formulated as logical propositions simulating intended effort, in the form of flow charts. The first model variant links two different processes. The first question is whether a positive or negative self-evaluation $SE\pm$ is anticipated in the task version in question, based on the outcome. As in the extended model (Heckhausen, 1977a), norm values (i.e., outcome standards) for the experience of failure $N-$ or success $N+$ and an internal causal attribution of the outcome CAi are the determining factors. Effort is not calculated until a positive or negative self-evaluation is anticipated, according to Kukla (1972a) and Meyer (1973a). In calculation of effort, subjects determine whether the experienced difficulty D will be too much for their own perceived ability even at maximal effort A_{Emax} or will require too little of them at minimal effort A_{Emin}. A constant can be inserted as a critical limiting value for the differences $A_{\text{Emax}} - D$ and $A_{\text{Emin}} - D$. If the differences are greater or less than the critical limiting values—that is, if the task is experienced as neither too difficult nor too easy—then an adequate degree of effort is intended. The second model variant involves only a calculation of effort, and the third takes into account only the self-evaluation consequence, as a determinant of effort intention. Every rhomboid in the flow chart contains personality and situation parameters that correspond to each other. (In Figure 7.5 these are specified only in the model of effort calculation.) With the aid of the model equation of the Rasch model (Rasch, 1960), the probability of a positive answer is calculated for each rhomboid. Since the test model is stochastic, a yes- or no-answer is generated for each of 100 to 1000 iterations in the computer simulation (each for a single task) for each question (rhomboid) on the basis of the probability value. The final result is a theoretical score distribution for a dependent variable such as intended effort. This theoretical distribution can be compared with the empirically determined intended-effort score. Table 7.6 shows for how many of the 105 subjects the empirical score for each of the four dependent variables did not deviate significantly from the theoretical score—that is, it indicates the extent of compatibility with the model in question. Only four of the eight model variants simulated by Kuhl are contrasted here:

1. self-evaluation and effort calculation (see Figure 7.5)
2. only self-evaluation

TABLE 7.6
Computer Simulation of Self-Evaluation, Intended Effort, and Performance[a,b]

| | Self-evaluation | | | |
Model variants	Positive	Negative	Intended effort	Performance
1. Self-evaluation plus effort calculation	38	22	28	66
2. Only self-evaluation	37	22	42	69
3. Only effort calculation	—	—	52	68
4. Risk-taking model	29	34	9	60

[a] Adapted from Kuhl, 1977, p. 301.
[b] Number of subjects conforming to four model variants. $N = 105$.

3. only effort calculation
4. Atkinson's risk-taking model

For the computer simulation of the fourth dependent variable (perform-ance), Kuhl appended to each of the four models an additional subprocess to reflect the degree of objective ability and intended effort.

As we can see from Table 7.6, self-evaluation was predicted for nearly equal numbers of subjects (20–35%) by the self-evaluation model (1 and 2) and the risk-taking model (4). The first model was somewhat superior in predicting positive self-evaluation and the second model in predicting nega-tive self-evaluation. With regard to intended effort, the pure self-evaluation model was hardly inferior to the pure effort-calculation model. In contrast, the risk-taking model explained the behavior of only a few subjects. With regard to performance, scores for more than half of the subjects were com-patible with all of the models.

As shown by the addition of superordinate goal consequences and side effects to the extended model, and by other examples above, with the aid of computer simulation model variants can be modified easily and even sup-plemented, in order to develop models that have explanatory value for as many subjects as possible. Nevertheless, different process models of moti-vation will probably always be required for different subject groups. Kuhl (1977) found that for his 105 subjects, intended effort corresponded for 21 subjects only to that predicted by the self-evaluation model, for 31 only to that predicted by the calculation-of-effort model, for 21 to both models, and finally, for 32 to neither model.

The next step, then, would be to look for differences between such subject groups. Kuhl found that subjects whose intended effort corresponded only to the calculation-of-effort model and not to the self-evaluation model had significantly higher scores for effort, estimates of ability, internal causal factors, negative evaluation of failure, and objective ability. It remains an open question why precisely these personality characteristics mark the valid-ity boundaries for various models of motivation. We must remember in future research that we cannot expect to find unlimited generalizability for any motivation model to all individuals. Such fictions, nurtured by tradi-tional statistical evaluation methods, disappear when we subject the individ-ual cases to a computer simulation on the basis of stochastic test models.

The Dynamic Theory of Achievement Motivation

Basing their work on the same facts and considerations that led to the addition of inertial tendencies to the original model (Atkinson & Cartwright, 1964), Atkinson and Birch (1970) developed a "dynamics of action" model (see Kuhl, in press a). This is a general, formalized motivational theory designed to explain subjects' transition from one action to another. Instead of episodic consideration of individual behavioral segments, as in Atkinson's old model (see Chapter 3) and — with few exceptions — in all other approaches in motivational psychology, for Atkinson and Birch the stream of behavior is the point of departure for their analysis. In a subsequent study they attempted to show that all behavioral phenomena in achievement-oriented situations that had previously been explained by the original and revised risk-taking models could also be explained by their new theory (Atkinson & Birch, 1974).

The new orientation introduced by Atkinson and Birch meant progress for achievement motivation research. In an apparent attempt to test models, achievement motivation researchers have tended to analyze only brief episodes of achievement-oriented behavior. As a rule they have not even analyzed the behavior itself, but only the completed behavioral product. In achievement-oriented situations, like any others, subjects change from one achievement-oriented way of behaving to another; or they perform actions with other orientations between one successful or unsuccessful completion of an achievement-motivated action and another. Interrupted and incomplete actions leave behind a tendency to persevere — that is, to resume the action. Motivation models must be formulated in such a way that they describe and explain the alternation of activities and the perseverance of tendencies. This demand by Atkinson and Birch cannot be emphasized enough.

What concepts are combined in the new dynamic model? First of all, the motivational tendency that is currently strongest is supposed to be reflected in behavior. If the behavior changes, we assume that a new tendency is dominant. Motivational tendencies are altered over time through the effect of arousing (instigating) and reducing (consummatory) forces. Instigating forces occur as the consequence of perceived situational factors, but also — according to Birch, Atkinson, and Bongort (1974) — as the consequence of thinking about possible behavioral goals. Consummatory forces occur as the consequence of carrying out an action or part of an action.

Behind every action is a behavioral tendency that is formed as a resultant action tendency $\overline{T}$ — as in the risk-taking model — constituted by the difference between an approach-oriented action tendency T that is altered over time by instigating and consummatory forces, and an avoidance-oriented tendency to inaction (N = "Negation").

$$\overline{T} = T - N.$$

The authors assume that in achievement-oriented behavior the forces behind the two tendencies T and N can be equated with the approach and avoidance tendencies of the risk-taking model. The instigating force F behind T would be

$$F = HS \times Is \times Ps,$$

and the inhibiting force I behind N would be

$$I = FF \times If \times Pf.$$

Thus tendencies to act or not to act change over time, depending on success and failure and on the perception of the achievement-oriented situation (which is determined by motive tendencies), on perceived goals of action, and on expectancies with regard to these. The instigating force determines the extent to which the action tendency T increases in strength over time; the same is true of the inhibiting force with the "negaction" tendency N.

As soon as a behavioral tendency becomes dominant it is no longer influenced only by an instigating force, but also by a consummatory force C. As in Lorenz' motivation model (1953), the performance of instrumental behaviors and goal behaviors reduces the original motivational strength — that is, consummatory force reduces the behavioral tendency. The stronger the behavioral tendency, the stronger the consummatory force becomes (otherwise a behavioral tendency would increase indefinitely). Since the consummatory force is also influenced by the particular nature of the activity to be carried out c, it is defined thus:

$$C = c \times T.$$

If a behavioral tendency becomes dominant, the difference between instigating F and consummatory force C determines the strength of the approach tendency T. However, since F and C grow with time — usually at different rates — the difference between the two forces, and thus the strength of the approach tendency, can change constantly. The alteration of the approach tendency over time is thus expressed as follows:

$$\frac{dT}{dt} = F - C.$$

The same is true of the avoidance tendency N. It is determined by the inhibiting force I, which — like the instigating force — can be aroused and strengthened by situational factors, thoughts, or ideas. The inhibiting force consumes itself in its continual resistance to the behavioral tendency in question. This process of self-consumption is caused by a consummatory force of the inaction tendency, the force of resistance R. Just as the consummatory force C is a product of the approach tendency T and the parameter c, the strength of the force of resistance is a product of the strength of the force of inaction (Negaction) multiplied by a parameter r for the kind of activity that is being suppressed:

$$R = N \times r.$$

Further assumptions and definitions are less important for our discussion here; they appear in the original studies (Atkinson & Birch, 1970, 1974, 1978).

Empirical Evidence: The Role of Consummatory Forces

The empirical testing of the dynamic model has so far been restricted to the role of consummatory forces. In two studies the authors used a computer program by Seltzer (1973) and others (Bongort, 1975; Seltzer & Sawusch, 1974) in the attempt to separate the consummatory force from the instigating force. This program simulated the behavioral stream in achievement-oriented choice situations on the basis of the assumptions and definitions of the dynamic model. The authors used the simulation to make predictions that could not be made on the basis of the old risk-taking model. Cases were constructed that would give the new model a chance to demonstrate its superiority.

One of the studies (Blankenship, 1979) demonstrates that easy tasks have a higher consummatory value c than difficult tasks and that this is the reason why less time is devoted to them under otherwise equal conditions. The other study (Kuhl & Blankenship, 1979a, 1979b) does not predict time allocated to a task, but rather preference for levels of difficulty of the same task when repeated choices must be made. According to computer-simulated derivations from the dynamic model, subjects should spend more time at the more difficult tasks in the first case, and choose increasingly difficult tasks in the second case. Neither of these behaviors can be derived from the risk-taking model. According to that model, in the first case success-motivated subjects would spend just as much time at easy tasks as at difficult tasks when the level of difficulty was equally far below and above $Ps = .50$. And in the second case the initial behavioral tendency would remain the same and the same level of difficulty would be chosen again each time. Let us describe each experiment in turn.

In order to show that easier tasks have a higher consummatory value than difficult tasks, Blankenship chose highly success-motivated subjects (n Ach > TAQ) and familiarized them with low, moderate, and high levels of difficulty of a computer target-shooting game (Ps of .70, .50, and .30). Then the main part of the experiment began, in the absence of the experimenter. Initially subjects were to rate the quality of jokes; then they were to resume

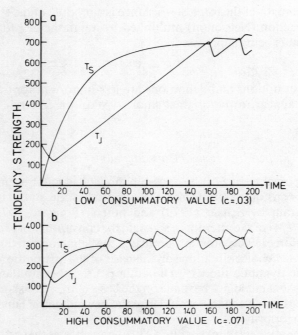

FIGURE 7.6 Computer simulation of the initial dura-
tion of an achievement-related activity (computer target-
shooting game) as a function of low (a) or high (b) probabil-
ity of success. T_S = tendency to continue with computer
target-shooting game. T_J = tendency to return to joke rat-
ing. c = consummatory value for the activity, by which the
approach tendency T is multiplied to obtain consummatory
force C. (Adapted from Blankenship, 1982, p. 911.)

the target-shooting game. They could return from the target-shooting game
to the jokes whenever they liked. In one condition the subjects were told
that they were being given the easy target-shooting games and in the other
condition they were told that they were being given only the difficult target-
shooting games. Actually they received tasks with a moderate rate of success
($Ps = .50$), so that the difference in time spent at the games could not be
attributed to a difference in frequency of successes.

The subjects could be expected to stay longer at the target-shooting games
before they returned to the evaluation of jokes if the consummatory value
were lower in the difficult condition than in the easy condition. Figure 7.6
shows two computer simulations of length of time spent at a task when the

consummatory value c was approximately equivalent to the two success rates of $Ps = .30$ and $Ps = .70$ ($c = .03$ vs. $.07$).

And indeed, the subjects in the difficult condition did spend more time than those in the easy condition at the repeated execution of tasks, before they returned to a non-achievement-oriented activity. As expected, we can conclude from this result that the more difficult tasks had less consummatory value, corresponding to the model derivation in Figure 7.6a, where $c = .03$ instead of $.07$. These results could be explained equally well with the aid of revisions of the risk-taking model which take into account that success-motivated subjects tend to choose difficult tasks rather than moderately difficult tasks (see Chapter 4).

In order to prevent such an alternative explanation, Blankenship attempted to show that the initial instigating force was equally strong under both difficulty conditions. Since the consummatory force can exert no influence before the subject begins carrying out the activity, the time until the target-shooting game is begun should be a nonconfounded index of instigating force. And indeed, the latencies were nearly the same under both difficulty conditions. Therefore, longer persistence at more difficult tasks should not be attributed to a stronger instigating force, but rather to a weaker consummatory force. (With a more difficult task, it takes longer before one feels that one has had enough.)

Blankenship's case rests entirely on the assumption that the period of latency is a valid indicator of the instigating force for a skill task that is ready to be performed, the difficulty of which has already been announced. One could easily object that the latency time is initially more an indicator of the behavioral tendency for the task that has already begun (joke rating) than for the achievement-related alternative activity; whether this is true has not yet been determined. Since the subjects were not able to choose between an easy achievement-related task and a difficult one, the subjects may initially have been thinking only of the difference between the two kinds of activities (reading and rating jokes vs. shooting down submarines in a computer game), and not of the level of difficulty of the alternative activity that had been assigned to them. In order to make a convincing case for Blankenship's position, it would be necessary to conduct further experiments.

Let us now examine the study by Kuhl and Blankenship (1979a, 1979b). It is based on the same deduction from the model — that is, that easier tasks (or tasks at which subjects are more successful) possess a higher consummatory value. The instigating force was assumed to consume itself more rapidly in a series of successes than in a series of failures (i.e., $cs > cf$).

Accordingly, repeated choices made among the levels of difficulty of a task should lead to a shift in the dominance relationship between the behavioral tendencies in favor of increasingly high levels of difficulty. The dynamic model thereby predicts a shift in the preference function of the various levels of difficulty even when situation factors (expectancies) remain the same. The expectancy-value model was not able to make such a prediction.

Kuhl and Blankenship (1979a, 1979b) used computer programs to predict that all subjects — both success-motivated and failure-motivated subjects — would tend increasingly to choose difficult tasks on the basis of the greater consummatory value of success at easy tasks. Let us discuss this study in more detail. The computer simulation demonstrates that, initially, success-motivated subjects show a preference for moderate levels of difficulty. That preference corresponds to the old model. After that, they should choose increasingly difficult tasks. Failure-motivated subjects should initially waver between quite easy tasks and quite difficult tasks. Then they should show a clear preference for easier tasks; this preference would disappear in favor of increasing preference for more difficult tasks.

In deriving their hypotheses for failure-motivated subjects, Kuhl and Blankenship also assumed that at the beginning of the free-choice situation the action and inaction tendencies for the various levels of difficulty had changed on the basis of the preceding practice phases. They assumed that the initial motivational situation corresponded to the second segment of the behavioral stream, as described in the computer simulation for failure-motivated subjects — that is, that behavioral tendencies to choose easy tasks would dominate.

On the basis of this additional assumption, the authors predicted that failure-motivated subjects given free choice of tasks would initially choose easy levels of difficulty and later begin to choose more difficult tasks.

This additional assumption has not been demonstrated to be correct. First of all, we must ask ourselves why the same assumption does not apply to success-motivated subjects. For success-motivated subjects Kuhl and Blankenship derived their hypotheses from the first segment of the simulated behavioral stream. In addition, the same study (Kuhl & Blankenship, 1979b, Figure 5) showed that a forced choice of levels of difficulty — and that was the case in the practice phase — apparently does not modify tendencies to action and inaction.

In order to test the hypotheses described above, Kuhl and Blankenship conducted a study in which subjects were able to choose 50 times which level of difficulty of an intellectual problem-solving task they wanted. Initially the subjects had enough opportunity to experience the various levels of difficulty of this task. In addition, they were told their individual probability of success at each task, which had been calculated by the experimenter. Thus we can assume that the subjective expectancies of success were well

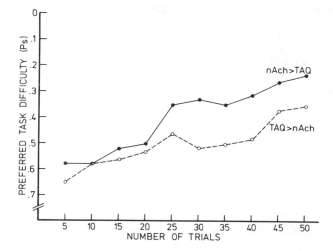

FIGURE 7.7 Median preferred subjective difficulties in a series of 50 choices made by success- (*n* Ach > TAQ) and failure-motivated (TAQ > *n* Ach) subjects. (Adapted from Kuhl & Blankenship, 1979b, p. 556.)

established when free choice began. Figure 7.7 shows the increase in levels of difficulty chosen, in relation to the individual probabilities of success of which the 40 male subjects had previously been informed.

Success- as well as failure-motivated subjects began at the easier levels and continued to the more difficult levels. Failure-motivated subjects initially chose somewhat easier tasks than success-motivated subjects; moreover, they did not increase task difficulty to levels as high as the highest difficulty levels chosen by success-motivated subjects.

Kuhl and Blankenship's results cannot be predicted on the basis of the original model or of the model revisions already discussed (see Chapter 4). In the earlier explanatory approaches no alterations in behavioral tendencies can be predicted when situation parameters stay the same. Kuhl and Blankenship (1979b) assumed, however, that the subjects' expectancies of success would no longer change during the 50 free choices; they questioned their subjects at the end of the experiment and excluded those subjects whose subjective expectancies deviated by more than 10% from the previously established probabilities of success.

Thus the findings confirm the authors' predictions. However, the confirmation value for the dynamic model seems low, since such a general and increasing preference for more difficult tasks was already documented in earlier studies (Heckhausen & Wagner, 1965; Jopt, 1974; Schneider & Posse, 1978c, 1982). Heckhausen and Wagner (1965) observed the dominance of ascending serial choice behavior in children $3\frac{1}{2}$ years old and older. In a postexperimental analysis summarizing seven studies, Schneider and Posse (1982) concluded that the assumption that subjects tend to choose in an ascending series predicted individual choice sequences better than did the risk-taking model.

Schneider and Posse (1982) interpret ascending serial choice behavior as the expression of a rational strategy of task processing, as do Heckhausen and Wagner. Like the choice of tasks of moderate difficulty, successive trying out of all levels of difficulty of a task (beginning with the easier tasks and then choosing increasingly more difficult tasks) is a suitable strategy for becoming familiar with a task and with one's own performance ability.

In a 1982 study by Schneider and Posse this ascending serial choice behavior appeared in a very noticeable form. Subjects in the target-shooting game described above were allowed to choose their level of difficulty 50 times. Nearly all subjects preferred increasingly more difficult tasks. This strategy was even more pronounced with the group of subjects who had been told that they should try to become familiar with the levels of difficulty of the task than with the group that received no such instructions (see Schneider & Posse, 1982). Such instructions to become familiar with the task were also given to the subjects in the study by Kuhl and Blankenship; it is thus impossible not to suspect that the observed choice behavior is the expression of a rational problem-solving strategy. The findings reported for the dynamic model could accordingly have been more convincing if the authors had not chosen for their demonstration a general behavioral phenomenon that has already been described and interpreted.

This concludes the description of the two empirical tests of the dynamic model. It is surely no coincidence that both studies dealt with consummatory force. Though neglected in the past, it is undoubtedly a decisive explanatory factor for the temporal sequence that characterizes achievement-oriented behavior. Achievement-oriented behavior varies in temporal sequence and differs in temporal sequence from many non-achievement-oriented behaviors. The simplest assumption is that consummatory force increases in a linear fashion over time and that the angle of ascent is determined by the strength of the behavioral tendency. This assumption, however, can hardly apply to all behavior that pursues a clearly defined end state as the achievement goal.

Instead, the characteristic sequence described is most likely to apply to the repetition of identical or similar tasks, as in Blankenship's study (1979), or to goalless activities such as daydreaming, or to simple satisfaction of needs. In the latter case, the sequence would apply to almost every activity in which behavioral time allocation follows de Villiers and Herrnstein's (1976) "law of relative effect." That is, it would apply to activities in which reinforcement rates have been established for the probable alternative reactions. In contrast, achievement-oriented actions are usually final actions that do not find their sudden consummation until the goal is attained, which is consistent with Ovsiankina's findings (1928) that the tendency to resume an activity is stronger, the nearer the activity is to completion when it is interrupted.

The dynamic model raises important questions: For example, what temporal sequences are associated with different kinds of actions? The model does need further empirical testing. However, independent of the outcome of such further research, motivational research is now unimaginable without the basic idea of a process-oriented analysis of achievement-oriented behavior.

Action Control: An Old Problem Revisited

Finally, we must turn to an old problem that is becoming relevant again in motivational research. After receiving considerable attention initially, it has been neglected for a half century. This is the question as to how a motivational tendency that is in essence fleeting eventually comes to guide behavior. Such a question can remain hidden as long as we fail to notice how many motivational tendencies are available to us, and how little time and how few resources we have available for acting according to our own intentions. We have deceived ourselves into believing in a nonexistent correspondence between motivations and intentions and actions, based on two forms of motivational research that are both extreme and common. One is the highly controlled laboratory experiment in which we induce all three at once (motivations, intentions, and actions), and thus are able to observe subjects behaving as we expect. And the other is the global relationships that exist between individual motive differences and life-outcome data that result over long spans of time and a variety of situations. Both forms of motivation research allow everything that may have happened after a motivational tendency is aroused, and before action is taken, to literally disappear into nothing.

Motivational theories have assumed tacitly or explicitly that the motivational tendency that is dominant at a given time determines behavior. The intention to act that is currently viewed as binding is carried out. But this assumption contradicts even our everyday experience. For example, we complete actions that we have begun, even when another goal has become even more important to us in the meantime. Above all, by no means do we always do what we have decided to do. Countless empirical findings con-

firm the relatively low correlation between intention and action (summa-
rized by Ajzen & Fishbein, 1977; Wicker, 1969). In the classical German
psychology of the will, the extent to which people realize their intentions was
considered to be the result of a number of mediating processes subsumed
under the concept of the will (Ach, 1905, 1910, 1935; Lindworsky, 1923).
Ach (1910) designated the relationship between the number of intentions
that are carried out and the total number of intentions to act that occur in a
particular period as the efficiency of the will.

Kuhl (1984) has formulated a model of action control in which some
hypothetical mediating processes are described. These processes are as-
sumed to determine the extent to which people carry out their intentions.
This model attempts to take into account classical research on volition as
well as supplementary processes that mediate between an intention and its
execution and to integrate the two. The model is an attempt to overcome a
tradition more than 50 years old in motivational psychology by which the
processes of action control are not assigned any independent mediating
status.

Lewin's theory (1926) is partly responsible for this tradition. Lewin at-
tempted to reduce the problem of action control to a problem of motiva-
tion. Lewin's inclination to overcome traditional dichotomies through ho-
mogenization (Lewin, 1931) even extended itself to the conceptual
distinction between intention and need (motivation). Since he conceived of
intentions as quasi-needs and thereby attributed to them the same dynamic
qualities as actual needs, he distorted our view of the special status of an
intention as opposed to a motivational tendency.

Control of Execution and Control of Intention

What is the special status of an intention as opposed to a motivational
tendency? Kuhl (1982a) finds that a motivational tendency acquires a
special quality of self-imposed commitment in the moment that it assumes
the status of an intention. This quality of self-imposed commitment
arouses a whole series of mediating processes that aim at protecting the
current intention from concurrent ("imposing") motivational tendencies
and preventing any one of these tendencies from displacing the current
intention before it has been carried out.

All of these processes are subsumed under the concept of control of inten-
tion, which is distinguished from the concept of control of execution. Kuhl
uses the term "control of execution" to describe the processes that control
the sequence of intended steps of action. Such processes are described in
cybernetically oriented models of behavioral regulation with hierarchical
levels of feedback loops (Carver & Scheier, 1981; Hacker, 1973; Miller,

Galanter, & Pribram, 1960; Volpert, 1974; von Cranach, 1980). While models of behavioral regulation describe how the execution of actions is controlled, control of intention is a matter of whether the current intention can be carried out at all despite the presence of resistance (concurrent tendencies, social constraints, difficulties that are inherent in the activity, etc.). That is, the question is whether the execution of the intended action will be realized. The concept of action control is understood as a higher-level concept, uniting the processes of control of intention and control of execution. At times it is also used in a more narrow sense to describe control of intention.

Volitional Mediating Processes

Kuhl (1982a) postulated a series of mediating processes that increase the probability that the current intention to act will be executed. The control of intention involves the following six processes.

1. Selective control of attention: Preferential attention is paid to information that has a relationship to the current intention.
2. Economy of information processing: This prevents excessive prolongation of the processes of weighing behavioral alternatives and the expectancy and incentive aspects that are connected with them.
3. Control of emotions: Feelings that promote the realization of the intended action are aroused; feelings that would tend to interfere with the course of action are avoided.
4. Encoding control: New information is encoded primarily according to the encoding categories that are suggested by the current intention to act.
5. Environmental control: This is a matter of supportive auxiliary measures that alter the environment in a way that facilitates the execution of the intention. This includes nearly everything that clinical psychologists describe as self-control (Kanfer & Hagerman, 1981; Thoresen & Mahoney, 1974). One example would be keeping no sweets in one's own house when one has decided to lose weight.
6. Motivation control: Here action control is supported by reference to the motivational source of the intention to act. This process, which is particularly interesting for motivational psychologists, involves the later regulation of the motivational tendency on the basis of which an intention to act has arisen. The purpose of regulation is protecting the intention from concurrent alternative tendencies. For example, this can take place through a process of incentive escalation, which is defined as selective focusing on positive consequences of the intended action (or on negative consequences that could be prevented by the action) that have not yet been taken into account.

Ach (1935) emphasized in his theory of activity of the will that volitional mediating processes cannot be activated unless they are necessary. Accordingly, the individual processes involved in control of intention come into play more forcefully, the stronger the resistance that needs to be overcome in the concrete situation. When the execution of the intended activity carries with it no difficulties of any kind, when there are no strong motivational tendencies that would support an alternative activity, and when the social pressure that is perceived in the concrete situation tends more to favor the execution of the intended action than to prevent it, then the realization of the intention hardly depends on the use of volitional mediating processes. In such a situation there can be a relatively close correlation between intention and behavior (e.g., Fishbein & Coombs, 1974). In order to explore the mediating role of volitional processes, however, it is necessary to choose precisely those situations in which the realization of the intention in question (1) is basically subject to volitional control (and thus does not exceed the abilities of the person in question), but (2) does require the overcoming of certain difficulties.

Action Orientation versus State Orientation

According to Kuhl (1984), the existence of difficulties that are basically capable of being overcome determines only in part whether the mediating processes described above will be used and whether they will be successful. In addition, the current structure of the intention to act is an important factor. The cognitive representation of intentions to act has received little attention in motivation models.

Whenever achievement motivation researchers have concerned themselves at all with the cognitive representation of that which could control action, the object of their attention has been the origin of a motivational state. This includes the early attempt by Heckhausen (1963b) to understand motivation as an emotional "expectancy gradient," an idea which has received little follow-up attention. In this approach the expectancy gradient was cognitively represented by awareness of an actual state, of a future (hoped-for or feared) state, and of a discrepancy between the two states. The discrepancy was thought to be based partly on the psychological temporal distance between both states. Characteristically, such an expectancy gradient was considered the basis not only of the motivation, but simultaneously also of the initiation and the course of the action. Thus it was overlooked that even a dominant motivational state that filled the subject's entire experience could be completely free of intention and far from being in a position to guide actual behavior. Motivations are a long way from actions. They start as wishes and must first become intentions — and intentions must become actions—before motivations have accomplished anything (see Heckhausen & Kuhl, 1985).

Kuhl (1982a) attempted to establish this transition through an elaboration of the concept of intention. He described the structure of an intention in the form of a volitional proposition, drawing on Anderson and Bowers' (1974) theory of semantic networks. In such a proposition the following are specified: (1) the conditions for execution (context), (2) the subject of the action (i.e., oneself), (3) the volitional relation (will), and (4) the action to be carried out. The action itself was further differentiated into the following four states: (1) the desired state, (2) the present state, (3) the discrepancy between the desired and present states, and (4) at least one step of action that could contribute to the removal of this discrepancy.

Traditional motivation models seem to be based on the implicit assumption that intentions are always complete—that is, that all of the elements named are present in the cognitive representation of an intention. Kuhl (1984) suggests, in contrast, that intentions can quite well be incomplete (degenerated), in the sense that one or more of the elements named are not sufficiently specified or are not activated strongly enough. For example, we may have the (complete) intention to solve a problem, but we may continually experience failure until eventually we can no longer recognize what steps of action could lead to the attainment of the desired state (solution of the problem). If the intention to solve the problem nevertheless remains—perhaps because the importance of success is experienced as being very high—then the intention degenerates (in this case, by loss of the action element). Kuhl (1984) describes the motivational state in which a degenerated intention exists as a state orientation, since the person's attention is concentrated in such a condition on a particular state. For example, the experience can involve a past or a present situation (the experience of failure and its emotional consequences) or a future state that is desired.

Various kinds of state orientation can be distinguished from each other according to which elements of the intention have degenerated or which of the remaining elements are the objects of attention. Kuhl (1982b) gives special emphasis to four cases that seem to occur with particular frequency. If attention is directed during the process of weighing alternatives too strongly and for an excessively long time toward anticipated consequences or other situational aspects, we can speak of a (1) "plan-related" state orientation. In contrast, if attention is directed too strongly toward the desired (end) goal of the action, we can speak of (2) "goal centering" (instead of activity centering). And finally, if past failures or successes remain in the center of attention, we have a (3) "failure-related" or (4) "success-related" state orientation.

What effect does the condition of state orientation have on action control? According to Kuhl (1982a), a state-oriented condition has a harmful effect on the realization of newly formed action intentions, since state-oriented cognitions possess a considerable tendency to persevere. Degenerated intentions cannot be carried out, and thus it is not so easy to dispose of them as it is after the realization of complete intentions. When the intention is to solve a problem that has not been solved after the exhaustion of all available action alternatives, fixation on the desired state leads to perseverance of the intention of solution — even when the person has already turned to a new goal (such as a different kind of task). The old intention of solution, persevering in degenerated form, can interfere with the realization of the new intention. That is particularly the case when the new intention is relatively complex, so that the persevering (old) intention occupies processing capacity that is actually needed in order to realize the new intention.

On the one hand, the assumption of perseverance is connected with traditional concepts of perseverance (Ach, 1935; Eysenck, 1967; Müller & Pilzecker, 1900); on the other hand, the new assumption elaborates the traditional concepts sufficiently that they can be used in the analysis of volitional mediating processes. For example, Eysenck's (1967) construct of introversion seems to be too general to be useful in an action model. The perseverance of state cognitions that interfere with realization cannot be reduced to a general tendency to perseverance that is conditioned by a reduced level of physiological inhibiting processes in the brain, such as the tendency that is expressed in such heterogeneous phenomena as a dislike for jokes or the perseverance of afterimages. Even a person who is extraverted in Eysenck's sense (low inclination for perseverance) can develop degenerated intentions, and the resulting perseverance can interfere with action control.

In addition to the effects of an action-oriented or state-oriented motivational state, Kuhl (1982a) also discusses various determinants of the two orientations. Questionnaires were constructed for the measurement of interindividual differences in the probability of finding oneself in an action-oriented or state-oriented condition in a given situation. The internal consistency, predictive validity, and discriminant validity of the questionnaires are satisfactory (Kuhl, in press b). These questionnaires were already discussed at the beginning of this chapter, in the section on action versus state orientation.

Subjects who show a high tendency toward action orientation in the questionnaire can naturally find themselves in a state-oriented condition when the situation produces massive arousal of such a condition. Among the most important situational determinants is confrontation with uncontrollable events, such as are manipulated in learned-helplessness experiments. Thus, in order to test his approach, Kuhl (1981, 1982a) carried out several experiments attempting to clarify theoretically the phenomenon of learned helplessness (see Seligman, 1975).

Empirical Studies: Action Orientation and Carrying Out
Intentions

Studies on the mediating role of action versus state orientation began by examining the influence of the postulated personality determinant of action control. In one experiment (Kuhl, 1982b), seventh graders in a German high school were given a list of activities with the request to show on a 6-point scale for each activity the extent to which they intended to carry out the activity in question after school. The next day the students indicated how much time they had actually spent on the various activities. In addition, they filled out the questionnaire for measuring plan-oriented action orientation.

For 11 of the 13 voluntary activities (i.e., those that are not initiated by social pressure, such as reading or playing with friends) the correlations between intention score and behavior score were in part considerably higher in the subgroup of action-oriented students than for state-oriented students. Action- and state-oriented students were distinguished from each other by whether their questionnaire scores were above or below the median. The study is also relevant for the postulated interaction between the personality trait being investigated and a situational factor. In seven out of nine activities that had tentatively been classified as primarily initiated by social norms, no higher correlations appeared between intention and behavior for action-oriented students than for state-oriented students. These findings are congruent with an exception made by Kuhl (1984), according to which instructions, commands, or social pressure are considered to be situational determinants of action control. When the execution of activities is regulated by social control, these activities require no dominant orientation toward action.

An additional test of the mediating role of plan-related action orientation came in an experiment designed to examine an aspect of Atkinson and Birch's (1970) dynamic model. In the present context the findings on the relationship between a motive measure and corresponding behavior correlates are interesting (Kuhl & Geiger, in press). Fourth graders in an elementary school had the opportunity throughout this experiment to change back and forth as often as they liked between three activities designed to arouse the achievement motive, the curiosity motive, or the help-giving motive. Just previously, the students had taken a projective multi-motive test developed for the experiment and designed to measure the three motives named.

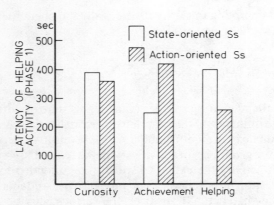

FIGURE 7.8 Latency preceding beginning of a helping activity (sorting game) as a function of the content of the dominant motive and the extent of action orientation. (Adapted from Kuhl & Geiger, in press.)

The general correlations between the motive measures and the corresponding behavioral measures were unusually low. However, the picture changed as soon as the subjects were divided into two groups, according to a median split on the questionnaire scores for plan-related action orientation. Action-oriented subjects showed some expected relationships between motive tendency and various behavioral measures. For example, with action-oriented subjects having a dominant helping motive, latency until they began a help-related sorting activity was significantly shorter than with action-oriented subjects having a dominant achievement motive. This correlation tended to be reversed for state-oriented subjects (Figure 7.8).

Mediating Processes

The findings reported so far have little to do with the mediating processes involved in the realization of an intention. How is it possible for action-oriented persons to realize more of their intentions than state-oriented persons? Findings exist on three of the six postulated mediating processes: on selective control of attention, economy of information processing, and control of emotions. They are presented in order.

The postulated mediating role of directing attention to action-related contents was explored in an experiment in which subjects who had just participated in a learning experiment were to reproduce not only "relevant" words they had been asked to learn, but also "irrelevant" words. Action-oriented subjects reproduced less irrelevant material than state-oriented subjects. However, this effect was reversed in another experimental condition in which the amount of material to be learned was so great that the subjects were overtaxed. The increased sensitivity to irrelevant information that was observed in action-oriented subjects in this condition was interpreted by Kuhl (1984) as an adaptive reaction in uncontrollable situations. If attention were to remain fixed on the uncontrollable goal in such situations, the realization of new (controllable) goals would be endangered.

Another study (Kuhl & Beckmann, 1983) supported the postulation of greater economy of information processing in action-oriented subjects. In this experiment action-oriented subjects made their decisions between various games of chance in a way that was dependent on a simpler decision rule than that used by state-oriented subjects. In their decisions, state-oriented subjects took into account information that could not increase their expected winnings to an appreciable extent. Such inclusive weighing of information before deciding in favor of an alternative action increases the danger that an intention once formed will be supplanted by alternative tendencies before it is realized.

The mediating function of feelings that interfere with realization was studied in an experiment involving patients who had just undergone a hernia operation (Kuhl, 1982a). In this study patients with high (failure-oriented) state orientation gave significantly higher estimates of postoperative pain and also requested more pain-killers than action-oriented patients. At the same time, scores for participation in various activities in the hospital (watching television, reading, short walks, physical exercise) were significantly lower in state-oriented patients than in action-oriented patients.

Action Control and Learned Helplessness

In many studies performance deficits have been observed after massed failure experience, even with tasks quite different from the training task. This phenomenon has been subjected to a number of quite different theoretical analyses, as we mentioned in Chapter 5. What most of these explanatory approaches have in common is the assumption of a motivational deficit, which itself is attributed to a generalized expectancy deficit. According to this model, the subjects acquired during helplessness training the expectancy of having no control over performance outcomes, and generalized this expectancy to the test task. Thereby this task was also subject to a motivational deficit and thus to interference with performance. As we have already shown in an experiment by Kuhl (1981), this explanatory approach is not sufficient. In addition to motivational aspects, functional aspects must also be taken into account. That is especially true when the test task is so different from the training task that it is hard to assume that anyone would transfer the low expectancy of control of the training task to the test task in every case. In processing different tasks subjects tend very quickly to form task-specific ability concepts (Kuhl, 1977).

In most experiments on learned helplessness there was no direct testing of the extent to which an expectancy deficit was transferred from the training task to the test task. In one study that did test the transfer hypothesis directly, there were no signs of a reduced expectancy of success at the test task before beginning it, even though a series of failures at a training task had been induced just before (Kuhl, 1981). Indeed, the subjects in an experimental group showed a significant performance drop on the test task after failure training in comparison with a control group. Nevertheless, they ranked the effort that they exerted in performance of the test task as significantly higher than subjects in the control group did. These findings cannot be reconciled with Seligman's (1975) hypothesis that generalized performance deficits after induction of failure are always brought about by a generalized deficit in expectancy and motivation.

What does mediate the observed performance deficits, if not a generalized deficit in expectancy and motivation? Kuhl's (1981) experiments indicate that the drops in performance are based on a deficit in action control. Apparently many subjects in the failure group were unable to direct their full attention to the information that was relevant to performing the test task, despite the presence of the intention to solve the task. The findings indicate that performance deficits appear when persevering (state-related) cognitions related to the experience of failure and its consequences place a burden on processing capacity. This conclusion is based on the observation that significant performance deficits occurred only when subjects were asked to write a short essay about the "present" situation after the failure training, or when a subject indicated in a questionnaire a disposition to state orientation after failure (i.e., if the score for action orientation lay below the median). In one condition the experimenter attempted to prevent the occurrence of state-related cognitions by requiring subjects to recite out loud the hypotheses that were being tested (explicit hypothesis testing). Here even state-oriented subjects showed no performance deficits.

The Process of Becoming Helpless

Kuhl and Weiss (1984) studied the process of the genesis of learned helplessness more closely. In an experiment involving action orientation after failure, 100 subjects were divided at the median into action-oriented and state-oriented groups. Within each of the two groups every 10 subjects was assigned to one of five experimental groups. These groups included three failure groups, of which one received failure feedback at a concept-for-

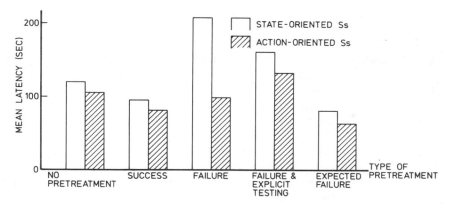

FIGURE 7.9   Median processing time (latency) for 10 anagrams as a function of type of pretreatment and extent of action or state orientation.   (Adapted from Kuhl & Weiss, 1984.)

mation task with no further intervention measures.   The other two not only experienced the failure induction, but they were also asked either to announce their hypotheses out loud ("explicit testing of hypotheses") or they were "informed" ahead of time that they were not expected to be able to solve the concept-building problem, on the basis of a test taken in a previous group meeting ("expected failure").   The manipulation was based on the notion that announcing that failure should be expected would either prevent the creation of a firm intention to solve the problem or at least would make it easier for subjects to completely give up such an intention.   Induced failure was expected to demonstrate to subjects the "validity" of the feedback. Thus no performance deficit was expected in either failure group on the basis of the theory of functional helplessness (Kuhl, 1981), despite the failure training.   Both intervention measures were expected to prevent the occurrence of state-related cognitions that could interfere with performance.

The findings corresponded fully to this prediction.   Only in the state-oriented subjects in the failure group without intervention was there a significant rise in average processing time of the anagrams worked on after the training phase, in comparison with the two control groups, one of which had not performed the training task and one of which had performed it successfully (Figure 7.9).

Similar findings appeared with other performance scores.   The interpretation of these findings that suggests a functional deficit rather than a motivational deficit is also supported by a postexperimental interview.   The subjects in whom a significant performance deficit had been observed (i.e., state-oriented subjects in the failure group without intervention) indicated, to a greater extent than did subjects in the control groups, that during work on the anagram tasks they had thought (1) about their performance, (2) about their state of mind, (3) about the length of the experiment, and (4) about their own ability to work anagram problems.

The interpretation of the findings that suggests interference with performance by self-centered cognitions is reminiscent of the attention theory of test anxiety (Morris & Liebert, 1970; Wine, 1971). This theory has also been used in the interpretation of helplessness findings (Lavelle, Metalsky, & Coyne, 1979). We should also mention here the motivational state measured by Heckhausen (1982a) in a critical achievement-related situation. When that state did involve fear of failure rather than hope of success, it was combined with increased occurrence of task-irrelevant self-doubt cognitions and with diminished performance.

However, the theory of functional helplessness goes beyond these approaches to the extent that it is able to specify, according to a theory of action control, the cause of emerging self-centered cognitions that interfere with performance. The cause of the perseverance of interfering state cognitions is not a state of anxiety, but rather the existence of a degenerated intention that has not been implemented but is still experienced as binding. The intention thus prevents a complete disengagement from the unsolved task. Naturally a state of intensified anxiety about an increase of irrelevant state cognitions can increase the performance deficit further. However, a study by Kuhl and Weiss (1984) has confirmed that interference with performance by state-related cognitions does not depend on the existence of a state of anxiety. In this study the performance deficits found in unreduced strength among state-oriented subjects within the failure group remained even when the analysis was restricted to a subgroup of success-motivated subjects (net hope > median; AMS by Gjesme & Nygard, 1970).

In the investigation by Kuhl and Weiss (1984) the process of becoming helpless was also examined more closely. During the four series of noncontingent feedback reports various measures were taken. In the failure groups — especially with state-oriented subjects without intervention — the strategy level decreased noticeably from the first through the fourth failure series. That was reflected, for example, in the increase in frequency of "hypothesis-less" trials in which no hypothesis was tested consistently.

The analysis of answers to the question of whether the subjects had thought about the causes of their performance while task processing was going on casts additional light on the process dynamics of the genesis of helplessness. In a study by Diener and Dweck (1978) it was precisely the helpless children — those who performed worse after experiencing failure — who thought more about causes. Heckhausen (1982a) found, in comparing various kinds of self-centered cognitions, that causal attributions for one's own performance were perceived as particularly disturbing by candidates for a university examination (see Figure 6.6).

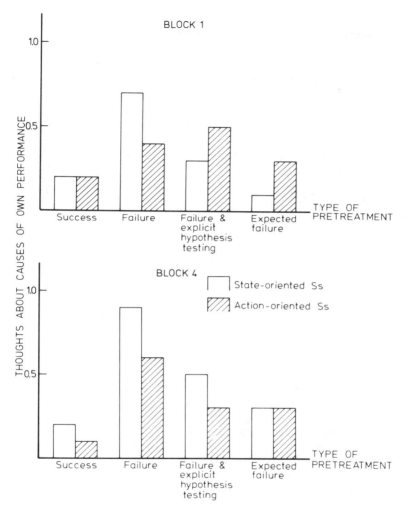

FIGURE 7.10   Relative frequency of thoughts about the causes of one's own performance in the 1st and 4th block of a pretreatment phase (concept-forming task) in relationship to type of pretreatment and dominance of action or state orientation.   (Adapted from Kuhl & Weiss, 1984.)

Here too it turned out that "thoughts about causes" were state cognitions that interfered with performance.   As we can see from Figure 7.10, while subjects were working the first problem, only the state-oriented subjects in the failure condition without intervention registered "thoughts about their own performance" significantly more often than did the entire group of subjects in the success condition. After failure at attempts to work the fourth problem, even action-oriented subjects in the failure group without intervention — as well as state-oriented (but not action-oriented) subjects in the failure group with explicit hypothesis testing — indicated significantly more frequently than the subjects in the success groups that they had thought about their own performance.

Apparently mere failure feedback to dispositionally state-oriented subjects was enough to initiate a state-oriented concern with causes of their experience of interference with performance. With action-oriented subjects such cognitions appeared only after four series of failures, and even then, only in the absence of any intervention (explicit hypothesis testing or announcement of failure) oriented toward reducing state-related cognitions. The explicit testing of hypotheses apparently immunized action-oriented (but not state-oriented) subjects against state-related cognitions even after four series of failures. Expected failure had this sort of immunizing function in both subject groups.

The process pattern illustrated in Figure 7.10 supports the interactionist interpretation of the process characteristic under investigation. Whether a subject in a specific situation is in a state-oriented or action-oriented condition depends on the interaction of personality and situational factors. Even a person with a strong disposition to action orientation can be found in a state-oriented condition after exposure to a massive stress situation.

Tracing behavior back to an interaction of internal and external conditions — that is, to an interaction of personality dispositions and influences of the current situation — was the contribution of achievement motivation research from the beginning (Nygard, 1981). Without an interactionist point of view, distinctions and relationships between motive and motivation would not have been recognized and would not have become so productive. The questions posed by motivation researchers may change as the chain of problems continues its formation, stretching out to include questions about individual motive differences, situational factors, and motivational states in order to increase our understanding of the origin of intentions and their implementation in actions. This exploration may eventually take place in an everyday context, with all its multiple current concerns (Klinger, 1971). Yet just as in the past, an interactionist point of view must be our guide, though certainly on more complex levels.

References

Abbey, A. (1982). Sex differences in attributions for friendly behavior: Do males misperceive females' friendliness? *Journal of Personality and Social Psychology, 42,* 830–838.

Abramson, L. Y., Seligman, M. E. P., & Teasdale, J. D. (1978). Learned helplessness in humans: Critique and reformulation. *Journal of Abnormal Psychology, 87,* 49–74.

Ach, N. (1905). *Über die Willenstätigkeit und das Denken: Eine experimentelle Untersuchung mit einem Anhang über das Hippsche Chronoskop.* Göttingen: Vandenhoeck & Ruprecht.

Ach, N. (1910). *Über den Willensakt und das Temperament.* Leipzig: Quelle und Meyer.

Ach, N. (1935). Analyse des Willens. In E. Abderhalden (Ed.), *Handbuch der biologischen Arbeitsmethoden. Vol. VI.* Berlin: Urban & Schwarzenberg.

Adam, E. E. (1972). An analysis of changes in performance quality with operant conditioning procedures. *Journal of Applied Psychology, 56,* 480–486.

Ajzen, J., & Fishbein, M. (1977). Attitude-behavior relation: A theoretical analysis and review of empirical research. *Psychological Bulletin, 5,* 888–918.

Alker, H. A. (1972). Is personality situationally specific or intrapsychically consistent? *Journal of Personality, 40,* 1–16.

Alloy, L. B., & Abramson, L. Y. (1979). Judgement of contingency in depressed and non-depressed students: Sadder but wiser? *Journal of Experimental Psychology: General, 108,* 441–458.

Alper, T. G. (1957). Predicting the direction of selective recall: Its relation to ego strength and *n* Achievement. *Journal of Abnormal and Social Psychology, 55,* 149–165.

Alper, T. G. (1974). Achievement motivation in college women: A now-you-see-it-now-you-don't phenomenon. *American Psychologist, 29,* 194–203.

Alpert, R., & Haber, R. N. (1960). Anxiety in academic achievement situations. *Journal of Abnormal and Social Psychology, 61,* 207–215.

Alschuler, A. S. (1973). *Developing achievement motivation in adolescents.* Englewood Cliffs, NJ: Educational Technology Publications.

Alschuler, A. S., Tabor, D., & McIntire, J. (1970). *Teaching achievement motivation.* Middletown, Conn: Educational Ventures.

Ames, C., Ames, R., & Felker, D. W. (1977). Effects of competitive reward structure and valence of outcome on children's achievement attribution. *Journal of Educational Psychology, 69,* 1–8.

Anderson, J., & Bower, G. (1974). *Human associative memory.* Washington: Hemisphere.

Andrews, J. D. W. (1967). The achievement motive and advancement in two types of organizations. *Journal of Personality and Social Psychology, 6,* 163–168.

Andrews, G. R., & Debus, R. L. (1978). Persistence and the causal perception of failure: Modifying cognitive attributions. *Journal of Educational Psychology, 70,* 154–166.

Angelini, A. L. (1959). Studies in projective measurement of achievement motivation of Brazilian students, males and females. Part of the proceedings of the 15th International Congress of Psychology, Brussels 1957, in *Acta Psychologica, XV,* 359–360.

Arkin, R. M., Appelman, A. J., & Burger, J. M. (1980). Social anxiety, self-presentation, and the self-serving bias in causal attribution. *Journal of Personality and Social Psychology, 38,* 23–35.

Arnold, M. B. (1960). *Emotion and personality.* New York: Columbia University Press.

Arsenian, S. (1942). Own estimate and objective measurement. *Journal of Educational Measurement, 33,* 291–302.

Atkinson, J. W. (1950). *Studies in projective measurement of achievement motivation.* Dissertation, University of Michigan.

Atkinson, J. W. (1953). The achievement motive and recall of interrupted and completed tasks. *Journal of Experimental Psychology, 46,* 381–390.

Atkinson, J. W. (1957). Motivational determinants of risk-taking behavior. *Psychology Review, 64,* 359–372.

Atkinson, J. W. (1958). *Motives in fantasy, action and society.* Princeton, NJ: Van Nostrand.

Atkinson, J. W. (1960). Personality dynamics. *Annual Review of Psychology, 11,* 255–290.

Atkinson, J. W. (1964). *An introduction to motivation.* Princeton, NJ: Van Nostrand.

Atkinson, J. W. (1967). *Strength of motivation and efficiency of performance: An old unresolved problem.* Paper presented at the APA congress in Washington.

Atkinson, J. W. (1974a). Strength of motivation and efficiency of performance. In J. W. Atkinson & J. O. Raynor (Eds.), *Motivation and achievement* (pp. 193–218). Washington, DC: Winston.

Atkinson, J. W. (1974b). Motivational determinants of intellective performance and cumulative achievement. In J. W. Atkinson & J. O. Raynor (Eds.), *Motivation and achievement* (pp. 389–410). Washington, DC: Winston.

Atkinson, J. W., Bastian, J. R., Earl, R. W., & Litwin, G. H. (1960). The achievement motive, goal setting and probability preferences. *Journal of Abnormal and Social Psychology, 60,* 27–36.

Atkinson, J. W., & Birch, D. (1970). *The dynamics of action.* New York: Wiley.

Atkinson, J. W., & Birch, D. (1974). The dynamics of achievement-oriented activity. In J. W. Atkinson & J. O. Raynor (Eds.), *Motivation and achievement* (pp. 271–326). New York: Wiley.

Atkinson, J. W., & Birch, D. (1978). *Introduction to motivation.* New York: Van Nostrand.

Atkinson, J. W., Bongort, K., & Price, L. H. (1977). Explanations using computer simulation to comprehend thematic apperceptive measurement of motivation. *Motivation and Emotion, 1,* 1–27.

Atkinson, J. W., & Cartwright, D. (1964). Some neglected variables in contemporary conceptions of decision and performance. *Psychological Reports, 14,* 575–590.

Atkinson, J. W., & Feather, N. T. (1966). *A theory of achievement motivation.* New York: Wiley.

Atkinson, J. W., Lens, W., & O'Malley, P. M. (1976). Motivation and ability: Interactive psychological determinants of intellective performance, educational achievement, and each other. In W. H. Sewell, R. M. Hauser & D. L. Featherman (Eds.), *Schooling and achievement in American society* (pp. 29–60). New York: Academic Press.

Atkinson, J. W., & Lens, W. (1980). Fähigkeit und Motivation als Determinanten momentaner und kumulativer Leistung. In H. Heckhausen (Ed.), *Fähigkeit und Motivation in erwartungswidriger Schulleistung* (pp. 129–192). Göttingen: Hogrefe.

Atkinson, J. W., & Litwin, G. H. (1960). Achievement motive and test anxiety conceived as motive to approach success and motive to avoid failure. *Journal of Abnormal and Social Psychology, 60,* 52–63.

Atkinson, J. W., & McClelland, D. C. (1948). The projective expression of needs. II: The effect of different intensities of the hunger drive on thematic apperception. *Journal of Experimental Psychology, 38,* 643–658.

Atkinson, J. W., & O'Connor, P. (1966). Neglected factors in studies of achievement-oriented performance: Social approval as incentive and performance decrement. In J. W. Atkinson & N. T. Feather (Eds.), *A theory of achievement motivation* (pp. 299–325). New York: Wiley.

Atkinson, J. W., & Raynor, J. O. (1974). *Motivation and achievement.* Washington, DC: Winston.

Atkinson, J. W., & Reitman, W. R. (1956). Performance as a function of motive strength and expectancy of goal attainment. *Journal of Abnormal and Social Psychology, 53,* 361–366.

Attneave, F. (1959). *Applications of information theory to psychology.* New York: Holt.

Bakan, D. (1966). *The duality of human existence.* Chicago: Rand McNally.

Bar-Tal, D., & Frieze, T. H. (1976). Attributions of success and failure for actors and observers. *Journal of Research in Personality, 10,* 256–265.

Bartmann, T. (1963). Der Einfluss von Zeitdruck auf die Leistung und das Denkverhalten bei Volksschülern. *Psychologische Forschung, 27,* 1–61.

Bavelas, J. B., & Lee, E. S. (1978). Effects of goal level on performance: A trade-off of quantity and quality. *Canadian Journal of Psychology, 32*(4), 219–240.

Beckman, L. J. (1970). Effects of students' performance on teachers' and of observers' attributions of causality. *Journal of Educational Psychology, 61,* 76–82.

Beit-Hallahmi, B. (1980). Achievement motivation and economic growth: A replication. *Personality and Social Psychology Bulletin, 6,* 210–215.

Bem, D. J., & Allen, A. (1974). On predicting some of the people some of the time: The search for cross-situational consistencies in behavior. *Psychological Review, 81,* 506–520.

Bem, S. (1977). On the utility of alternative procedures for assessing psychological androgyny. *Journal of Consulting and Clinical Psychology, 45,* 196–205.

Berglas, S., & Jones, E. E. (1978). Drug choice as a self-handicapping strategy in response to noncontingent success. *Journal of Personality and Social Psychology, 36,* 405–417.

Berlyne, D. E. (1960). *Conflict, arousal and curiosity.* New York: McGraw-Hill.

Bernstein, W. M., Stephan, W. G., & Davis, M. H. (1979). Explaining attributions for achievement: A path analytic approach. *Journal of Personality and Social Psychology, 37,* 1810–1821.

Bieri, J. (1961). Complexity–simplicity as a personality variable in cognitive and preferential behavior. In D. W. Fiske & S. R. Maddi (Eds.), *Functions of varied experience.* Homewood, IL: Dorsey.

Birch, D., Atkinson, J. W., & Bongort, K. (1974). Cognitive control of action. In B. Weiner (Ed.), *Cognitive views of human motivation.* New York: Academic Press.

Birney, R. C., Burdick, H., & Teevan, R. C. (1969). *Fear of failure motivation.* New York: Van Nostrand.

Blankenship, V. (1979). *Consummatory value of success, task difficulty, and substitution.* Unpublished doctoral dissertation, University of Michigan.

Blankenship, V. (1982). The relationship between consummatory value of success and achievement-task difficulty. *Journal of Personality and Social Psychology, 42,* 901–914.

Bludau, H. -F. (1976). *Mobilitätstendenzen im Gefangenen-Dilemma-Spiel.* Diplomarbeit (thesis), Psychologisches Institut der Ruhr-Universität Bochum.

Bolles, R. C. (1972). Reinforcement, expectancy, and learning. *Psychological Review, 79,* 394–409.

Bolles, R. C. (1974). Cognition and motivation: Some historical trends. In B. Weiner (Ed.), *Cognitive views of human motivation* (pp. 1–20). New York: Academic Press.

Bongort, K. (1975). *Most recent revision of computer program for dynamics of action.* Unpublished computer program, University of Michigan, Ann Arbor.

Borg, G. (1962). *Physical performance and perceived exertion.* Lund: Gleerup.

Bowers, K. S. (1977). There's more to Iago than meets the eye: A clinical account of personal consistency. In D. Magnusson & N. S. Endler (Eds.), *Personality at the crossroads: Current issues in interactional psychology* (pp. 65–81). Hillsdale, NJ: Erlbaum.

Brackhane, R. (1976). *Bezugssysteme im Leistungsverhalten.* Dissertation, Philosophische Fakultät der Universität Münster.

Bradley, G. W. (1978). Self-serving biases in the attribution process: A re-examination of the fact or fiction question. *Journal of Personality and Social Psychology, 36,* 56–71.

Brauckmann, L. (1976). *Erstellung und Erprobung eines Lehrerverhaltenstrainings zur Veränderung der motivanregenden Bedingungen des Unterrichts.* Diplomarbeit (thesis), Psychologisches Institut der Ruhr-Universität Bochum.

Brim, O. G. (1955). Attitude content-intensity and probability expectations. *American Social Review, 20,* 68–76.

Broadhurst, P. I. (1959). The interaction of task difficulty and motivation: The Yerkes-Dodson law revived. *Acta Psychologica, 16,* 321–338.

Brody, N. (1963). N-Achievement, test anxiety and subjective probability of success in risk-taking behavior. *Journal of Abnormal and Social Psychology, 66,* 413–418.

Brookover, W. B., Thomas, S., & Paterson, A. (1966). Self-concept of ability and school achievement. *Sociology of Education, 37,* 271–278.

Brunswick, E. (1952). *The conceptual framework of psychology.* Chicago: University of Chicago Press.

Buckert, U., Meyer, W.-U., & Schmalt, H.-D. (1979). Effects of difficulty and diagnosticity on choice among tasks in relation to achievement motivation and perceived ability. *Journal of Personality and Social Psychology, 37,* 1172–1178.

Buggle, F., & Baumgärtl, F. (1972). *Hamburger Neurotizismus- und Extraversionsskalen für Kinder und Jugendliche.* Göttingen: Hogrefe.

Burnstein, E. (1963). Fear of failure, achievement motivation, and aspiring to prestigeful occupations. *Journal of Abnormal and Social Psychology, 67,* 189–193.

Butzkamm, J. (1972). *Informationseinholung über den eigenen Leistungsstand in Abhängigkeit vom Leistungsmotiv und von der Aufgabenschwierigkeit.* Diplomarbeit (thesis), Psychologisches Institut der Ruhr-Universität Bochum.

Butzkamm, J. (1981). *Motivierungsprozesse bei erwartungswidrigen Rückmeldungen.* Dissertation, Gesamthochschule Duisburg.

Butzkamm, J., Halisch, F., & Posse, N. (1978). Selbstregulationsforschung und Selbstkonzepte. In S. H. Filipp (Ed.), *Selbstkonzeptforschung: Probleme, Befunde, Perspektiven.* Stuttgart: Klett-Cotta.

Campbell, D. J., & Ilgen, D. R. (1976). Additive effects of task difficulty and goal setting on subsequent task performance. *Journal of Applied Psychology, 61,* 319–324.

Carver, C. S., & Scheier, M. F. (1981). *Attention and self-regulation: A control-theory approach to human behavior.* New York: Springer.

Carver, S. C., & Scheier, M. F. (1982). Control theory: A useful conceptual framework for personality, social, clinical, and health psychology. *Psychological Bulletin, 92,* 111–135.

Chandler, T. A., Shama, D. D., Wolf, F. M., & Planchard, S. K. (1981). Multiattributional causality: A five cross-national samples study. *Journal of Cross-Cultural Psychology, 12,* 207–221.

Cooper, H. M., & Burger, J. M. (1980). How teachers explain students' academic performance. *American Educational Research Journal, 12,* 95–109.

Cooper, W. H. (1983). An achievement motivation nomological network. *Journal of Personality and Social Psychology, 44*(4), 841–861.

Covington, M. V., & Omelich, C. L. (1979). Are causal attributions causal? A path analysis of the cognitive model of achievement motivation. *Journal of Personality and Social Psychology, 37,* 1487–1504.

Crandall, V. C. (1969). Sex differences in expectancy of intellectual and academic reinforcement. In C. P. Smith (Ed.), *Achievement-related motives in children* (pp. 11–45). New York: Russell Sage Foundation.

Crandall, V. C., Katkovsky, W., & Crandall, V. J. (1965a). A children's social desirability questionnaire. *Journal of Consulting Psychology, 29,* 27–36.

Crandall, V. C., Katkovsky, W., & Crandall, V. J. (1965b). Children's beliefs in their own control of reinforcements in intellectual–academic achievement situations. *Child Development, 36,* 91–109.

Crandall, V. C., Katkovsky, W., & Preston, A. (1962). Motivational and ability determinants of young children's intellectual achievement behaviors. *Child Development, 33,* 643–661.

Cunningham, J. D., Starr, P. A., & Kanouse, P. A. (1979). Self as actor, active observer, and passive observer: Implications for causal attributions. *Journal of Personality and Social Psychology, 37,* 1146–1152.

Dambauer, J. (Ed.) (1971–1984). *Bibliographie der deutschsprachigen psychologischen Literatur.* Frankfurt/Main: Vittorio Klostermann.

Damm, J. (1968). Effects of interpersonal contexts on relationships between goal-setting behavior and achievement motivation. *Human Relations, 21,* 213–226.

Deaux, K. & Emswiller, T. (1974). Explanations of successful performance on sex-linked tasks: What's skill for the male is luck for the female. *Journal of Personality and Social Psychology, 29,* 80–85.

Deaux, K., & Farris, E. (1977). Attributing causes for one's performance: The effects of sex, norms, and outcome. *Journal of Research in Personality, 11,* 59–72.

deCharms, R. (1968). *Personal causation.* New York: Academic Press.

deCharms, R. (1972). Personal causation training in the schools. *Journal of Applied Social Psychology, 2,* 95–113.

deCharms, R. (1976). *Enhancing motivation: Change in the classroom.* New York: Irvington.

deCharms, R., & Davé, P. N. (1965). Hope of success, fear of failure, subjective probability, and risk-taking behavior. *Journal of Personality and Social Psychology, 1,* 558–568.

deCharms, R., & Moeller, G. H. (1962). Values expressed in American children's readers: 1800–1950. *Journal of Abnormal and Social Psychology, 64,* 136–142.

Depeweg, W. (1973). *Die Wirkung von Erfolg und Misserfolg auf die Leistung bei einer Kartensortieraufgabe in Abhängigkeit von Leistungsmotivation und Schwierigkeit der Aufgabe.* Diplomarbeit (thesis), Psychologisches Institut der Ruhr-Universität Bochum.

de Villiers, P. A., & Herrnstein, R. J. (1976). Toward a law of response strength. *Psychological Bulletin, 83,* 1131–1153.

de Zeeuw, G., & Waagenar, W. A. (1974). Are subjective probabilities probabilities? In C. -A. S. Stäel von Holstein (Ed.), *The Concept of Probability in Psychological Experiments.* Dordrecht: Reidel.

Diener, C. J., & Dweck, C. S. (1978). An analysis of learned helplessness: Continuous changes in performance, strategy, and achievement cognitions following failure. *Journal of Personality and Social Psychology, 36,* 451–462.

Diggory, J. C. (1966). *Self-evaluation: Concepts and studies.* New York: Wiley.

Dörner, D. (1976). *Problemlösen als Informationsverarbeitung.* Stuttgart: Kohlhammer.

Donley, R. E., & Winter, D. G. (1970). Measuring the motives of public officials at a distance: An exploratory study of American presidents. *Behavioral Sciences, 15,* 227–236.

Düker, H. (1963). Über reaktive Anspannungssteigerung. *Zeitschrift für experimentelle und angewandte Psychologie, 10,* 46–72.

Duffy, E. (1962). *Activation and behavior.* London: Wiley.

Dunnette, M. D. (Ed.) (1976). *Handbook of industrial and organizational psychology.* Chicago: Rand McNally.

Duval, S., & Wicklund, R. A. (1973). Effects of objective self-awareness on attribution of causality. *Journal of Experimental Social Psychology, 9,* 17–31.

Dweck, C. S. (1975). The role of expectations and attributions in the alleviation of learned helplessness. *Journal of Personality and Social Psychology, 31,* 674–685.

Dweck, C. S., & Repucci, N. D. (1973). Learned helplessness and reinforcement of responsibility in children. *Journal of Personality and Social Psychology, 25,* 109–116.

Dweck, C. S., & Wortman, C. B. (1982). Learned helplessness, anxiety, and achievement motivation: Neglected parallels in cognitive, affective, and coping responses. In H. W. Krohne & L. Laux (Eds.), *Achievement, stress, and anxiety* (pp. 93–125). Washington, DC: Hemisphere.

Edwards, W. (1954). The theory of decision-making. *Psychological Bulletin, 51,* 380–417.

Eisen, S. V. (1979). Actor-observer differences in information inference and causal attribution. *Journal of Personality and Social Psychology, 37,* 261–272.

Elashoff, J. D., & Snow, R. E. (1971). *Pygmalion reconsidered. A case study in statistical inference: Reconsideration of the Rosenthal–Jacobson data on teacher expectancy.* Belmont, CA: Wadsworth.

Elig, T. W., & Frieze, I. H. (1975). A multi-dimensional scheme for coding and interpreting perceived causality for success and failure events: The Coding Scheme of Perceived Causality (CSPC). SAS: *Catalog of Selected Documents in Psychology, 5,* 313.

Elke, G. (1978). *Die Erfassung und Dimensionierung des Kausalfaktoren-Repertoires zur "naiv"-psychologischen Ursachenerklärung von Schülerleistungen.* Diplomarbeit (thesis), Psychologisches Institut der Ruhr-universität Bochum.

Entin, E. E. (1974). Effects of achievement-oriented and affiliative motives on private and public performance. In J. W. Atkinson & J. O. Raynor (Eds.), *Motivation and achievement* (pp. 219–236). Washington, DC: Winston.

Entin, E. E., & Raynor, J. O. (1973). Effects of contingent future orientation and achievement motivation on performance in two kinds of tasks. *Journal of Experimental Research in Personality, 6,* 314–320.

Entwisle, D. R. (1972). To dispel fantasies about fantasy-based measures of achievement motivation. *Psychological Bulletin, 77,* 377–391.

Enzle, M. W., Harvey, M. D., & Wright, E. F. (1980). Personalism and distinctiveness. *Journal of Personality and Social Psychology, 39,* 542–552.

Ertel, S. (1964). Die emotionale Natur des "semantischen Raumes." *Psychologische Forschung, 28,* 1–32.

Escalona, S. K. (1940). The effect of success and failure upon the level of aspiration and behavior in manic–depressive psychoses. University of Iowa, *Studies of Child Welfare, 16,* 199–302.

Eysenck, H. J. (1966). Personality and experimental psychology. *Bulletin of the British Psychological Society, 19,* 1–28.

Eysenck, H. J. (1967). *The biological bases of personality.* Springfield: Thomas.

Farmer, H. S., & Fyans, L. J. (1980). Women's achievement and career motivation: Their risk-taking patterns, home–career conflict, sex role orientation, fear of success, and self-concept. In L. J. Fyans (Ed.), *Achievement motivation: Recent trends in theory and research* (pp. 390–414). New York: Plenum.

Feather, N. T. (1958). Level of aspiration and achievement imagery. *Australian Journal of Psychology, 10,* 319–328.

Feather, N. T. (1961). The relation of persistence at a task to expectation of success and achievement related motives. *Journal of Abnormal and Social Psychology, 63,* 552–561.

Feather, N. T. (1962). The study of persistence. *Psychological Bulletin, 59,* 94–115.

Feather, N. T. (1963a). Persistence at a difficult task with alternative task of intermediate difficulty. *Journal of Abnormal and Social Psychology, 66,* 604–609.

Feather, N. T. (1963b). The relationship of expectation of success to reported probability, task structure, and achievement related motivation. *Journal of Abnormal and Social Psychology, 66,* 231–238.

Feather, N. T. (1965). The relationship of expectations of success to need achievement and test anxiety. *Journal of Personality and Social Psychology, 1,* 118–126.

Feather, N. T. (1966). Effects of prior success and failure on expectations of success and subsequent performance. *Journal of Personality and Social Psychology, 3,* 287–298.

Feather, N. T. (1967). Valence of outcome and expectation of success in relation to task difficulty and perceived locus of control. *Journal of Personality and Social Psychology, 7,* 372–386.

Feather, N. T. (1968). Change in confidence following success or failure as a predictor of subsequent performance. *Journal of Personality and Social Psychology, 9,* 38–46.

Feather, N. T. (1969). Attribution of responsibility and valence of success and failure in relation to initial confidence and task performance. *Journal of Personality and Social Psychology, 13,* 129–144.

Feather, N. T. (Ed.). (1981). *Expectations and actions: Expectancy-value models in psychology.* Hillsdale, NJ: Erlbaum.

Feather, N. T., & Saville, M. R. (1967). Effects of amount of prior success and failure on expectations of success and subsequent task performance. *Journal of Personality and Social Psychology, 5,* 226–232.

Feather, N. T., & Simon, J. G. (1971). Causal attributions for success and failure in relation to expectations of success based upon selective or manipulative control. *Journal of Personality, 39,* 527–541.

Feather, N. T., & Simon, J. G. (1975). Reactions to male and female success and failure in sex-linked occupations: Impressions of personality, causal attributions, and perceived likelihood of different consequences. *Journal of Personality and Social Psychology, 31,* 20–31.

Federoff, N. A., & Harvey, J. H. (1976). Focus of attention, self-esteem and the attribution of causality. *Journal of Research in Personality, 10,* 336–345.

Feldman, N. S., Higgins, E. T., Karlovac, M., & Ruble, D. N. (1976). Use of consensus information in causal attribution as a function of temporal presentation and availability of direct information. *Journal of Personality and Social Psychology, 34,* 694–698.

Fenigstein, A., Scheier, M. F., & Buss, A. H. (1975). Public and private self-consciousness: Assessment and theory. *Journal of Consulting and Clinical Psychology, 43,* 522–527.

Festinger, L. (1942). A theoretical interpretation of shifts in level of aspiration. *Psychological Review, 49,* 235–250.

Festinger, L. (1954). A theory of social comparison processes. *Human Relations, 7,* 117–140.

Festinger, L. (1957). *A theory of cognitive dissonance.* Stanford: Stanford University Press.

Fiedler, K. (1982). Causal schemata: Review and criticism of research on a popular construct. *Journal of Personality and Social Psychology, 42,* 1001–1013.

Fineman, S. (1977). The achievement motive construct and its measurement: Where are we now? *British Journal of Psychology, 68,* 1–22.

Fisch, R., & Schmalt, H. -D. (1970). Vergleich von TAT- und Fragebogendaten der Leistungs-motivation. *Zeitschrift für experimentelle und angewandte Psychologie, 17,* 608–634.

Fischer, G. H. (1974). *Einführung in die Theorie psychologischer Tests.* Bern: Huber.

Fischhoff, B. (1976). Attribution theory and judgement under uncertainty. In J. H. Harvey, W. J. Ickes, & R. F. Kidd (Eds.), *New directions in attribution research, I* (pp. 421–452). Hillsdale, NJ: Erlbaum.

Fishbein, M., & Coombs, F. S. (1974). Basis for decision: An attitudinal analysis of voting behavior. *Journal of Applied Social Psychology, 4,* 95–124.

Folkes, V. S. (1982). Communicating the reasons for social rejection. *Journal of Experimental Social Psychology, 18,* 235–252.

Folkman, S., Schaefer, C., & Lazarus, R. S. (1979). Cognitive processes as mediators of stress and coping. In L. Hamilton & D. M. Waburton (Eds.), *Human stress and cognition: An information-processing approach.* London: Wiley.

Fontaine, G. (1974). Social comparison and some determinants of expected personal control and expected performance in a novel task situation. *Journal of Personality and Social Psychology, 29,* 487–496.

Fontaine, G. (1975). Causal attribution in simulated versus real situations: When are people logical, when are they not? *Journal of Personality and Social Psychology, 32,* 1021–1029.

Frankel, A., & Snyder, M. C. (1978). Poor performance following unsolvable problems: Learned helplessness or egotism? *Journal of Personality and Social Psychology, 36,* 1415–1423.

French, E. G. (1955). Some characteristics of achievement motivation. *Journal of Experimental Psychology, 50,* 232–236.

French, E. G. (1958a). The interaction of achievement motivation and ability in problem solving success. *Journal of Abnormal and Social Psychology, 57,* 306–309.

French, E. G. (1958b). Effects of the interaction of motivation and feedback on task performance. In J. W. Atkinson (Ed.), *Motives in fantasy, action, and society* (pp. 400–408). Princeton, NJ: Van Nostrand.

French, E., & Lesser, G. S. (1964). Some characteristics of the achievement motive in women. *Journal of Abnormal and Social Psychology, 68,* 119–128.

French, E. G., & Thomas, F. H. (1958). The relation of achievement motivation to problem solving effectiveness. *Journal of Abnormal and Social Psychology, 56,* 46–48.

Freud, S. (1915). Triebe und Triebschicksale, *Internationale Zeitschrift für Psychoanalyse, 3,* 84–100.

Frieze, I. (1973). *Studies of information processing and the attributional process.* Dissertation, University of California, Los Angeles.

Frieze, I., & Weiner, B. (1971). Cue utilization and attributional judgements for success and failure. *Journal of Personality, 39,* 591–605.

Frost, P. J., & Mahoney, T. A. (1976). Goal setting and the task process, I: An interactive influence on individual performance. *Organizational Behavior and Human Performance, 17,* 328–350.

Fuchs, R. (1963). Funktionsanalyse der Motivation. *Zeitschrift für Experimentelle und Angewandte Psychologie, 10,* 626–645.

Fuchs, R. (1965). Über die Darstellung motivierender Erwartungen. *Psychologische Beiträge, 8,* 516–563.

Fuchs, R. (1976). Furchtregulation und Furchthemmung des Zweckhandelns. In A. Thomas (Ed.), *Psychologie der Handlung und Bewegung* (pp. 97–162). Meisenheim: Hain.

Galbraith, J., & Cummings, L. (1967). An empiric investigation of the motivational determinants of past performance: Interactive effects between instrumentality-valence, motivation, and ability. *Organizational Behavior and Human Performance, 2*, 237–257.

Gavin, J. F. (1970). Ability, effort, and role perception as antecedents of job performance. *Experimental Publication System, 5* (manuscript 190A).

Georgopolous, B. S., Mahoney, G. M., & Jones, N. W. (1957). A path-goal approach to productivity. *Journal of Applied Psychology, 41*, 345–353.

Gilmor, T. M., & Minton, H. L. (1974). Internal versus external attribution of task performance as a function of locus of control, initial confidence and success-failure outcome. *Journal of Personality, 42*, 159–174.

Gjesme, T. (1971). Motive to achieve success and motive to avoid failure in relation to school performance for pupils of different ability levels. *Scandinavian Journal of Educational Research, 15*, 81–99.

Gjesme, T. (1973). Achievement-related motives and school performance for girls. *Journal of Personality and Social Psychology, 26*, 131–136.

Gjesme, T. (1974). Goal distance in time and its effects on the relations between achievement motives and performance. *Journal of Research in Personality, 8*, 161–171.

Gjesme, T. (1975). Slope of gradients for performance as a function of achievement motive, goal distance in time, and future time orientation. *Journal of Psychology, 91*, 143–160.

Gjesme, T. (1976). Future-time gradients for performance in test anxious individuals. *Perceptual and Motor Skills, 42*, 235–242.

Gjesme, T. (1981). Is there any future in achievement motivation? *Motivation and Emotion, 5*, 115–138.

Gjesme, T., & Nygard, R. (1970). *Achievement-related motives: Theoretical considerations and constructions of a measuring instrument.* Unpublished manuscript, University of Oslo.

Goffman, E. (1967). *Stigma.* Frankfurt/Main: Suhrkamp.

Goodman, P. S., Rose, J. H., & Furcon, J. E. (1970). Comparison of motivational antecedents of the work performance of scientists and engineers. *Journal of Applied Psychology, 14*, 491–495.

Gray, J. (1971). *Angst und Stress. Entstehung und Überwindung von Neurosen und Frustrationen.* München: Kindler.

Groeben, N., & Scheele, B. (1977). *Argumente für eine Psychologie des reflexiven Subjekts.* Darmstadt: Steinkopff.

Grossmann, S. (1973). *Essentials of physiological psychology.* New York: Wiley.

Guilford, J. P. (1964). *Persönlichkeit.* Weinheim: Beltz.

Haber, R. N. (1958). Discrepancy from adaptation level as a source of affect. *Journal of Experimental Psychology, 56*, 370–375.

Hacker, W. (1973). *Allgemeine Arbeits- und Ingenieurpsychologie.* Berlin: Deutscher Verlag der Wissenchaften.

Hackmann, J. R., & Porter, L. W. (1968). Expectancy theory predictions of work effectiveness. *Organizational Behavior and Human Performance, 3*, 417–426.

Halisch, F. (1976). Die Selbstregulation leistungsbezogenen Verhaltens: Das Leistungsmotiv als Selbstbekräftigungssystem. In H. -D. Schmalt und W. -U. Meyer (Eds.), *Leistungsmotivation und Verhalten* (pp. 137–164). Stuttgart: Klett.

Halisch, F. (1982). *Über die Güteeigenschaften des LM-Gitters für Kinder (Schmalt): Kritische Anmerkungen zu einer Analyse von Krug & Wolter (1979).* Diagnostica, 28, 146–153.

Halisch, F., Butzkamm, J., & Posse, N. (1976). Selbstbekräftigung: I. Theorieansätze und experimentelle Erfordernisse. *Zeitschrift für Entwicklungspsychologie und Pädagogische Psychologie, 8*, 145–164.

Halisch, F. & Heckhausen, H. (1977). Search for feedback information and effort regulation during task performance. *Journal of Personality and Social Psychology, 35,* 724–733.

Hallermann, B. (1975). *Untersuchungen zur Anstrengungskalkulation.* Diplomarbeit (thesis), Psychologisches Institut der Ruhr-Universität Bochum.

Hamilton, J. O. (1974). Motivation and risk-taking behavior. *Journal of Personality and Social Psychology, 29,* 856–864.

Hancock, J. G., & Teevan, R. C. (1964). Fear of failure and risk-taking behavior. *Journal of Personality, 32,* 200–209.

Hansen, R. D. (1980). Commonsense attribution. *Journal of Personality and Social Psychology, 39,* 996–1009.

Hansen, R. D. & Donoghue, J. M. (1977). The power of consensus: Information, derived from one's own and others' behavior. *Journal of Personality and Social Psychology, 35,* 294–302.

Hansen, R. D., & Lowe, C. A. (1976). Distinctiveness and consensus: The influence of behavioral information on actors' and observers' attributions. *Journal of Personality and Social Psychology, 34,* 425–433.

Hansen, R. D., & Stonner, D. M. (1978). Attributes and attributions: Inferring stimulus properties, actors' dispositions, and causes. *Journal of Personality and Social Psychology, 36,* 657–667.

Harvey, J. H., Town, J. P., & Yarkin, K. L. (1981). How fundamental is "The fundamental attribution error"? *Journal of Personality and Social Psychology, 40,* 346–349.

Hayashi, T., & Habu, K. A. (1962). A research on achievement motive: An experimental test of the "thought sampling" method by using Japanese students. *Japanese Psychological Research, 4,* 30–42.

Hebb, D. O. (1955). Drives and the C.N.S. (Conceptual nervous system). *Psychological Review, 62,* 243–254.

Hecker, G. (1971). *Leistungsentwicklung im Sportunterricht.* Weinheim: Beltz.

Hecker, G. (1974). Bericht über eine Untersuchung zur Leistungsentwicklung im Sportunterricht des 1. und 2. Schuljahres. *Sportunterricht, 6,* 191–197.

Hecker, G., Kleine, W., Wessling-Lünnemann, G., & Beier, A. (1979). Interventionsstudien zur Entwicklungsförderung der Leistungsmotivation im Sportunterricht. *Zeitschrift für Entwicklungspsychologie und Pädagogische Psychologie, 11,* 153–169.

Heckhausen, H. (1955). Motivationsanalyse der Anspruchsniveausetzung. *Psychologische Forschung, 25,* 118–154.

Heckhausen, H. (1963a). *Hoffnung und Furcht in der Leistungsmotivation.* Meisenheim: Hain.

Heckhausen, H. (1963b). Eine Rahmentheorie der Motivation in zehn Thesen. *Zeitschrift für experimentelle und angewandte Psychologie, 10,* 604–626.

Heckhausen, H. (1964). Über die Zweckmässigkeit einiger Situationsbedingungen bei der inhaltsanalytischen Erfassung der Motivation. *Psychologische Forschung, 27,* 244–259.

Heckhausen, H. (1967a). *The anatomy of achievement motivation.* New York: Academic Press.

Heckhausen, H. (1967b). *The Atkinson model reshaped.* Lecture at the APA convention, Washington.

Heckhausen, H. (1968a). Achievement motive research: Current problems and some contributions towards a general theory of motivation. In W. J. Arnold (Ed.), *Nebraska Symposium on Motivation* (pp. 103–174). Lincoln: University of Nebraska Press.

Heckhausen, H. (1968b). Förderung der Lernmotivierung und der intellektuellen Tüchtigkeit. In H. Roth (Ed.), *Begabung und Lernen* (pp. 175–211). Stuttgart, Klett.

Heckhausen, H. (1971). Trainingskurse zur Erhöhung der Leistungsmotivation und der unternehmerischen Aktivität in einem Entwicklungsland: Eine nachträgliche Analyse des erzielten Motivwandels. *Zeitschrift für Entwicklungspsychologie und Pädagogische Psychologie, 3,* 253–268.

Heckhausen, H. (1972a). Die Interaktion der Sozialisationsvariablen in der Genese des Leistungsmotivs. In C. F. Graumann (Ed.), *Handbuch der Psychologie* (Vol. 7/2, pp. 955–1019). Göttingen: Hogrefe.

Heckhausen, H. (1972b). *Soziale und individuelle Bezugsnorm.* Unpublished manuscript, Netherlands Institute of Advanced Study, Wassenaar.

Heckhausen, H. (1972c). *Attribuierungsbedingungen für affektive Konsequenzen.* Unpublished manuscript, Psychologisches Institut der Ruhr-Universität Bochum.

Heckhausen, H. (1973). Intervening cognitions in motivation. In D. E. Berlyne & K. B. Madsen (Eds.), *Pleasure, reward, preference* (pp. 217–242). New York: Academic Press.

Heckhausen, H. (1974). *Leistung und Chancengleichheit.* Göttingen: Hogrefe.

Heckhausen, H. (1975a). Fear of failure as a self-reinforcing motive system. In I. G. Sarason & C. Spielberger (Eds.), *Stress and anxiety* (Vol. II, pp. 117–128). Washington, DC: Hemisphere.

Heckhausen, H. (1975b). *Effort expenditure, aspiration level and self-evaluation before and after unexpected performance shifts.* Preliminary draft, Psychologisches Institut der Ruhr-Universität Bochum.

Heckhausen, H. (1975c). *Perceived ability, achievement motive and information choice: A study by Meyer reanalyzed and supplemented.* Unpublished manuscript, Ruhr-Universität Bochum.

Heckhausen, H. (1976a). Lehrer-Schüler-Interaktion. In F. E. Weinert, C. F. Graumann, H. Heckhausen, & M. Hofer (Eds.), *Pädagogische Psychologie* (Part IV, pp. 85–124). Weinheim: Beltz.

Heckhausen, H. (1976b). Kompetenz. In *Historisches Wörterbuch der Philosophie* (Vol. IV, pp. 922–923). Basel: Karger.

Heckhausen, H. (1977a). Achievement motivation and its constructs: A cognitive model. *Motivation and Emotion, 1,* 283–329.

Heckhausen, H. (1977b). Motivation: Kognitionspsychologische Aufspaltung eines summarischen Konstrukts. *Psychologische Rundschau, 28,* 175–189.

Heckhausen, H. (1978a). Selbstbewertung nach erwartungswidrigem Leistungsverlauf: Einfluss von Motiv, Kausalattribution und Zielsetzung. *Zeitschrift für Entwicklungspsychologie und Pädagogische Psychologie, 10,* 191–216.

Heckhausen, H. (1978b). Ein kognitives Motivationsmodell und die Verankerung von Motivkonstrukten. In H. Lenk (Ed.), *Handlungstheorien in interdisziplinärer Perspektive* (Vol. 3). München: Fink.

Heckhausen, H. (1978c). Kommentar zum Beitrag von Meyer. In D. Görlitz, W. -U. Meyer, & B. Weiner (Eds.), *Bielefelder Symposium über Attribution* (pp. 89–92). Stuttgart: Klett-Cotta.

Heckhausen, H. (Ed.) (1980a). *Fähigkeit und Motivation in erwartungswidriger Schulleistung.* Göttingen: Hogrefe.

Heckhausen, H. (1980b). *Motivation und Handeln.* Berlin: Springer-Verlag.

Heckhausen, H. (1982a). Task-irrelevant cognitions during an exam: Incidence and effects. In H. W. Krohne & L. Laux (Eds.), *Achievement, stress, and anxiety* (pp. 247–274). Washington, DC: Hemisphere.

Heckhausen, H. (1982b). The development of achievement motivation. In W. W. Hartup (Ed.), *Review of Child Development Research* (Vol. 6). Chicago: University of Chicago Press.

Heckhausen, H., & Krug, S. (1982). Motive modification. In A. Stewart (Ed.), *Motivation and Society* (pp. 274–318). San Francisco: Jossey-Bass.

Heckhausen, H. & Kuhl, J. (1985). From wishes to action: The dead ends and short cuts on the long way to action. In M. Frese & J. Sabini (Eds.), *Goal-directed behavior: Psychological theory and research on action.* Hillsdale, NJ: Erlbaum.

Heckhausen, H., & Rheinberg, F. (1980). Lernmotivation im Unterricht, erneut betrachtet. *Unterrichtswissenschaft, 8,* 7–47.

Heckhausen, H., & Wagner, I. (1965). Anfänge der Entwicklung der Leistungsmotivation: (II) In der Zielsetzung des Kleinkindes. Zur Genese des Anspruchsniveaus. *Psychologische Forschung, 28,* 179–245.

Heckhausen, H., & Weiner, B. (1972). The emergence of a cognitive psychology of motivation. In P. C. Dodwell (Ed.), *New horizons in psychology* (pp. 126–147). London: Penguin.

Heider, F. (1958). *The psychology of interpersonal relations.* New York: Wiley.

Heneman, H., & Schwab, D. P. (1972). Evaluation of research in expectancy theory predictions of employee performance. *Psychological Bulletin, 78,* 1–9.

Herbart, J. F. (1913). *Pädagogische Briefe oder Briefe über die Anwendung der Psychologie auf die Pädagogik (1831).* O. Willmann and T. Fritsch (Eds.) (Vol. II). Osterwieck, Leipzig: A. W. Zickfeld.

Hermans, H. J. M. (1970). A questionnaire measure of achievement motivation. *Journal of Applied Psychology, 54,* 353–363.

Higgins, E. T., & Bryant, S. L. (1982). Consensus information and the fundamental attribution error: The role of development and in-group versus out-group knowledge. *Journal of Personality and Social Psychology, 43,* 889–900.

Hillgruber, A. (1912). Fortlaufende Arbeit und Willensbetätigung. *Untersuchungen zur Psychologie und Philosophie, 1,* (6).

Hockey, R. (1979). Stress and the cognitive components of skilled performance. In V. Hamilton & D. M. Warburton (Eds.), *Human stress and cognition: An information processing approach.* New York: Wiley.

Hoffman, L. W. (1974). Fear of success in males and females: 1965 and 1972. *Journal of Consulting and Clinical Psychology, 42,* 353–358.

Hoffman, L. W. (1977). Fear of success in 1965 and 1974: A follow-up study. *Journal of Consulting and Clinical Psychology, 45,* 310–321.

Horner, M. S. (1968). *Sex differences in achievement motivation and performance in competitive and non-competitive situations.* Doctoral dissertation, University of Michigan.

Horner, M. S. (1969). Fail: Bright woman. *Psychology Today, 3*(6), 36–38, 62.

Horner, M. S. (1970). Femininity and successful achievement: A basic inconsistency. In J. M. Bardwick, E. Douvan, M. S. Horner, & D. Gutmann (Eds.), *Feminine personality and conflict.* Belmont, CA: Brooks/Cole.

Horner, M. S. (1974a). The measurement and behavioral implications of fear of success in women. In J. W. Atkinson & J. O. Raynor (Eds.), *Motivation and achievement* (pp. 91–117). Washington, D.C.: Winston.

Horner, M. S. (1974b). Performance of men in noncompetitive and interpersonal competitive achievement-oriented situations. In J. W. Atkinson & J. O. Raynor (Eds.), *Motivation and achievement* (pp. 237–254). Washington, DC: Winston.

Horner, M. S., Tresemer, D. W., Berens, A. E., & Watson, R. I. (1973). *Scoring manual for an empirically derived scoring system for motive to avoid success.* Unpublished manuscript, Harvard University.

Howell, W. S. (1972). Compounding uncertainty from internal sources. *Journal of Experimental Psychology, 95,* 6–13.

Hoyos, C. (1965). *Motivationspsychologische Untersuchungen an Kraftfahrern mit dem TAT nach McClelland* (7th supplementary volume of the Archiv für die gesamte Psychologie). Frankfurt: Akademische Verlagsanstalt.

Hoyos, C. (1969). *Risikowahlverhalten bei industriellen Präzisionsarbeiten.* Bern: Huber.

Hoyos, C. (1974). *Arbeitspsychologie.* Stuttgart: Kohlhammer.

Hull, C. C. (1930). Knowledge and purpose as habit mechanisms. *Psychological Review, 37,* 511–525.

Hunn, A. (1925). Über die Gesetzmässigkeit der Beeinflussung von Exaktheitsarbeit durch das Tempo. *Psychotechnische Zeitschrift, 1,* 177–180.

Hunt, J. McV. (1964). The psychological basis for using pre-school enrichment as an antidote for cultural deprivation. *Merrill-Palmer Quarterly, 10,* 209–248.

Ickes, W. J., & Kidd, R. F. (1976). An attributional analysis of helping behavior. In J. H. Harvey, W. J. Ickes, & R. F. Kidd (Eds.), *New directions in attribution research* (pp. 311–334). Hillsdale, NJ: Erlbaum.

Isaacson, R. L. (1964). Relation between *n* achievement, test anxiety, and curricular choices. *Journal of Abnormal and Social Psychology, 68,* 447–452.

Isaacson, R. L., & Raynor, J. O. (1966). *Achievement-related motivation and perceived instrumentality of grades to future career success.* Unpublished manuscript, University of Michigan, Ann Arbor.

Iseler, A. (1970). *Leistungsgeschwindigkeit und Leistungsgüte.* Weinheim: Beltz.

Jardine, E., & Winefield, A. H. (1981). Achievement motivation, psychological reactance, and learned helplessness. *Motivation and Emotion, 5,* 99–113.

Jones, E. E. (1979). The rocky road from acts to dispositions. *American Psychologist, 34,* 107–117.

Jones, E. E., Goethals, G. R., Kennington, G. E., & Severance, I. J. (1972). Primacy and assimilation in the attribution process: The stable entity proposition. *Journal of Personality, 40,* 250–274.

Jones, E. E., & Nisbett, R. E. (1971). *The actor and the observer: Divergent perceptions of the causes of behavior.* New York: General Learning Press.

Jones, E. E., Rock, L., Shaver, K. G., Goethals, G. R., & Ward, L. M. (1968). Pattern of performance and ability attribution: An unexpected primacy effect. *Journal of Personality and Social Psychology, 10,* 317–340.

Jopt, U. (1970). *Die Abhängigkeit des Anreizes von Erfolgswahrscheinlichkeit und Leistungsmotivation in einem Geschicklichkeitsspiel.* Diplomarbeit (thesis), Psychologisches Institut der Ruhr-Universität Bochum.

Jopt, U. -J. (1974). *Extrinsische Motivation und Leistungsverhalten.* Dissertation, Fakultät für Philosophie, Pädagogik, Psychologie der Ruhr-Universität Bochum.

Jopt, U. -J., & Ermshaus, W. (1977). Wie generalisiert ist das Selbstkonzept eigener Fähigkeit? Eine motivationspsychologische Untersuchung zur Aufgabenabhängigkeit der Fähigkeitswahrnehmung. *Zeitschrift für Experimentelle und Angewandte Psychologie, 24,* 578–601.

Jopt, U. -J., & Sprute, J. (1978). Schulische Verhaltens- und Attribuierungskonsequenzen naiver Fähigkeitswahrnehmung. *Newsletter "Selbstkonzepte,"* Universität Trier, *2,* (1).

Kanfer, F. H. (1971). The maintenance of behavior by self-generated stimuli and reinforcement. In A. Jacobs & L. B. Sachs (Eds.), *The psychology of private events* (pp. 39–59). New York: Academic Press.

Kanfer, F. H., & Hagerman, S. (1981). The role of self-regulation. In L. P. Rehm (Ed.), *Behavior therapy for depression: Present status and future directions.* New York: Academic Press.

Karabenick, S. A. (1972). Valence of success and failure as a function of achievement motives and locus of control. *Journal of Personality and Social Psychology, 21,* 101–110.

Karabenick, S. A. (1977). Fear of success, achievement and affiliation dispositions, and the performance of men and women under individual and competitive conditions. *Journal of Personality, 45,* 117–149.

Karabenick, S. A., & Youssef, Z. I. (1968). Performance as a function of achievement levels and perceived difficulty. *Journal of Personality and Social Psychology, 10,* 414–419.

Kassin, S. M. (1979). Consensus information, prediction, and causal attribution: A review of the literature and issues. *Journal of Personality and Social Psychology, 37,* 1966–1971.

Kelley, H. H. (1967). Attributional theory in social psychology. In D. Levine (Ed.), *Nebraska symposium on motivation, 1967* (pp. 192–238). Lincoln: University of Nebraska Press.

Kelley, H. H. (1972). *Causal schemata and the attribution process.* New York: General Learning Press.

Kelley, H. H. (1973). The process of causal attribution. *American Psychologist, 28,* 107–128.

Kelley, H. H. (1976, April). *Recent research in causal attribution.* Invited address, Western Psychological Association, Los Angeles.

Kelley, H. H., & Michela, J. L. (1980). Attribution theory and research. *Annual Review of Psychology, 31,* 457–501.

Kleinbeck, U. (1975). *Motivation und Berufswahl.* Göttingen: Hogrefe.

Kleinbeck, U. (1977). Berufserfolg — Berufszufriedenheit — berufliche Entwicklung. In K. H. Seifert (Ed.), *Handbuch der Berufspsychologie* (pp. 345–396). Göttingen: Hogrefe.

Kleinbeck, U., & Schmidt, K. -H. (1979). Aufgabenwahl im Ernstfall einer betrieblichen Ausbildung: Instrumentalitätstheoretische Ergänzung zum Risikowahl-Modell. *Zeitschrift für Entwicklungspsychologie und Pädagogische Psychologie, 11,* 1–11.

Kleine, W. (1976). *Förderung der Leistungsmotivation im Sportunterricht der Grundschule.* Dissertation, Pädagogische Hochschule Rheinland, Abteilung Aachen.

Kleine, W., & Hecker, G. (1977). Zur Förderung der Leistungsmotivation und der Sportmotorik im Sportunterricht der Grundschule. *Sportwissenschaft, 7,* 63–76.

Klinger, E. (1966). Fantasy need achievement as a motivational construct. *Psychological Bulletin, 66,* 291–308.

Klinger, E. (1971). *Structure and functions of fantasy.* New York: Wiley.

Knapp, R. H., & Garbutt, J. T. (1958). Time imagery and the achievement motive. *Journal of Personality, 26,* 426–434.

Kock, S. E. (1965). *Företagsledning och motivation.* Helsingfors: Svenska Handelshögskolan, Affärsekonomiska Förlagsföreningen.

Kock, S. E. (1974). Företagsledning och motivation. *Nordisk Psykologi, 26,* 211–219.

Kogan, N., & Wallach, M. A. (1967). Risk taking as a function of the situation, the person, and the group. In T. M. Newcomb (Ed.), *New directions in psychology III* (pp. 111–278). New York: Holt, Rinehart and Winston.

Kolb, D. A. (1965). Achievement motivation training for underachieving high-school boys. *Journal of Personality and Social Psychology, 2,* 783–792.

Kraeft, U., & Krug, S. (1979). Beeinflussung von Lehrerattribuierungen und ihre Auswirkung. In L. Eckensberger (Ed.), *Bericht über den 31. Kongress der DGfPs, Mannheim, 1978.* Göttingen: Hogrefe.

Krampen, G. (1979). Zur prognostischen Bedeutung kognitiv-motivationaler Affekte von Zensuren in einer Deutscharbeit bei Hauptschülern. *Zeitschrift für Entwicklungspsychologie und Pädagogische Psychologie, 11,* 250–260.

Krau, E. (1982). Motivational feedback loops in the structure of action. *Journal of Personality and Social Psychology, 43,* 1030–1040.

Krug, B. (1972). *Misserfolgsattribuierungen und deren Auswirkungen auf Erwartungs- und Leistungsänderungen sowie auf Persistenz.* Diplomarbeit (thesis), Psychologisches Institut der Ruhr-Universität Bochum.

Krug, S. (1971). *Der Einfluss von kognitiven Variablen auf Determinanten leistungsmotivier-*

ten Verhaltens. Diplomarbeit (thesis), Psychologisches Institut der Ruhr-Universität Bochum.

Krug, S., Hage, A., & Hieber, S. (1978). Anstrengungsmotivation in Abhängigkeit von der Aufgabenschwierigkeit, dem Konzept eigener Tüchtigkeit und dem Leistungsmotiv. *Archiv für Psychologie, 130,* 265–278.

Krug, S., & Hanel, J. (1976). Motivänderung: Erprobung eines theoriegeleiteten Trainingsprogramms. *Zeitschrift für Entwicklungspsychologie und Pädagogische Psychologie, 8,* 274–287.

Krug, S., & Peters, J. (1977). Persönlichkeitsänderung nach Sonderschuleinweisung. *Zeitschrift für Entwicklungspsychologie und Pädagogische Psychologie, 9,* 181–184.

Krug, S., Peters, J., & Quinkert, H. (1977). Motivförderungsprogramm für lernbehinderte Sonderschüler. *Zeitschrift für Heilpädagogik, 28,* 667–674.

Krug, S., Rheinberg, F., & Peters, J. (1977). Einflüsse der Sonderbeschulung und eines zusätzlichen Motivänderungsprogramms auf die Persönlichkeitsentwicklung von Sonderschülern. *Zeitschrift für Heilpädagogik, 28,* 431–439.

Kuhl, J. (1972). *Zum Problem der Eindimensionalität der Messung von Leistungsmotivation mittels des Heckhausen-TAT.* Diplomarbeit (thesis), Psychologisches Institut der Ruhr-Universität Bochum.

Kuhl, J. (1977). *Mess- und prozesstheoretische Analysen einiger Person- und Situationsparameter der Leistungsmotivation.* Bonn: Bouvier.

Kuhl, J. (1978a). Standard setting and risk preference: An elaboration of the theory of achievement motivation and an empirical test. *Psychological Review, 85,* 239–248.

Kuhl, J. (1978b). Situations-, reaktions- und personbezogene Konsistenz des Leistungsmotivs bei der Messung mittels des Heckhausen-TAT. *Archiv für Psychologie, 130,* 37–52.

Kuhl, J. (1981). Motivational and functional helplessness: The moderating effect of state versus action orientation. *Journal of Personality and Social Psychology, 40,* 155–170.

Kuhl, J. (1982a). Handlungskontrolle als metakognitiver Vermittler zwischen Intention und Handeln: Freizeitaktivitäten bei Hauptschülern. *Zeitschrift für Entwicklungspsychologie und Pädagogische Psychologie, 9,* 141–148.

Kuhl, J. (1982b). Action- vs. state-orientation as a mediator between motivation and action. In W. Hacker, W. Volpert, & M. von Cranach (Eds.), *Cognitive and motivational aspects of action* (pp. 67–85). Berlin: VEB Deutscher Verlag der Wissenschaften.

Kuhl, J. (1983). *Motivation, Konflikt, und Handlungskontrolle.* Heidelberg: Springer.

Kuhl, J. (1984). Volitional aspects of achievement motivation and learned helplessness: Toward a comprehensive theory of action-control. In B. A. Maher (Ed.), *Progress in Experimental Personality Research* (Vol. 12, pp. 99–170). New York: Academic Press.

Kuhl, J. (in press a). Integrating cognitive and dynamic approaches: A prospectus for a unified motivational psychology. In J. Kuhl & J. W. Atkinson (Eds.), *Motivation, thought, and action: Personal and situational determinants.* New York, Praeger.

Kuhl, J. (in press b). Volitional mediators of cognition-behavior consistency: Self-regulatory processes and action vs. state orientation. In J. Kuhl & J. Beckmann (Eds.), *Action control: From cognition to behavior.* New York: Springer.

Kuhl, J., & Beckmann, J. (1983). Handlungskontrolle und Umfang der kognitiven Informationsverarbeitung: Wahl einer vereinfachten (nicht-optimalen) Entscheidungsregel zugunsten rascher Handlungsbereitschaft. *Zeitschrift für Sozialpsychologie, 14,* 241–250.

Kuhl, J., & Blankenship, V. (1979a). The dynamic theory of achievement motivation: From episodic to dynamic thinking. *Psychological Review, 86,* 141–151.

Kuhl, J., & Blankenship, V. (1979b). Behavioral change in a constant environment: Moving to more difficult tasks in spite of constant expectations of success. *Journal of Personality and Social Psychology, 37,* 551–563.

Kuhl, J., & Geiger, E. (in press). The dynamic theory of the anxiety-behavior relationship: A study on resistance and time allocation. In J. Kuhl & J. W. Atkinson (Eds.), *Motivation, thought, and action.* New York: Praeger.

Kuhl, J., & Weiss, M. (1984). Performance deficits following uncontrollable failure: Impaired action control or global attributions and generalized expectancy deficits. Max-Planck-Institute for Psychological Research, München, Paper 5.

Kukla, A. (1972a). Foundations of an attributional theory of performance. *Psychological Review, 79,* 454–470.

Kukla, A. (1972b). Attributional determinants of achievement-related behavior. *Journal of Personality and Social Psychology, 21,* 166–174.

Kukla, A. (1974). Performance as a function of resultant achievement motivation (perceived ability) and perceived difficulty. *Journal of Research in Personality, 7,* 374–383.

Kukla, A. (1977). *Self-perception of ability and resultant achievement motivation.* Unpublished manuscript, Scarborough College, University of Toronto.

Kukla, A. (1978). An attributional theory of choice. In L. Berkowitz (Ed.), *Advances in Experimental Social Psychology* (Vol. 11, pp. 862–873). New York: Academic Press.

Kun, A., & Weiner, B. (1973). Necessary versus sufficient causal schemata for success and failure. *Journal of Research in Personality, 7,* 197–207.

Lanzetta, J. T., & Hannah, T. E. (1969). Reinforcing behavior of "naive" trainers. *Journal of Personality and Social Psychology, 11,* 245–252.

LaPorte, R. E., & Nath, R. (1976). Role of performance goals in prose learning. *Journal of Educational Psychology, 68,* 260–264.

Lau, R. R., & Russell, D. (1980). Attributions in the sport pages. *Journal of Personality and Social Psychology, 39,* 29–38.

Laufen, A. (1967). *Validierungsstudie des TAT-Verfahrens zur Erhebung der Anschlussmotivation.* Diplomarbeit (thesis), Psychologisches Institut der Ruhr-Universität Bochum.

Lavelle, T. L., Metalsky, G. J., & Coyne, J. C. (1979). Learned helplessness, test anxiety, and acknowledgement of contingencies. *Journal of Abnormal Psychology, 88,* 381–387.

Lawler, E. E., & Porter, L. W. (1967). Antecedent attitudes of effective managerial job performance. *Organizational Behavior and Human Performance, 2,* 122–142.

Lazarus, R. S. (1968). Emotion and adaptation: Conceptual and empirical relations. In W. J. Arnold (Ed.), *Nebraska Symposium of Motivations* (pp. 175–270). Lincoln: University of Nebraska Press.

Lee, W. (1971). *Decision theory and human behavior.* New York: Wiley.

Lerner, M. J., & Miller, D. T. (1978). Just world research in the attribution process: Looking back and ahead. *Psychological Bulletin, 85,* 1030–1051.

Lesser, G. S., Krawitz, R., & Packard, R. (1963). Experimental arousal of achievement motivation in adolescent girls. *Journal of Abnormal and Social Psychology, 65,* 59–66.

Lewin, K. (1926). Untersuchungen zur Handlungs- und Affekt-Psychologie, II: Vorsatz, Wille und Bedürfnis. *Psychologische Forschung, 7,* 330–385.

Lewin, K. (1931). The conflict between Aristotelian and Galilean modes of thoughts in contemporary psychology. *Journal of General Psychology, 5,* 141–177.

Lewin, K. (1935). *Dynamic theory of personality.* New York: McGraw Hill.

Lewin, K. (1938). *The conceptual representation and the measurement of psychological forces.* Durham, NC: Duke University Press.

Lewin, K. (1951). *Field theory in social science.* New York: Harper & Row.

Lewin, K., Dembo, T., Festinger, L., & Sears, P. S. (1944). Level of aspiration. In J. McHunt (Ed.), *Personality and behavior disorders* (Vol. I, pp. 333–378). New York: Ronald Press.

Leyhausen, P. (1965). Das Motivationsproblem in der Ethologie. In H. Thomae (Ed.), *Handbuch der Psychologie* (Vol. II, pp. 794–816). Göttingen: Hogrefe.

Liebert, R. M., & Morris, L. W. (1967). Cognitive and emotional components of test anxiety: A distinction and some initial data. *Psychological Reports, 20,* 975–978.

Liebhart, E. H. (1977). Fähigkeit und Anstrengung im Lehrerurteil: Der Einfluss inter- versus intraindividueller Perspektive. *Zeitschrift für Entwicklungspsychologie und Pädagogische Psychologie, 9,* 94–102.

Lindworsky, J. (1923). *Der Wille. Seine Erscheinung und Beherrschung nach den Ergebnissen der experimentellen Forschung.* Leipzig: Barth.

Littig, L. W. (1963). Effects of motivation and probability preferences. *Journal of Personality, 31,* 417–427.

Litwin, G. H. (1966). *Motives and expectancy as determinants of preference for degree of risk.* Unpublished honors thesis, University of Michigan, 1958. In J. W. Atkinson & N. T. Feather (Eds.), *A theory of achievement motivation,* New York: Wiley.

Litwin, G. H., & Stringer, R. A. (1968). *Motivation and organizational climate.* Boston: Harvard University, Graduate School of Business Administration, Division of Research.

Lobsien, M. (1914). *Die experimentelle Ermüdungserforschung.* Langensalza: Beyer.

Locke, E. A. (1968). Toward a theory of task motivation and incentives. *Organizational Behavior and Human Performance, 3,* 157–189.

Locke, E. A., Shaw, K. N., Saari, L. M., & Latham, G. P. (1981). Goal setting and task performance: 1969–1980. *Psychological Bulletin, 90,* 125–152.

Lorenz, K. (1953). Die Entwicklung der vergleichenden Verhaltensforschung in den letzten 12 Jahren. *Zoologischer Anzeiger, 17,* 36–58.

Lorenz, K. (1963). *Das sogenannte Böse.* Wien: Borotha-Schoeler.

Lorenz, K. (1969). Innate bases of learning. In K. H. Pribram (Ed.), *On the biology of learning* (pp. 13–93). New York: Harcourt, Brace & World.

Lösel, F. (1975). Prozesse der Stigmatisierung in der Schule. In M. Brusten & J. Hohmeier (Eds.), *Stigmatisierung 2* (pp. 7–34). Darmstadt: Luchterhand.

Lowell, E. L. (1952). The effect of need for achievement on learning and speed of performance. *Journal of Psychology, 33,* 31–40.

Ludwig, S. (1982). Die Parameter des Leistungsmotivs und ihre Relation zu leistungsbezogenen Verhaltens- und Sozialisationsmerkmalen. *Zeitschrift für Entwicklungspsychologie und Pädagogische Psychologie, 14,* 149–160.

Luginbuhl, J. E. R., Crowe, D. H., & Kahan, J. P. (1975). Causal personality attribution for success and failure. *Journal of Personality and Social Psychology, 31,* 86–93.

Lührmann, J. V. (1977). *Bezugsnorm: Perzeption und Orientierung bei Schülern.* Diplomarbeit (thesis), Psychologisches Institut der Ruhr-Universität Bochum.

Madsen, K. B. (1974). *Modern theories of motivation.* Copenhagen: Munksgaard.

Magnusson, D. (1976). *Consistency and coherence in personality: A discussion of lawfulness at different levels.* Reports from the Psychological Department, the University of Stockholm, No. 472.

Magnusson, D., & Endler, N. S. (1977). Interactional psychology: Present status and future prospects. In D. Magnusson & N. S. Endler (Eds.), *Personality at the crossroads: current issues in interactional psychology* (pp. 3–31). Hillsdale, NJ: Erlbaum.

Mahone, C. H. (1960). Fear of failure and unrealistic vocational aspiration. *Journal of Abnormal and Social Psychology, 60,* 253–261.

Major, B. (1980). Information acquisition and attribution process. *Journal of Personality and Social Psychology, 39,* 1010–1023.

Mandler, G., & Sarason, S. B. (1952). A study of anxiety and learning. *Journal of Abnormal and Social Psychology, 47,* 166–173.

Markus, H. (1977). Self-schemata and processing information about the self. *Journal of Personality and Social Psychology, 35,* 63–78.

Marlowe, D., & Crowne, D. P. (1960). A new scale of social desirability independent of psychopathology. *Journal of Consulting Psychology, 24,* 349–354.

Masters, J. C., Furman, W., & Barden, R. C. (1977). Effects of achievement standards, tangible rewards, and self-dispensed achievement evaluations on children's task mastery. *Child Development, 48,* 217–224.

McArthur, L. A. (1972). The how and what of why: Some determinants and consequences of causal attribution. *Journal of Personality and Social Psychology, 22,* 171–193.

McClelland, D. C. (1951a). *Personality.* New York: Holt, Rinehart, & Winston.

McClelland, D. C. (1951b). Measuring motivation in fantasy: The achievement motive. In H. Guetzkow (Ed.), *Groups, leadership, and men.* New York: Carnegie Press.

McClelland, D. C. (1958a). Methods of measuring human motivation. In J. W. Atkinson (Ed.), *Motives in fantasy, action, and society* (pp. 7–42). Princeton, NJ: Van Nostrand.

McClelland, D. C. (1958b). Risk taking in children with high and low need for achievement. In J. W. Atkinson (Ed.), *Motives in fantasy, action, and society* (pp. 306–321). Princeton, NJ: Van Nostrand.

McClelland, D. C. (1961). *The achieving society.* Princeton, NJ: Van Nostrand.

McClelland, D. C. (1965). Toward a theory of motive acquisition. *American Psychologist, 20,* 321–333.

McClelland, D. C. (1971). *Assessing human motivation.* New York: General Learning Press.

McClelland, D. C. (1972a). What is the effect of achievement motivation training in the schools? *Teachers College Record, 74,* 129–145.

McClelland, D. C. (1972b). Opinions predict opinions: So what else is new? *Journal of Consulting and Clinical Psychology, 38,* 325–326.

McClelland, D. C. (1975). *Power: The inner experience.* New York: Irvington.

McClelland, D. C. (1978). Managing motivation to expand human freedom. *American Psychologist, 33,* 201–210.

McClelland, D. C. (1980). Motive dispositions: The merits of operant and respondent measures. In L. Wheeler (Ed.), *Review of Personality and Social Psychology* (Vol. 1, pp. 10–41). Beverly Hills, CA: Sage.

McClelland, D. C., & Alschuler, A. S. (1971). *Achievement motivation development project.* Unpublished manuscript, Harvard University, Cambridge, MA.

McClelland, D. C., Atkinson, J. W., Clark, R. A., & Lowell, E. L. (1953). *The achievement motive.* New York: Appleton–Century–Crofts. (2nd ed., 1976)

McClelland, D. C., Clark, R. A., Roby, T. B., & Atkinson, J. W. (1949). The projective expression of needs, IV: The effects of need for achievement on thematic apperception. *Journal of Experimental Psychology, 39,* 242–255.

McClelland, D. C., & Liberman, A. M. (1949). The effects of need for achievement on recognition of need-related words. *Journal of Personality, 18,* 236–251.

McClelland, D. C., & Winter, D. G. (1969). *Motivating economic achievement.* New York: Free Press.

McFarland, C., & Ross, M. (1982). Impact of causal attributions in affective reactions to success and failure. *Journal of Personality and Social Psychology, 43,* 937–946.

McMahan, I. D. (1973). Relationship between causal attributions and expectancy of success. *Journal of Personality and Social Psychology, 28,* 108–114.

Medway, F. J., & Lowe, C. A. (1976). The effect of stimulus person valence on divergent self–other attributions for success and failure. *Journal of Research in Personality, 10,* 266–278.

Mehrabian, A. (1968). Male and female scales of the tendency to achieve. *Educational and Psychological Measurement, 28,* 493–502.

Mehrabian, A. (1969). Measures of achieving tendency. *Educational and Psychological Measurement, 29,* 445–451.

Mehta, P. (1968). Achievement motivation training for educational development. *Indian Educational Review, 3,* 1–29.

Mehta, P. (1969). *The achievement motive in high school boys.* New Delhi: National Council of Educational Research and Training.

Mehta, P., & Kanade, H. M. (1969). Motivation development for educational growth: A follow-up study. *Indian Journal of Psychology, 46,* 1–20.

Meichenbaum, D. (1972). Cognitive modification of test-anxious college students. *Journal of Consulting and Clinical Psychology, 39,* 370–380.

Mento, A. J., Carteledge, N. D., & Locke, E. A. (1980). Maryland vs. Michigan vs. Minnesota: Another look at the relationship of expectancy and goal difficulty to task performance. *Organizational Behavior and Human Performance, 25,* 419–440.

Meyer, H. H., Walker, W. B., & Litwin, G. H. (1961). Motive patterns and risk preferences associated with entrepreneurship. *Journal of Abnormal and Social Psychology, 63,* 570–574.

Meyer, J. P. (1980). Causal attribution for success and failure: A multivariate investigation of dimensionality, formation, and consequences. *Journal of Personality and Social Psychology, 38,* 704–718.

Meyer, J. P., & Koelbl, S. L. M. (1982). Dimensionality of students' causal attributions for test performance. *Personality and Social Psychology, 8,* 31–36.

Meyer, W. -U. (1969). Anspruchsniveau und erlebte Selbstverantwortlichkeit für Erfolg und Misserfolg. *Psychologische Beiträge, 11,* 328–348.

Meyer, W. -U. (1972). Überlegungen zur Konstruktion eines Fragebogens zur Erfassung von Selbstkonzepten der Begabung. Unpublished manuscript, Psychologisches Institut der Ruhr-Universität Bochum.

Meyer, W. -U. (1973a). *Leistungsmotiv und Ursachenerklärung von Erfolg und Misserfolg.* Stuttgart: Klett.

Meyer, W. -U. (1973b). Anstrengungsintention in Abhängigkeit von Begabungseinschätzung und Aufgabensschwierigkeit. *Archiv für Psychologie, 125,* 245–262.

Meyer, W. -U. (1976). Leistungsorientiertes Verhalten als Funktion von wahrgenommener eigener Begabung und wahrgenommener Schwierigkeit. In H. -D. Schmalt & W. -U. Meyer (Eds.), *Leistungsmotivation und Verhalten* (pp. 101–135). Stuttgart: Klett.

Meyer, W. -U. (1978). Der Einfluss von Sanktionen auf Begabungskonzeptionen. In D. Görlitz, W. -U. Meyer, & B. Werner (Eds.), *Bielefelder Symposium über Attribution* (pp. 71–87). Stuttgart: Klett-Cotta.

Meyer, W. -U. (1981). Leistung, Leistungseinschätzung und Ursachenzuschreibung in Abhängigkeit vom Konzept eigener Begabung. Unpublished manuscript, Universität Bielefeld.

Meyer, W. -U. (1982). Indirect communications about perceived ability estimates. *Journal of Educational Psychology, 74,* 888–897.

Meyer, W. -U., Bachmann, M., Biermann, U., Hempelmann, M., Plöger, F. -O. & Spiller, H. (1979). The informational value of evaluative behavior: Influences of praise and blame on perceptions of ability. *Journal of Educational Psychology, 71,* 259–268.

Meyer, W. -U., & Butzkamm, A. (1975). Ursachenerklärung von Rechennoten: I. Lehrerattribuierungen. *Zeitschrift für Entwicklungspsychologie und Pädagogische Psychologie, 7,* 53–66.

Meyer, W. -U., Folkes, V., & Weiner, B. (1976). The perceived informational value and affective consequences of choice behavior and intermediate difficulty task selection. *Journal of Research in Personality, 10,* 410–423.

Meyer, W. -U., & Hallermann, B. (1974). Anstrengungsintention bei einer leichten und schweren Aufgabe in Abhängigkeit von der wahrgenommenen eigenen Begabung. *Archiv für Psychologie, 126,* 85–89.

Meyer, W. -U., & Hallermann, B. (1977). Intended effort and informational value of task outcome. *Archiv für Psychologie, 129,* 131–140.

Meyer, W. -U., Heckhausen, H., & Kemmler, L. (1965). Validierungskorrelate der inhaltsanalytisch erfassten Leistungsmotivation guter und schwacher Schüler des dritten Schuljahres. *Psychologische Forschung, 28,* 301–328.

Meyer, W. -U., & Plöger, F. -O. (1979). Scheinbar paradoxe Wirkungen von Lob und Tadel auf die wahrgenommene eigene Begabung. In S. H. Filipp (Ed.), *Selbstkonzept-Forschung: Probleme, Befunde und Perspektiven* (pp. 221–235). Stuttgart: Klett-Cotta.

Meyer, W. -U., & Schmalt, H. -D. (1978). Die Attributionstheorie. In D. Frey (Ed.), *Kognitive Theorien der Sozialpsychologie* (pp. 98–136). Bern: Huber.

Mierke, K. (1955). *Wille und Leistung.* Göttingen: Hogrefe.

Miessler, M. (1976). *Leistungsmotivation und Zeitperspektive.* München: Oldenbourg.

Mikula, G., Uray, H., & Schwinger, T. (1976). Die Entwicklung einer deutschen Fassung der Mehrabian Achievement Risk Preference Scale. *Diagnostica, 22,* 87–97.

Miller, D. T. (1976). Ego involvement and attribution for success and failure. *Journal of Personality and Social Psychology, 34,* 901–906.

Miller, D. T., Norman, S. A., & Wright, E. (1978). Distortion in person conception as a consequence of the need for effective control. *Journal of Personality and Social Psychology, 36,* 598–607.

Miller, D. T., & Porter, C. A. (1980). Effects of temporal perspective on the attribution process. *Journal of Personality and Social Psychology, 39,* 532–541.

Miller, D. T., & Ross, M. (1975). Self-serving biases in the attribution of causality: Fact or fiction? *Psychological Bulletin, 82,* 213–225.

Miller, G. A., Galanter, E., & Pribram, K. H. (1960). *Plans and the structure of behavior.* New York: Holt, Rinehart & Winston.

Miller, I. W. III, & Norman, W. H. (1979). Learned helplessness in humans: A review and attribution-theory model. *Psychological Bulletin, 86,* 93–118.

Miller, N. E. (1944). Experimental studies of conflict. In J. McV. Hunt (Ed.), *Personality and the behavioral disorders* (Vol. I, pp. 431–465). New York: Ronald Press.

Mischel, W. (1973). Toward a cognitive social learning reconceptualization of personality. *Psychological Review, 80,* 252–283.

Mitchell, T. R., & Albright, D. (1972). Expectancy theory predictions of job satisfaction, job effort, job performance, and retention of naval aviation officers. *Organizational Behavior and Human Performance, 8,* 1–20.

Mitchell, T. R., & Biglan, A. (1971). Instrumentality theories: Current uses in psychology. *Psychological Bulletin, 76,* 432–454.

Moede, W. (1920). *Experimentelle Massenpsychologie: Beiträge zur Experimentalpsychologie der Gruppe.* Leipzig: Hirzel.

Monahan, L., Kuhn, D., & Shaver, P. (1974). Intrapsychic versus cultural explanations of the "fear of success" motive. *Journal of Personality and Social Psychology, 29,* 60–64.

Monson, T. C., & Snyder, M. (1977). Actors, observers, and the attribution process: Toward a reconceptualization. *Journal of Experimental Social Psychology, 13,* 89–111.

Morgan, S. W., & Mausner, B. (1973). Behavioral and fantasied indicators of avoidance of success in men and women. *Journal of Personality, 41,* 457–469.

Morris, J. L. (1966). Propensity for risk taking as a determinant of vocational choice: An extension of the theory of achievement motivation. *Journal of Personality and Social Psychology, 3,* 328–335.

Morris, L. W., & Liebert, R. M. (1969). Effects of anxiety on timed and untimed intelligence tests. *Journal of Consulting and Clinical Psychology, 33,* 240–244.

Morris, L. W., & Liebert, R. M. (1970). Relationship of cognitive and emotional components of test anxiety to physiological arousal and academic performance. *Journal of Consulting and Clinical Psychology, 35,* 332–337.

Morrison, H. W. (1954). *Validity and behavioral correlates of female need for achievement.* Unpublished master's thesis, Wesleyan University.

Moulton, R. W. (1958). Notes for a projective measure for fear of failure. In J. W. Atkinson (Ed.), *Motives in fantasy, action, and society* (pp. 563–571). Princeton, NJ: Van Nostrand.

Moulton, R. W. (1965). Effects of success and failure on level of aspiration as related to achievement motives. *Journal of Personality and Social Psychology, 1,* 399–406.

Moulton, R. W. (1967). *Age group and ability group norms as determinants of level of aspiration.* Unpublished manuscript, University of California, Berkeley.

Moulton, R. W. (1974). Motivational implications of individual differences in competence. In J. W. Atkinson & J. O. Raynor (Eds.), *Motivation and achievement* (pp. 77–82). Washington: Winston.

Mücher, H., & Heckhausen, H. (1962). Influence of mental activity and achievement motivation on skeletal muscle tonus. *Perceptual and Motor Skills, 14,* 217–218.

Müller, G. E., & Pilzecker, A. (1900). *Experimentelle Beiträge zur Lehre vom Gedächtnis.* Suppl. vol. of *Zeitschrift für Psychologie.*

Murray, H. A. (1938). *Explorations in personality.* New York: Oxford University Press.

Murray, H. A. (1951). Toward a classification of interaction. In T. Parsons & E. A. Shils (Eds.), *Toward a general theory of action* (pp. 434–464). Cambridge, MA: Harvard University Press.

Newson, D., & Rindner, R. J. (1979). Variation in behavior perception and ability attribution. *Journal of Personality and Social Psychology, 37,* 1847–1858.

Nicholls, J. G. (1975). Causal attribution and other achievement related cognitions: Effects of task outcome, attainment value and sex. *Journal of Personality and Social Psychology, 31,* 379–399.

Nicholls, J. G. (1976). Effort is virtuous, but it's better to have ability: Evaluative responses to perceptions of effort and ability. *Journal of Research in Personality, 10,* 306–315.

Nicholls, J. G. (1978). The development of the concepts of effort and ability, perception of academic attainment and the understanding that difficult tasks require more ability. *Child Development, 49,* 800–814.

Nicholls, J. G. (1979). Quality and equality in intellectual development: The role of motivation in education. *American Psychologist, 34,* 1071–1084.

Nicholls, J. G. (1980). The development of the concept of difficulty. *Merrill-Palmer Quarterly, 26,* 271–281.

Nickel, T. W. (1974). The attribution of intention as a critical factor in the relation between frustration and aggression. *Journal of Personality, 42,* 481–492.

Nisbett, R. E., Borgida, E., Crandall, R., & Reed, H. (1976). Popular induction: Information is not necessarily informative. In J. Carroll & J. Payne (Eds.), *Cognitive and social behavior* (pp. 113–133). Hillsdale, NJ: Erlbaum.

Nisbett, R. E., & Wilson, T. D. (1977). Telling more than we can know: Verbal reports on mental processes. *Psychological Review, 84,* 231–259.

Nuttin, J. (1964). The future time perspective in human motivation and learning. *Acta Psychologica, 23,* 60–82.

Nuttin, J. (1978). La perspective temporelle dans le comportement humain. In P. Fraisse (Ed.), *Du temps biologique au temps psychologique* (pp. 1–62). Paris: Presses Universitaire de France.

Nygard, R. (1977). *Personality, situation, and persistence.* Oslo: Universitetsforlaget.

O'Connor, D. A., Atkinson, J. W., & Horner, M. (1966). Motivational implications of ability grouping in schools. In J. W. Atkinson & N. T. Feather (Eds.), *A theory of achievement motivation* (pp. 231–248). New York: Wiley.

Olweus, D. (1977). A critical analysis of the "modern" interactionist position. In D. Magnusson & N. S. Endler (Eds.), *Personality at the crossroads: Current issues in interactional psychology* (pp. 221–233). Hillsdale, NJ: Erlbaum.

Orvis, B. R., Cunningham, J. D., & Kelley, H. H. (1975). A closer examination of causal inference: The role of consensus, distinctiveness, and consistency information. *Journal of Personality and Social Psychology, 32,* 605–616.

Ovsiankina, M. (1928). Die Wiederaufnahme unterbrochener Handlungen. *Psychologische Forschung, 11,* 302–379.

Pachella, R. G. (1974). The interpretation of reaction time in information-processing research. In B. H. Kantowitz (Ed.), *Human information processing: Tutorials in performance and cognition* (pp. 41–82). New York: Wiley.

Parsons, J., & Goff, S. B. (1980). Achievement motivation and values: An alternative perspective. In L. J. Fyans (Ed.), *Achievement motivation: Recent trends in theory and research* (pp. 349–373). New York: Plenum.

Passer, M. W., Kelley, N. H., & Michela, J. H. (1978). Multidimensional scaling of the causes for negative interpersonal behavior. *Journal of Personality and Social Psychology, 36,* 951–962.

Patten, R. L., & White, L. A. (1977). Independent effects of achievement motivation and overt attribution on achievement behavior. *Motivation and Emotion, 1,* 39–59.

Peak, H. (1955). Attitude and motivation. In M. R. Jones (Ed.), *Nebraska Symposium on Motivation* (pp. 148–189). Lincoln: University of Nebraska Press.

Peplau, L. A. (1976). Impact of fear and sex-role attitudes on women's competitive achievement. *Journal of Personality and Social Psychology, 34,* 561–568.

Peter, R. (1978). *Motivationale Effekte der Bezugsnorm-Orientierung von Lehrern: Eine Längsschnittstudie an Hauptschulen der 5. und 7. Klassenstufen.* Diplomarbeit (thesis), Psychologisches Institut der Ruhr-Universität Bochum.

Pettigrew, T. F. (1967). Social evaluation theory. In D. Levine (Ed.), *Nebraska Symposium on Motivation 1967* (pp. 241–311). Lincoln, Nebraska.

Phares, E. D. (1976). *Locus of control in personality.* Morristown, NJ: General Learning Press.

Pittman, T. S., & Pittman, N. L. (1980). Deprivation of control and the attribution process. *Journal of Personality and Social Psychology, 39,* 377–389.

Poppelreuter, W. (1918). *"Die Arbeitsschauuhr." Ein Beitrag zur praktischen Psychologie.* Langensalza, Wardt & Klauwell.

Poppelreuter, W. (1923). *Allgemeine methodische Richtlinien der praktischen psychologischen Begutachtung.* Leipzig: Kröner.

Pottharst, B. C. (1955). *The achievement motive and level of aspiration after experimentally induced success and failure.* Doctoral dissertation, University of Michigan.

Pritchard, R. D., & Sanders, M. S. (1973). The influence of valence, instrumentality, and expectancy of effort and performance. *Journal of Applied Psychology, 57,* 55–60.

Quattrone, G. A., & Jones, E. E. (1980). The perception of variablity within in-groups and out-groups: Implications for the law of small numbers. *Journal of Personality and Social Psychology, 38,* 141–152.

Rand, P. (1978). Some validation data of the Achievement Motives Scales (AMS). *Scandinavian Journal of Educational Research, 22,* 155–171.

Rasch, G. (1960). *Probabilistic models for some intelligence and attainment tests.* Kopenhagen: Nielson & Lydicke.

Raynor, J. O. (1969). Future orientation and motivation of immediate activity: An elaboration of the theory of achievement motivation. *Psychological Review, 76,* 606–610.

Raynor, J. O. (1970). Relationship between achievement-related motives, future orientation, and academic performance. *Journal of Personality and Social Psychology, 15,* 28–33.

Raynor, J. O. (1974). Future orientation in the study of achievement motivation. In J. W. Atkinson & J. O. Raynor (Eds.), *Motivation and achievement* (pp. 121–154). Washington: Winston.

Raynor, J. O. (1976). *Future orientation, self-evaluation, and motivation for achievement.* Unpublished manuscript, State University of New York, Buffalo.

Raynor, J. O., Atkinson, J. W., & Brown, M. (1974). Subjective aspects of achievement motivation immediately before an examination. In J. W. Atkinson & J. O. Raynor (Eds.), *Motivation and achievement* (pp. 155–171). Washington: Winston.

Raynor, J. O., & Entin, E. E. (1972). *Achievement motivation as a determinant of persistence in contingent and noncontingent paths.* Unpublished manuscript, State University of New York, Buffalo.

Raynor, J. O., & Rubin, I. S. (1971). Effects of achievement motivation and future orientaton on level of performance. *Journal of Personality and Social Psychology, 17,* 36–41.

Raynor, J. O., & Smith, C. P. (1966). Achievement-related motives and risk taking in games of skill and chance. *Journal of Personality, 34,* 176–198.

Raynor, J. O., & Sorrentino, R. M. (1972). *Effects of achievement motivation and task difficulty on immediate performance in contingent paths.* Unpublished manuscript, State University of New York, Buffalo.

Reiss, G. (1968). Der Einfluss von Erfolgs- und Misserfolgsmotivierung auf das Behalten eigener Leistungen. Dissertation, Philosophische Fakultät der Universität Münster.

Reitman, W. R. (1960). Motivational induction and the behavioral correlates of the achievement and affiliation motives. *Journal of Abnormal and Social Psychology, 60,* 8–13.

Reitman, W. R., & Atkinson, J. W. (1958). Some methodological problems in the use of thematic apperceptive measures of human motives. In J. W. Atkinson (Ed.), *Motives in fantasy, action, and society* (pp. 664–693). Princeton, NJ: Van Nostrand.

Rest, S., Nierenberg, R., Weiner, B., & Heckhausen, H. (1973). Further evidence concerning the effects of perceptions of effort and ability on achievement evaluation. *Journal of Personality and Social Psychology, 28,* 187–191.

Reuman, D. A. (1982). Ipsative behavioral variability and the quality of thematic apperceptive measurement of the achievement motive. *Journal of Personality and Social Psychology, 43,* 1098–1110.

Rheinberg, F. (1975). Zeitstabilität und Steuerbarkeit von Ursachen schulischer Leistung in der Sicht des Lehrers. *Zeitschrift für Entwicklungspsychologie und Pädagogische Psychologie, 7,* 180–194.

Rheinberg, F. (1977). Soziale und individuelle Bezugsnorm. *Zwei motivierungsbedeutsame Sichtweisen bei der Beurteilung von Schülerleistungen.* Dissertation, Fakultät für Philosophie, Pädagogik, Psychologie an der Ruhr-Universität Bochum.

Rheinberg, F. (1979). Bezugsnormen und Wahrnehmung eigener Tüchtigkeit. In S. H. Filipp (Ed.), *Selbstkonzept-Forschung: Probleme, Befunde und Perspektiven* (pp. 237–252). Stuttgart: Klett.

Rheinberg, F. (1980). *Schulleistungsbewertung und Lernmotivation.* Göttingen: Hogrefe.

Rheinberg, F. (1982). Zweck und Tätigkeit: Motivationspsychologische Analysen zur Handlungsveranlassung. Habilitationsschrift (postdoctoral thesis). Psychologisches Institut der Ruhr-Universität Bochum.

Rheinberg, F. (1983). Achievement evaluation: A fundamental difference and its motivational consequences. *Studies in Educational Evaluation* (pp. 185–194). Vol. 9. Oxford: Pergamon Press.

Rheinberg, F., Duscha, R., & Michels, U. (1980). Zielsetzung und Kausalattribution in Abhängigkeit vom Leistungsvergleich. *Zeitschrift für Entwicklungspsychologie und Pädagogische Psychologie, 12,* 177–189.

Rheinberg, F., & Enstrup, B. (1977). Selbstkonzept der Begabung bei Normal- und Sonderschülern gleicher Intelligenz: Ein Bezugsgruppeneffekt. *Zeitschrift für Entwicklungspsychologie und Pädagogische Psychologie, 9,* 171–180.

Rheinberg, F., & Krug, S. (1978a). Innere und äussere Differenzierung, Motivation und Bezugsnorm-Orientierung. In K. J. Klauer & H. J. Kornadt (Eds.), *Jahrbuch für empirische Erziehungswissenschaft 1978* (pp. 165–195). Düsseldorf: Schwann.

Rheinberg, F., & Krug, S. (1978b). Bezugsgruppenwechsel: Übernahme eines Stigmas oder neuer Vergleichsmaßstab zur Selbsteinschätzung (Replik auf Casparis). *Zeitschrift für Entwicklungspsychologie und Pädagogische Psychologie, 10,* 269–273.

Rheinberg, F., Krug, S., Lübbermann, E., & Landscheid, K. (1980). Beeinflussung der Leistungsbewertung im Unterricht: Motivationale Auswirkungen eines Interventionsversuchs. *Unterrichtswissenschaft, 8,* 48–60.

Rheinberg, F., Lührmann, J. V., & Wagner, H. (1977). Bezugsnorm-Orientierung von Schülern der 5.–13. Klasse bei der Leistungsbeurteilung. *Zeitschrift für Entwicklungspsychologie und Pädagogische Psychologie, 9,* 90–93.

Rheinberg, F., Schmalt, H. -D., & Wasser, I. (1978). Ein Lehrerunterschied, der etwas ausmacht. *Zeitschrift für Entwicklungspsychologie und Pädagogische Psychologie, 10,* 3–7.

Riemer, B. S. (1975). Influence of causal beliefs on affect and expectancy. *Journal of Personality and Social Psychology, 31,* 1163–1167.

Rollett, B., & Bartram, M. (1976). *Anstrengungsvermeidungstest AVT.* Braunschweig: Westermann.

Ronis, D. L., Hansen, R. D., & O'Leary, V. E. (1983). Understanding the meaning of achievement attributions: A test of derived locus and stability scores. *Journal of Personality and Social Psychology, 4,* 702–711.

Rorer, L. G. (1965). The great response style myth. *Psychological Bulletin, 63,* 129–156.

Rosenbaum, R. M. (1972). A dimensional analysis of the perceived causes of success and failure. Dissertation, University of California, Los Angeles.

Rosenthal, R., & Jacobson, L. J. (1968). *Pygmalion in the classroom.* New York: Holt, Rinehart & Winston.

Rösler, F., Jesse, J., Manzey, D., & Grau, U. (1982). Ist das LM-Gitter nur ein LM-Test?— Eine dreimodale Faktorenanalyse des LM-Gitters für Kinder (Schmalt). *Diagnostica, 28,* 131–145.

Ross, L. (1977). The intuitive psychologist and his shortcomings: Distortions in the attribution process. In R. Green & M. Quanty (Eds.), *Advances in Experimental Social Psychology* (Vol. 10) (pp. 173–220). New York: Academic Press.

Roth, S. (1980). A revised model of learned helplessness in humans. *Journal of Personality, 48,* 103–133.

Rothbaum, F., Weisz, J. R., & Snyder, S. S. (1982). Changing the world and changing the self: A two-process model of perceived control. *Journal of Personality and Social Psychology, 42,* 5–37.

Rothkopf, E. Z., & Kaplan, R. (1972). Exploration of the effect of density and specificity of instructional objectives on learning from text. *Journal of Educational Psychology, 63,* 295–302.

Rotter, J. B. (1954). *Social learning and clinical psychology.* Englewood Cliffs, NJ: Prentice-Hall.

Rotter, J. B. (1955). The role of the psychological situation in determining the direction of human behavior. In M. R. Jones (Ed.), *Nebraska Symposium on Motivation* (pp. 245–269). Lincoln: University of Nebraska Press.

Rotter, J. B (1966). Generalized expectancies for internal versus external control of reinforcement. *Psychological Monographs, 80* (1, Whole No. 609).

Ruble, D. N. (1980). A developmental perspective on theories of achievement motivation. In L. J. Fyans (Ed.), *Achievement motivation: Recent trends in theory and research* (pp. 225–245). New York: Plenum.

Ruble, D. N., & Feldman, N. S. (1976). Order of consensus, distinctiveness, and consistency information and causal attribution. *Journal of Personality and Social Psychology, 34,* 930–937.

Russell, D. (1982). The causal dimension scale: A measure of how individuals perceive causes. *Journal of Personality and Social Psychology, 42,* 1137–1145.

Sabini, J., & Silver, M. (1981). Introspection and causal accounts. *Journal of Personality and Social Psychology, 40,* 171–179.

Sader, M., & Keil, W. (1968). Faktorenanalytische Untersuchungen zur Projektion der Leistungsmotivation. *Archiv für die gesamte Psychologie, 120,* 25–53.

Sader, M., & Specht, H. (1967). Leistung, Motivation und Leistungsmotivation. Korrelationsstatistische Untersuchungen zur Leistungsmotivmessung nach Heckhausen. *Archiv für Psychologie, 119,* 90–130.

Sarason, I. G. (1972). Experimental approaches to test anxiety: Attention and the uses of information. In C. D. Spielberger (Ed.), *Anxiety and behavior: Current trends in theory and research* (Vol. 2). New York: Academic Press.

Sarason, I. G. (1975). Anxiety and self-preoccupation. In I. G. Sarason & C. D. Spielberger (Eds.), *Stress and anxiety* (Vol. 2). Washington, DC: Hemisphere.

Savage, L. J. (1954). *The foundations of statistics.* New York: Wiley.

Sawusch, J. R. (1974). Computer simulation of the influence of ability and motivation on test performance and cumulative achievement and the relation between them. In J. W. Atkinson & J. O. Raynor (Eds.), *Motivation and achievement* (pp. 425–438). Washington, DC: Winston.

Saxe, L., Greenberg, M. S., & Bar-Tal, D. (1974). Perceived relatedness of trait dispositions to ability and effort. *Perceptual and Motor Skills, 38,* 39–42.

Schachter, S. (1964). The interaction of cognitive and physiological determinants of emotional state. In L. Berkowitz (Ed.), *Advances in experimental social psychology* (Vol. I, pp. 49–80). New York: Academic Press.

Scherer, J. (1972). *Änderungen von Lehrerattribuierungen und deren Auswirkungen auf Leistungsverhalten und Persönlichkeitsmerkmale von Schülern.* Diplomarbeit (thesis), Psychologisches Institut der Ruhr-Universität Bochum.

Schmale, H., & Vukovich, A. (1961). Skalometrische Untersuchungen über die erlebte Anstrengung bei dynamischer Muskelarbeit. *Psychologische Beiträge, 6,* 3–25.

Schmalt, H. -D. (1973). Die GITTER-Technik—ein objektives Verfahren zur Messung des Leistungsmotivs bei Kindern. *Zeitschrift für Entwicklungspsychologie und Pädagogische Psychologie, 5,* 231–252.

Schmalt, H. -D. (1974). *Entwicklung und Validierung einer neuen Technik zur Messung verschiedener Aspekte des Leistungsmotivs—das LM-GITTER.* Dissertation, Fakultät für Philosophie, Pädagogik, Psychologie, Ruhr-Universität Bochum.

Schmalt, H. -D. (1975). Selbständigkeitserziehung und verschiedene Aspekte des Leistungsmotivs. *Zeitschrift für Entwicklungspsychologie und Pädagogische Psychologie, 7,* 24–37.

Schmalt, H. -D. (1976a). *Das LM-GITTER, Ein objektives Verfahren zur Messung des Leistungsmotivs bei Kindern: Handanweisung.* Göttingen: Hogrefe.

Schmalt, H. -D. (1976b). *Die Messung des Leistungsmotivs.* Göttingen: Hogrefe.

Schmalt, H. -D. (1978). Leistungsthematische Kognitionen I: Kausalerklärungen für Erfolg und Misserfolg. *Zeitschrift für experimentelle und angewandte Psychologie, 25,* 246–272.

Schmalt, H. -D. (1979a). Leistungsthematische Kognitionen II: Kausalattribuierungen, Erfolgserwartungen und Affekte. *Zeitschrift für experimentelle und angewandte Psychologie, 26,* 509–531.

Schmalt, H. -D. (1979b). Machtmotivation. *Psychologische Rundschau, 30,* 269–285.

Schmalt, H. -D. (1982). The two concepts of fear of failure motivation. In R. Schwarzer, H. M. van der Ploeg, & C. D. Spielberger (Eds.), *Advances in test-anxiety research* (Vol. 1, pp. 45–52). Lisse: Swets and Zeitlinger.

Schmalt, H. -D. (in prep.). Fear of failure motivation and causal attributions of success and failure.

Schmalt, H. -D., & Oltersdorf, G. (in prep.). *Motivspezifische und kognitive Determinanten des Ausdauerverhaltens.*

Schmalt, H. -D., & Schab, W. (1984). Methodenkritische Untersuchungen zum LM-GITTER für Kinder (Schmalt). *Diagnostica, 4,* 482–498.

Schmidt, H. D. (1966). *Leistungschance, Erfolgserwartung und Entscheidung.* Berlin: VEB Deutscher Verlag der Wissenschaften.

Schneider, K. (1971). *Leistungs- und Risikoverhalten in Abhängigkeit von situativen und überdauernden Komponenten der Leistungsmotivation: Kritische Untersuchungen zu einem Verhaltensmodell.* Dissertation, Fakultät für Philosophie, Pädagogik, Psychologie, Ruhr-Universität Bochum.

Schneider, K. (1972). The relationship between estimated probabilities and achievement motivation. *Acta Psychologica, 36,* 408–416.

Schneider, K. (1973). *Motivation unter Erfolgsrisiko.* Göttingen: Hogrefe.

Schneider, K. (1974). Subjektive Unsicherheit und Aufgabenwahl. *Archiv für Psychologie, 126,* 147–169.

Schneider, K. (1976). Leistungsmotiviertes Verhalten als Funktion von Motiv, Anreiz und Erwartung. In H. -D. Schmalt & W. -U. Meyer (Eds.), *Leistungsmotivation und Verhalten* (pp. 33–59). Stuttgart: Klett.

Schneider, K. (1977). Leistungsmotive, Kausalerklärungen für Erfolg und Misserfolg und erlebte Affekte nach Erfolg und Misserfolg. *Zeitschrift für experimentelle und angewandte Psychologie, 24,* 613–637.

Schneider, K. (1978). Die Wirkung von Erfolg und Misserfolg auf die Leistung bei einer visuellen Diskriminationsaufgabe und auf physiologische Anstrengungsindikatoren. *Archiv für Psychologie, 130,* 69–88.

Schneider, K. (1979). Die Wirkungen von Erfolg und Misserfolg auf die Leistung in Intelligenztestaufgaben bei unterschiedlichem Leistungsmotiv. *Psychologische Beiträge, 21,* 261–276.

Schneider, K. (1978c). Atkinson's "Risk Preference" Model. *Motivation and Emotion, 2,* (4) 333–343.

Schneider, K., & Eckelt, D. (1975). Die Wirkung von Erfolg und Misserfolg auf die Leistung bei einer einfachen Vigilanzaufgabe. *Zeitschrift für experimentelle und angewandte Psychologie, 22,* 263–289.

Schneider, K., & Gallitz, H. (1973). Leistungsänderungen nach Erfolg und Misserfolg bei leichten und schwierigen Aufgaben. In K. Schneider (Ed.), *Motivation unter Erfolgsrisiko* (pp. 80–106). Göttingen: Hogrefe.

Schneider, K., & Heckhausen, H. (1981). Subjective uncertainty and task preference. In H. J. Day (Ed.), *Advances in intrinsic motivation and aesthetics* (pp. 149–167). New York: Plenum.

Schneider, K., & Heggemeier, D. (1978). Die Wirkung von Erfolg und Misserfolg auf die Güte- und Mengenleistung bei motorischen Aufgaben in Abhängigkeit von der überdauernden Leistungsmotivation. *Zeitschrift für experimentelle und angewandte Psychologie, 15,* 291–301.

Schneider, K., & Kreuz, A. (1979). Die Effekte unterschiedlicher Anstrengung auf die Mengen- und Güteleistung bei einer einfachen und schweren Zahlensymbolaufgabe. *Psychologische Praxis, 23,* 34–50.

Schneider, K., & Meise, C. (1973). Leistungs- und anschlussmotiviertes Risikoverhalten bei der Aufgabenwahl. In K. Schneider, *Motivation unter Erfolgsrisiko* (pp. 212–238). Göttingen: Hogrefe.

Schneider, K., & Posse, N. (1978a). Subjektive Unsicherheit, Kausalattribuierung und Aufgabenwahl I. *Zeitschrift für experimentelle und angewandte Psychologie, 25,* 302–320.

Schneider, K., & Posse, N. (1978b). Subjektive Unsicherheit, Kausalattribuierungen und Aufgabenwahl II. *Zeitschrift für experimentelle und angewandte Psychologie, 25,* 474–499.

Schneider, K., & Posse, N. (1978c). Der Einfluss der Erfahrung mit einer Aufgabe auf die Aufgabenwahl, subjektive Unsicherheit und die Kausalerklärungen für Erfolge. *Psychologische Beiträge, 20,* 228–250.

Schneider, K., & Posse, N. (1982). Risk taking in achievement-oriented situations: Do people really maximize affect or competence motivation? *Motivation and Emotion, 6,* 259–271.

Schneider, K., & Rieke, K. (1976). *Entscheidungszeit, Konfidenz, subjektive Wahrscheinlichkeit und Aufgabenwahl bei einem Glücksspiel.* Arbeitsbericht (unpublished report), Psychologisches Institut der Ruhr-Universität Bochum.

Schönpflug, W., & Heckhausen, H. (1976). *Lärm und Motivation.* Opladen: Westdeutscher Verlag.

Scott, W. A. (1956). The avoidance of threatening material in imaginative behavior. *Journal of Abnormal and Social Psychology, 52,* 338–346.

Seligman, M. E. P. (1975). Helplessness: On depression, development, and death. San Francisco: Freeman.

Seltzer, R. A. (1973). Simulation of the dynamics of action. *Psychological Reports, 32,* 859–872.

Seltzer, R. A., & Sawusch, J. R. (1974). Appendix A. Computer program written to simulate the dynamics of action. In J. W. Atkinson & J. O. Raynor (Eds.), *Motivation and achievement* (pp. 411–423). New York: Wiley.

Shannon, C. E., & Weaver, W. (1949). *The mathematical theory of communication.* Urbana: University of Illinois Press.

Shrable, K., & Moulton, R. W. (1968). Achievement fantasy as a function of variations in self-rated competence. *Perceptual and Motor Skills, 27,* 515–528.

Simon, H. A. (1955). A behavioral model of rational choice. *Quarterly Journal of Economics, 69,* 99–118.

Simon, J. G., & Feather, N. T. (1973). Causal attributions for success and failure at university examinations. *Journal of Educational Psychology, 64,* 45–56.

Smedslund, J. (1972). *Becoming a psychologist.* Oslo: Universitetsforlaget.

Smith, C. P. (1963). Achievement-related motives and goal setting under different conditions. *Journal of Personality, 31,* 124–140.

Smith, C. P. (1966). The influence of testing conditions and need for achievement scores and their relationship to performance scores. In J. W. Atkinson & N. T. Feather (Eds.), *A theory of achievement motivation* (pp. 277–297). New York: Wiley.

Smith, C. P. (1969). The origin and expression of achievement-related motives in children. In C. P. Smith (Ed.), *Achievement related motives in children* (pp. 102–150). New York: Russell Sage Foundation.

Smith, C. P., & Feld, S. C. (1958). How to learn the method of content analysis for n Achievement, n Affiliation and n Power. In J. W. Atkinson (Ed.), *Motives in fantasy, action, and society.* Princeton, NJ: Van Nostrand.

Smith, R. L., & Troth, W. A. (1975). Achievement motivation: A rational approach to psychological education. *Journal of Counseling Psychology, 22,* 500–504.

Smits, B., & Schmalt, H. -D. (1978). Dimensionsanalytische Untersuchungen des LM-GIT-TERs für Kinder (SCHMALT). *Diagnostica, 24,* 146–161.

Snyder, M. L., Stephan, W. G., & Rosenfield, D. (1976). Egotism and attribution. *Journal of Personality and Social Psychology, 33,* 435–441.

Sohn, D. (1977). Affect generating powers of effort and ability self attributions of academic success and failure. *Journal of Educational Psychology, 69,* 500–505.

Sohn, D. (1984). The empirical base of Trope's position on achievement-task choice: A critique. *Motivation and Emotion, 8,* 91–107.

Sorrentino, R. M., & Sheppard, B. H. (1978). Effects of affiliation-related motives on swimmers in individual versus group competition: A field experiment. *Journal of Personality and Social Psychology, 36,* 704–714.

Sorrentino, R. M., & Short, J. A. C. (1977). The case of the mysterious moderates: Why motives sometimes fail to predict behavior. *Journal of Personality and Social Psychology, 35,* 478–484.

Spence, J. T., & Helmreich, R. L. (1978). *Masculinity and femininity.* Austin: University of Texas Press.

Spence, J. T., & Spence, K. W. (1966). The motivational components of manifest anxiety: Drive and drive stimuli. In C. D. Spielberger (Ed.), *Anxiety and behavior* (pp. 291–326). New York: Academic Press.

Spielberger, C. D. (1966). Theory and research on anxiety. In C. D. Spielberger (Ed.), *Anxiety and behavior* (pp. 3–20). New York: Academic Press.

Spielberger, C. D., Gorsuch, R. L., & Lushene, R. E. (1970). *STAI manual for the State-Trait Anxiety Inventory.* Palo Alto: Consulting Psychologists Press.

Stamps, L. (1973). The effects of intervention techniques on children's fear of failure behavior. *Journal of Genetic Psychology, 123,* 85–97.

Starke, E. (1975). *Informationseinholung über die eigene Leistung in Abhängigkeit vom Leistungsmotiv und wahrgenommener eigener Begabung.* Diplomarbeit (thesis), Psychologisches Institut der Ruhr-Universität Bochum.

Stein, A. M., & Bailey, M. N. (1973). The socialization of achievement orientation in women. *Psychological Bulletin, 80,* 345–364.

Stevens, L., & Jones, E. E. (1976). Defensive attribution and the Kelley cube. *Journal of Personality and Social Psychology, 34,* 809–820.

Stigler, G. J. (1950). The development of utility theory. *Journal of Political Economy, 58,* 307–327, 373–396.

Strang, H. R., Lawrence, E. C., & Fowler, P. C. (1978). Effects of assigned goal level and knowledge of results on arithmetic computation: A laboratory study. *Journal of Applied Psychology, 63,* 446–450.

Strodtbeck, F. L., McDonald, M. R., & Rosen, B. (1957). Evaluation of occupations: A reflection of Jewish and Italian mobility differences. *American Social Review, 22,* 546–553.

Susen, G. R. (1972). *Die Wirkung von Erfolg und Misserfolg auf die intellektuelle Leistung in Abhängigkeit von Leistungsmotivation und Schwierigkeit der Aufgabe.* Diplomarbeit (thesis), Psychologisches Institut der Ruhr-Universität Bochum.

Taylor, J. A. (1953). A personality scale of manifest anxiety. *Journal of Abnormal and Social Psychology, 48,* 285–290.

Tennen, H., & Eller, S. J. (1977). Attributional components of learned helplessness and facilitation. *Journal of Personality and Social Psychology, 35,* 265–271.

Terborg, J. R., & Miller, H. E. (1978). Motivation, behavior, and performance: A closer examination of goal setting and monetary incentives. *Journal of Applied Psychology, 63,* 29–39.

Terhune, K. W. (1968a). Motives, situation, and interpersonal conflict within Prisoner's Dilemma. *Journal of Personality and Social Psychology Monograph Supplement, 8* (3, Pt. 2).

Terhune, K. W. (1968b). Studies of motives, cooperation, and conflict within laboratory microcosms. *Buffalo Studies, 4* (1), 29–58.

Terhune, K. W. (1970). The effects of personality in cooperation and conflict. In P. Swingle (Ed.), *The structure of conflict* (pp. 193–234). New York: Academic Press.

Thomas, C., & Teevan, R. C. (1969). Level of aspiration and motive patterns (Tech. Rep. No. 2, 1964). Quoted from R. C. Birney, H. Burdick, & R. C. Teevan: *Fear of failure motivation.* New York: Van Nostrand.

Thoresen, C. E., & Mahoney, M. J. (1974). *Behavioral self-control.* New York: Holt, Rinehart & Winston.

Thorndike, R. L. (1963). *The concepts of over- and under-achievement.* New York: Bureau of Publications, Teachers College, Columbia University.

Thurstone, L. L. (1937). Ability, motivation, and speed. *Psychometrika, 2,* 249–254.

Tolman, E. C. (1932). *Purposive behavior in animals and men.* New York: Appleton.

Tolman, E. C. (1955). Principles of performance. *Psychological Review, 62,* 315–326.

Tolman, E. C. (1959). Principles of behavior. In S. Koch (Ed.), *Psychology: A study of a science* (Vol. II). New York: McGraw-Hill.

Tomkins, S. S. (1961). Discussion of Dr. Murstein's paper. In J. Kagan & G. S. Lesser (Eds.), *Contemporary issues in thematic apperceptive methods* (pp. 274–287). Springfield: Thomas.

Touhey, J. C., & Villemez, W. J. (1975). Need achievement and risk-taking preference: A clarification. *Journal of Personality and Social Psychology, 32,* 713–719.

Touhey, J. C., & Villemez, W. J. (1980). Ability attribution as a result of variable effort and achievement motivation. *Journal of Personality and Social Psychology, 38,* 211–216.

Tresemer, D. (1974, March). Fear of success: Popular but unproven. *Psychology Today,* 82–85.

Triandis, H. (1972). *The analysis of subjective culture.* New York: Wiley.

Trope, Y. (1975). Seeking information about one's own ability, as a determinant of choice among tasks. *Journal of Personality and Social Psychology, 32,* 1004–1013.

Trope, Y. (1979). Uncertainty-reducing properties of achievement tasks. *Journal of Personality and Social Psychology, 37,* 1505–1518.

Trope, Y. (1980). Self-assessment, self-enhancement, and task preference. *Journal of Experimental Social Psychology, 16,* 116–129.

Trope, Y., & Brickman, P. (1975). Difficulty and diagnosticity as determinants of choice among tasks. *Journal of Personality and Social Psychology, 31,* 918–926.

Trudewind, C. (1982). The development of achievement motivation and its interindividual differences: Ecological determinants. In W. W. Hartup (Ed.), *Review of Child Development Research* (Vol. 6). Chicago: University of Chicago Press.

Trudewind, C., & Kohne, W. (1982). Bezugsnorm-Orientierung der Lehrer und Motiventwicklung: Zusammenhänge mit Schulleistung, Intelligenz und Merkmalen der häuslichen Umwelt in der Grundschulzeit. In F. Rheinberg (Ed.), *Bezugsnormen zur Schulleistungsbewertung: Analyse und Intervention* (pp. 115–141). Düsseldorf: Schwann.

Tversky, A. (1967a). A general theory of polynomial conjoint measurement. *Journal of Mathematical Psychology, 4,* 1–20.

Tversky, A. (1967b). Utility theory and additivity analysis of risk choices. *Journal of Experimental Psychology, 75,* 27–36.

Ungar, S. (1980). The effects of certainty of self-perceptions on self-presentational behaviors: A test of the strength of self-enhancement motives. *Social Psychology Quarterly, 43,* 165–172.

Valins, S., & Nisbett, R. E. (1971). *Some implications of attribution processes for the development and treatment of emotional disorders.* New York: General Learning Press.

Valle, V. A., & Frieze, I. (1976). Stability of causal attributions as a mediator in changing expectations for success. *Journal of Personality and Social Psychology, 33,* 579–587.

Varga, K. (1977). Who gains from achievement motivation training? *Vikalpa* (The Journal for Decision Makers). Indian Institute of Management, Ahmedabad, *2,* 187–200.

Veroff, J. (1957). Development and validation of a projective measure of power motivation. *Journal of Abnormal and Social Psychology, 54,* 1–8.

Veroff, J. (1969). Social comparison and the development of achievement motivation. In C. P. Smith (Ed.), *Achievement related motives in children* (pp. 46–101). New York: Russell Sage Foundation.

Veroff, J., Atkinson, J. W., Feld, S. C., & Gurin, G. (1960). The use of thematic apperception to assess motivation in a nationwide interview study. *Psychological Monographs, 74* (12, Whole No. 499).

Veroff, J., Wilcox, S., & Atkinson, J. W. (1953). The achievement motive in high school and college-age women. *Journal of Abnormal and Social Psychology, 48,* 103–119.

Volpert, W. (1974). *Handlungsstrukturanalyse als Beitrag zur Qualifikationsforschung.* Köln: Pahl-Rugenstein.

von Cranach, M., Kalbermatten, U., Indermühle, K., & Gugler, B. (1980). *Zielgerichtetes Handeln.* Stuttgart: Huber.

von Holst, E. (1937). Bausteine zu einer vergleichenden Physiologie der lokomotorischen Reflexe bei Fischen: II. Mitteilung. *Zeitschrift für vergleichende Physiologie, 24,* 532–562.

Vontobel, J. (1970). *Leistungsbedürfnis und soziale Umwelt.* Bern: Huber.

Vorwerg, M. (1977). Adaptives Training der Leistungsmotivation. *Zeitschrift für Psychologie, 185,* 230–236.

Vroom, V. H. (1964). *Work and motivation.* New York: Wiley.

Wahba, M. A., & House, R. J. (1974). Expectancy theory in work and motivation: Some logical and methodological issues. *Human Relations, 27,* 121–147.

Wagner, H. (1977). *Entwicklung und Erprobung eines Beobachtungsschlüssels zur Erfassung bezugsnormspezifischer Aspekte im Lehrerverhalten.* Diplomarbeit (thesis), Psychologisches Institut der Ruhr-Universität Bochum.

Wahl, D. (1975). *Erwartungswidrige Schulleistungen.* Weinheim: Beltz.

Wainer, H. A., & Rubin, I. M. (1971). Motivation of research and development entrepreneurs: Determinants of company success. In D. A. Kolb, I. M. Rubin, & J. McIntire (Eds.), *Organizational Psychology* (pp. 131–139). Englewood Cliffs, NJ: Prentice-Hall.

Walster, E. (1966). Assignment of responsibility for an accident. *Journal of Personality and Social Psychology, 3,* 73–79.

Walter, H. (1968). *Die Verwendung technischer Lernhilfen in Abhängigkeit von der Leistungs-motivation der Schüler.* Burgsteinfurt: Kreisverwaltung.
Wasna, M. (1972). *Motivation, Intelligenz und Lernerfolg.* München: Kösel.
Watson, D. (1982). The actor and the observer: How are their perceptions of causality divergent? *Psychological Bulletin, 92*(3), 682–700.
Weary, G. (1980). Examination of affect and egotism as mediators of bias in causal attributions. *Journal of Personality and Social Psychology, 38,* 348–355.
Weber, M. (1904, 1905). Die protestantische Ethik und der Geist des Kapitalismus. *Archiv für Sozialwissenschaft und Sozialpolitik, 20,* 1–54; *21,* 1–110.
Weiner, B. (1965a). The effects of unsatisfied achievement motivation on persistence and subsequent performance. *Journal of Personality, 33,* 428–442.
Weiner, B. (1965b). Need achievement and the resumption of incompleted tasks. *Journal of Personality and Social Psychology, 1,* 165–168.
Weiner, B. (1966). The role of success and failure in the learning of easy and complex tasks. *Journal of Personality and Social Psychology, 3,* 339–343.
Weiner, B. (1967). Implications of the current theory of achievement motivation for research and performance in the classroom. *Psychology in the Schools, 4,* 164–171.
Weiner, B. (1970). New conceptions in the study of achievement motivation. In B. Maher (Ed.), *Progress in Experimental Personality Research* (Vol. 5, pp. 67–109). New York: Academic Press.
Weiner, B. (1972). *Theories of motivation. From mechanism to cognition.* Chicago: Markham.
Weiner, B. (1973). From each according to his abilities: The role of effort in a moral society. *Human Development, 16,* 53–60.
Weiner, B. (1974a). *Achievement motivation and attribution theory.* New York: General Learning Press.
Weiner, B. (1974b). An attributional interpretation of expectancy-value theory. In B. Weiner (Ed.), *Cognitive view of human motivation* (pp. 51–69). New York: Academic Press.
Weiner, B. (1977). An attributional model for educational psychology. In L. Shulman (Ed.), *Review of research in education* (Vol. 4, pp. 179–209). Itasca, IL: Peacock.
Weiner, B. (1979). A theory of motivation for some classroom experiences. *Journal of Educational Psychology, 71,* 3–25.
Weiner, B. (1980a). A cognitive (attribution)-emotion-action model of motivated behavior: An analysis of judgments of help giving. *Journal of Personality and Social Psychology, 39,* 186–200.
Weiner, B. (1980b). *Human motivation.* New York: Holt, Rinehart & Winston.
Weiner, B. (1982). The emotional consequences of causal attributions. In M. S. Clark & S. T. Fiske (Eds.), *Affect and cognition* (pp. 185–209). Hillsdale, NJ: Erlbaum.
Weiner, B., Frieze, I., Kukla, A., Reed, L., Rest, S., & Rosenbaum, R. M. (1971). *Perceiving the causes of success and failure.* New York: General Learning Press.
Weiner, B., Heckhausen, H., Meyer, W. -U., & Cook, R. E. (1972). Causal ascriptions and achievement behavior: A conceptual analysis of effort and reanalysis of locus of control. *Journal of Personality and Social Psychology, 21,* 239–248.
Weiner, B., & Kukla, A. (1970). An attributional analysis of achievement motivation. *Journal of Personality and Social Psychology, 15,* 1–20.
Weiner, B., & Litman-Adizes, T. (1980). An attributional expectancy-value analysis of learned helplessness and depression. In J. Garber & E. P. Seligman (Eds.), *Human Helplessness: Theory and Applications* (pp. 35–57). New York: Academic Press.
Weiner, B., Nierenberg, R., & Goldstein, M. (1976). Social learning (locus of control) versus attributional (causal stability) interpretations of expectancy of success. *Journal of Personality, 44,* 52–68.

Weiner, B., & Potepan, P. A. (1970). Personality characteristics and affective reactions toward exams of superior and failing college students. *Journal of Educational Psychology, 61,* 144–151.

Weiner, B., & Rosenbaum, R. M. (1965). Determinants of choice between achievement and non-achievement-related activities. *Journal of Experimental Research in Personality, 1,* 114–121.

Weiner, B., Russel, D., & Lerman, D. (1978). Affektive Auswirkungen von Attributionen. In D. Görlitz, W. -U. Meyer, & B. Weiner (Eds.), *Bielefelder Symposion über Attribution* (pp. 139–174). Stuttgart: Klett-Cotta.

Weiner, B., Russel, D., & Lerman, D. (1979). The cognition–emotion process in achievement-related contexts. *Journal of Personality and Social Psychology, 37,* 1211–1220.

Weiner, B., & Schneider, K. (1971). Drive versus cognitive theory: A reply to Boor and Harmon. *Journal of Personality and Social Psychology, 18,* 258–262.

Weiner, B., & Sierad, J. (1975). Misattribution for failure and enhancement of achievement strivings. *Journal of Personality and Social Psychology, 31,* 415–421.

Weisfeld, G. E., & Beresford, J. M. (1982). Erectedness of posture as an indicator of dominance or success in humans. *Motivation and Emotion, 6,* 113–131.

Welford, A. T. (1962). Arousal, channel capacity, and decision. *Nature, 194,* 165–166.

Welford, A. T. (1976). *Skilled performance: Perceptual and motor skills.* Glenview, IL: Scott, Foresman.

Wells, G. L., & Harvey, J. H. (1977). Do people use consensus information in making causal attributions? *Journal of Personality and Social Psychology, 35,* 279–293.

Wendt, H. W. (1967). Verhaltensmodelle des Nichtwissenschaftlers: Einige biographische und Antriebskorrelate der wahrgenommenen Beziehung zwischen Erfolgswahrscheinlichkeit und Zielanreiz. *Psychologische Forschung, 30,* 226–249.

Wetzel, C. G. (1982). Self-serving biases in attribution: A Bayesian analysis. *Journal of Personality and Social Psychology, 43,* 197–209.

White, R. W. (1959). Motivation reconsidered: The concept of competence. *Psychological Review, 66,* 297–333.

Wickelgren, W. A. (1977). Speed–accuracy tradeoff and information processing dynamics. *Acta Psychologica, 41,* 67–85.

Wicker, A. W. (1969). Attitudes versus actions: The relationship of verbal and overt behavioral responses to attitude objects. *Journal of Social Issues, 25,* 41–78.

Wicker, W. (1970). Soziales Verhalten als ökologische Anpassung. *Verhandlungen der Deutschen Zoologischen Gesellschaft, 64,* 291–304.

Wicklund, R. A. (1975). Objective self-awareness. In L. Berkowitz (Ed.), *Advances in experimental social psychology* (Vol. 8, pp. 235–275). New York: Academic Press.

Wieczerkowski, W., Nickel, H., Janowski, A., Fittkau, B., & Rauer, W. (1974). *AFS-Handanweisung für die Durchführung und Auswertung und Interpretation.* Braunschweig: Westermann.

Wimer, S., & Kelley, H. H. (1982). An investigation of the dimensions of causal attribution. *Journal of Personality and Social Psychology, 43,* 1142–1162.

Windmöller, O. (1930). Die Beziehungen zwischen Arbeitsschnelligkeit und Arbeitsgüte. *Psychotechnische Zeitschrift, 5,* 1–13, 65–78.

Wine, J. (1971). Test anxiety and direction of attention. *Psychological Bulletin, 76,* 92–104.

Wine, J. D. (1980). Cognitive-attentional theory of test anxiety. In J. G. Sarason (Ed.), *Test anxiety* (pp. 349–385). Hillsdale, NJ: Erlbaum.

Wine, J. D. (1982). Evaluation anxiety: A cognitive-attentional construct. In H. W. Krohne & L. Laux (Eds.), *Achievement, stress, and anxiety* (pp. 207–219). Washington, DC: Hemisphere.

Winefield, A. H., & Jardine, E. (1982). Effects of differences in achievement motivation and amount of exposure on responses to uncontrollable rewards. *Motivation and Emotion, 6,* 245–257.

Winter, D. G. (1973). *The power motive.* New York: The Free Press.

Winter, D. G., & Stewart, A. (1977). Power motive reliability as a function of retest instructions. *Journal of Consulting and Clinical Psychology, 45,* 436–440.

Winter, D. G., & Wiecking, F. A. (1971). The new Puritans: Achievement and power motives of New Left radicals. *Behavioral Science, 16,* 523–530.

Wise, J. A. (1970). Estimated and scaled judgements of subjective probabilities. *Organizational Behavior and Human Performance, 5,* 85–92.

Wish, P. A. (1970). *The motive to approach success and the motive to avoid failure: Psychological determinants of choosing a college major.* Unpublished doctoral dissertation, Boston College.

Witte, W. (1976). Ist all das, was man umgangssprachlich Handeln nennt, Verhalten spezifischer Art? In A. Thomas (Ed.), *Psychologie der Handlung und Bewegung* (pp. 23–55). Meisenheim: Hain.

Wolk, S., & DuCette, J. (1973). The moderating effect of locus of control in relation to achievement-motivation variables. *Journal of Personality, 41,* 59–70.

Wollert, R. W. (1979). Expectancy shifts and the expectancy confidence hypothesis. *Journal of Personality and Social Psychology, 37,* 1888–1901.

Wong, P. T. P., & Weiner, B. (1981). When people ask "why" questions, and the heuristics of attributional search. *Journal of Personality and Social Psychology, 40,* 650–663.

Woodworth, R. S. (1958). *Dynamics of behavior.* New York: Holt, Rinehart, & Winston.

Wortman, C. B. (1976). Causal attributions and personal control. In J. H. Harvey, W. J. Ickes, & R. F. Kidd (Eds.), *New directions in attribution research* (pp. 23–52). Hillsdale, NJ: Erlbaum.

Wortman, C. B., & Brehm, J. W. (1975). Responses to uncontrollable outcomes: An interpretation of reactance theory and the learned helplessness model. In L. Berkowitz (Ed.), *Advances in Experimental Social Psychology* (Vol. 8, pp. 277–336). New York: Academic Press.

Wright, P., & Rip, P. D. (1981). Retrospective reports on the causes of decisions. *Journal of Personality and Social Psychology, 40,* 601–614.

Wylie, R. C. (1968). The present status of self theory. In E. F. Borgatta & W. W. Lambert (Eds.), *Handbook of personality theory and research* (pp. 728–787). Chicago: Rand McNally.

Yerkes, R. M., & Dodson, J. D. (1908). The relation of strength of stimulus to rapidity of habit-formation. *Journal of Comparative and Neurological Psychology, 18,* 459–482.

Zajonc, R. B. (1980). Feeling and thinking: Preferences need no inferences. *American Psychologist, 35,* 151–175.

Zeigarnik, B. (1927). Über das Behalten von erledigten und unerledigten Handlungen. *Psychologische Forschung, 9,* 1–85.

Zuckerman, M. (1978). Actions and occurrences in Kelley's cube. *Journal of Personality and Social Psychology, 36,* 647–656.

Zuckerman, M. (1979). Attribution of success and failure revisited, or: The motivational bias is alive and well in attribution theory. *Journal of Personality, 47,* 245–287.

Zuckerman, M., Brown, R. H., Fischler, G. L., Fox, G. A., Lathin, D. R., & Minasian, A. (1979). Determinants of information-seeking behavior. *Journal of Research in Personality, 13,* 161–174.

Zuckerman, M., & Wheeler, L. (1975). To dispel fantasies about the fantasy-based measure of fear of success. *Psychological Bulletin, 82,* 932–946.

Author Index

Numbers in *italic* are page numbers of complete references.

Subject Index